HARDY THE WRITER

By the same author

*ONE RARE FAIR WOMAN
Thomas Hardy's letters to
Florence Henniker, 1893–1922
(edited with Evelyn Hardy)

*A COMMENTARY ON
THE POEMS OF THOMAS HARDY
*THOMAS HARDY: ART AND THOUGHT

Edited for the New Wessex Edition
*THOMAS HARDY: TWO ON A TOWER
*THE STORIES OF THOMAS HARDY (3 vols)

Edited for the Thomas Hardy Society
THOMAS HARDY AND THE MODERN WORLD
BUDMOUTH ESSAYS ON THOMAS HARDY
THE THOMAS HARDY SOCIETY REVIEW (1975–84)

---

*A HARDY COMPANION
*A JANE AUSTEN COMPANION
*A BRONTË COMPANION
*A GEORGE ELIOT COMPANION
*A GEORGE ELIOT MISCELLANY
*A D. H. LAWRENCE COMPANION
*A WORDSWORTH COMPANION
*A TENNYSON COMPANION
*A T. S. ELIOT COMPANION
*A WORDSWORTH CHRONOLOGY
*THE COLLECTED SONNETS OF
CHARLES (TENNYSON) TURNER
(edited with M. Pinion)
*A TENNYSON CHRONOLOGY
*A THOMAS HARDY DICTIONARY

*Also published by Macmillan

Hardy the Writer

Surveys and Assessments

F. B. PINION

MACMILLAN

First published 1990

Published by
THE MACMILLAN PRESS LTD
Houndmills, Basingstoke, Hampshire RG21 2XS
and London
Companies and representatives
throughout the world

Typeset by Wessex Typesetters
(Division of The Eastern Press Ltd)
Frome, Somerset

Printed and bound in Great Britain at
The Camelot Press plc, Southampton

British Library Cataloguing in Publication Data
Pinion. F. B. (Francis Bertram), 1908–
Hardy the writer.
1. Fiction in English. Hardy, Thomas, 1840–1928–
Critical studies
I. Title
823'.8
ISBN 0–333–47362–0

To the Wightman family
for their long and dedicated service
to the Thomas Hardy Society

Contents

Preface

Most of these essays were written in the winter of 1987–8 in order to create a volume which would present the major aspects of Hardy's work as a whole, in a progressive, anticipative manner, with introductory and concluding surveys, and with illustrative material drawn from his poetry and prose at all appropriate stages. In this way numerous links have been established between Hardy's fiction and his poems, some of which receive close critical analysis. None of his novels is neglected, though special attention is given to the last four he wrote. Important references are made throughout to his *Life* and *Collected Letters*.

The principal aim has been to reflect Hardy's intentions and assess his achievements. The essays suggest that his formative thought, the product of a period of conflict between new scientific philosophy and humanism on the one hand, and traditional Christian theology combined with Victorian restraints on the other, developed when England was not nearly as intellectually provincial as Matthew Arnold had affirmed. Above all, they illustrate the extent to which the creative imagination and the style of Hardy the writer were stimulated and strengthened by literary influences, particularly from the Bible, a wide range of poetry, and great works from classical times to his own.

In their first versions, four of the essays have been published separately: 'The Ranging Vision' in *Thomas Hardy After Fifty Years* (ed. Lance St John Butler), London and Basingstoke, 1977; 'Hardy and George Eliot' in the author's *A George Eliot Companion*, London and Totowa, New Jersey, 1981; '*Two on a Tower*' as the introduction to the New Wessex Edition, London, 1975; and '*Jude the Obscure*: Origins in Life and Literature' in *Thomas Hardy Annual No. 4* (ed. Norman Page), London and Basingstoke, 1986. Part of the essay on Mrs Henniker is drawn from my introduction to *One Rare Fair Woman* (London and Basingstoke, 1972, now out of print), an edition of Hardy's letters to her which was prepared in collaboration with Evelyn Hardy. Certain topics which appeared in my *Thomas Hardy: Art and Thought* (London and Basingstoke, now out of print) have been included in revised and abridged forms. Brief notes on resemblances between *The Mayor of Casterbridge* and *Les Misérables* have been extracted from the same publication, and the study of 'Neutral Tones' is based on part of an article which I contributed to *Cahiers Victoriens & Edouardiens*, no. 12, October 1980.

Four of the essays were given in their original form as lectures: 'The Uniqueness of *The Woodlanders*' at a meeting of the Hardy Society in 1987, to mark the centenary of the novel's first publication; 'Philosophy in Fiction' at Western Washington University, Bellingham, 1980; 'Hebraism and Hellenism' as 'Hardy and "Hellenic Paganism"' at the Hardy Society School, 1982; and 'Hardy's Novel-Endings' at the Hardy Society Conference, 1988.

All twenty essays have been revised, some considerably, to ensure, first, that repetition of substance is reduced to a minimum consonant with clarity and completeness of individual subjects, and, secondly, that references and illustrations are as varied as possible.

Grateful acknowledgments are made to my wife for helpful recommendations on the final text, and for welcome assistance in proof-reading; to Simon Gatrell, Professor of English at the University of Georgia, for confirming a manuscript item on which I made a note at the New York Public Library in 1969; and to Sarah Roberts-West and Mrs Valery Rose for their ready assistance on behalf of the publishers.

1

The Ranging Vision

To say that Hardy's style is not responsible for the steady growth of interest in his work would be specious; it can no more be dissociated from his imaginative thinking than form can be separated from expression in sculpture. His literary longevity owes much to his thoughtfulness and verbal economy, more to a creative gift which is often poetic, but most to his vision of life. Many of Hardy's poems are based on his own emotional experiences, and most of his stories are set in very circumscribed areas. Yet one does not think of him as egotistical or provincial. As an artist he often shows the rare faculty of combining imaginative experience relative to the individual (himself included) with an unwavering sense of man's place in space and time. Such a vision imparts grandeur to the local and relatively insignificant; it can make his Wessex world transcend topographical limits, and endow human action with universal significance.

Hardy's early poetic imagination was largely literary in origin, and the familiar images he adopted from Shakespeare and other poets tend to convey that sense of generality which made him feel their appropriateness to situations in his own prose and poetry. Among them are gardens and the ravages of frost and blight, wintry severities, and the suffering of birds. A superb early example is to be found in 'Neutral Tones'. He tells us that he knew little about love when he began to write poetry;[1] if he could write the 'She, to Him' sonnets in 1866, he could imagine the situation for 'Neutral Tones' soon afterwards. As a creative writer, he looked beyond the limitations of direct experience long before the essays of Carlyle, Walter Bagehot, Leslie Stephen, Arnold, and Pater guided his reading and enlarged his critical independence.

Arnold's strictures on the provinciality of English writers are well known. In 'The Literary Influence of Academies' and 'The Function of Criticism' he charged them with egocentricity, quirkishness of style, lack of proportion, and lack of precision. Aeschylus, Sophocles, and Shakespeare had been fortunate to live in epochs of quickening ideas; the weakness of Byron and even Wordsworth was that, unlike Goethe, 'they had their source in a great movement of feeling, not in a great movement of mind'. He therefore stressed the role of the critic as a disinterested seeker and disseminator of 'the best that is known and thought in the world'.

On one form of provincialism Hardy took issue with Arnold:

> A certain provincialism of feeling is invaluable. It is of the essence of individuality, and is largely made up of that crude enthusiasm without which no great thoughts are thought, no great deeds done.[2]

One could wish Hardy had been more explicit. His 'crude enthusiasm' must be largely commensurate with that local appeal which commends elements of setting, character, or incident for artistic re-creation in accordance with the author's theme and his vision of life. It is clear from 'The Profitable Reading of Fiction' that 'thoughts' cannot be dissociated from 'deeds'. They are creative and not extrinsic or didactic; they affect the course of action as well as the portrayal of character. A novel is not 'the thing' but 'a view of the thing'; and 'characters, however they may differ, express mainly the author, his largeness of heart or otherwise, his culture, his insight, and very little of any other living person'. Hardy's standards of greatness may be judged by his definition of 'good fiction' as 'that kind of imaginative writing which lies nearest to the epic, dramatic, or narrative masterpieces of the past', and by his reference to 'the old masters . . . from Aeschylus to Shakespeare'.

If a particular region appeals to an author (Hardy or Robert Frost), however limited it may be, it can be adapted to imaginative settings and situations far more successfully than less familiar scenes. Wessex supplied 'quite enough human nature . . . for one man's literary purpose', Hardy wrote. Even though he derived a special satisfaction from preserving its old superstitious beliefs and customs, the artist in him was opposed to representative fidelity as a general rule. His subject was 'life' and not its 'garniture'. He thought he might be driven to write about 'social and fashionable life as other novelists did. Yet he took no interest in manners, but in the substance of life only.' He might have said with Wordsworth that 'the essential passions of the heart find a better soil in which they can attain their maturity' in rural life than in society. 'The domestic emotions have throbbed in Wessex nooks with as much intensity as in the palaces of Europe', he wrote in 1912, recalling, no doubt, his claim in *The Woodlanders* that, in a sequestered spot like Little Hintock, 'from time to time, dramas of a grandeur and unity truly Sophoclean are enacted in the real, by virtue of the concentrated passions and closely-knit interdependence of the lives therein'. His characters 'were meant to be typically and essentially those of any and every place where

Thought's the slave of life, and life time's fool,

– beings in whose hearts and minds that which is apparently local should be really universal'.[3]

Arnold exaggerated the extent of English intellectual provincialism, and gloomily assumed that contemporary writers were doomed to 'die in the wilderness'. In his formative period Hardy was capable of finding (in Arnold's words) 'a current of ideas in the highest degree animating and nourishing to the creative power'. The new scientific philosophy gave a formidable cogency to Shelley's thought; and the task of the tragic writer was admirably enunciated by Pater.[4] There was, in fact, a considerable weight of 'scientific opinion' in the country for the discerning thinker, and in none was it more constructive than in J. S. Mill, whose new 'religion of humanity' was rooted in the Positivism of Auguste Comte. Hardy's ideas came from these and other sources; they confirmed a philosophy of chance as opposed to Providence, and underlined the need for altruism through co-operation and education. Mischance and pity are the key to his most serious work, and he showed that the conflict between natural law and social and other circumstantial factors is capable of a tragic view which is essentially similar to that of the Greeks. Confirmation of this is to be found in Richard le Gallienne's conclusion that *Jude the Obscure* is 'an indictment of much older and crueller laws than those relating to marriage, the laws of the universe. It is a Promethean indictment of that power, which, in Omar's words,

with pitfall and with gin,
Beset the path we were to wander in,

and to conceive it merely as a criticism of marriage is to miss its far more universal tragic significance.'[5]

Despite fits of depression, Hardy never really lost his sense of humour or relativity, 'as if there were no cakes and ale in the world'.⁶ On a philosophical level, two contrasting visions co-existed in his mind: the individual as the centre of his own world and as an insignificant entity in the scientific dimensions of space and time. Both are to be found in 'At Castle Boterel'. As *Two on a Tower* exemplifies, the individual must assume a greater importance from the human angle than the immensities of the stellar universe. Hardy never forgot this viewpoint even when his subject was the fate of millions in *The Dynasts*; the duality of his vision is represented by the Spirit of the Pities and the Spirit of the Years. There is a reminder of it in the tragi-comedy of Jocelyn Pierston:

> How incomparably the immaterial dream dwarfed the grandest of substantial things, when here, between those three sublimities – the sky, the rock, and the ocean – the minute personality of this washer-girl filled his consciousness to its extremest boundary, and the stupendous inanimate scene shrank to a corner therein.

Particularly poignant is Sue Bridehead's heartfelt comment on little Father Time: 'There's more for us to think about in that one little hungry heart than in all the stars of the sky.'⁷

The other view is inescapable. It comes to Knight in a flash of geological time as he hangs perilously on the Cliff without a Name. Whatever the sufferings of Mrs Yeobright, or Eustacia, or Clym, Egdon Heath remains 'a face on which time makes but little impression'. In *Desperate Remedies* and *Tess of the d'Urbervilles* the ephemerality of love is poetically translated into the glory of gnats quickly passing through the sunshine. 'Mary's birthday. She came into the world . . . and went out . . . and the world is just the same . . . not a ripple on the surface left', Hardy wrote on 23 December 1925, remembering his poem 'Just the Same'. The thought is inherent in 'Life and Death at Sunrise', and in what Bathsheba hears and sees when she wakes near the pestilential swamp after discovering the extent of Troy's perfidy. Hardy's sense of his own insignificance plays a key part in 'A Commonplace Day' and 'To Meet, or Otherwise', a love poem to Florence Dugdale.

A drab wintry view of Tess and Marian at Flintcomb-Ash reveals them as flies crawling over the landscape. The adverse 'circumstantial will' which determines their lot is not equated with the gods, but the reminder of *King Lear* ('As flies to wanton boys are we to the gods') is echoed in the Aeschylean reference to the President of the Immortals' ending his 'sport' with Tess when she is hanged. The tragic gravamen in the satirical ' "Justice" was done' is that victims of chance such as Tess have, as Swinburne stressed, but one life to live; it is 'her every and only chance'. On her futile journey in blazing sunshine across Egdon Heath, Mrs Yeobright is associated with 'independent worlds of ephemerons'. She does not recognise her son in the distant furze-cutter; he seems to be 'of no more account in life than an insect'. To the Spirit of the Years such men as Napoleon are no more than 'meanest insects on obscurest leaves' in the chart of 'the elemental ages'. Such perspectives are inseparable from natural law and the great web of cause–effect which spreads through the universe and society. Middleton Murry was right in affirming that Hardy's 'reaction to an episode has behind and within it a reaction to the universe'.[8]

Local history extended the range of Hardy's vision of life. Around Dorchester he could not escape prehistoric burial-mounds and fortifications; Maumbury Ring and the discoveries of excavators reminded him of 'the power, the pride, the reach of perished Rome'; and aged country people still remembered defensive preparations against the Napoleonic invasion. His historical sense of proportion is seen in the aerial pictures of *The Dynasts*; a longer perspective still, in the Spirit of the Years. Human folly continues, and Hardy would not have ended this work as he did had he foreseen the 1914–18 war. He had met politicians, and was depressed to think how far a people's destiny depended on men of such limited views; for twenty years he had advocated a League of Nations. As nationalistic greed and public indifference made a second major war seem inevitable, he concluded near the end of his life that it was time to end 'visioning The impossible within this universe';

> And if my vision range beyond
> The blinkered sight of souls in bond,
> – By truth made free –
> I'll let all be,
> And show to no man what I see.[9]

Whatever it was that filled Hardy with most gloomy pessimism, it may not be irrelevant to state that this veiled or obscurant prediction came from one who in his early years (cf. 'Childhood Among the Ferns') had shrunk anticipatively from the ills of life, who more than once expressed the view that it was better not to be born (cf. 'Thoughts from Sophocles', an uncollected verse translation), and who had preferred to withdraw from the world. He continually invented excuses for not attending meetings in his later years, and was happiest as bookworm or writer in his study at Max Gate. 'A Private Man on Public Men', published and probably written about the same time as 'Childhood Among the Ferns', confirms the impression that Hardy was most himself 'far from the madding crowd'. The tenor of the poem he wrote on his eighty-sixth birthday is that, having never expected much of the world, he has never been disappointed. Towards the end he contemplated it with growing dismay.

Though, as we see in 'Drinking Song', Hardy's knowledge of the fallaciousness of beliefs about the universe and other mysteries, from the time 'when thought began', made him sceptical of Einstein's theories, he accepted scientific truth uncompromisingly, believing with John the evangelist that 'the truth shall make you free'. Truth, he believed, would undermine Christian theology, though the religion of the future would have to preserve the best of Christian ethics (charity, altruism, or loving-kindness), and combine it with scientific endeavour for the general good, to save western civilization.[10]

It is not surprising that Hardy's love of the Church, its music, and the language of its services, never failed, despite the growth of his scepticism. The parish church, especially in the country, was the centre of community life; the close ties which he and his family had with Stinsford Church during his early boyhood and youth helped to hallow its associations, and its moral and spiritual teaching; his subsequent architectural interest in churches and their renovation enhanced his aesthetic appreciation of all that the Church of England offered. It is no wonder that he wished to be a country curate. If he was high-minded, shrewd observations on church dignitaries and actions saved him from being priggish. As a result of such an upbringing the Church is often an important feature in his novels and short stories, and the background of memorable scenes from *Desperate Remedies* to *Jude the Obscure*; it provides his most humorous tales in 'Old Mrs Chundle', 'Absent-Mindedness in a Parish Choir', 'Andrey Satchel and the Parson and Clerk', and delightful presentations in *Under the Greenwood Tree* and the opening of *Two on a Tower*. As that novel daringly illustrates, Hardy's later disrespect for theological dogma made him think a bishop fair game. Later still, in 'The Son's Veto', he was roused to strong satire against the unchristian snobbery of clergymen. In *Jude the Obscure* the object of his attack is High Church unenlightenment, superstitious ritualism, and inflexible illiberalism *vis-à-vis* the marriage bond. He regretted that Positivism had not made greater progress, and felt that the best work being done by the Church was that of humble clergy in poor parishes and city slums. As he tells us in his *Life*, the hopes which he held at various times from 1920 to 1925 that the Church of England would become rationalized and 'comprehensive enough to include the majority of thinkers of the previous hundred years who had lost all belief in the supernatural' were raised only to be disappointed.

Hardy had been 'churchy' all his life, and the Bible remained his major book of wisdom. His Biblical quotations, allusions, and references far outnumber those from any other source, including Shakespeare. Frequently he makes us think, as St Paul urged the Philippians to do, on things lovely, true, and of good report (cf. 'The Souls of the Slain', 'The To-Be-Forgotten'). His familiarity with the Bible probably did more to enlarge his historical sense than any other literature. He shares the psalmist's view that 'a thousand years' are but 'as yesterday', and sees the continuity of life ('seed-time and harvest shall not cease') 'though Dynasties pass'. Where Biblical echoes in Hardy's fiction refer to well-known events and figures (Cain and Job, for example) they still have a universalizing effect. Their aptness is such that often, in a flash, they supply an imaginative release which confirms the immutability of human nature, as when, at the end of 'Old Mrs Chundle', the curate, stunned by the realization of his false Church standards, goes out 'like Peter at the cock-crow'. It is easy to miss the implications and aptness of Hardy's Biblical quotations. When Bathsheba looks at the white face of the coffined Fanny Robin, she fancies that it shows a consciousness of the retaliatory pain it inflicts 'with all the merciless rigour of the Mosaic law'. Only by studying the whole context of the slightly inaccurate quotation which follows (cf. Exodus, xxi.22–5) can one see how it applies to Troy (about to enter) as much as to Bathsheba.[11] Hardy's Biblical references seem least convincing where they are most ambitious: in the Jude-Jesus parallels which were dictated by his Christminster–Crucifixion theme.

Hardy achieves a considerable degree of universality through his use of literature. The major actions of *The Return of the Native* and *The Mayor of Casterbridge* are imagined within short distances from his birthplace. In the former the perennial conflict between hedonistic selfishness and altruistic zeal is adapted from Arnold and Pater, and heightened by Hardy's sense of natural defect in a Darwinian world. In the latter his immediate aim was a successful weekly serial with continual excitement and suspense. His main purpose was to please at a much higher level, and with this in view he drew Wessex parallels to the old Old Testament story of Saul and David, to the *Oedipus Rex* of Sophocles, to *King Lear*, and even more notably to *Les Misérables*.[12] After experiment in various directions, in long short stories and novels, he gives the impression of setting himself high tragic standards, and of aiming to enhance the imaginative appeal of his story through the creation of elements suggested by scenes and situations which had proved their worth in various countries from ancient to modern times. Hardy is no mere borrower, however closely the final philosophy of Elizabeth-Jane resembles that which concludes Sophocles' play. He adapts and transmutes, and the critical question relates not to the means but to the result. Only a creative writer with imaginative vision can re-create effectively in this way, and only situations which are essentially the same throughout the ages can respond to this kind of treatment. The artistry of *Tess of the d'Urbervilles* cannot be fully appreciated without a realization of its indebtedness in idea and imagery to Shakespeare's 'The Rape of Lucrece' and Richardson's *Clarissa*.[13] Though F. R. Leavis omits him from his 'great tradition' of English novelists, it is doubtful whether any of them had a stronger traditional awareness of this kind than Hardy.

Readers familiar with *The Waste Land* will appreciate the generalizing dimensions which literary quotations and allusions can give to the particular. Hardy's works are strewn with them from many sources, ancient and contemporary, English and foreign. Henchard's jealousy of Farfrae makes him brood until he becomes 'cankered in soul' like Bellerophon; 'his nature to extenuate nothing' gives him the noble bearing of Othello in adversity. A similar but more extended universalizing effect is obtained by Hardy's association of his tempters and villains with Goethe's Mephistopheles or Milton's Satan. In the scene which precedes the rape of Tess (the opening of an episode first published as 'Saturday Night in Arcady') we are reminded of rural Greece in classical literature as rushing couples in the reel are metamorphosed by the

haze into 'satyrs clasping nymphs', 'a multiplicity of Pans whirling
a multiplicity of Syrinxes', 'Lotis attempting to elude Priapus, and
always failing', while 'Sileni of the throng' sit by the walls.

Hardy's literary allusiveness can be far-reaching. In 'A Singer
Asleep' he stresses the influence of Sapphic fragments, those
'orts' which are 'love incarnadine', on Swinburne's poetry. 'The
Impercipient' loses immeasurably if the echoes of Tennyson's *In
Memoriam* and Wordsworth's 'Intimations of Immortality' are not
fully realized. The heaven of pre-existence which it virtually denies
is hinted at in 'Midnight on the Great Western', where the boy's
raptness on his life's journey between one unknown and another,
and the question whether he knows 'a sphere' far above our 'rude
realms', recall the young traveller of Wordsworth's poem, happily
lost in the light of heaven though 'shades of the prison-house' are
closing in on him.

Two pastoral scenes with classical references have remarkable
overtones. At Talbothays the declining sun casts shadows of the
cows in the milking-sheds 'with as much care over each contour
as if it had been the profile of a Court beauty on a palace wall;
copied them as diligently as it had copied Olympian shapes on
marble *façades* long ago, or the outline of Alexander, Caesar, and
the Pharaohs'. This time perspective carries the same connotation
as Shirley's.

> The glories of our blood and state
> Are shadows, not substantial things.

After the sheep-shearing supper in *Far from the Madding Crowd*,
Jacob Smallbury 'volunteered a ballad as inclusive and interminable
as that with which the worthy toper old Silenus amused on a
similar occasion the swains Chromis and Mnasylus, and other jolly
dogs of his day'. 'The sun went down in an ochreous mist', but
the shearers 'talked on, and grew as merry as the gods in Homer's
heaven'. With the Virgilian reference we glimpse *inter alia* the
continuity of essential occupations through the ages, and are
reminded (incidentally) of a timelessness which Hardy's rustics
often acquire from choice comments expressing the wit, wisdom,
humour, and foolishness of the common people. They may derive
something from his Wessex, more from his imagination; they are,
as he says of the best fiction, 'more true . . . than history or nature
can be'.[14]

The range of Hardy's vision is multiple, and the result is frequent, sometimes juxtaposed, changes of perspective. The classical associations of the sheep-shearing supper have a rich imaginative effect, but more significant for the story than Smallbury's ballad is Bathsheba's singing of the verse 'For his bride a soldier sought her' from a traditional song. When the feverish Clym Yeobright, convinced that Eustacia is responsible for his mother's death, sets off to confront her at Alderworth, we are reminded of the tragic expression of Oedipus, and almost immediately afterwards we are arrested by 'the imperturbable countenance of the heath, which, having defied the cataclysmal onsets of centuries, reduced to insignificance by its seamed and antique features the wildest turmoil of a single man'. Nothing expresses the artistic function of Egdon Heath more vividly than this image. Similarly, before the classical associations of Talbothays, we have a distant view of Tess in the flat pastoral valley, 'like a fly on a billiard-table of indefinite length, and of no more consequence to the surroundings than that fly'. Perspectives like the last are continually found in *The Dynasts*, as either spoken or implied (visualized) comment.

Hardy's vision ranges from the minute to the universal, from vernal leaves like new-spun silk to 'the full-starred heavens' of winter in 'Afterwards', from fern sprouts 'like bishops' croziers' to the varicoloured constellations over Norcombe Hill, and from Drummer Hodge, the unknown Wessex soldier, to the wonder excited by the 'strange-eyed constellations' which remain 'his stars eternally' in the southern hemisphere.

The poetry or romance of the contemporary world of railways and new technology is found in Hardy's verse, and formed an important element in his conception of *A Laodicean*. It is most distinctly felt near the opening of the novel, when the 'dying falls and melodious rises' in the singing of the telegraph wire which is seen overhead against 'the stars in their courses', as it links the medievalism of Stancy Castle with the modernity of London, are associated with the 'quiring' of the stars 'to the young-eyed cherubim' in Shakespeare.

'In a Museum' and 'A Kiss' show Hardy's scientific imagination lost in wonder at sounds travelling from earth through space or starting from widely different areas to mingle in 'the full-fugued song of the universe unending'. In 'According to the Mighty Working' he thinks of the web of cause–effect for ever woven throughout the universe by the Spinner of the Years. It is responsible for disasters such as the loss of the *Titanic* or the international tragedy of *The Dynasts*; for hereditary characteristics which determine so much in life ('Discouragement', 'The Pedigree'); and for strange physical transformations from death and burial ('Voices from Things Growing in a Churchyard').

Hardy's altruism extends to the whole living world, just as his patriotism applies to the whole globe regardless of race ('The wind blew words'). In 'The Darkling Thrush' (influenced perhaps by Keats's 'What the Thrush said'[15]), and 'An August Midnight' he recognises that the humblest creatures may have insights beyond the reach of human senses and intellect. Waterloo makes him think not only of human carnage but of distress and destruction before the outbreak of battle, in birds and butterflies, animals above and below ground, flowers in bud, and unripened fruit and corn.

The general in the particular may be found in Hardy scenes relative to marriage. The woman of 'She Revisits Alone the Church of Her Marriage' is any one of a countless number who have happy recollections of their wedding-services; the poem is a wonderful evocation of a common experience. The road which Henchard and his wife follow at the opening of *The Mayor of Casterbridge* is dusty and worn; by it a weak bird sings 'a trite old evening song' such as could have been heard there at the same time for centuries; the couple are strangely individualized but the staleness of their marriage is a commonplace of time. Unlike them, the pair in the poem 'John and Jane' are generic; their parental expectations and experience are all too common. Even in 'She Hears the Storm', which is so specifically localized that the widow must be Hardy's mother, no attempt is made to reduce the general reference to the imagined experience.

Hardy can look at his own private sorrow in a detached way. His marriage proved to be unhappy, and with hindsight he often regretted that he had not married this person or that (always assuming, it seems, that each would have married him). So he thought when Helen Paterson, the illustrator of *Far from the Madding Crowd*, married. His poem on the subject, 'The Opportunity', shows no self-pity; its jaunty measure proclaims a wry acceptance of a common plight, and the acknowledgment is more defined when it is seen that the form of the poem is based on Browning's 'Youth and Art', which has exactly the same theme.

Another Browning theme, that of 'The Statue and the Bust', becomes the subject of 'The Waiting Supper', a story which, like so many of Hardy's, shows the hold of boyhood memories. The original of the hissing waterfall which expresses the tragic irony of situation came to his notice when his father was employed by the architect Benjamin Ferrey in the rebuilding of Stafford House near Lower Bockhampton. Hardy felt impelled to use places connected with forebears in his stories. In *Jude the Obscure* he was tempted to use the names of relatives at Fawley of whom he had heard from his grandmother; he abandoned them, but it was filial piety which determined the precise Marygreen setting of that novel, just as interest in three generations of Hardys suggested *Under the Greenwood Tree*, and his mother's childhood the setting for *The Woodlanders*. All these stories, ranging from the relatively idyllic to the tortured and tragic, enjoy a universality of appeal which transcends their Wessex topography.

One can have local attachment without having a provincial outlook. Hardy discovered in Italy that he had taken 'Dorchester and Wessex life' with him. At Fiesole the sight of an ancient coin reminded him of Roman remains unearthed in his grounds at Max Gate. In Venice he noticed that the bell of St Mark's campanile had 'exactly that tin-tray *timbre* given out by the bells of Longpuddle and Weatherbury, showing that they are of precisely the same-proportioned alloy'. His historical sense was assisted by his architectural knowledge. After a few days in Rome, he felt that its 'measureless layers of history' lay upon him 'like a physical weight'.[16] One reason he did not wish to visit the United States was that he preferred places with historical layers, and this interest is to be found in some of his more amusing poems such as 'Aquae Sulis', 'The Coronation', and 'Christmas in the Elgin Room'.

In 'After the Fair' Hardy sees the High Street of Casterbridge deserted at midnight by all but the ghosts of its buried citizens,

> From the latest far back to those old Roman hosts
>   Whose remains one yet sees . . . .

The stories of *A Group of Noble Dames* have a basis in Wessex history, and we are asked to imagine their narration in the Dorset County Museum, where finally they assume their appropriate place in the long perspective of time, as 'a single pirouetting flame on the top of a single coal' makes 'the bones of the ichthyosaurus seem to leap, the stuffed birds to wink', and 'the varnished skulls of Vespasian's soldiery' to smile.

The sundial design which Hardy used to illustrate 'The Temporary the All' aptly serves as an introduction to his poetry. It was clearly planned for Max Gate, but not executed until after his death. From his study window he could see Conquer Barrow, a prehistoric mound, not far away. His poems show that he often thought of the dead he had known, and particularly of his wife, his parents, and his sister Mary, buried at Stinsford, across the valley. Near their burial-ground is Kingston Maurward, the manor house where, in his early boyhood, he had fallen in love with the lady whose ageing (imaginatively recalled in the tragic ending of *Two on a Tower*) shocked him unforgettably in London. It is of her and fleeting time that he had thought in 'The Dream-Follower':

> A dream of mine flew over the mead
> To the halls where my old Love reigns;
> And it drew me on to follow its lead:
> And I stood at her window-panes;

> And I saw but a thing of flesh and bone
> Speeding on to its cleft in the clay;
> And my dream was scared, and expired on a moan,
> And I whitely hastened away.

A barrow is excavated on Bincombe Down, a few miles off, and he writes 'The Clasped Skeletons', recalling famous lovers in Hebrew, classical, and medieval history, and reflecting that they are but of yesterday compared with the fossils near the pair whose bones have recently been brought to light. In 'Evening Shadows' he thinks of shadows cast by Max Gate after his death, and how the shadow of Conquer Barrow is likely to outlast the Christendom which superseded the pagan myths of the period when it was constructed. Implicit in the thought of 'Waiting Both' is the web of natural law which extends through stellar space and the individual; a star looks down and agrees with Hardy that they must each wait, and let time go by, until the inevitable change comes. Max Gate is 'The House of Silence', and the 'visioning powers' which he attributes to his phantom self in this poem are not exaggerated:

'It is a poet's bower,
Through which there pass, in fleet arrays,
Long teams of all the years and days,
Of joys and sorrows, of earth and heaven,
That meet mankind in its ages seven,
An aion in an hour.'

Hardy's statements on fiction and poetry square with his finest achievements. The 'whole secret' of the former lies in an adjustment to 'things eternal and universal'; 'a poet should express the emotion of all the ages and the thoughts of his own'.[17] Great art springs from an alliance between the local and the contemporary and those relatively timeless issues which remain essentially unchanged because they are true to life. Mythical interpretations of life and the universe have in the end become scientific, and the principal key to Hardy's continuing success as a writer is that he combines to an unusual degree a scientific vision of man's place in the universe with an artistic realization of the greatness in writing which has commanded assent through the ages. The humanitarianism of his imaginative appeal has been taken for granted. It is because Pater, in drawing a distinction between 'good art' and 'great art', stresses this aspect of literature, and implies such perspectives as this introductory essay attempts to illustrate, that his conclusion to 'Style' is particularly appropriate:

Given the conditions I have tried to explain as constituting good art; – then, if it be devoted further to the increase of men's happiness, to the redemption of the oppressed, or the enlargement of our sympathies with each other, or to such presentment of new or old truth about ourselves and our relation to the world as may ennoble and fortify us . . . it will be also great art; if, over and above those qualities I summed up as mind and soul – that colour and mystic perfume, and that reasonable structure, it has something of the soul of humanity in it, and finds its logical, its architectural place, in the great structure of human life.

In the end one is left wondering whether heart, imagination, and intellect combined in Hardy to achieve what Arnold regarded as 'the element by which the modern spirit, if it would live right, has chiefly to live'. He defined this as 'the imaginative reason'; Pater, more precisely, as 'the imaginative intellect'.[18]

2
Hardy and George Eliot

The influence of literature on Hardy's novels was great, and a study of the evidence suggests that his indebtedness to George Eliot, especially in his early writing, was considerable. One must allow for coincidences, even more for what can be retained by the subconscious memory, but there can be little doubt that Hardy took hints from George Eliot's fiction, and developed them for his own artistic ends.

Perhaps this explains his apprehension when the opening chapters of *Far from the Madding Crowd*, published anonymously in the January 1874 number of *The Cornhill Magazine*, reminded a reviewer of George Eliot. A year later, when the novel appeared as a whole, attention was drawn to similarities with *Adam Bede* by one critic; another began with Hardy's pastoral vein, and described *Under the Greenwood Tree* as 'a series of rustic sketches – Dutch paintings . . . after the manner of *Silas Marner*'. The result was that Hardy decided to set aside the rural subject he had intended for his next novel, and to experiment with *The Hand of Ethelberta*, showing that 'he did not mean to imitate anybody'.

So he wrote nearly half a century later when preparing his *Life*. At the time he seems to have forgotten what George Eliot had meant to him, and to subscribe to the current view (represented by his friend Edmund Gosse) that George Eliot was a philosopher rather than a novelist. He is on safe ground in expressing surprise that the reviewer had detected her pen in the opening chapters of *Far from the Madding Crowd*, just as he is in asserting that 'she had never touched the life of the fields', but the remainder of his comments are less reliable. The reviews of 1875 were nearer the mark, and it was for this reason that Hardy decided to postpone the story he had planned, the plot of which he returned to more than ten years later when he began *The Woodlanders*.

His assessment of George Eliot's rustics and their speech is less convincing than that of a reviewer who in 1872 referred to 'the wonderful village talk which the author of "Adam Bede" has evolved out of her consciousness, and which sounds as good as if she had waited in taprooms all her life'. George Eliot's rich evocations of farm life in that novel came from her imaginative memory; Hardy's, mainly from direct impressions. *Adam Bede* shows that rustic speech came more readily to her; Hardy's is more selective, more artfully fashioned, at times comparable to Shakespeare's. His conjecture that Positivist expressions must have been responsible for the reviewer's judgment in January 1874 is surprising; he must have been thinking of Positivist characteristics in some of his later novels. They are not noticeable in the opening chapters of *Far from the Madding Crowd*, or in the work as a whole, though towards the end, with the memorable feats of Black Bess at Greenhill Fair, there is a reference to the subjective view of immortality which could have been written after reading George Eliot's 'O may I join the choir invisible', first published in May 1874.

It is hard to imagine that Hardy was not familiar with *Adam Bede*, one of the greatest immediate successes of all time, long before he became anxious to succeed as a writer of fiction. This did not happen until after the rejection of *The Poor Man and the Lady* in 1869, when, following Meredith's advice, he began to consider a novel with a more complicated plot. For *Desperate Remedies* he took hints from more popular authors such as Miss Braddon and Wilkie Collins, but it would have been most unlike him to neglect the works of George Eliot, the most eminent British novelist after the death of Dickens in 1870. *Felix Holt* had been published in 1866. It is one of those rare novels which have tragic scenes as awe-inspiring as anything in classical drama, and Hardy could not fail to respond to the Transome story, or to such chapter epigraphs as this from the *Agamemnon* of Aeschylus: ''Tis law as steadfast as the throne of Zeus – Our days are heritors of days gone by.' *Felix Holt* may have given Hardy greater assurance in adopting a complicated criminal plot. He was most probably further emboldened by George Eliot's example in rooting her tragedy in a lady's affair which leads to the anguish of concealment (and extreme bitterness of grief when her illegitimate son hardens his heart against her), for he turns a similar but more romantic complication into the mingled tragedy and villainy of Miss Aldyclyffe and her illegitimate son Manston. Aware of hardships in the youth of his paternal grandmother, he would have been particularly susceptible to a passage on *Felix Holt* in *The Saturday Review* (which he read regularly) on 'the evil usage which women receive at the hands of men'. Miss Aldclyffe's tragedy comes to the fore in the bedroom scene at Knapwater House (vi.1), and it is here, particularly in the detail, that the similarity to *Felix Holt* (xlix–1) is most remarkable, though Hardy's adaptation is more psychologically complex. Mrs Transome is a proud woman who yearns for affection; Miss Aldclyffe is a haughty, impatient woman who is overcome by long-checked feelings, and wishes to love as well as be loved. Her passion shows no lesbian propensity, but the sudden reawakening of the love she had felt for Cytherea's father, the thwarting of which in her youth had gradually warped her nature.

The possibilities of the old village instrumental choir in Hardy's second surviving novel *Under the Greenwood Tree* may well have been suggested by George Eliot's humorous reminiscence at the opening of 'Amos Barton'. Three of the choir, the wheelwright leader, the bassoon, and one of the key-bugles, appear at the Rainbow in *Silas Marner*, in a scene which had an immense influence on the development of Hardy's rustic chorus. *Silas Marner* recalls Christmas carols and the Christmas service in the country, but the great social event of the season is the dance at Squire Cass's on New Year's Eve. With Solomon the fiddler leading the procession into the White Parlour (after some preliminary fiddling and 'Sir Roger de Coverley') and social priorities being observed in the dance, we are reminded of the Christmas party at the tranter's in *Under the Greenwood Tree*. Humorous comments from observers, and details of dress, supply other parallels. Ben Winthrop's description of Mrs Osgood, tripping along with little steps as if she had wheels on her feet, recalls Hardy's Mrs Crumpler, who 'moved so smoothly through the figure that her feet were never seen', making the imaginative think that 'she rolled on castors'. John Morley's approval of the Christmas Eve pictures at the tranter's in *The Poor Man and the Lady* and high praise for his rustic humour in a review of *Desperate Remedies* had not been forgotten by Hardy. He revised the first for *Under the Greenwood Tree*, and planned his story in accordance with the reviewer's recommendation that he should give himself greater scope to present more pictures of 'consequential village worthies, and gaping village rustics', figures reminiscent of Wilkie's paintings and 'still more perhaps of those of Teniers'. This advice lent weight to the views expressed by George Eliot in *Adam Bede* (xvii), and the first effect of both may be seen in the sub-title of *Under the Greenwood Tree*, 'A Rural Painting of the Dutch School'. George

Eliot's enthusiastic digression on Dutch paintings, with its zeal for truthfulness to life, and the presentation of common people, in art, continued to support Hardy in his novels, in tragic as in humorous scenes, long after he had ceased to give it conscious heed.

Would he have chosen 'Far from the Madding Crowd' for the title of his fourth novel but for George Eliot? His interest in Greek drama must have made him dwell on the penultimate paragraph of her introduction to *Felix Holt*. The 'pain that is quite noiseless', 'unknown to the world' and remote from 'the roar of hurrying existence', recalls Gray's lines 'Far from the madding crowd's ignoble strife . . . They kept the noiseless tenor of their way.' Hardy expresses George Eliot's thought when he writes in *The Woodlanders* of 'dramas of a grandeur and unity truly Sophoclean' which are enacted in 'sequestered spots outside the gates of the world'.

Other brief literary passages kindled Hardy's imagination. In the introduction to *Felix Holt* he read, about the shepherd: 'his solar system was the parish; the master's temper and the casualties of lambing-time were his region of storms'. There are events of the latter kind on Norcombe Hill and with Bathsheba at Weatherbury. Although its dimension is spatial, 'his solar system was the parish' is reminiscent of those seemingly changeless times when the uprooting of a great cider-bearing tree or the demolition of Dicky Hill's cider-house was a major event to the frequenters of Warren's malthouse; reminiscent too of a visual harmony between the shearers and the great barn that had scarcely changed for centuries. The introductory words, 'To-day the large side doors were thrown open', echo with less rousing resonance 'For the great barn-doors are thrown wide open' in *Adam Bede*, where the scene within (unlike Hardy's) is given only passing notice. The same novel presents a great harvest supper, with songs, which is altogether more realistic, though less imaginatively fused with the story, than Hardy's shearing-supper. There, as the evening wears on, the rustics grow as merry as the gods in Homer's heaven, a comparison as felicitous as bold, anticipated in *Scenes of Clerical Life*, with the oak table in the housekeeper's room at Cheverel Manor high enough for Homer's gods, and Mr Bates a latter-day Bacchus from Olympus. Passing over the harvest supper in *Far from the Madding Crowd*, Hardy presents the results of the revels which follow, thereby confirming the realization of disaster which comes premonitorily to Bathsheba as she helps Gabriel to save her corn. A pregnant metaphor in *Adam Bede* may have sown the seed for this remarkably imaginative scene: 'and yet the time of harvest and ingathering is not come, and we tremble at the possible storms that may ruin the precious fruit in the moment of its ripeness'. The picture here is of the corn before it is harvested, but Hardy's mind was as imaginatively fertile as it was imaginatively receptive.

Tragic seduction in *Adam Bede* may obviously have helped to initiate Hardy's plot, but correspondences between Hetty, Arthur Donnithorne, and Adam Bede relationships on the one hand, and those between Fanny Robin, Sergeant Troy, and Gabriel Oak on the other, do not go very far. Donnithorne is an army man like Troy, but more important is the similarity between Adam Bede and Gabriel Oak. The quality they share is epitomized in Gabriel's surname, and suggested in a description of a glimpse of the chase, the scene of Arthur and Hetty's seduction: 'Those beeches and smooth limes – there was something enervating in the very sight of them; but the strong knotted old oaks had no bending languor in them – the sight of them would give a man some energy.' Idea and image may have fused in Hardy's memory after reading the conclusion of 'Mr Gilfil's Love-Story'. 'But it is with men as with trees', George Eliot wrote; alone, in his old age, Mr Gilfil was like a 'poor lopped oak', but he had been 'sketched out by nature as a noble tree. The heart of him was sound, the grain was of the finest'; the main trunk of his nature remained loyal to 'a first and only love'.

Perhaps nothing in George Eliot created more artistic emulation in Hardy than the Rainbow scene in *Silas Marner*. *The Saturday Review* thought it worthy of Shakespeare, and its resemblance to the Warren malthouse scenes is significant. Some of the worthies who meet at the Rainbow are closely connected with the Church, and their communicative example contributed to Hardy's inspiration in *Under the Greenwood Tree*. In *Far from the Madding Crowd* and *The Return of the Native* the role of the rustic group is extended. They are an unfailing source of humour, and help signally to create a sense of parish background. In their comments on the course of the main action, they also function more like the Greek chorus, the drift of their conversation being artfully contrived to reveal relevant portions of the past or hint at developments to come. Hardy's style and presentation are crisper and livelier than George Eliot's; he has a greater fund of humour. He was more indebted to Shakespeare, but technically, in all respects, he was influenced chiefly by the manner in which she introduced light relief in the Rainbow scene, and even more by her method of relating it closely to the story. The way in which her dialogue leads to its climax, with the ghostlike appearance of Silas after his loss of gold, has its nearest parallel in Hardy when Boldwood unexpectedly enters the malthouse with the letter announcing Fanny Robin's sudden departure in the hope of marrying Troy; the artistic comparison is here much in George Eliot's favour.

This brings us to 1875, when Hardy chose to write *The Hand of Ethelberta*, and prove that 'he did not mean to imitate anybody'. Further experimentation followed until he found his strength in *The Mayor of Casterbridge*. Hardy's novel benefited, as *The Return of the Native* had done, from his taking time to read, relax, and study artistic presentation. There seems to be little doubt that he read *The Mill on the Floss*, for he quotes Novalis in words which are much nearer George Eliot's than they are to the original.[1] The maxim 'Character is Fate' applies as much to Mr Tulliver as to Henchard. A man of strong feeling, kind-hearted but rashly impulsive and rather superstitious, Tulliver is temperamentally akin to the mayor. Like him he belongs to the old rule-of-thumb world of provincial business; 'if the world had been left as God made it', he says, he could have seen his way and held his own. He trusts to luck, and takes great risks, as Henchard does, when things go wrong. *Vis-à-vis* the Dodsons he may have suggested the Henchard–Farfrae polarity. His natural lack of foresight, particularly when he borrows money from his enemy's client, means that he has 'a destiny as well as Oedipus', and qualifies him to 'plead, like Oedipus, that his deed was inflicted on him rather than committed by him'; these words apply even more to Henchard. Tulliver's dependence on his 'little wench' Maggie, at the time of his downfall, is more touching than Henchard's on Elizabeth-Jane; and his curse on Wakem reminds us of the terrible imprecation dramatically produced by the unwitting choir on Farfrae. Tulliver's thirst for revenge drives him to sadistic rage; Henchard is on the brink of murder when he saves himself.

The possibility of George Eliot's influence on Hardy through scattered and incidental images must be considered. The 'crystallising feather-touch' which shook Lydgate's flirtation into love was probably remembered in the poem 'At the Word "Farewell" '. An epigraph in *Felix Holt* –

'Twas town, yet country too; you felt the warmth
Of clustering houses in the wintry time;
Supped with a friend, and went by lantern home.
Yet from your chamber window you could hear
The tiny bleat of new-yeaned lambs, or see
The children bend beside the hedgerow banks
To pluck the primroses

– may have seemed so appropriate to Dorchester that Hardy
thought of it in *The Mayor of Casterbridge*.[2] Combined with Carlyle's
image of 'the Soul of Man' lacerating itself 'like a captive bird,
against the iron limits which Necessity has drawn round it', that
of Caterina as a poor bird 'beginning to flutter and vainly dash its
soft breast against the hard iron bars of the inevitable'[3] probably
ensured that the trapped and helpless bird as an expression of the
heroine's plight found its place in *Desperate Remedies* and, more
often, in *Tess of the d'Urbervilles*. A description in *Daniel Deronda* of
'girl-tragedies that are going on in the world, hidden, unheeded,
as if they were but tragedies of the copse or hedgerow, where the
helpless drag wounded wings forsakenly, and streak the shadowed
moss with the red moment-hand of their own death' probably
resulted in such a scene, after a battue, on the night when Tess
seeks to sleep in a plantation, as the tragedy of her life takes her
to Flintcomb-Ash. Alec d'Urberville's threat to her in the final act
of that tragedy is initiated in a manner reminiscent of the 'ugly
black spot on the landscape' which images that of the sinister
Raffles to Bulstrode: he is first noticed as a 'black speck' in the
distance as he seeks out Tess on high exposed farmland at
Flintcomb-Ash.[4]

Elsewhere other possible or indubitable George Eliot influences
on Hardy will be discussed, including the reduction of a whole
scene in *Romola* to a single image. Another in *Daniel Deronda*, when
Gwendolen is tempted to let her loathed and dreaded husband
drown, and hesitates before making a hopeless attempt to save
him, has its parallel in 'A Tragedy of Two Ambitions'. When Daniel
hears her story, he is certain that her remorse is 'the precious sign
of a recoverable nature', 'the culmination of that self-disapproval
which had been the awakening of a new life within her'. He did
not wish to say anything which would diminish the 'sacred
aversion' she felt towards 'her worst self – that thorn-pressure
which must come with the crowning of the sorrowful Better,

suffering because of the Worse'. These last words, and their presentation, could well have contributed to Hardy's 'if way to the Better there be, it exacts a full look at the Worst' in the second of his 'In Tenebris' poems. George Eliot's words, '*Caritas*, the highest love or fellowship, which I am happy to believe that no philosophy will expel from the world' may have influenced him when he made Jude declare, after Sue's penitential return to the Church, and the announcement of her intended re-marriage to Phillotson, that the verses on charity will 'stand fast' when all that she calls 'religion' has passed away.[5]

Daniel Deronda appeared in 1876, and it seems unlikely that Hardy, who wished above all to succeed as a poet, would miss two of George Eliot's comments. Most conspicuously, in the opening paragraph of the third book, she wrote:

> And perhaps poetry and romance are as plentiful as ever in the world except for those phlegmatic natures who I suspect would in any age have regarded them as a dull form of erroneous thinking. They exist very easily in the same room with the microscope and even in railway carriages: what banishes them is the vacuum in the gentleman and lady passengers.

She repeated the idea in the following book: 'Here undoubtedly lies the chief poetic energy: – in the force of imagination that pierces or exalts the solid fact, instead of floating among cloud-pictures.' (Ruskin had expressed very similar views.) In June 1877 Hardy wrote: 'There is enough poetry in what is left, after all the false romance has been abstracted, to make a sweet pattern.' The following April he cited Hobbema's method of 'infusing emotion into the baldest external objects'. His next novel was *A Laodicean*, a novel of intrigue in which his most serious aim was to convince the reader that the new world of technology, including railways, can acquire aesthetic appeal if we have eyes to see and ears to hear.

Hardy regarded George Eliot as one of the greatest thinkers of her time. When she died near the end of 1880, he wrote:

> If Comte had introduced Christ among the worthies in his calendar it would have made Positivism tolerable to thousands who, from position, family connection, or early education, now decry what in their heart of hearts they hold to contain the germs

of a true system. It would have enabled them to modulate gently into the new religion by deceiving themselves with the sophistry that they still continued one-quarter Christians, or one-eighth, or one-twentieth, as the case might be: This is a matter of *policy*, without which no religion succeeds in making way.

Both Hardy and George Eliot were Positivist in sympathy, believing that the welfare of mankind depends on an enlightened altruism. Their philosophical positions were similar; each had a scentific outlook, assuming that life on earth is the only life of which one can be assured. People are too much subject to the chance of birth and circumstance. The higher aim therefore is to do everything possible for the less fortunate, for the general good, and for the generations to come. Hardy was less optimistic. In his fiction he puts the emphasis on chance (including heredity), whereas George Eliot stresses the importance of moral choice; in his later years he concluded that mankind was swayed too much by 'unreason'. Inspired by greater resolution, and in no way blinded to human shortcomings and dangers, George Eliot believed in 'the slow stupendous teaching of the world's events', and did not doubt 'the efficacy of feeling in stimulating to ardent co-operation' for humanitarian ends.

3

Psychological Pictorialism

Hardy the novelist is less dramatic in technique than Jane Austen, and relies much more on settings for his effects. Among these, however, the merely pictorial, those of the backcloth type, are rather minimal, the longer and the more important reflecting human situations and feelings. By such means he usually conveys a deeper, more imaginative, and more memorable awareness of characters at critical points in the action than a writer such as Henry James who depends largely on the refinements of psychological analysis.

Hardy had seen no doubt the value of such a technique in contemporary fiction, including works by Wilkie Collins and George Eliot. It was impressed upon him further as a result of studying the works of great painters, a habit which began during the period of his architectural apprenticeship in London, when he made a practice of devoting twenty minutes after lunch to the close inspection of 'a single master' on each of his many visits to the National Gallery. In the visual conception of his characters he often recalls pictures he had studied, and occasionally his imagined scenes remind him of period characteristics in painting. As Cytherea makes her way to the old manor house where she is to meet Manston, a thunderstorm threatens, and 'livid grey shades, like those of the modern French painters', make 'a mystery of the remote and dark parts of the vista', seeming 'to insist upon a suspension of breath'. Years after recording this artistic recollection, Hardy became interested in the French Impressionists, as is evident not only in his *Life* but also in *The Woodlanders*, where Marty South is presented as 'an impression-picture of extremest type, wherein the girl's hair alone, as the focus of observation, was depicted with intensity and distinctness, while her face, shoulders, hands, and figure in general, were a blurred mass of unimportant detail, lost in haze and obscurity'. Among the rarer sunny scenes in the woods of this novel, the Impressionist mode of regard is noticeable in this vignette:

Just about here the trees were large and wide apart, and there was no undergrowth, so that she could be seen to some distance a sylph-like greenish-white creature, as toned by the sunlight and leafage.[1]

The view of Marty differs from this in being psychological; its artistic concentration reflects the one interest and purpose of barber Percomb, who is about to enter, on his Loki-mission as Mrs Charmond's agent.

It is, not surprisingly, easy to find reminders of Hardy's pictorial effects in paintings, but impossible to decide whether any such resemblances are more than coincidental. Too often insufficient allowance is made for his creative powers. He was unusually sensitive to colour, and some of his more incidental description suggests that he tended to exaggerate tones for the sake of effect. The western light adds a tint of orange to the vivid purple of heather at the very climax of its bloom, and so intensifies the colours that they seem 'to stand above the surface of the earth and float in mid-air like an exhalation of red'. The general colour of a carriage in Hyde Park is the rich indigo of a midnight sky. Early on a bright October morning semi-opaque screens of blue haze make mysteries of 'the commonest gravel-pit, dingle, or recess', and, a little later, the smoke of newly lit fires ascends from cottage chimneys 'like the stems of blue trees'.[2] Styles of paintings may have influenced Hardy in such descriptions, but, where his main concern is psychologically bound to character, the probability is strong that he himself created the outer scenes to express inner worlds of mood, or of that indivisible conjunction of thought and emotion which crises bring.

Ambitious to succeed, Hardy in his first published novel attempted to translate feelings into one of his most poetic and ambitious landscapes. Circumstance and altruism combine to make the heroine Cytherea feel that she has no alternative but to marry the sensual Manston, from whose 'hot voluptuous nature' she instinctively shrinks. Such character is represented by 'the cloak of rank broad leaves' under which the stream flows from 'the ruinous foundations of an old mill' by which they stand in a meadow, stream and ruin symbolizing time and decay, the passing of the only life which human beings can expect with certitude.[3] The symbolism continues:

On the right hand the sun, resting on the horizon-line, streamed across the ground from below copper-coloured and lilac clouds, stretched out in flats beneath a sky of pale soft green. All dark objects on the earth that lay towards the sun were overspread by a purple haze, against which a swarm of wailing gnats shone forth luminously, rising upward and floating away like sparks of fire.

The purple haze is made explicit in a former scene, when Edward Springrove and Cytherea fall in love. At this 'supremely happy moment' in their lives, 'the "bloom" and the "purple light" were strong on the lineaments of both'. (Here Hardy clearly expected many of his readers to recognise the reference to 'The Progress of Poesy' by Thomas Gray in *The Golden Treasury*.) Cytherea believes that Manston loves her, and hopes she will be able to love him. For a moment she is optimistic: the 'dark objects' on the earth are 'overspread by a purple haze', but the wailing gnats, remembered from Keats's autumn ode, are like evanescent sparks of fire. The sunset is inevitably close.

Cytherea's euphoria is equally ephemeral. Oppressed by the stillness and humidity of the atmosphere, she is reduced to passivity.

The helpless flatness of the landscape gave her, as it gives all such temperaments, a sense of bare equality with, and no superiority to, a single entity under the sky.

When Manston takes her by the hand and implores her to love him, she is aware of his trembling, and pities him. She realizes that her brother's hospital treatment depends on his kindness, and she remembers Edward's fickleness. In her dilemma she discerns in the autumnal haze over the marshy ground all that remains of the Swinburnian garden which spells joyless love. Like Tess, when she has lost her lover and is condemned to another, she feels as if she is in 'a boat without oars, drifting with closed eyes down a river – she knew not whither'.[4]

Such were the reviews of *Desperate Remedies* that Hardy did not expect it to be reprinted, and transferred two contrasting passages from this poetic landscape to *The Return of the Native*. Clym's decision to abandon his career in Paris and settle with Eustacia on Egdon, with scant prospects of earning an adequate income as a teacher, results in a bitter exchange of words with his mother. He is infatuated with Eustacia, and they meet, just after this quarrel, on 'a perfect level' of the heath. Again, with hardly a change, we have the setting sun, a sky of pale soft green, dark objects overspread by a purple haze, and the wailing gnats that dance like sparks of fire. Here the sun's rays stream across the ground from 'between' copper-coloured and lilac clouds, the copper contrasting with the softer hues, and suggestive rather of menace, as in *Desperate Remedies*. The euphoria of Clym and Eustacia is decisive; they 'will be married at once'. Clym sees the luminous rays enwrap Eustacia as she departs, but gradually the 'dead flat of the scenery' overpowers him, and 'something in its oppressive horizontality' reminds him of the 'arena of life', giving him 'a sense of bare equality with, and no superiority to, a single living thing under the sun'. He has cooled, and can now look at his prospects soberly; Eustacia is 'no longer the goddess but the woman to him', someone he has to protect and provide for, even be 'maligned for'.[5]

Having, as she thought, lost Edward Springrove irrecoverably, Cytherea decides there is no course left her but that of self-abnegation for the sake of her brother and Manston. Ill and worn out, she becomes indifferent to her future, and drifts towards marriage. For her therefore 'the ordinary sadness of an autumnal evening-service' seems to be doubled when she attends church with Miss Aldclyffe, with Manston sitting two seats forward from their pew. After the service she and Manston leave together, and take a secluded walk through the churchyard, returning by another gate to enter the church just as the sexton is locking up. She knows intuitively that her consent to marriage will be sought, and the hopelessness of her situation is reflected by her surroundings and the minatory glare of the sun as they walk up the nave:

> Everything in the place was the embodiment of decay: the fading red glare from the setting sun, which came in at the west window, emphasizing the end of the day and all its cheerful doings, the mildewed walls, the uneven paving-stones, the wormy pews, the sense of recent occupation, and the dank air of death which had gathered with the evening, would have made grave a lighter mood than Cytherea's was then.

The wintry scenes which follow immediately before and after her wedding emphasize the adversity of chance and the barrier between Cytherea and Edward on his 'Too late, beloved' return.

Scenes in *A Pair of Blue Eyes* are rather different, several having a recurrently proleptic significance. An unusually coloured one, related more incidentally to this series, has a psychological import, serving as an imaginative pointer to the growing disillusionment of Knight, the hard-hearted purist in love. Just after moonrise on a chilly October evening he walks with Elfride, determined to pry further into her past. He takes her to the church, where the restorers have demolished one side of the tower. They sit by the altar steps, looking at the heavy arch spanning the junction of the nave and eastern side of the tower, which stands firm. Beyond the arch can be seen, first the pile of fallen stones, 'then a portion of moonlit churchyard, then the wide and convex sea behind'. From the east window behind them, 'wherein saints and angels vied with each other in primitive surroundings of landscape and sky', rays of crimson, blue, and purple shine upon the pair, throwing upon the pavement at their feet 'a softer reproduction of the same translucent hues'. The scene recalls the casement of Keats's 'The Eve of St Agnes', with its rich colours thrown on the kneeling Madeline. As if consciously drawing a difference between the rapture of Keats's lovers and the ill-fated love of Elfride and Knight, Hardy creates an incongruity in his romantic setting by showing the shadowed heads of his couple as 'opaque and prominent blots' amid the softer reflections on the floor of the church. 'Presently the moon became covered by a cloud, and the iridescence died away.' When moonlight returns it brightens the foreground of the visible churchyard, and reveals the white tomb of Mrs Jethway's son against the unlit background. The suggestion is wholly funereal, and the sight is enough to initiate Knight's relentless search for the truth. Elfride, rather like Tess in submitting to 'the stream of events', is not strong enough to withstand his persistent inquiries. She protests but, though he has no inkling of her former relations with Stephen Smith, Knight is convinced that the girl he has loved is second-hand, and not the embodiment of honesty and innocence he had assumed. When he escorts her home, the iridescence, or the 'glory' and the 'dream', has 'passed away'.[6]

But for its pictorialism *Far from the Madding Crowd* would be little more than an exciting but rather melodramatic story. Its natural scenery ranges from the starry sky to the rural, and to the more minute and unusual observations of an author whose sharpness of perception was devoted to the promotion of descriptive definition and originality. Some of the ampler scenes, notably those of the clear night-sky from Norcombe Hill, the great barn at shearing-time, and the violent thunderstorm during which Oak and Bathsheba work together to save her stacked corn,[7] are among Hardy's most memorable. The most telling include several that are steeped in human significance, and remembered in conjunction with the leading characters, at critical points in their lives or relationships. In this respect, in the depth of emotion with which scenes are impregnated, *Far from the Madding Crowd* shows an assurance and impressiveness from which there is no later advance on a comparable scale except in *Tess of the d'Urbervilles*. Such scenes endow these two novels with great imaginative appeal.

There can be little doubt that certain features of the scene above the chalk-pit where Oak's flock of sheep perished, after panicking over the edge to escape the attentions of his untrained dog, reflect his thoughts and feelings. He quickly realizes that the ewes had not been insured, and that 'his hopes of being an independent farmer' have been 'laid low – possibly for ever'. Recovering from his stupor, he raises his head, and surveys the scene listlessly, noticing an oval pond near the rim of the pit, and above it 'the attenuated skeleton of a chrome-yellow moon', dogged by the morning star. The pool glitters like a dead man's eye, and a breeze ruffles its waters, shaking and elongating the moon's reflection, 'and turning the image of the star to a phosphoric streak'. The moon and the star, and their reflection in a pond like the eye of a corpse, express the extinction of Gabriel's hopes so vividly that he cannot forget the scene. Hardy's imagery and its associations bear such a resemblance to those of a passage in 'The Ancient Mariner' that it is doubtful whether the likenesses could be the product of any but conscious recollection. Coleridge presents a horned moon which is 'star-dogged' (once an ill-omen to superstitious sailors) at the point when 'four times fifty living men' drop dead one by one on the deck. The wedding-guest who listens spell-bound to the ancient mariner's story intervenes to tell him that he fears him and his 'glittering eye'. Hardy associates a star-dogged horned moon, which had only a few days to last, with a pond that glitters like a dead man's eye, and with the loss of most of Gabriel's sheep, four times fifty in fact. More significant probably in the evocation of Hardy's scene is 'the curse in a dead man's eye' which the ancient mariner is fated to see 'seven days, seven nights'.[8]

The question raised by the more elaborate and colourless scene 'Outside the Barracks' is whether it expresses the diminishing hopes of Fanny Robin or whether it is intended to impart a feeling of the tragic hopelessness of her mission. A public path is presented one dreary snowy evening; on the left hand it is bordered by a river behind which rises a wall; on the immediate right there is a tract of land which is partly meadow, partly moor. The winter has reached its climax, and the irregularities of the moorland have become featureless. It seems to be no more than 'the lowest layer of a firmament of snow', the dark arch of cloud gradually sinking, as if the snow in the heavens 'and that encrusting the earth would soon unite into one mass without any intervening stratum of air at all'. In this way the imminence of hope's extinction is evoked. To the left the wall is even darker than the sky, and the river gloomier still. The form that moves along its brim seems human. It is referred to as a 'spot' in the snow, but when Fanny secures the attention of Sergeant Troy in the barracks (which are on the other side of the river and closed for the night) their colloquy reveals her distress at his repeated failure to marry her, as he had promised. As the 'little spot' moves away (reduced as a reminder of the individual's insignificance in the sum of things) a low peal of laughter from listeners in the barracks is hardly distinguishable from 'the gurgle of the tiny whirlpools outside'.

The scene, in short, anticipates the Spirit of the Years, the Spirit of the Pities, and the Spirits Sinister and Ironic. Its presentation is highly objective, but so artistically selective that it does more than communicate a victim's suffering; it defines an authorial view of life. If it derives from any source outside Hardy's imagination, it most probably originated from his appreciation of some brief poetic effects in *Middlemarch*, where George Eliot chooses a wintry scene, with snow falling and the 'distant flat' shrinking 'in uniform whiteness and low-hanging uniformity of cloud' – a 'white vapour-walled landscape' – to express the 'stifling oppression' of Dorothea's life, the 'moral imprisonment' which extinguishes her hopes of walking on 'clear heights' in full communion with Mr Casaubon, the man whom she had idealistically misjudged and married.[9]

Snowy surroundings with moonlight and incipient sunrise are strikingly used to show the effect of Bathsheba's valentine on Boldwood, a gentlemanly bachelor whose temperament is such that when his equilibrium is disturbed he is 'in extremity at once'. By the evening which follows its arrival he has felt 'the symmetry of his existence to be slowly getting distorted in the direction of an ideal passion'. When he goes to bed he places the valentine in the corner of his looking-glass. The 'mysterious influences of night' invest its writing 'with the presence of the unknown writer'. As he dozes, her vision takes form; when he wakes, the moonlight is unusual. His window admits only its reflection,

> and the pale sheen had that reversed direction which snow gives, coming upward and lighting up his ceiling in an unnatural way, casting shadows in strange places, and putting lights where shadows had used to be.

In this way the mental *bouleversement* of Boldwood which is to result in the neglect of his farm and the shooting of Troy is emphasized. Early next morning he goes outside and watches the slow sunrise. Only half the sun is visible; it burns rayless 'like a red and flameless fire shining over a white hearthstone', hinting at the passion that will be roused in him. The sky, 'pure violet in the zenith', is leaden to the north and murky to the east, the effect of the whole resembling a sunset 'as childhood resembles age'. This general inversion clearly bodes ill for Boldwood's love; it is repeated around the horizon, which the snow makes difficult to distinguish:

> in general there was here, too, that before-mentioned preternatural inversion of light and shade which attends the prospect when the garish brightness commonly in the sky is found on the earth, and the shades of earth are in the sky.

The unpropitiousness of the valentine's effect is projected in the last feature of Hardy's skyscape, the wasting moon, 'now dull and greenish-yellow, like tarnished brass', in the west.

The mysterious influences of an unusually dark night invest the first meeting of Bathsheba and Troy with romance. Not until her lantern is opened does she know who it is she brushed against in the first plantation. (Her dress has been caught by the rowel of his spur.) The light reveals to her astonishment that the man to whom she is 'hooked' is a soldier, brilliant in brass and scarlet.

> His sudden appearance was to darkness what the sound of a trumpet is to silence. Gloom, the *genius loci* at all times hitherto, was now totally overthrown, less by the lantern-light than by what the lantern revealed. The contrast of this revelation with

her anticipations of some sinister figure in sombre garb was so great that it had upon her the effect of a fairy transformation.

Troy is bold in his gallantry. He thanks Bathsheba for 'the sight of such a beautiful face' and, after being freed from the tangle in the gimp of her dress, tells her he wishes 'it had been the knot of knots, which there's no untying'. When she hears what Liddy knows of him, she is ready to think favourably of him. She has been 'hooked' indeed, as Hardy's last remark on this luckless meeting indicates: it was 'a fatal omission of Boldwood's that he had never once told her she was beautiful'.

Bathsheba's bedazzlement by Sergeant Troy is the subject of 'The Hollow amid the Ferns', a brilliant *tour de force* which reveals the lightning play and evolutions of Troy's swordsmanship as an *aurora militaris* in the 'long, luxuriant rays' of the setting sun. Her impulsive folly leads to quarrels with both Oak and Boldwood, the latter's jealous rage and threats making her fearful for Troy. Left alone, she walks up and down in distraction, then sits on a heap of stones by the wayside. 'There she remained long', and the nature of her thoughts is reflected in the skyscape:

> Above the dark margin of the earth appeared foreshores and promontories of coppery cloud, bounding a green and pellucid expanse in the western sky. Amaranthine glosses came over them then, and the unresting world wheeled her round to a contrasting prospect eastward, in the shape of indecisive and palpitating stars.

The forebodings inspired by Boldwood which threaten Bathsheba's peace of mind are glossed over by hopes of love, but she cannot decide what to do. She gazes upon the 'silent throes' of the stars without realization, her spirit by this time being far away with Troy. It is 'troubled', however; his nature, she knows intuitively, is to be fickle in love.[10]

The first dramatic revelation of Bathsheba's folly in marrying Troy is made as it were by lightning strokes during the storm when she helps Oak to save her corn while her husband and his men lie in drunken stupor after their harvest revels. Her final disillusionment comes when she discovers the extent of his heartless perfidy towards Fanny Robin, and is rejected by Troy in his fit of remorse. She runs from home, heedless of direction, and takes refuge for the night in a withering fern-brake beneath large beech and oak trees. Early in the morning she finds that she has recovered, sounds of animated natural life, and then of a cheerful ploughboy, harmonizing with her new mood. Fallen autumnal leaves suggest that a phase of her life is ending. The swamp she finds she has rested near, full of decay and unpleasantly vivid fungi, seems like 'a nursery of pestilences', and reflects her thoughts on the moral evil with which she has been associated. The schoolboy who is heard trying to recite the collect he has to learn introduces us to Bathsheba's fervent hope that she may be given grace to 'cast away the works of darkness'. She is encouraged by the sight of Liddy, who crosses the swamp without sinking while 'iridescent bubbles of dank subterranean breath' rise from the sweating surface beside her feet. She tells her not to flinch if she finds herself in 'a fearful situation' through marriage, but to stand her ground. Strength has come to Bathsheba after the most fearful crisis in her life.

Scenes which express feeling are more incidental in *The Return of the Native*. The acoustic 'picture' introducing Eustacia consists of plaintive notations of the November wind over the heath, their most impressive and peculiar feature being the 'worn whisper' of the 'mummied' heath-bells which is joined indistinguishably by the lengthened sighing of a heroine who is weary with life on Egdon. Clym Yeobright's distress on quarrelling with his mother is expressed in the plantation which suffers damage in the high winds; wet young beeches undergo 'amputations, bruises, cripplings, and harsh lacerations' from which the wasting sap will 'bleed for many a day to come'. The plantation represents modern man, more sensitive and prone to suffer than his primitive ancestors; the gusts that tear its trees wave the natural growth of furze and heather 'in a light caress'. His mother's suffering when she vainly tries to effect a reconciliation with him and Eustacia is presented at greater length in a Darwinian blaze of exhausting heat; when her end nears, the sight of a heron rising and winging its way radiantly towards the sun makes her yearn for release from earthly pain. The storm when Eustacia is lost in the darkness of Egdon parallels the chaos of her mind just before her death.

The Mayor of Casterbridge opens with a visual study of a young man and his wife walking one late summer evening to Weydon-Priors fair. She carries their child, a baby girl, but they keep apart, though his elbow almost touches her shoulder at times. There is no communication between them; she has not thought of taking her husband's arm, or he of taking hers. With the tools of his trade in a rush-basket at his back, he walks in a 'measured, springless' manner indicative of ability, determination, and 'a dogged and cynical indifference', apparent also in his reading, or pretence of reading, a ballad sheet which he keeps in front of him as best he can with the hand that holds his basket strap. The perpendicularity of his stern, swarthy, slightly inclined face suggests hardness and purposeful strength. The chief attraction of his wife's face is its mobility of responsiveness when she looks at her child. This, the only natural feeling observable in the parents, is enhanced in the rays of the setting sun. As the mother, silently thinking, plods along in the shade of the hedge, she wears 'the hard, half-apathetic expression of one who deems anything possible at the hands of Time and Chance except, perhaps, fair play'. His lack of interest in wife and child is due, as the sequel shows, to his resentment that their dependence on him balks his freedom and selfish ambition. The scantiness of her expectation can be gauged by the fixity of her look, with little interest, ahead; the road has no special features, and its grassy dust-covered margins serve to accentuate the 'stale familiarity' which accompanies the trio, with hedges, trees, and other wayside vegetation in 'the blackened-green stage of colour' that foreshadows their autumnal doom. To emphasize still further the near-extinction of feeling in the couple, a weak old bird sings 'a trite old evening song' that might have been heard at the same place and 'at any sunset of that season' for centuries. Marriage has so little to offer the wife that, when Henchard, the worse for drink, sells her with the child at the fair, she accepts what she thought had begun as a joke as an opportunity for a new life; she is freed like the bird that escapes from the tent where she is sold chattel-wise to the sailor Newson.

When Henchard, after the death of his wife, whom he had reinstated for the sake of Elizabeth-Jane, discovers that the latter is not his daughter but Newson's, he concludes that fate is bent on punishing him, and looks out at the night 'as at a fiend'. He then walks by the river, 'the Schwarzwasser of Casterbridge', towards the hangman's cottage. 'The lugubrious harmony of the spot with his domestic situation' is too much to bear. The square mass in front of the buildings above the cliff seems like a pedestal without a statue; it is the base for the gallows at the entrance of the county gaol, and his observation suggests that he identifies himself with its missing human complement. A similar harmony

expresses his feelings when, after sparing the life of his successful
rival Farfrae, and hearing of Lucetta's critical illness as a result of
the skimmington-ride, he runs out to Weatherbury, hoping to meet
him and expedite his return to his wife. Only the moan of Yalbury
Wood is heard above his heart-throbs as he hurries on his wasted
mission. Farfrae distrusts 'this repentant sinner', and makes his
intended business detour, leaving Henchard to curse himself like
'a less scrupulous Job'.

When Newson returns, Henchard, fearful of losing Elizabeth-
Jane, 'the new-sprung hope of his loneliness', tells him she is dead.
Newson believes him, and leaves Casterbridge, but the fear of his
return and discovery of the truth preys on Henchard's mind, and
makes him think of suicide. Music has a 'regal power' over him,
and in his present state the allurement of audible waters outside
Casterbridge is music to his ears. Hardy therefore gives the
direction of his suicidal thoughts in orchestral terms:

The whole land ahead of him was as darkness itself; there was
nothing to come, nothing to wait for. Yet in the natural course
of life he might possibly have to linger on earth another thirty
or forty years – scoffed at; at best pitied.

The thought of it was unendurable.

To the east of Casterbridge lay moors and meadows, through
which much water flowed. The wanderer in this direction, who
should stand still for a few moments on a quiet night, might
hear singular symphonies from these waters, as from a lampless
orchestra, all playing in their sundry tones, from near and far
parts of the moor. At a hole in a rotten weir they executed a
recitative; where a tributary brook fell over a stone breastwork
they trilled cheerily; under an arch they performed a metallic
cymballing; and at Durnover Hole they hissed. The spot at
which their instrumentation rose loudest was a place called Ten
Hatches, whence during high springs there proceeded a very
fugue of sounds.

The skimmington-ride which had killed Lucetta saves Henchard's
life. He is about to drown himself in Ten Hatches Hole when he
sees his effigy, which has been thrown in the river and floated
down to the pool. What he sees is *himself*; he is so superstitious
that he thinks it a sign of divine intervention, and, after taking up

his coat and hat, walks off as if he had been 'in the actual presence
of an appalling miracle'.

  An audio-visual scene near the beginning of *The Woodlanders* has
a proleptic significance, expressing the hopelessness of self-denying
Marty South when she overhears enough to indicate that Giles
Winterborne, whom she silently loves, is not for her, and sacrifices
her one attractive feature, her beautiful locks, for the future
adornment and pleasure of Mrs Charmond. As she toils till three
in the morning, the two sovereigns left by Percomb for the coveted
tresses 'suggest a pair of jaundiced eyes on the watch for an
opportunity'. Whenever she looks up and sighs for weariness they
tempt her, but she quickly withdraws her gaze. She has been
working by the blaze of her fire, and when she opens the door the
night 'in all its fulness' meets her 'flatly' on the threshold, as if it
were 'the very brink of an absolute void' like the Ginnung-Gap of
Teutonic myth before the world's creation. The grief of stoical
endurance is heard in 'the vocalized sorrows of the trees, . . . the
screech of owls, and the fluttering tumble of some awkward wood-
pigeon ill-balanced on its roosting-bough'. Other incidental scenes
reflect human unfulfilment in *The Woodlanders*, but its sharpest
Darwinian presentation expresses the gnawing suspicion of
Fitzpiers' infidelity that oppresses his wife Grace and her father as
they halt 'beneath a half-dead oak, hollow and disfigured with
white tumours, its roots spreading out like claws grasping the
ground'. This picture of canker Care[11] is reinforced by a chill wind.

  Here the 'dim atmosphere of unnaturalness' and the ominous
'livid curtain edged with pink' in the eastern sky contrast with the
previous scene in the same vale, when Winterborne, the 'fruit-
god' of 'Pomona's plain' appears 'like Autumn's very brother' to
Grace as they walk together behind his cider-mill. Instinctively she
sheds 'the veneer of artificiality which she had acquired at the
fashionable schools', and becomes her natural self, her heart rising
'from its late sadness like a released bough'. The bounty of fruitful
nature, she impulsively feels (with evident irony), is reflected in
her circumstances; no sooner has she been 'cast aside by Edred
Fitzpiers than another being, impersonating chivalrous and undilu-
ted manliness, had arisen out of the earth ready to her hand'.
The supreme, most unalloyed happiness she and Winterborne
experience in each other is depicted in a scene which stands out
colourfully against the general greyness of the novel, especially in
the prospect of the western sky before them. Such is their felicity

that all obstacles and chances of mishap in the way of its future attainment are forgotten, and they are one in heavenly and unfathomable bliss:

> Between the broken clouds they could see far into the recesses of heaven as they mused and walked, the eye journeying on under a species of golden arcades, and past fiery obstructions, fancied cairns, loganstones, stalactites and stalagmite of topaz. Deeper than this their gaze passed thin flakes of incandescence, till it plunged into a bottomless medium of soft green fire.

It is as if they have attained, in Wordsworth's words, 'that serene and blessed mood' in which 'the affections gently lead' them on, while 'with an eye made quiet by the power of harmony, and the deep power of joy' they 'see into the life of things'.

The most memorable fusions of scene with thought and feeling in *Tess of the d'Urbervilles* are related to summer lushness in the Valley of the Great Dairies and the hard, flinty upland of Flintcomb-Ash in its wintry severity, before and after Angel's desertion of Tess. The 'brim-fulness' of Froom Vale in Thermidorean heat is matched by the sensuousness of Tess's beauty as he observes her at 'a moment when a woman's soul is more incarnate than at any other time'; yet their love remains on an ideal or spiritual level which Tess has no wish to change. An original sunset picture expresses her torture, when, after Angel's repeated entreaty that she should marry him, she fears she is drifting into acquiescence out of jealousy, and is tempted to assent without revealing her past, 'to snatch ripe pleasure before the iron teeth of pain could have time to shut upon her':

> At half-past six the sun settled down upon the levels, with the aspect of a great forge in the heavens, and presently a monstrous pumpkin-like moon arose on the other hand. The pollard willows, tortured out of their natural shape by incessant chop-pings, became spiny-haired monsters as they stood up against it.

As Angel and Tess walk together in the evening, the low rays of sunshine form 'a pollen of radiance over the landscape'. She wishes that it would always be summer and autumn', with Angel courting her, a 'perpetual betrothal' without any change.

When winter comes Tess works with Marian on the highest field
of Flintcomb-Ash farm, above lynchets where flints in 'bulbous,
cusped, and phallic shapes' are an incidental reminder of the
misfortune destined to dog the whole of her brief womanhood
until she is freed by death. Her forlornness is seen in the 'desolate
drab' of a featureless field which confronts the 'white vacuity' of a
sky without lineaments. The two girls crawling over the surface of
the former have no more consequence than flies. They can talk 'of
the time when they lived and loved together at Talbothays Dairy,
that happy green tract of land where summer had been liberal in
her gifts', for both are young enough to retain 'the inherent will to
enjoy', though 'the circumstantial will against enjoyment' is strong.
Tess's suffering, as day after day passes with nothing to sustain
her hope that Angel will return, is given its intensest expression
in a close-up of those Arctic birds that have been driven south by
the cruelty of 'the circumstantial will':

> gaunt spectral creatures with tragical eyes – eyes which had
> witnessed scenes of cataclysmal horror in inaccessible polar
> regions of a magnitude such as no human being had ever
> conceived, in curdling temperatures that no man could endure;
> which had beheld the crash of icebergs and the slide of snow-
> hills by the shooting light of the Aurora; been half blinded by
> the whirl of colossal storms and terraqueous distortions; and
> retained the expression of feature that such scenes had engen-
> dered.

During the interval of the long threshing-scene at Flintcomb-Ash,
after being taunted by Alec, and slapping him sharply across the
face with her leather glove, Tess cries out, 'Once victim, always
victim – that's the law!' Her suffering, past, present, and to come,
at the hands of the Prime Mover or Immanent Will is indicated by
all that she has had to endure to the point of exhaustion on the
thresher driven by the engine which is 'the *primum mobile*' of her
'little world'. Alec can no longer resist her, and the sequel is
suggested in the ominous hues which invest the scene later in the
action:

> From the west a wrathful shine – all that wild March could afford
> in the way of sunset – had burst forth after the cloudy day,
> flooding the tired and sticky faces of the threshers, and dyeing

them with a coppery light, as also the flapping garments of the women, which clung to them like dull flames.

Whatever hopes the distant prospect of Christminster illuminations raises in the boy Jude, he is to find it a city of dim light and disappointment. The final tragedy which befalls him and Sue is related to its Tractarian superstition, and to the way in which Sue, whose intellect had 'scintillated like a star', is so emotionally distraught after the horror of seeing her hanged children that she considers their loss God's retribution for sin, and decides she must do penance by remarrying, and prostituting herself to, Phillotson, to whom she is physically averse. Side by side with this self-crucifixion is that of Jude in his drunken remarriage to Arabella, whose only attraction has been her sexuality. That two such unnatural degradations were considered right in the sight of Heaven by the Church, High Church especially, makes Jude protest to Sue:

> 'You make me hate Christianity, or mysticism, or Sacerdotalism, or whatever it may be called, if it's that which has caused this deterioration in you. That a woman-poet, a woman-seer, a woman whose soul shone like a diamond – whom all the wise of the world would have been proud of, if they could have known you – should degrade herself like this! I am glad I had nothing to do with Divinity – damn glad – if it's going to ruin you in this way!'

He has just found her in the darkness of the ritualistic church of St Silas. Hardy's thought on the subject, which conveys Jude's views and Sue's feelings, is subsumed in one of his most unilluminated Christminster scenes. Jude enters the church, and hears a sound as of sobbing in the general silence as he moves towards it in an obscurity 'broken only by the faintest reflected night-light from without':

> High overhead, above the chancel steps, Jude could discern a huge, solidly constructed Latin cross – as large, probably, as the original it was designed to commemorate. It seemed to be suspended in the air by invisible wires; it was set with large jewels, which faintly glimmered in some weak ray caught from outside, as the cross swayed to and fro in a silent and scarcely

perceptible motion. Underneath, upon the floor, lay what appeared to be a heap of black clothes, and from this was repeated
the sobbing that he had heard before. It was Sue's form, prostrate
on the paving.

The scene registers Hardy's most imaginative indictment of the
Church's unenlightened inflexibility on the marriage question.

The above scenes may be divided into the bright and the sombre.
Only one bright scene expresses unalloyed bliss, and it cannot last
long. Most of the more colourful landscapes or skyscapes have
ominous tones, and this is not surprising from one whose interest
in pictures was not in scenic beauty but in deeper realities, those
tragical mysteries of life which he found in the later works of
Turner. Hardy's sombre scenes are characteristic of one who
believed that orthodox beauty was losing its appeal, and that
modern thinkers would find themselves more in harmony with
'the chastened sublimity of a moor, a sea, or a mountain', the
sand-dunes of Scheveningen or spots like Iceland.[12]

4

Two on a Tower

In January 1882, when Hardy agreed to write *Two on a Tower*, he had reached a point almost exactly midway in his career as a writer of prose fiction. He had shown his creative gifts in a number of works, most of all in *Far from the Madding Crowd* and *The Return of the Native*, but his greatest tragedies were still to come. The kind of 'charity' or altruism which inspires them is more clearly and confidently voiced in *Two on a Tower*, their immediate forerunner, than ever before. More than any other of his novels it combines all those elements, including tragedy and humour, which Hardy had in mind when he divided his fiction into three categories: 'Novels of Character and Environment', 'Romances and Fantasies', and 'Novels of Ingenuity'.

Though not ranked among Hardy's major achievements, *Two on a Tower* is certainly one of his most readable and remarkable. It is a moving romance which makes admirable and ingenious use of rather limited resources to provide a story which is economical in presentation and continually enlivened with suspense or surprising turns of event. On reading it in 1920, Mrs Henniker, a novelist herself, found it strange that it was not '*more* talked of', and thought the interest of the story 'wonderfully well maintained'. By Victorian standards it was daring enough; but to embark on a romance conceived with reference to cosmic space was even more venturesome, arguing a knowledge of astronomy which was far from superficial.

Hardy's interest in stellar space went much deeper than the visual as it is seen in the northern sky of *Far from the Madding Crowd* and the southern sky of 'Drummer Hodge'. Both express the 'poetry of motion' felt by their author in 'the panoramic glide of the stars', but pre-eminently these scenes are presented as they appeared to Wessex rustics. One is familiar, the other foreign; Gabriel Oak has learned to tell the time from the direction of the stars, while the drummer is lost in wondering ignorance. Hardy's adolescent interest in astronomy had been stimulated by Cassell's *The Popular Educator* and telescope observations with the Moules at Fordington.[1] Ten years later, when contemporary scientific philosophy had overthrown his belief in Providence, he had realized, like the hero of *Maud*, the 'sad astrology, the boundless plan' that makes the stars 'tyrants' in 'iron skies',

> Innumerable, pitiless, passionate eyes,
> Cold fires, yet with power to burn and brand
> His nothingness into man.

Two poems of the period illustrate Hardy's philosophical fascination with the world of space. 'At a Lunar Eclipse' (186–) gives a foretaste of *The Dynasts*, emphasizing the relative insignificance of the earth, its tragic wars and heroism, its geniuses and 'women fairer than the skies'. The central idea of 'In vision I roamed' (1866) is more akin to that of *Two on a Tower*: after sweeping imaginatively through

> ghast heights of sky,
> To the last chambers of the monstrous Dome,

the poet takes comfort in the thought that someone dear to him, though far away, is relatively near.

In *The Return of the Native* Hardy presented a tragic story against an Egdon background designed to suggest not only mankind's endurance but also the insignificance of the individual in time, whereas in *Two on a Tower* he 'set the emotional history' of two cosmologically 'infinitesimal lives against the stupendous background of the stellar universe', hoping 'to impart to readers the sentiment that of these contrasting magnitudes the smaller might be the greater to them as men'. With the harsh indifference of nature's laws, and the impact of what appears from limited knowledge to be chance in human affairs, these dimensions form the general context of Hardy's tragedy. The Spirit of the Pities is heard against the Spirit of the Years.

Features of the story had appealed to him at various times before he began to plot the novel. The tower on Black Down to the memory of Admiral Hardy was a distant landmark which must have excited Hardy's attention when he set off to his school in Dorchester, partly from its Napoleonic associations, and even more from the glow he felt as a collateral descendant of one of the great figures in the battle of Trafalgar. A jotting among his memoranda for fiction shows that he had this monument in mind for a story in November 1878. Eight years earlier he had made a note on a wife who pined for her husband, though he had treated her roughly; when at last he sent for her, she died for joy at the news. Possibilities could have been suggested by a passage in George Eliot's *The Mill on the Floss*, where Maggie Tulliver, after asking questions on the astronomer in *The Eton Latin Grammar* 'who hated women generally', remarks:

> 'I suppose it's all astronomers [who hate women]: because, you
> know, they live up in high towers, and if the women came there,
> they might talk and hinder them from looking at the stars.'

Hardy's fictional interest in the subject may have been stimulated by hearing the surgeon Sir Henry Thompson expatiate on his astronomical pursuits when he visited him for a consultation after the long illness which made it necessary for him to dictate much of *A Laodicean* to his wife.[2] If so, as seems most likely, it was filliped soon after they moved from Upper Tooting to Wimborne, Dorset, in June 1881. During the first night in their new home they watched Tebbutt's Comet. Soon afterwards Hardy became interested in the high tower a few miles away in Charborough Park; it provided a setting which he chose to disguise, and revived 'the poor man and the lady' motif which had been the subject of his first (unpublished) novel. He probably anticipated the eager expectations which the second transit of Venus would arouse in the later part of 1882. There could have been little doubt about the subject of his next novel when he was invited in October 1881 to provide a serial for *The Atlantic Monthly*, for the following month he wrote to the Astronomer Royal requesting permission to visit the observatory at Greenwich. How he obtained it is best told in his own words:

> He was requested to state before it could be granted if his
> application was made for astronomical and scientific reasons or
> not. He therefore drew up a scientific letter, the gist of which
> was that he wished to ascertain if it would be possible for him
> to adapt an old tower, built in a plantation in the West of England
> for other objects, to the requirements of a telescopic study of the
> stars by a young man very ardent in that pursuit (this being the

imagined situation in the proposed novel). An order to view
Greenwich Observatory was promptly sent.[3]

Expressions and facts in the novel show that one of the books
Hardy studied was R. A. Proctor's *Essays on Astronomy* (1872). His
aim, he told his friend Edmund Gosse (who later suggested the
epigraph from Richard Crashaw's 'Love's Horoscope'), was 'to
make science, not the mere padding of a romance' but its 'actual
vehicle'.[4]

In devising his story Hardy conformed to two principles he had
observed from the outset of his career as a novelist. The first he
postulated ingenuously in July 1868 when he offered *The Poor Man
and the Lady* to Macmillan: 'as a rule no fiction will considerably
interest readers poor or rich unless the passion of love forms a
prominent feature in the thread of the story'. The second is found
in notes he wrote in the summer preceding his Greenwich visit:

> The real, if unavowed, purpose of fiction is to give pleasure by
> gratifying the love of the uncommon in human experience. . . .
>   The writer's problem is, how to strike the balance between
> the uncommon and the ordinary so as on the one hand to give
> interest, on the other to give reality.
>   In working out this problem, human nature must never
> be made abnormal, which is introducing incredibility. The
> uncommonness must be in the events, not in the characters;
> and the writer's art lies in shaping that uncommonness while
> disguising its unlikelihood, if it be unlikely.[5]

The seeds of romance in the story of a beautiful widow who falls
in love with a handsome young astronomer and marries him
secretly are obvious: the 'uncommonness' lies in the circumstances
which compel her, a lady of the most laudable principles, to rise
above self-interest, insist that her husband shall travel abroad to
further his career and, finding that she is with child, accept a
deceived bishop's proposal of marriage without infringing the law.
Hardy's artistic problem was related not to such ingenuities of plot
but to his theme: two people whose lives we follow with interest
will naturally seem more important than the immensities of outer
space, but it is extraordinarily difficult for the novelist, however
great his astronomical knowledge, to create concurrently rather

than intermittently an imaginative realization of the infinitesimality of those lives in the universe at large.

Readers in the post-Lawrentian era can hardly appreciate a writer's restrictions in the Victorian world. Hardy's audacity had not yet reached its climax, and he had still to learn how to accommodate his stories to magazine readers. The reception of *Desperate Remedies*, his first published novel, made him realize the danger of offending upper-class moral susceptibilities. Eleven years later, in creating circumstances which made a lady reveal her love despite the restraints of propriety, Hardy knew what risks he was running, but it is doubtful whether he realized his offence in making the same lady, even though a passive victim, a party to the deception of a bishop. The best that can be said for Hardy is that he draws a veil over it; his excuse that Lady Constantine succumbed to 'convention' remains unconvincing. It could only have rubbed salt into the wound of the contemporary society reader. The editor of *The Atlantic* was perturbed, readers were offended, and reviewers were 'acid'. Hardy took comfort, however, when eminent critics wrote, telling him in private that the novel was his most original work, and 'the affair of the Bishop' 'a triumph in tragi-comedy'.[6]

By January 1882 he had agreed to arrange the story for American serialization in eight monthly parts, the first to appear in May. This programme required a careful scrutiny of the story as a whole, with readjustments no doubt, before the first instalment was completed and sent off to Boston in February. It was a happy period in Hardy's life, according to Sir George Douglas, who first met him at Wimborne; and this happiness is reflected in the rather high-spirited detachment which occasionally characterizes the presentation, as well as in the humour of the rustic scenes. The first of these is such that one wishes it were longer; but an eight-part serial imposed limits on all aspects of the novel.

It is typical of Hardy that he accepted the pressures of serial demand, agreed to publication in book form as soon as possible, and later regretted his shortcomings. Professionally he did his best in the circumstances; had he known what interest would develop in his work he might have pursued a more circumspect policy. The novel appeared in October 1882 before the serial was concluded. The following January he informed Gosse that,

though the plan of the story was carefully thought out, the actual writing was lamentably hurried – having been produced month by month, and the MS. dispatched to America, where it was printed without my seeing the proofs. It would have been rewritten for the book form if I had not played truant and gone off to Paris.

It seems most unlikely that he seriously contemplated rewriting the novel, for agreement to publish the book was reached as early as July 1882. To promote interest in the work after its publication, he wrote a neat narrative abstract for his publisher:

Being the story of the unforeseen relations into which a lady and a youth many years her junior were drawn by studying the stars together; of her desperate situation through generosity to him; and of the reckless *coup d'audace* by which she effected her deliverance.

The criticism roused by this *coup d'audace* seems to have astonished Hardy, who, in answer to the charge that he was hostile to the Church, rightly but evasively pointed out that 'one of the most honourable characters', the hero's friend, is a clergyman, and that the heroine's 'most tender qualities' are inseparable from her religious feelings.

At the beginning of June, when he had probably not reached the halfway stage in *Two on a Tower*, Hardy wrote one of his most famous notes on the artist:

As, in looking at a carpet, by following one colour a certain pattern is suggested, by following another colour, another; so in life the seer should watch that pattern among general things which his idiosyncrasy moves him to observe, and describe that alone. This is, quite accurately, a going to Nature; yet the result is no mere photograph, but purely the product of the writer's own mind.

Hardy implies that the creative artist must remain true to his own nature or personality. Inevitably, in writing for the entertainment of magazine-readers, he was compelled to include narrative items and links against his better judgement; and readers familiar with the scene in *Tess of the d'Urbervilles* which expresses his abhorrence of blood sports may be astonished that he could have detailed

Swithin's methods of improvising supper, when he and his wife
were forced to take refuge in the tower to avoid recognition by
Louis Glanville, as if bird-killing were as unexceptionable to the
author as to most countrymen of the period. One can applaud his
dexterity in resolving the involutions of the coral-bracelet menace,
but it is no more than a trivial device for keeping the reader on
tenterhooks. *Two on a Tower* is not one of Hardy's most serious
novels. It is a romantic tragi-comedy, but it reveals the main facets
of his artistic personality and 'idiosyncratic mode of regard'.

It would be a mistake to overlook his humour; it was part of his
rural inheritance. He would enjoy the story of the parson's bride
who couldn't avoid blushing deeply when a certain psalm was
sung at her wedding, or of the yokel who, when told to rehearse
the articles of his belief during preparations for Confirmation,
knew no better than to answer the parson as the irreverent Sir
Blount Constantine prompted. This was a colour in Hardy's
temperament that was to become more and more interwoven with
his tragic patterns until it assumed a rather sombre general hue.
As one of his earliest novels, *Under the Greenwood Tree*, illustrates
abundantly, his rustics often utter perennial sense in incomparable
language which raises a smile and goes straight to its mark. Happily
he made such expression the pivotal point for the main turn in the
romantic events which precede the tragi-comedy of *Two on a Tower*:

'But the young man himself?'
'Planned, cut out, and finished for the delight of 'ooman!'
'Yet he must be willing.'
'That would soon come. If they get up this tower ruling
plannards together much longer, their plannards will soon rule
them together, in my way o' thinking. If she've a disposition
towards the knot, she can soon teach him.'
'True, true, and lawfully. What before mid ha' been a wrong
desire is now a holy wish!'
The scales fell from Swithin St Cleeve's eyes as he heard the
words of his neighbours. . . .

The most important pattern Hardy saw in life was the complex
web of chance. In such a world the fortunes of people are regulated
at critical stages by the interaction of character, environmental
opportunities past and present, and events. In the passage already
quoted from the jottings on fiction which Hardy made in the
summer of 1881, it is stressed that anything unusual must be in

events, not character. He expressed this view more memorably when, anticipating criticism of his next novel, *The Mayor of Casterbridge*, he took comfort in the thought that 'it is not improbabilities of incident but improbabilities of character that matter'. Truth is even stranger than fiction, and unusual events (such as the illegality of Swithin and Lady Constantine's marriage owing to the false reporting of her former husband's death in Africa about three months before its actual occurrence) determine the plot of *Two on a Tower*. Had the hero and heroine differed radically in one respect from what they are, had Viviette not been endowed with a more mature sense of responsibility than Swithin's, for example, the story could not have remained the same, however.

The critical importance of chance is illustrated when Swithin receives the letter outlining the terms of his great-uncle's legacy. Had it arrived a month earlier, there is no telling what effect the prospect of a large annuity might have had on one 'whose love for celestial physics was second to none'. It reached him when he was on his way to his marriage at Bath; 'his bosom's lord sat lightly in his throne', and 'it affected him about as much as the view of horizons shown by sheet-lightning. He saw an immense prospect; it went, and the world was as before.' (Swithin's readiness to sacrifice his career again for love is revealed insistently when the marriage is discovered to be illegal, but Viviette's altruism prevails.) This is but the first in a series of chances which create the gin in which the heroine finds herself desperately caught. As the tragedy tightens its hold, Hardy's nobler nature is expressed. It is seen in Viviette's sacrifice of her happiness for her husband's future. 'To love St Cleeve so far better than herself as this was to surpass the love of women as conventionally understood', but it is this subjection of self-love to 'benevolence' that leads to disaster. Superficially Hardy's language may seem detached, but its overtones reveal deep imaginative feeling. In Swithin's absence, could Viviette 'singly meet her impending trial, despising the shame' when she finds she is pregnant, and could he wish to marry her when she was 'fading to middle-age'? 'A fear sharp as a frost settled down upon her, that in any such scheme as this she would be building upon the sand.' In altruism and self-denial she displays that most excellent gift of charity; in the final trial of her fortitude she falters. Marty South and Tess were to demonstrate these virtues unswervingly, and Hardy's heart went out to all of them in their distresses.

Though not the most tragic, Viviette is perhaps the most
attractive, of Hardy's heroines. The following passage suggests that
an explanation is to be found in his life:

> Lady Constantine, in being nearly ten years his senior, was an
> object even better calculated to nourish a youth's first passion
> than a girl of his own age, superiority of experience and ripeness
> of emotion exercising the same peculiar fascination over him as
> over other young men in their first ventures in this kind.

Part of the final tragedy of Viviette is her immediate awareness
from Swithin's look that, in losing her beauty's bloom during his
long absence, she has lost his heart. The pathos of the situation
was known to Hardy from experience. Even as a young boy he
had fallen in love with the lady of the local manor who had
mothered him, but so great was the change in her appearance
when he met her years later in London that he made it the subject
of early poems such as 'Amabel' and 'She, to Him'. The opening
lines of the latter prove conclusively that one of the minor themes
of *Two on a Tower* struck plaintive chords:

> When you shall see me in the toils of Time,
> My lauded beauties carried off from me,
> My eyes no longer stars as in their prime . . .

How deep were his resurrected feelings on the subject may be
seen in his 1895 preface.

The novel was not planned predominantly as a tragedy. Lady
Constantine was destined to be a pawn in a game of dupery which
may, from one angle, have appeared to Hardy as one of life's little
ironies. She was spared the shame of public gossip and slander,
but the off-stage episode of her married life in a bishop's palace
leaves one wondering what misery and guilt she suffered, and
whether a slightly malicious humour got the better of Hardy's
judgment when he planned this phase of the novel. Perhaps he
could take the consequential, self-seeking Bishop Helmsdale little
more seriously than we can Mr Collins in *Pride and Prejudice*, whom
he somewhat resembles. Louis Glanville's intrigue is regarded as
'Puck-like', as if the author's attitude is summed up in the words
'Lord, what fools these mortals be!' Planes and perspectives have

changed. The door is closed on tragic feelings, and conspiracy triumphs.

With chance as an important element in a writer's philosophy, a predisposition to irony of situation is almost inevitable. In the plot of *Two on a Tower* much depends on the time-factor in Swithin's receipt of his great-uncle's letter and in the unexpected arrival of new information on Sir Blount Constantine's death. The tragic consequences of actions to which Lady Constantine would never have consented had she known the truth may indeed be regarded as cruel 'satires of circumstances'. More ordinary and incidental irony occurs when she entertains the bishop, and the serenity of her manner (arising from her secret marriage) makes her all the more attractive to him. It continues when this self-important dignitary finds a clue for his repulse in the synchronization of his first proposal and the receipt of the more circumstantial account of her husband's death. The last little irony in Louis Glanville's plans to save his sister (and still, like the brother in 'A Tragedy of Two Ambitions', to exploit her marriage to his advantage') is the bishop's complacent comment on Lady Constantine's acceptance of him: 'A good and wise woman, she perceived what a true shelter from sadness was offered in this, and was not the one to despise Heaven's gift.'

Hardy's inability to expand within the limits imposed by his serial agreement is particularly noticeable in the economy of scenic effects. His keen observation is seen more often in detail than in landscape. Yet one of the more dominant features of his later novels, the harmonization of setting and situation, may be glimpsed at intervals. The opening scene seems to augur both happiness and sorrow; in the sunshine of an early winter afternoon the tower is 'bright and cheerful' above a gloomy wood where skeletal trees sob and moan. 'Darker grew the evenings, tearfuller the moonlights, and heavier the dews' when the lovesick hero found he was unable to concentrate on his life-work as a result of his lady's absence. At his marriage proposal, the wind shakes the building, and starts up an intenser moan in the firs. The lovers are swayed by emotion much as the candleflame in the lantern is swayed by 'the tempest without'. When they agree to marry secretly (not knowing that such a course would wreck Swithin's opportunities for a distinguished career), the wind roars and shakes the tower until suddenly it reaches hurricane force and whirls away the dome.

The insignificance of the individual in space and time was axiomatic for Hardy, but in *Two on a Tower* his main aim was to create an 'emotional history', and by limiting himself to two principal characters he gave himself greater scope for making their romance and tragedy loom large in the reader's imagination. To provide the contrasting viewpoints in a single vision proved not surprisingly, especially under the pressure of serialization, beyond his grasp. With this theme in mind, he chose an ancient camp for the site of his tower, with 'palaeolithic dead men' feeding the roots of the trees around its base. Swithin's wedding-preparations

> accorded well with the prehistoric spot on which they were made. Embedded under his feet were possibly even now rude trinkets that had been worn at bridal ceremonies of the early inhabitants. Little signified those ceremonies to-day . . . That his own rite, nevertheless, signified much, was the inconsequent reasoning of Swithin, as it is of many another bridegroom besides.

Brief statements of this kind can give the reader no lasting impression of individual insignificance relative to archaeological time.

The main background, however, is the stellar universe. In his attempt to express how relatively infinitesimal individual human life is, Hardy chose for his astronomer a youthful enthusiast, so absorbed in his studies that he is detached from the world and insusceptible to a woman's charms. Their first sweeps of space and subsequent discussions emphasize that nothing was made for man, that the universe continues until grandeur is lost eventually in ghastliness, and all human affairs lose their importance. Yet, however much Lady Constantine feels 'annihilated' by it, the effect on the reader is little more than conceptual. During their next observations they

> more and more felt the contrast between their own tiny magnitudes and those among which they had recklessly plunged, till they were oppressed with the presence of a vastness they could not cope with even as an idea, and which hung about them like a nightmare.

Such reductive impressions are occasional and little more than a backcloth. With one slight exception (the scene on the tower immediately after Viviette's discovery of Swithin's legacy), celestial immensities are not linked with human plight in moving situations, as landscape and time are in *The Return of the Native* and *Tess of the d'Urbervilles*. A brief reference to 'the cruelty of the natural laws' which had been Swithin's study does nothing imaginatively to reinforce an intermittent theme.

To some extent it is reinforced by astronomical allusion. When Swithin realizes that, in thinking of the heaven above, he had not perceived 'the better heaven beneath', and proclaims that Viviette's eyes are henceforth to be his stars, we are reminded of the line already quoted from 'She, to Him'. The astronomer's terms and imagery recall his studies. He tells Lady Constantine that the shattering of the lens he had brought from London fills but a degree in the circle of her thoughts but covers the whole circumference of his; to him the streak of her cheek from Louis's whiplash is as 'straight as a meridian'. A long bed of snowdrops 'looked up at him like a nether Milky Way'; the following autumn, when Welland House suffered neglect, tufts of grass in the gravel walks appeared like black stars in the gloaming. Elsewhere in his narration Hardy frequently alludes to the heavens and astronomy. The 'modern Eudoxus' rises above 'the embarrassing horizon of Lady Constantine's great house' and becomes himself when he enlarges on the scintillation of the stars. His astronomical ardour renewed by marriage, the telescope becomes 'the *primum mobile* of his gravitation'. When she insists on their separation for the sake of his career,

> He turn'd and saw the terror in her eyes,
> That yearn'd upon him shining in such wise
> As a star midway in the midnight fix'd.

As Swithin travels abroad and becomes increasingly interested in the southern skies, Viviette, who had stood high in his heaven, sinks 'like the North Star, lower and lower with his retreat southward'. When he returns years later, time has brought unexpected changes:

> Her cheeks had lost for ever that firm contour which had been
> drawn by the vigorous hand of youth, and the masses of hair

that were once darkness visible had become touched here and there by a faint grey haze, like the Via Lactea in a midnight sky.

The discipline which characterizes the general style (despite some minor lapses) may be seen in Hardy's other associative imagery. It is never lush or excessive. Concise, apt, and often idiosyncratic, it shows a wide range of interest and sensibility. Recollections of what he had heard or seen in his boyhood occur in the reference to muffs 'large as smugglers' tubs' and in the parallel between Swithin's ready response to the question on equatorial manufacturers and the drawing of a weir-hatch which speedily inundates Lady Constantine with the information she seeks. Hardy's commonest imagery proclaims the countryman and poet. How impressively he evokes the evanescent effect of the opportunities conjured up by his great-uncle's letter on Swithin will already have been noticed. The link between the faint grey haze in Viviette's hair and the Via Lactea recalls their first joint observation of the Milky Way, 'stretched across over their heads with the luminousness of a frosted web'. A few of the illustrative images show a familiarity with paintings and architectural drawing. Many derive from Shakespeare, more from the Bible; their register extends from 'the mishap of Tobit' to tragic tones and evocations. The aptness of humorous similitudes ranges from the more obvious (in, for example, the clearing of throats like the noise of atmospheric hoes and scrapers) to the wittier, when, with a swift change of aspect as he leaves Lady Constantine to reprimand Swithin, the bishop appears 'like an evangelized King of Spades come to have it out with the Knave of Hearts'. The swaying 'in seconds' of the 'thin straight stems' of trees 'like inverted pendulums' has a fascinating oddity, but more admirable is the fine precision of

her intention wheeled this way and that like the balance of a watch. His unexpected proposition had brought about the smartest encounter of inclination with prudence, of impulse with reserve, that she had ever known.

As a reflection of character and mood, the letters form an interesting variety, those from Lady Constantine, Bishop Helmsdale, and Swithin's misogynist great-uncle being the most memorable. Not surprisingly, Viviette's are moving or tragic. Her 'Romance' nature contrasts with the Laodicean temperament of

Hardy's previous heroine. The 'Eve' in her shows itself in her
occasional pique at Swithin's unflattering ingenuousness, in the
thought (rapidly following a twinge of conscience) that by marriage
she had raised him socially, and in her jealousy of Tabitha Lark.
Despite his youth and differences in their social background,
the lovers make an excellent match. Their astronomical pursuits
dissolve mundane distinctions and promote a sense of equality.
Each has a nobility of nature and a readiness to put the interests
of the other first. Their physical contrast has its temperamental
parallel. Swithin is an intellectual, remarkably detached from
sublunary affairs before he realizes what love is. Viviette is warm
and affectionate, swayed by generous feelings, 'either lover or
dévote'; any realization she has of the 'ephemeral trivialities' of her
problems in the infinite sum of things must be slight and transitory.
Ironically, Swithin's scientific outlook, the 'inexorably simple logic'
which makes him accept Viviette's self-denying wishes literally
when he returns after years of absence, contributes to the final
catastrophe.

   In its concluding stages, the pace of the novel quickens admirably.
The account of Swithin's travels and work is kept to an effective
minimum, in the interests of both author and reader. Swithin
learns enough from England to satisfy the curiosity of the reader
before his return, and the ending is worked out with commendable
artistry. Speaking for the rustic 'chorus', Hezzy Biles asserts that
little has happened at Welland during Swithin's absence: 'when
you've said that a few stripling boys and maidens have busted
into blooth, and a few married women have plimmed and chimped
(my lady among 'em), why, you've said anighst all, Mr San Cleeve'.
Yet no one is overlooked, and we learn all that is relevant, not
least with reference to Tabitha Lark. Its context may seem slightly
unrealistic, though Viviette is a religious woman, but the simple
question asked by her son in the hearing of Swithin as he ascends
the tower, 'You made a mistake, didn't you, mother?', remains
haunting in its dramatic irony. Shocks follow, leading to one of
Hardy's most tragic climaxes. The final pages combine story and
theme. The 'loneliness' of the southern sky seemed more lonely
to Swithin than the 'north stellar region', and we are reminded of
the 'ephemeral trivialities' of life. On his return, the theme is the
effect of time and change. It is largely through Time's revenges,
and the immediate effect of physical change in Viviette on Swithin,
that the bishop is avenged. On this note the novel ends, suggesting

that, if we can detach ourselves and look at life from a more macrocosmic viewpoint, the tragedy wears a comic aspect.

The astronomical topicality of *Two on a Tower* must have increased its interest in 1882–3. The only transits of Venus in the nineteenth century occurred in December 1874 and December 1882. If Swithin did not have the first of these in mind when he referred to the next (xxix), the concluding events of the story must be imagined to have taken place after the complete novel was published. It would be unwise to assume that Hardy kept close to contemporary astronomical chronology (no eclipse of the moon fits in with a time scheme relating to either transit of Venus), yet he seems to have utilized two events of 1881, the appearance of Tebbutt's Comet (xii) and the publication of important work by an American on variable stars (ix).

The reception of the novel did much to make Hardy realize what a 'fearful price' the contemporary novelist had to pay for 'the privilege of writing in the English language'.[7] Yet he did not mind outraging readers who judged by the letter of the law, for, thirteen years later, when revising for the first uniform edition of his novels, he took steps to show conclusively that Lady Constantine's child was conceived when she and Swithin knew that their marriage was illegal.[8] On this issue, even after completing *Jude the Obscure*, he preferred an evasive half-truth in his preface of 1895.

5
Mephistophelian and Satanic

Hardy's two poems 'The Dead Quire' and 'The Paphian Ball' present local and legendary tales which are minor offshoots of the Christian tradition, notably exemplified in Milton's 1629 ode, of the dumbfounding of the pagan gods when the birth of Christ was heralded by the angels. In the first of them revelry is suspended in shame when the departed Mellstock choir is heard playing the old carol 'While shepherds watch'd their flocks by night'. When, in the second, they strike up the tune by chance at the hallucinatory ball they have been accompanying, its voluptuous paintings, its half-naked women, and their handsome partners, all vanish, and the members of the choir find themselves on Egdon Heath, with Christmas Day dawning red behind dark Rainbarrow, which bulges 'like a supine negress' breast Against Clyffe-Clump's faint far-off crest'. Hours before this, it seemed, they had been on their usual Christmas rounds when, near Rushy-Pond, a figure stood up against the moon, tempting them to play for gold at a grand ball. Though it meant serving the Devil, they had found themselves there after walking blindfold by unknown ways, and seen heaps of shining guineas before them as they wore themselves out with playing until, too drowsy to think, they had struck up their carol with miraculous dispelling effect. The strange figure against the moon is a Mephistophelian tempter; the tune he hums is 'weird-some' or fatal. He entices men from God's ways.

An imaginative link in *The Mayor of Casterbridge* (when everyone and everything connected with the skimmington-ride vanish like the crew of *Comus* as 'executors of the law' appear in the streets) suggests that the revellers of the heath fantasy, the 'crew' of the ballroom that had vanished with its 'heaped-up' guineas, had some kinship with the rout or rabble of Comus in Milton's masque, whose rites to Hecate, the classical goddess of the moon presiding over magic and enchantments, included

Midnight Shout and Revelry,
Tipsy Dance and Jollity.

The moon very evidently plays an important role when the most attractive and mysterious of Hardy's Mephistophelian characters, Baron von Xanten in 'The Romantic Adventures of a Milkmaid' (his Germanic origin further accentuated by appeals to his 'Gott' in the final version), agrees to take Margery Tucker to a distant ball. A 'great' moon floods her face with light as she expresses her wish to attend the Yeomanry Ball; later it has replaced the sun as the illuminator of her father's diary when she agrees to accompany him to a dance in the next county where they will be unknown. There is something 'magical and compulsory' about him, she finds when they practise the polka, the new dance which has become the London craze, as moon-shadows race over them from the twigs. The story blends fantasy with Wessex realism, and it is probably for this reason that its topography, first centred in the Swenn (Frome) valley east of Casterbridge, then transferred to 'Lower Wessex', remains confusing. In the first main episode, the Cinderella portion of the tale, Margery changes for the ball within a hollow tree in Chillington Wood, not far originally, it seems, from the Clyffe-Clump of 'The Paphian Ball'.[1] The coachman of the waiting carriage is a foreigner; as she and the baron leave country familiar to her, darkness sets in, growing thicker and thicker with the night. When they reach the lordly mansion where the ball takes place, steam ascends from the flanks of the horses, whose hot breath jets forth like smoke out of volcanoes, and the Drum Polka is heard, its 'deep and mighty note' throbbing through the air at every fourth beat. As in 'Reminiscences of a Dancing Man', the author remembers his youthful excitement in London:

> Who now recalls those crowded rooms
>   Of old yclept 'The Argyle',
> Where to the deep Drum-polka's booms
>   We hopped in standard style?
> Whither have danced those damsels now!
> Is Death the partner who doth moue
>   Their wormy chaps and bare?
> Do their spectres spin like sparks within
> The smoky halls of the Prince of Sin
>   To a thunderous Jullien air?

Margery thinks the polished floor consists of black ice; the musicians sit in the gallery 'with romantic mop-heads of raven hair', under which their faces and eyes shine 'like fire under coals', the suggestion being that the extra energy brought into dancing by the polka was the counterpart of steam, the new motive power in industry. Margery is reluctant to leave, but Baron von Xanten is adamant. He mounts to his seat on the box, lights a cigar, and they plunge under the trees. It is almost daylight when they reach Chillington Wood, where, after she has changed dress in the hollow tree, he ruthlessly sets fire to all her ballroom finery. He is a gentleman, a literary scion of the prince of darkness in *King Lear*,[2] who does not behave like 'the Prince of Sin'. He is grateful to the dairymaid for saving his life, and acts as though he were her moral guardian. Had he known she was engaged, he would have never taken her to the ball; she is a wicked deceiver. He promotes her wedding, but their mutual fascination remains. Originally Hardy had intended her to leave England in the baron's yacht, never to return, but he gave way to Victorian propriety, the baron restoring her to her husband, reconciliation with whom is achieved in a most elaborate final episode. In this Margery is seen in a grand coach drawn by coal-black horses, sitting beside 'a fine dark gentleman with black mustachios, and a very pale prince-like face'. Once on the hard road they rattle out of sight 'like hell-and-skimmer'; after her return, the horses and carriage are seen looking 'black and daemonic against the slanting fires of the western sun'. Whatever the propriety of Baron von Xanten's behaviour, the temptation he poses is recurrently linked through imagery with darkness, smoke, and fire, hinting at Hell, and specifically, in a scene wearing 'the aspect of some unholy assignation in Pandaemonium', at Milton's.

Diggory Venn is a weirdsome frequenter of Egdon Heath, but he does not belong to the world of the strange figure against the moon in 'The Paphian Ball'. In describing the old Wessex reddlemen as 'Mephistophelian visitants', Hardy does no more than compare their bright ruddy appearance with the fiery red cloak which was the token of Mephistopheles' provenance in Goethe's *Faust*. When he refers to Diggory's 'weird character' he alludes to his almost uncanny habit of appearing suddenly in the right place at a critical juncture, and even more to the part he plays as Thomasin Yeobright's protector in determining the lives or fate of Wildeve and Eustacia Vye. His guardian role is good and altruistic; he is in love with Thomasin.[3]

From the outset Hardy's villains are associated with the Devil. When the heroine of *Desperate Remedies* first meets Manston, she experiences a 'general unearthly weirdness' as he plays the organ against a violent storm of 'thunder, lightning, and rain'. Less obvious than the reference here to the weird sisters of *Macbeth* is the absorption of the popular superstition relating to Mephistopheles or the Devil. Early in *The Woodlanders* Marty South, resisting the temptation to sell her locks for gold, tells the hairdresser Mr Percomb that he goes on talking 'like the Devil to Doctor Faustus in the penny book'. In this, after a fearful storm, with lightning and thunder, which seemed to threaten the end of the world, he was wont to cheer Faustus and his friend with music such as they had never heard. Hardy's 'Manston' was most probably suggested by 'Mannion', the name of the villain in Wilkie Collins' *Basil*; the two characters have physical resemblances, and Mannion's Satanism is reinforced at appropriate junctures by darkness and storm, with lightning and thunder.[4]

In his later fiction (with the exception of 'The Romantic Adventures of a Milkmaid', where he works out the Mephistophelian role more lightly and freely than elsewhere) Hardy uses smoking as a device for announcing his tempter or villain. He had introduced the technique late in *The Return of the Native*, where Wildeve, before resorting to the moth-signal in the hope of inducing Eustacia, Clym's wife, to join him, appears looking over the garden gate, with a cigar in his mouth. Felice Charmond, the worldly temptress of *The Woodlanders*, in a dressing-gown of deep purple (love's colour), with 'a pile of magnificent hair on the crown of her head' (from the locks sacrificed by Marty South), is seen holding a cigarette between the fingers of her right hand while idly breathing a thin stream of smoke from her delicately curved lips. Both her lovers, the Italianized American and Fitzpiers, are cigar-smokers.

In *A Laodicean* and *Two on a Tower*, the two major works which immediately preceded 'The Romantic Adventures of a Milkmaid', Hardy introduces two parasitical tricksters, William Dare, Captain de Stancy's illegitimate son, whose defamatory plotting almost succeeds in contriving a marriage between his father and the wealthy heroine Paula Power, and Louis Glanville, engineer of the *coup d'audace* whereby his high-principled sister Lady Constantine (after finding herself pregnant and quite unable, as a result of her own altruistic insistence, to communicate with her illegitimate husband) is saved from dishonour when, with enhanced prospects for his own foreseeable future, he fools her former admirer, the infatuated Bishop of Melchester, into marrying her with little delay.

Lady Constantine's husband died in Africa much later than she had first been informed (after her marriage to the young astronomer Swithin St Cleeve, she was shocked to find). It was when they were returning from this by train that Louis Glanville made his first dramatic appearance, lashing his horses in a way that suggests he would be relentless in the prosecution of his designs. When the union of the bishop and his sister is on his mind, or when he suspects a relationship between her and Swithin that will balk his plans, he resorts to a cigar. Returning after her futile dash to prevent Swithin's departure for the southern hemisphere, she sees 'a red coal' in the arbour, Louis's favourite haunt; he is smoking his 'Havannah'. Lost in thought when he hears her plight, he lets his cigar go out, and stands looking intently at the ground. The bishop's arrival the next morning to hear her answer to his epistolary proposals provides the way to save Swithin's reputation and her own. 'A tempter had shown it to her', and convention forces her hand. She becomes the 'spiritual queen of Melchester', as her brother had hoped.

Dare is more disadvantaged than Glanville, and cigarette-smoking is the outward sign of his diabolical reflections. Secretly for his own security he plans to ensure that his father marries the affluent Paula Power, owner of Stancy Castle. The first obstacle to be removed is the young architect George Somerset who enjoys her favour. The initiation of Dare's partnership with Havill against him takes place in a darkened recess of the summer-house to the accompaniment of sheet-lightning and thunder during her garden-party. After losing money to him by card-play in church, his father, Captain de Stancy, tells him he is 'quite a Mephistopheles'. When they met, Dare had told him that he had come 'From going to and fro in the earth, and walking up and down in it, as Satan said to his Maker'. Previously this 'cosmopolite' had hinted at such overtones when he informed Havill that he is a citizen of the world, and at home everywhere. If, as seems most likely, his addition, 'A man whose country has no boundary is your only true gentleman', was intended as an allusion to the prince of darkness in *King Lear*, it fails adequately to convey the significance its context suggests.[5]

Dare's Mephistophelian role is most evident when, after plying his father with intoxicating liquor, he induces him to peer into

Paula's gymnasium as the noonday sunlight pours down through the lantern, 'irradiating her with a warm light that was incarnadined by her pink doublet and hose'. In creating this species of 'optical poem' Hardy adapted the scene in Goethe where Faust, after gazing voluptuously on the mirrored form of lovely woman, drinks the witch's potion, and is assured by Mephistopheles that he will soon see the model of all womankind in flesh and blood, adding (in an aside) 'With this draught in your body, you will soon see a Helen in every woman.' Hardy comes to terms with Victorian convention by clothing the attractive Paula in a costume of fleshly pink; she practises a Hellenist physical cult, and becomes another Helen for the inflammable de Stancy.

With his 'broad forehead, vertical as the face of a bastion', Dare resembles Wilkie Collins' villain Mannion. The defamation of Somerset by this *chevalier d'industrie* is on the point of succeeding when his nefarious role is disclosed to Paula on the morning scheduled for her wedding with Captain de Stancy, who, after a night of 'thick-coming fancies' (like Lady Macbeth's), is 'as full of apprehension as one who has a league with Mephistopheles'. Paula does not know whether to regard Dare as man, boy, or demon. After her marriage to Somerset, he punningly hints at his revenge, telling his father that he has another *match* for him, and that it will be a *light* night, as indeed it is when he sets fire to Stancy Castle. Hardy's diabolic additives do not create the ambience he aimed at in *A Laodicean*, but the evidence of the novel and of the *coup d'audace* in *Two on a Tower* indicates the great appeal which the Mephistophelian had for him. This is confirmed not only in 'The Romantic Adventures of a Milkmaid' but also, much later, in *The Dynasts*, where, in conformity with Goethe's Mephistopheles as a commentator on human kind and events, Hardy expresses part of his variable self through the Spirits Sinister and Ironic.

Alec d'Urberville shows some of the characteristics of earlier Hardy villains, but he belongs to more serious fiction than that in which Hardy had essayed his more Mephistophelian roles, and has close links with Milton's Satan. He first appears as a tall young man, smoking a cigar, his lips full and red like those of the sensual Manston, his complexion 'almost swarthy', and his 'well-groomed black moustache' reminiscent of Baron von Xanten. When he regales Tess inside his tent he watches her through the skeins of his smoke; she has no idea that 'there behind the blue narcotic haze was potentially the "tragic mischief" of her drama – one who stood fair to be the blood-ray in the spectrum of her young life'. His sadistic nature is revealed in his driving when he conveys Tess and her luggage to the Slopes, nipping his cigar between his teeth at the prospect; 'the teeth are the instruments of our sensual will', writes D. H. Lawrence.[6] The garden where she tends Mrs Stoke d'Urberville's poultry is notable for its inclusion of environmental features associated with Richardson's Clarissa and her rapist Lovelace; Alec's wall-leaping entry recalls Satan's irruption into the garden of Eden. On the Saturday night of Tess's rape 'the red coal of a cigar' shows Alec waiting for his opportunity.

When, after her desertion by Angel Clare, he comes as a tempter to the Durbeyfield allotment at Marlott, he works in the smoke as darkness falls; flares from a burning heap of weeds light up the steel prongs of his fork, which is introduced as a reminder of popular superstition on the Devil and Hell-fire such as Hardy heard when he was a child.[7] Tess is the victim of circumstances, her first fall inflicted ruthlessly upon her, her second assented to involuntarily. Hardy the novelist has to create a sense of inevitability throughout, but, philosophically, he is not a determinist. However much the course of things follows the chances of character and circumstance, his use of 'potentially' and 'stood fair' when he brings Alec and Tess together for the first time implies that there are times in life when individuals are free to make choices which will affect their destinies.

6

The Uniqueness of *The Woodlanders*

There are, of course, factors common to all Hardy's novels, in some more obvious than in others, but it is more critically interesting to consider how the novels differ from each other. Each has its special identity, setting it apart from all the others in subject or theme, in tone or atmosphere. It is true that some minor imaginative effects and some more important fictional ideas in *Desperate Remedies* are repeated, the former in *The Return of the Native*, the latter in *Tess of the d'Urbervilles*, yet the contrast between Hardy's first published story, a mystery-thriller with a sensational and tightly complicated plot, and the others, or with the idyllicism of his second, *Under the Greenwood Tree*, far outweighs whatever they have in common. In no other of his novels do we find anything comparable to the London 'Upstairs, Downstairs' situations of *The Hand of Ethelberta*. *The Trumpet-Major* is his one historical novel, ironically of the type (since *The Hand of Ethelberta* failed to ensure a continuation of Hardy in *The Cornhill Magazine*) which Leslie Stephens preferred, with George III 'just round the corner'.[1] In his next, *A Laodicean*, Hardy turns from Dorset and the past to his contemporary world of technological advance and European travel. The change from both of these to the passionate love-story of *Two on a Tower* is remarkable, but even more striking is Hardy's bold venture into the world of 'the full-starred heavens', which had fascinated him ever since he made his own observations through the Moules' telescope at Fordington. *The Mayor of Casterbridge* is anything but a love-story; it stands apart in the Hardy canon by virtue of its Casterbridge setting, its commercial plot, and the dominance of character, rather than chance, in the rise and fall of its tragic hero. Chance is crucial in both *Tess of the d'Urbervilles* and *Jude the Obscure*; in a sense, which is obvious almost from the outset, they are complementary, but they are diverse in tone, texture, and settings. Above all, they differ in imaginative conception and purport; the Crucifixion theme of *Jude* has no parallel in *Tess*.

63

The more familiar we are with Hardy's novels, the more we realize those idiosyncratic features and characteristics which give them their individualities; the more likely also are we to appreciate his artistic efforts not to be repetitive and facile. When Angel Clare is becoming acquainted with the inmates of Crick's dairy-farm, he realizes a truth stated by Pascal, that 'the more intelligent one is, the more original people one finds'; it is rather like saying 'the more individuality we find in others'. So it is with Hardy's novels. Early critics, however, relying on early impressions, were apt to be struck by his similarities; and some of their conclusions, especially with reference to his characters, are astonishing. 'Gabriel Oak, Diggory Venn, and Giles Winterborne are clearly brothers', Lascelles Abercrombie wrote;[2] 'indeed, a family so identical in feature, physical, mental, and spiritual is beyond the accomplishment of human generation'. 'These three men', he continued, 'are but three disguises of a single piece of psychological imagination; and the disguising is scarcely more than a difference in name, in trade, and fortune'. 'Taken in a bunch', another critic wrote much later,[3] Hardy's men and women 'show surprisingly little individuality. Which is Giles and which is Gabriel? Is the girl in the corner Grace Melbury or Anne Garland or Fancy or Elfride?' After Roy Morrell's *Thomas Hardy, the Will and the Way* (1965) no one is likely to confuse the passive Giles of *The Woodlanders* with the enterprising, never long downcast, Gabriel Oak of *Far from the Madding Crowd*. Resemblances between Fancy Day and Grace Melbury are rather accidental and superficial. Albert J. Guerard is more discriminating, but his genealogy of Hardy's young women, which places them in simple categories,[4] as if Marty South and Tess are of the same type, again illustrates the danger of assessments which are too general and remote to have important critical value.

The term 'unique' is too absolute and exclusive to be applied to any of Hardy's novels. If one is to be isolated for its essential and dominant quality, it must be *The Well-Beloved*, the last of his to be completed (in its final form). Though its settings are real enough, it belongs to a world of fantasy and illusion. Its persistent theme, the pursuit of the ideal woman, is traceable as far back as *Desperate Remedies*, but it assumes its Shelleyan Platonic form, that of the elusive, migratory Idea, first in *The Woodlanders* – only in a different mode. Specialities of this kind, and others more accidental and external, constitute the 'uniqueness' of *The Woodlanders*; several factors and characteristics relate to it alone among Hardy's novels.

The Woodlanders is the only novel which Hardy set aside after planning it, and took up several years later. When the first instalment of *Far from the Madding Crowd* appeared anonymously in *The Cornhill Magazine*, one reviewer thought it the work of George Eliot. Hardy had, in fact, borrowed from George Eliot in both this novel and *Under the Greenwood Tree*. Not surprisingly he deemed it expedient to give up the projected story 'which later took shape in *The Woodlanders*', and turn from rural life 'in a new and untried direction' with *The Hand of Ethelberta*. After he had completed *The Mayor of Casterbridge* and taken his usual long holiday in London, preoccupation with the Max Gate removal in 1885 may have made him think (as he had probably done already) that it would be advantageous to choose for his next novel the story which was already planned. He seems to have attempted a revision of the plot, but, after working three long days in November 'in a fit of depression, as if enveloped in a leaden cloud' (rather like Winterborne, when lopping the tree which seems fetishistically to threaten John South's life), he decided 'after all' to return to the original, and concentrated on working out the details. (The novel is extremely well structured, and there is nothing to suggest that he overlooked anything important.)

Hardy first planned the novel when the writing of *Far from the Madding Crowd* at Higher Bockhampton was well in hand. At the time he had only to take a short walk in one of the neighbouring woods to see signs in plenty of the natural struggle for existence. This is the main tenor of his poem 'In a Wood', which carries with it a reference to *The Woodlanders*. Juxtaposed to it in *Wessex Poems* we have 'Middle-Age Enthusiasms', dedicated to his sister Mary; it recalls their delight in watching 'strange sheens' leaping 'from quaint leaves in shade'. Whether she accompanied him to the Bockhampton plantation when he visited it two days before Christmas 1883 or on his birthday the following year is conjectural. His notes on the second of these visits contain details of strange leafy sheens, and of an auditory image, which were included in *The Woodlanders*.[5]

This is the one novel in which Hardy makes woods and their Darwinian aspects the main setting for his story; it is the only one, moreover, in which the setting is the wooded country his mother knew so well during her early years in and around Melbury

Osmond. The question of topography brings us to one of the most interesting features of the novel, though it has little significant bearing on its substance. In no other novel did he subsequently try to mislead readers about his true setting; he transferred that of 'The Romantic Adventures of a Milkmaid' in order to avoid incongruous associations in the reader's mind with the tragedy of Tess. His motivation for the apparent transfer of the background in *The Woodlanders*, however, was anything but artistic.

The change is more illusory than real, extending to little beyond the alteration of Wessex place-names, to give the impression that High Stoy, instead of the original 'Rubdon' or Bubb Down east of Melbury (or 'Hintock') House, is the 'axis of so many critical movements' in the action. In the first edition Fitzpiers, returning from Mrs Charmond at Middleton Abbey (Milton Abbas) allows the horse Darling to stop at Holy Spring, where he hears Owlscombe (i.e. Batcombe) church-clock strike midnight; in the revised version the corresponding places are Lydden Spring and Newland Buckton (i.e. Buckland Newton). Of special interest is Melbury's visit to Hintock House to bring back Fitzpiers early one gloomy April evening. He follows Darling's tracks, and enters one side of the park by a bridle-gate until he sees Darling indistinctly by a clump of trees. He damns Fitzpiers for not riding honestly up to the house, and tethers his horse to a neighbouring tree. Without ringing he enters Mrs Charmond's mansion, and tries various doors, finally to see Fitzpiers and Felice stepping out through an open window. They part at the railing between the lawn and the park, Fitzpiers disappearing in the dusky trees. He mistakes his horse and is thrown; Melbury follows on Darling, and finds him stunned and stupefied. He gets him astride Darling, and escorts him towards their home at Hintock. In the first edition they proceed past Great Willy, the largest oak in the wood, towards Tutcombe Bottom, 'intensely dark now with overgrowth, and popularly supposed to be haunted by the spirits of the fratricides exorcised from Hintock House'. 'Tutcombe Bottom' is clearly Stutcombe Bottom, a swampy hollow half a mile or so south-west of Melbury House. Hardy left a reference to it in the fourth chapter: the cramp in Melbury's left shoulder 'had come of carrying a pollard, unassisted, from Tutcombe Bottom home'. There can be no doubt then that Hintock House, with Bubb Down to one side and Stutcombe on the other, occupied the same site in Hardy's imagination as Melbury House, the home of the Ilchesters.

He had disguised it by placing it in a deep hollow, like the house he knew (now demolished) at Turnworth near Blandford. When preparing 'The First Countess of Wessex' for magazine publication (with recognizable illustrations of Melbury House and the entrance to the park from sketches made by Alfred Parsons when Hardy accompanied him there in January 1889), he probably realized not only the risk he ran of offending the Ilchesters by that story[6] but also the possibility of their eventually discovering his earlier association of their home with the seductive Felice Charmond. The ending of 'The First Countess of Wessex' shows that he was already anticipating further concealment in *The Woodlanders* by pretending to transfer its setting to another woodland area about five miles further east. The opportunity for this revision did not come until 1895, when Hardy prepared the novel for issue in the first uniform edition of the Wessex Novels. In this, at the outset, Mrs Dollery's route from Sherton to Abbot's Cernel creates considerable confusion for any literary topographer, but such changes are practically insignificant, alterations in background being slight and infrequent. The most interesting new landscape feature (xxiii) arises from the replacement of 'that plantation reaching over the hill like a great slug' by 'that hill rising out of the level like a great whale', a reference to Dungeon Hill east of Middlemarsh.

If further evidence is needed to prove that the background of the novel was not imagined in the High Stoy region, it comes at the end. The churchyard on the hill where Marty lays her flowers on Winterborne's grave is not at Hermitage, as used to be thought, but at Melbury Osmond, the village north of Melbury Park of which Hardy heard so much from his mother. What he did not dare to state publicly he admitted to his friend Edmund Gosse in a letter written from Florence on 5 April 1887: 'Great Hintock' is Melbury Osmond.

The Woodlanders is the first novel in which Hardy raises an important sociological issue. In *Jude the Obscure* he was to show a preoccupation with the ties of marriage; in *The Woodlanders*, and here only, he dramatizes a protest against the inadequacies of contemporary legislation on divorce. This question is inseparable from the chronology of events within the novel, a subject which has singled out *The Woodlanders* for special consideration, though the issue is less important than recent controversy suggests, if we study the evidence supplied by Hardy. It arises from Fred Beaucock's reference to the divorce act of 1857 as 'the new statute' passed 'last year', after, in fact, the extraordinary appearance in the woods on old Midsummer Eve of an American who had left the States years earlier, in 1865, at the end of the American Civil War. After sojourning in southern Europe he is now stout and Italianized; his statement that he had 'never' returned to his native country since the failure of 'the Southern cause' seems to imply the passing of several years, and suggests that we are in the early 1870s, a period confirmed by Hardy when, replying evasively in 1926 to a query on the location of 'Little Hintock', he wrote, 'However, to be more definite, it has features which were to be found fifty years ago . . . .' The phrase 'fifty years ago' can have no relevance apart from the period of the novel; fifty is a 'round' number which takes us back to the time when Hardy first planned the novel (not later than 1874), when the visit of the disappointed and Europeanized South Carolinian expatriate would not have been inappropriate.

To suggest that Hardy mistook the period of the American war is unwarrantable. In England, where many people had American relatives, interest in the subject was considerable. Hardy must have heard and read a great deal about it when he was in London. He kept up with current affairs mainly by reading *The Saturday Review*, which devoted a leader to the civil war almost every week during its last year, and every week as it approached its end. Whether he included the ex-American in his plot less than ten years after 'the failure of the Southern cause' (as seems most probable, since he was introduced chiefly for its *dénouement*), or little more than twenty years (which seems less likely, since Hardy tells us he went back to his original plot), it seems quite incredible that he could have forgotten when the war ended. His writing generally shows a keen historical sense, and he prepared the ground for *The Woodlanders* with great care. No contemporary critic found his chronology implausible and, had he been guilty of a serious lapse, he had ample opportunity to make all the necessary revisions, affecting only a few lines of the text, when he worked on his topographical changes in 1895.

We do not need to resort to the whimsical explanation of the New Wessex Edition that Hardy presents a dream-world in which historical sequence is irrelevant. Even in a fantasy such as *The Well-Beloved* he keeps both feet firmly on the ground, with sedulous regard for details of background change in a three-generation period. 'Let Time roll backward if it will', he wrote in one of his last poems; the idea might appeal to 'magians', but not to him. He was orthodox; Einstein made him feel that the universe of mathematical philosophy was becoming 'too comic for words'. Again, bearing in mind *The Trumpet-Major*, and fictional statements about railways in *A Pair of Blue Eyes* and *The Mayor of Casterbridge*, we cannot assume that 'Wessex' events coincide with historical chronology. Even if we suppose that Sherton is Sherborne, the new railway of 1860 to the latter fits in with no internal chronology of *The Woodlanders* which is calculated on whether or not Beaucock was correct in saying that the 1857 divorce act was passed 'last year'.

The fact that contemporary readers and critics, who were far more conversant with the 1857 act and the American Civil War than we are, found nothing controversial in the time-sequence of *The Woodlanders* suggests that any answer to the problem must be found in the novel. Hardy does not play the role of an omniscient author, but he twice sounds warnings on the illusions created by the pretender Beaucock; the precise reference to the act ('twenty and twenty-one Vic.') would put the intelligent reader on guard. 'How much of the exaggerated information on the then new divorce laws imparted by Beaucock to his listeners was the result of ignorance, and how much of dupery, was never ascertained', Hardy tells us, too tersely perhaps, indicating in 'the then new divorce laws . . . imparted by Beaucock' that the 1857 act was new then only according to a plausible rogue, who, even when he was a lawyer's clerk, had sought to create the impression that he was a clever fellow. He had taken to drink and lost his post; now he earns a living, mainly in public-houses, drawing up wills at half-a-crown a time. 'An idea implanted early in life is difficult to uproot, and many elderly tradespeople still clung to the notion that Fred Beaucock knew a great deal of law', Hardy warns us. From this it is clear that Beaucock had had little to do with the law for a long time; he knew the title at least of the 1857 act, which he repeats parrot-fashion. If it is not abracadabra to him, it is to Melbury. We are left to guess whether Beaucock was ignorant or deceitful when he spoke of the new court 'established last year'. He clearly knew nothing fundamentally about the act, for he continues, 'no longer one law for the rich and another for the poor'. The 1857 act set up a new civil court for divorce proceedings in London, but it did not extend the range of those who could afford them beyond the middle class, and it introduced no new principles. Had Beaucock known the law, he would have realized that it offered nothing to raise Melbury's hopes, and he would have taken care not to risk consulting a London lawyer on the case. He may have read newspaper reports in the 1870s on battered wives in industrial areas, and the mounting pressures on their behalf which were to lead to the Matrimonial Causes Act of 1878.

Set in country familiar to Hardy's mother in her youth, *The Woodlanders* contains superstitions and superstitious practices which she related at Higher Bockhampton. Others are to be found in some of the short stories, notably in 'The Superstitious Man's Story', 'Interlopers at the Knap', and (though its setting is in the Frome valley) in 'The Withered Arm'. The aged friend who reminded the author that Rhoda Brook's incubus dream had occurred while she was lying down on a hot afternoon, and not while asleep at midnight, was almost certainly his mother. Superstitions are slow to die; most of them lasted into the twentieth century. Nowhere in Hardy's novels do they play a more important part than in *The Woodlanders*. It is gratifying to learn from the first edition that the swamp to which the two fratricidal brothers were exorcised by a priest after haunting King's Hintock Court was Tutcombe Bottom; more difficult to remember that the old local saying 'On new-year's tide, a cock's stride' was linked to the rate of their return year by year to their old quarters. The bark-rippers who tell the story recount other mysterious sights explicable only in terms of such supernatural agencies as white and black witches; elsewhere we hear of witches and demons. Many no doubt, like Marty South, were familiar with the story of Doctor Faustus in the penny book. Melbury's workmen are convinced that the new doctor Fitzpiers has sold his soul to the Devil, and that he had ordered books on the black art from London. A parcel of them had been sent by mistake to the parson; his wife dipped into them, and became hysterical, thinking he had turned heathen and their children would be ruined. The hour for marriage-divination is midnight on old Midsummer Eve; then the young women hope to gain glimpses of their future partners for life. As a company of them are about to weave their spell – the black art on this occasion involving the sowing of hempseed – one who had feared they were dealing with the Devil wishes they had stayed at home, and been contented with hole-digging, which would disclose their future husbands' trades (from noises in the hole). The Midsummer 'larry' is notable for the Fitzpiers–Suke Damson encounter, and for the strange appearance of the lost gentleman in evening-dress. Catching sight of him, one girl mistakes him for Satan with his hour-glass. The appeal of witchcraft and of the Mephistophelian and Satanic to Hardy was rooted in boyhood memories of tales told at home, many by his mother on superstitious customs and beliefs in and around Melbury Osmond.

More surcharged in 'The Son's Veto', Hardy's insistence on the harmful snobbish effect of higher-class education is a feature which distinguishes *The Woodlanders* from his other novels. Grace Melbury's father is a merchant who regards her education at 'fashionable schools' as an investment on which he hopes to make 'a better return'. Fond, well-meaning, but foolish, he thinks it would be *'wasting her* to give her to a man of no higher standing' than Winterborne. Her values are falsified by the artificial 'veneer' of her education, and, with full encouragement from Melbury, she finds herself 'as it were in mid-air between two storeys of society'; she turns to the genteel, to Mrs Charmond and Fitzpiers, to be disappointed by one and betrayed by the other. Too late she discovers the happiness of being her natural self with Winterborne; experience has taught her the difference between the 'great and little in life', between 'two sophisticated beings – versed in the world's ways' and the sincerity of such men as Winterborne:

> Honesty, goodness, manliness, tenderness, devotion, for her only existed in their purity now in the breasts of unvarnished men; and here was one who had manifested such towards her from his youth up.

Nature, Hardy tells us, had striven to join them together; he wrote from experience, knowing what divisions and inhibitions could be created by artificial values and distinctions. His first wife's sense of superior social accomplishments and endowment was the source of disparagements which he may already have suffered, and he had observed London society for years, sufficiently to detect the false concomitants of breeding, sophistication, affluence, and convention. Grace Melbury may recall Fancy Day, who is tempted to marry one socially superior to Dick Dewy. Fancy has not been sent to a fashionable boarding-school, and, put to the test, she proves that education has not spoilt her nature. Grace has acquired new standards; she is ambivalent. Soon after Winterborne's death she returns to her class-superior husband; she cannot escape the

man-trap of Fitzpiers' cultivated flattery and charm, however
superficial and cynical. Hardy's impatience with her is well-known;
he voices it through her father near the end of the novel, but what
he could only hint at there he states clearly elsewhere: 'the heroine
is doomed to an unhappy life with an inconstant husband. I
could not accentuate this strongly in the book, by reason of the
conventions of the libraries, etc.'[7]

Hardy had seen too much of nature on the heath and in the
woodlands near his birthplace to be astonished by *The Origin of
Species*. There is little of the idyllic in *The Woodlanders*. In spring,
when the orchards are pink with bloom, the nightingale pours out
'all the intensity of his eloquence' one evening, and primroses are
palely visible among the copses, but the barked branches of oaks
look spectral in the woodland gloom as the enamoured Fitzpiers
leaves with Grace. After discovering her purse, they had been
standing silently together, when two large birds, apparently engrossed in a quarrel while roosting or nesting, had tumbled one
over the other into the ashes at their feet. 'That's the end of what
is called love', someone says. It is Marty, who has been watching
the pigeons, unaware of Grace's presence, and assuming, when
she catches sight of him in the background, that the other person
is Winterborne.

In no other novel does Hardy present so much of the natural
world in its Darwinian features:

> On older trees . . . huge lobes of fungi grew like lungs. Here, as
> everywhere, the Unfulfilled Intention, which makes life what it
> is, was as obvious as it could be among the depraved crowds of
> a city slum. The leaf was deformed, the curve was crippled, the
> taper was interrupted; the lichen ate the vigour of the stalk, and
> the ivy strangled to death the promising sapling.

The last detail may remind us of 'The Ivy-Wife', but it is far more
important to notice how the Unfulfilled Intention counterpoints
critical phases in the lives of the chief protagonists. When Melbury
and Grace walk one evening, both deeply anxious over her
husband's late-night returns from alleged medical missions, they
halt beneath 'a half-dead oak, hollow and disfigured with white
tumours, its roots spreading out like claws grasping the ground';
a chilly wind encircles them. The Unfulfilled Intention applies to
the plot generally; it may have been consciously intended as the

theme. The plot, to use Hardy's phrase in *The Hand of Ethelberta*, shows concatenated affections, in which A follows B (Marty South, Winterborne), B follows C (Winterborne, Grace Melbury), and C . . . . Extended interlinking of this kind is found in no other work by Hardy. When he refers to courses in Hintock lives which 'were part of the pattern in the great web of human doings then weaving in both hemispheres from the White Sea to Cape Horn' he probably had in mind what he had been thinking, not long before he began work on *The Woodlanders*, of how the novel could give an impression of the human race 'as one great network or tissue which quivers in every part when one point is shaken, like a spider's web if touched'.[8] The result is that all the lovers, if such a term may serve to include relationships as diverse as those between Marty and Winterborne, Winterborne and Grace Melbury, Grace and Fitzpiers, Fitzpiers and Mrs Charmond, are doomed, ultimately or from first to last, to deprivation or unfulfilment. Neither Grace nor Mrs Charmond can be permanently happy, and the pursuit of the well-beloved by the Italianized gentleman from Carolina ends only in catastrophe.

The range from Winterborne and Marty South to this intrusive and unreal stage figure is great. Grace Melbury occupies a central place; she is, as Hardy says, midway between two storeys; they are social but also moral. The question is one of integrity. The poem 'In a Wood', begun in 1887 (the year *The Woodlanders* was published) but not concluded until 1896, gives illustrations of the Unfulfilled Intention in nature, and concludes:

> Since, then, no grace I find
> Taught me of trees,
> Turn I back to my kind,
> Worthy as these.
> There at least smiles abound,
> There discourse trills around,
> There, now and then, are found
> Life-loyalties.

Giles Winterborne enjoys some happy meetings with Grace, but Marty South is one who never told her love. Her life-loyalty is expressed most movingly at the very end, when Grace no longer visits his grave.

The Woodlanders is the only novel in which Hardy presents the

Idealist in love as a libertine; he had learnt the difference between the real and the visionary romanticism which haunted him in his early years of authorship at Weymouth.[9] A dilettante scientist and philosopher, the Shelleyan Fitzpiers is haunted by the Idea, or the perfect imaginary form, of woman, which he is sceptical of finding in the flesh. His first sight of Grace Melbury is a mirror-reflection, not her real self; the vision convinces him that Nature had at last recovered her lost union with the Idea. He thinks mistakenly that he catches sight of her in the wood on old Midsummer Eve, and again he is enchanted to think that the impossible has happened, the Idea being 'for once completely fulfilled . . . in the objective substance'. One of Hardy's comments on the philosophical idealism which is capable of such deceptive metamorphosis is heard in the sarcastic whirr of the night-hawk as this Tannhäuser of Little Hintock addresses himself to Suke Damson in the haycock. Another is applied to him as the lonely outsider, with no local interests and little to do; a young man in such circumstances, Hardy writes, 'may dream of his ideal friend', but 'some humour of the blood will probably lead him to think rather of an ideal mistress, and at length the rustle of a woman's dress, the sound of her voice, or the transit of her form against the field of his vision, will enkindle his soul with a flame that blinds his eyes'.

'Regarding his own personality as one of unbounded possibilities, because it was his own', Fitzpiers has studied German metaphysics, hoping to discover where the physical and the transcendental meet. He indulges his imagination, the Idea being nurtured by Shelley's poetry; like that of the lover in Hardy's poem 'The Chosen' his 'conjoint emotion' is such that he can be possessed by several 'distinct infatuations at the same time'. German philosophy has made him believe that love is wholly subjective, and that it would affect him equally whoever the woman he met, just as the rainbow iris falls indifferently against an oak, ash, or elm tree. The significance of this idealizing image is not propounded outside *The Woodlanders*, but Hardy uses it in its more general illusory sense several times later in his poetry with reference to love and romantic views of nature. Hardy's more mature views on the question of love are made explicit in the novel: when Grace's idealization of Fitzpiers had been 'demolished by the intimacy of common life' in her marriage, and she had found him 'as merely human as the Hintock people themselves, a new foundation was in demand for an enduring and staunch affection – a sympathetic interdependence, wherein mutual weaknesses are made the grounds for a defensive alliance'.

Another special feature of *The Woodlanders* is the employment of Norse imagery to reinforce the theme; it is not used to the same extent or with comparable imaginative significance elsewhere in Hardy's writings. Initially the images combine with evidence of the Unfulfilled Intention to accentuate the tomblike stillness, the note of hopelessness with which the novel opens. At three o'clock on a winter's morning, exhausted with spar-gad cutting, Marty South opens the door. As 'the night in all its fulness met her flatly on the threshold, like the very brink of an absolute void, or the ante-mundane Ginnung-Gap believed in by her Teuton forefathers', she hears in the wind the 'vocalized sorrows of the trees, together with the screech of owls, and the fluttering tumble of some awkward wood-pigeon ill-balanced on its roosting-bough'. The day emerges sunless 'like a dead-born child'. Two days later the hectic leaves of beeches are heard rustling 'with a sound almost metallic, like the sheet-iron foliage of the fabled Jarnvid wood'. Whatever Hardy's knowledge of Icelandic myth, its main influence in *The Woodlanders* derives from Matthew Arnold's 'Balder Dead'.[10] The dripping woodland sound which was part of the universal mourning for Balder's death is to be found in Hardy's novel from the beginning. It is strongly emphasized when Grace sets out, for the sake of Grammer Oliver, to meet Fitzpiers for the first time: 'the battle between snow and thaw' continued in mid-air, and 'trees dripped on the garden plots, where no vegetables would grow for the dripping'. When Melbury, disillusioned with his son-in-law, tells Winterborne that Grace has lost her taste for refinements, and still loves him, he does not know 'what fires' he is 'recklessly stirring up'. Darkness closes round them, 'and the monotonous drip of the fog from the branches' quickens as it turns to fine rain. A 'regular dripping' of such fog is heard on the first morning of the story. A few hours earlier Marty, the unfulfilled, has cut off her locks after losing hope of marrying Giles Winterborne; she dreads seeing her 'deflowered visage' in the mirror as much as Thor's wife did her reflection in a pool after the rape of her locks by Loke the Malicious. (Loke is associated with the wood of Jarnvid in 'Balder Dead'.) Giles's deprivation is anticipated in the scene where, while lopping off boughs from the tree which appears to threaten the life of Marty's bedridden father, he is suddenly enveloped in a fog where he remains as darkness falls, not responding to Grace, who has just communicated her father's wish that they forget their informal engagement. The fog is another 'gloomy Niflheim', the abode of Norse heroes who die unfulfilled.

The Woodlanders is the exception among Hardy's novels in having a title-page epigraph by its author. Hardy composed it eight and a half years after the novel was completed, when he was preparing it for the uniform edition of 1895–6.[11] By this time he had given up all hope of a loving relationship with his wife. The pines he had planted at Max Gate were growing fast, and he wrote:

> Not boskiest bow'r
> When hearts are ill affin'd
> Hath tree of pow'r
> To shelter from the wind!

While planting some of those trees, and hearing them sigh in the wind, he had thought as Marty was to do when assisting Giles in the same occupation. 'It seems to me', she says, 'as if they sigh because they are very sorry to begin life in earnest.' The boy Hardy had wished like Jude never to grow up; in retrospect, confirmed by experience, he could utter the same wish. Each tree, he wrote years later in 'The Pine Planters', will continue to sigh.

> Grieving that never
> 　Kind Fate decreed
> It should for ever
> 　Remain a seed,
> And shun the welter
> 　Of things without,
> Unneeding shelter
> 　From storm and drought.

The epigraph, with its emphasis on 'When hearts are ill affin'd', is more apposite to Hardy at Max Gate in 1895 than it is to the novel, with Winterborne as its hero.

The Woodlanders enjoys the distinction of being Hardy's favourite among his novels. His note on completing it at 8.20 p.m. on 4 February 1887 is followed by the sentence, 'In after years he often said that in some respects The Woodlanders was his best novel.' In April 1912, when making his last careful revision (for the Wessex Edition), he wrote to Florence Dugdale, 'On taking up The Woodland-

ers and reading it after many years I think I like it, *as a story*, the best of all'; he had reached page 140, it should be said.[12] Many will wonder why he gave special emphasis to his liking it best as a story, since it is rather a series of situations than a great action. He gives part of the answer in the next sentence: 'Perhaps that is owing to the locality and scenery of the action, a part I am very fond of.' It delighted him in recalling places which had excited his interest during visits from boyhood onwards, because they were associated with his mother's life, and with all he had heard from her of events, customs, and strange traditions in her homeland area. Hardy had reason to be satisfied too with the structuring of the novel, especially in the opening chapters, and with writing which continually discloses sensitive observation, mature reflection, and fine imaginative effects. Deeper and more personal reasons may be suspected, as the title-page epigraph suggests.

Despite such extravaganzas as the theatrical appearance of the Italianized American in Hintock woodland, and the hysterical comicality of the scene in which Fitzpiers' extra-marital lovers of low and high degree, almost distraught with alarm at the news of his accident, are ushered by Grace into his empty bedroom with the dramatic flourish 'Wives all, let's enter together!', there is nothing wholly incongruous or discordant in *The Woodlanders*. It needs relief, for the prevailing tone is grey and wintry; whenever hope is engendered, it is not long sustained. The novel's moods vary from the tragic to the humorous, from the pathos of the deluded Melbury's hopes to the grimness of the man-trap vengeance threatened by Timothy Tangs; above all, from the serenity of the scene in which Giles appears as Autumn's brother, and the evening sky reflects the instinctive happiness he and Grace at last find in each other's company – her senses revelling 'in the sudden lapse back to Nature unadorned' – to the hopeless resignation of the aptly named Winterborne in those wet, cold, fatal Darwinian conditions outside One Chimney Hut.

One critic maintains that 'Nature, as manifested in the woodlands' of the novel, is 'calm, temperate, almost idyllic'; another, while admitting that its atmosphere is melancholy, concludes that the key, summarizing word for it is 'mellow'.[13] In what sense, it is not easy to see. The majority of scenes are wintry or wet, with recurrent gloom, fog-dripping trees, and a varied selection of Darwinian reminders. A mellow scene such as that of Grace and Giles in the cider season is all the more memorable by contrast with the tones which predominate. Trees are 'haggard', grey phantoms' in winter, or 'weird' and 'spectral' in the leafy season. For the most part Hardy is not interested in seeing Nature 'as a Beauty'; his imaginative eyes are focused, rather, on 'the tragical mysteries of life'. His note on the 'late-Turner' style was written in January 1887 when, as a writer, he was still preoccupied with *The Woodlanders*.[14] In this novel Hardy finds kinship with what Shelley imaged in 'Epipsychidion' as 'the wintry forest of our life'. He may have had his father in mind when he wrotes of Giles 'As one, in suffering all, that suffers nothing', but, his imagination activated by his own felt experience, he could readily empathize with Winterborne's 'When the sun shines flat on the north front of Sherton Abbey – that's when my happiness will come to me!', and with his renunciation of life, just as he had done with Henchard's last wish, 'that no man remember me'.

The recovery of Oak and Bathsheba after setback and disaster makes one wonder how different in spirit *The Woodlanders* would have been had it been written immediately after *Far from the Madding Crowd*. As it is, it presents a relationship of tragic lives rather than the kind of tragic action which is found in *The Mayor of Casterbridge* or *Tess of the d'Urbervilles* or *Jude the Obscure*. It has been compared with *Under the Greenwood Tree*. Whatever their similarities, the differences are enormous. One is Hardy's happiest story; the other, I believe, is his saddest. This does not imply that it is depressing; Giles and Marty South have a nobility – a grandeur perhaps – which elevates and consoles. The sad music of humanity uplifts as much as it chastens and subdues. *The Woodlanders* appealed to Hardy's spirit; he liked it because it contains, on the one hand, so much with which he sympathized, and on the other, much that he condemned. A well-known passage in a letter written by his second wife to Sydney Cockerell on 26 December 1920 runs: 'He is now . . . writing a poem with great spirit: always a sign of well-being with him. Needless to say it is an intensely dismal poem.'

The Woodlanders is not dismal, nor was Hardy quite the Jaques of *As You Like It* who could suck melancholy out of a song as a weasel sucks eggs; he was variable, but often, like Shelley, he found solace in the expression of sadness. A few days after working over his old plot for *The Woodlanders* he wrote: 'a tragedy exhibits a state of things in the life of an individual which unavoidably causes some natural aim or desire of his to end in a catastrophe when carried out'. The formulation is too tethered to the Unfulfilled Intention in human life to have great literary value; it is relevant to Melbury and Grace rather than to the passively enduring Marty South and Giles Winterborne, with whom we have deeper sympathies if we submit to Hardy's orchestration of the story. It could have expressed his own feelings; he had not proceeded far with his novel when he wrote:

> This evening, the end of the old year 1885 finds me sadder than many previous New Year's Eves have done. Whether building this house at Max Gate was a wise expenditure of energy is one doubt, which, if resolved in the negative, is depressing enough. And there are others. But:
> 'This is the chief thing: Be not perturbed; for all things are according to the nature of the universal.'

The conclusion of this quotation from Marcus Aurelius voices Hardy's resignation. It corresponds to words from the *Agamemnon* of Aeschylus which are remembered by Jude after he has lost his children: 'Things are as they are, and will be brought to their destined issue.'

7

Philosophy in Fiction

When literature begins to teach or preach it quickly threatens boredom, unless it appeals to a member of a particular group to whom moral earnestness, religious zeal, or political partisanship is the crusading breath of life. Commenting on sentimental comedy in the eighteenth century (a period when writers, following the example of *The Spectator*, believed in their civilizing mission), Fielding, through Parson Adams in *Joseph Andrews*, found 'things almost solemn enough for a sermon' in one play. The tendency to make the theatre 'a school of morality' led to Garrick's protest in his prologue to Hugh Kelly's *False Delicacy*:

> Write moral plays – the blockhead! – why, good people,
> You'll soon expect this house to wear a steeple!
> For our fine piece, to let you into facts,
> Is quite a Sermon, – only preach'd in Acts.

Many of us can think of twentieth-century plays in which the action leads up to an address directed at the audience for propaganda purposes. At such times the listener or reader, feeling he is being 'got at', resents the breaking of dramatic illusion and wonders if it can be recovered; he prefers to reflect for himself on any questions which may be implicit in a significant presentation of life. Functionally this sudden shift in an actor's role is not comparable to those recurrent occasions when Fielding or Thackeray or Meredith draws the curtain (as it were) and suspends the action while discoursing on subjects which arise; their combined role of novelist and essayist is confessed and justifiable, though it may not please the reader who is impatient to know the next development in the story.

George Eliot showed the same inclination to comment, without ever indulging it unduly. Writing to Mrs Peter Taylor on 18 July 1878, she said, 'It is one thing to feel keenly for one's fellow-beings; another to say, "This step, and this alone, will be the best to take for the removal of particular calamities."' Rightly she concluded that her function as a novelist was that of 'the *aesthetic*, not the doctrinal teacher – the rousing of the nobler emotions, which make mankind desire the social right, not the prescribing of special measures, concerning which the artistic mind, however strongly moved by social sympathy, is often not the best judge'. Like Sidney in *The Defence of Poesie* she held that 'aesthetic teaching is the highest of all teaching', but that 'if it ceases to be purely aesthetic – if it lapses anywhere from the picture to the diagram – it becomes the most offensive of all teaching'.

All great art is moral in its implications; it is, as Matthew Arnold said, 'a criticism of life', since it reflects its creator's values. To some degree or other, it will rouse sympathy, approval, ridicule, or condemnation; it will appeal to a sense of misfortune or injustice, of social rightness and proportion, promoting those higher, disinterested, humanitarian perceptions without which no propaganda or philosophy can be wise or perennially convincing. Through comic satire and tragedy Jane Austen and Shakespeare make us realize human absurdity and error, evil and injustice, more intensely and agreeably than any writer who sacrifices art to overt writing for any cause or for the assertion of his own point of view. Thomas Hardy had a ready gift of humour, but *The Hand of Ethelberta* and the general course of his fiction suggest very strongly that the writing of comic satire appealed to him less than the writing of tragedy. Adverting in his General Preface of 1912 to 'what has been called the present writer's philosophy of life', he writes: 'Some natures become vocal at tragedy, some are made vocal by comedy, and it seems to me that to whichever of these aspects of life a writer's instinct for expression the more readily responds, to that he should allow it to respond.' The bias of his genius is best indicated in his 'Candour in English Fiction':

All really true literature directly or indirectly sounds as its refrain the words in the *Agamemnon*: 'Chant Aelinon, Aelinon! but may the good prevail.'

The present essay seeks to exemplify ways in which Hardy, to use George Eliot's expression, sought to 'incarnate' ideas, indicating points of view through artistic presentations of life, either pictorially or through human action. At its most successful, the informing idea does not modify the functioning of the scene or action in itself. It cannot spoil the effect on the reader whose imaginative range is limited to narrative and spectacle, and it cannot but deepen, intensify, and enlarge the vision of more intellectually imaginative readers. The crucial question for the novelist is how to dissolve philosophical import in scenes and images which play a necessary or significant part in the main action of his story.

The philosophy which informs the scenes selected to illustrate Hardy's varying degrees of success in 'aesthetic' modes of presentation may appear to be an impression of life appropriate to a character at a particular time or in a given situation, or it may be that of the author contemplating the circumstances in which a character is involved. The implicit philosophy may extend further, giving the author's view, as far as it is definable, of the ultimate cause of things, and particularly of those chances (as they seem) which determine, for better or worse, so much in the course of people's lives. Since Hardy's philosophy was conditioned by the scientific discovery of his age (geological, cosmic, and Darwinian), it may be externalized fictionally in natural scenes with a scientific emphasis. Lives may be presented with reference to the infinite dimensions of space and time. The lovers of *Two on a Tower* are 'infinitesimal' against 'the stupendous background of the stellar universe', yet, as Hardy says in his preface, the smaller of the 'contrasting magnitudes' is the greater to us 'as men' or readers. This is usually taken for granted, since each of us is the centre of his own universe. Hardy's ambivalence is often found in reverse, the relative insignificance of human individuals in times of stress being shown with reference to insect life.

It is not unlikely that Hardy associated a sensationally climactic scene in Wilkie Collins' *Basil* with the high cliffs of Cornwall which he saw for the first time in 1870, for it was from a steep shelving rock on a high Cornish promontory that the villain Mannion, in pursuit of the hero, fell to his death in waves at an unfathomable depth below, after a frantic struggle to secure his hold. Such a threat to Knight in *A Pair of Blue Eyes* is the occasion for a passage which brings home to the reader the insignificance of man in geological time. The heroine's resourcefulness in rescuing Knight by a rope discreetly contrived from her underwear was authorially calculated to give Grundyan readers a *frisson* rather than a thrill. If Hardy had forgotten the circumstances of Mannion's death, as seems very unlikely, they were probably recalled by Leslie Stephen's 'A Bad Five Minutes in the Alps', which appeared in the November 1872 number of *Fraser's Magazine*. Resemblances between this and Hardy's *tour de force* are not very significant; they are far outweighed by striking differences between imaginative, excitingly dramatized narrative and the rather tedious philosophizing of an essay which is so abstract, methodical, and prolonged within a fictional framework ending in anticlimax that the concept as a whole fails to carry conviction.

Suspended on a slope of rock above the Cliff without a Name, with only a tuft of vegetation saving him from certain death, Knight finds himself, by 'one of those familiar conjunctions of things wherewith the inanimate world baits the mind of man when he pauses in moments of suspense', face to face with an imbedded fossil with eyes which seem to regard him; it is a trilobite. 'Separated by millions of years in their lives, Knight and this underling' seem 'to have met in their place of death'. We are asked to believe that, being a geologist, Knight by force of habit, even at this 'dreadful juncture', had time to consider 'the varied scenes that had had their day between this creature's epoch and his own':

> Time closed up like a fan before him. He saw himself at one extremity of the years, face to face with the beginning and all the intermediate centuries simultaneously. Fierce men, clothed in the hides of beasts, and carrying, for defence and attack, huge clubs and pointed spears, rose from the rock, like the phantoms before the doomed Macbeth. They lived in hollows, woods, and mud huts – perhaps in caves of the neighbouring rocks. Behind them stood an earlier band. No man was there. Huge elephantine forms, the mastodon, the hippopotamus, the tapir, antelopes of monstrous size, the megatherium, and the myledon – all, for the moment, in juxtaposition. Further back, and overlapped by these, were perched huge-billed birds and swinish creatures as large as horses . . . .

Hardy's technique works, but it does not present an integration of action and idea, such as obtains in some of the most imaginative forms of fusing philosophy and fiction. The events, external and internal, are linked but appositional or sequential. His intention is clear, and his viewpoint is so striking and final that we rarely pause to consider the probability, in the circumstances, of such concentration on prehistoric life even for 'less than half a minute'. The possibility must have seemed indubitable to Hardy after reading in Stephen's essay 'It is often said that persons in similar situations have seen their whole past existence pass rapidly before them.'[1]

The sequential mode of presenting fiction philosophically is found in the Darwinian example which follows from *The Return of the Native*. Mrs Yeobright makes her way across Egdon Heath in torrid sunshine, hoping for reconciliation with Eustacia. Circumstances combine in an extraordinary manner to make her believe that Eustacia has deliberately kept the door closed against her, and she begins her return journey depressed, exhausted, and without refreshment. She is found too late, suffering fatally from toxaemia after being stung by an adder. On her outward journey, the air had been 'pulsating silently, and oppressing the earth with lassitude':

> Occasionally she came to a spot where independent worlds of ephemerons were passing their time in mad carousal, some in the air, some on the hot ground and vegetation, some in the tepid and stringy water of a nearly dried pool. All the shallower ponds had decreased to a vaporous mud amid which the maggoty shapes of innumerable obscure creatures could be indistinctly seen, heaving and wallowing with enjoyment.

The author hints at his descriptive purpose by telling us that Mrs Yeobright, 'being a woman not disinclined to philosophize', sometimes sat down under her umbrella 'to rest and to watch their happiness'. She then asks her way, and is told to follow a furzecutter. It is her son Clym, and he appears in the distance 'not more distinguishable from the scene around him than the green caterpillar from the leaf it feeds on'. As he stops to cut brambles for tying his furze into bundles, he seems to be 'of no more account in life than an insect'. So, briefly, idea is fused with image, and humanity is scaled down to a level of significance in the natural order which makes Mrs Yeobright rather like the ephemerons she has observed. Nature is indifferent: conditions which are life-giving to one species are life-denying to another.

To Mrs Yeobright, on her return journey, the sun appears 'like some merciless incendiary, brand in hand, waiting to consume her'. Then 'all visible animation' disappears from the landscape, though husky notes of male grasshoppers indicate that 'amid the prostration of the larger animal species' there is 'an unseen insect world' which is vigorously active. Mrs Yeobright sits on a 'perfumed mat' of shepherd's thyme. She has reached a state of passivity. Her last thoughts are dictated by what catches her eye; a bustling colony of ants in front of her reminds her that such activity as theirs had been in progress for years at the same spot. A heron then flies towards the sun, and she wishes she could enjoy its freedom and a happy release from earth. 'Had the track of her next thought been marked by a streak in the air, like the path of a meteor, it would have shown a direction contrary to the heron's, and have descended to the eastward upon the roof of Clym's house.' In this way, after re-emphasizing the relative insignificance of the mortal lot in the context of creation, the scene closes with one of those 'contrasting magnitudes', the undying love of a mother for her son.

Mrs Yeobright's fatal journey is the main subject of 'The Closed Door', the fourth book of *The Return of the Native*. This section opens with the gorgeousness of Egdon in the happy first weeks of Clym and Eustacia's marriage, when the July sun 'fired its crimson heather to scarlet'. The heath harmonizes with moods. Its significant mood for Hardy is set in the opening chapter of the novel; for him 'the great and particular glory of the Egdon waste' began when the shades of the heath fraternized with the growing darkness of night.

> Only in summer days of highest feather did its mood touch the level of gaiety. Intensity was more usually reached by way of the solemn than by way of the brilliant, and such a sort of intensity was often arrived at during winter darkness, tempests, and mists. Then Egdon was aroused to reciprocity; for the storm was its lover, and the wind its friend.

Before summoning up resolution to call, Mrs Yeobright sits beneath a clump of fir trees on the knoll near Clym and Eustacia's home, and for a few minutes dismisses 'thoughts of her own storm-broken and exhausted state' to contemplate that of the trees, 'splintered, lopped, and distorted by the fierce weather that there held them at its mercy whenever it prevailed'. In the opening paragraph of 'The Closed Door' we find that the flowering period of the heath is the second of three seasons, representing morning, noon, and eve, which create a cycle of superficial changes. Egdon's deeper reality can be felt most when it assumes 'the dark hue of the winter period, representing night'. Only then can 'its true tale' be fully understood; the gaiety of life and all its milder seasons are superficial.

The Egdon scene of the opening chapter, in November as twilight darkens, almost foreshadows the scene in 'The Darkling Thrush', when, at the end of the day, at the end of the last year of the century, the poet gazes on a sombre scene which seems devitalized and dispirited, until suddenly the joyous note of a frail, wind-beruffled thrush startles him into the thought that his philosophy of life may be wrong, and that the happy bird, instinctively in touch with nature, may be wiser than he. The *Leitmotiv* struck in the opening chords of 'A Face on which Time makes but Little Impression' is darker in tone than Hardy's philosophical retrospect in 'He Never expected Much', where he confirms that the world has faithfully maintained the limited promise it made in his childhood:

> 'I do not promise overmuch,
>   Child; overmuch;
> Just neutral-tinted haps and such',
>   You said to minds like mine.
> Wise warning for your credit's sake!
> Which I for one failed not to take,
> And hence could stem such strain and ache
>   As each year might assign.

Yet the thought is similar: the 'strain and ache' are imaged in the trees which suffer on a heath loved by the storm; and 'to minds like mine' recalls the affinity of the heath's sombreness with 'the more thinking among mankind', but not with 'our race when it was young'.

Egdon Heath therefore is associated with 'the ache of modernism', as Hardy defined it in *Tess of the d'Urbervilles*. It was the product of Darwinism and the loss of faith consequent on the clash between science and superannuated Christian theology. Hardy lost his faith in Providence about 1865, and concluded, as he expresses it in 'Hap', that Crass Casualty or blind insensitive Chance obstructs 'the sun and rain' (which bring life and hope), and 'dicing Time for gladness casts a moan'. (The maimed trees under which Mrs Yeobright sits keep up a perpetual moan.) The defects of natural law, especially in heredity, made Hardy feel with Keats that 'but to think is to be full of sorrow And leaden-eyed despairs'. In Walter Pater's essay on Winckelmann[2] a contrast is drawn between the serenity attained by the Greeks (which Hardy had in mind when he wrote of the time when 'our race' was young) and the fever and fret of modernity. The fever and fret are depicted in Clym Yeobright: his beauty would 'in no long time be ruthlessly overrun by its parasite, thought'; 'he already showed that thought is a disease of the flesh, and indirectly bore evidence that ideal physical beauty is incompatible with emotional development and a full recognition of the coil of things'. To this Hardy adds, in a more general vein,

> What the Greeks only suspected we know well; what their Aeschylus imagined our nursery children feel. That old-fashioned revelling in the general situation grows less and less possible as we uncover the defects of natural laws, and see the quandary that man is in by their operation.

The conflict between 'the ache of modernism' and the desire to return to pagan joyousness is centred in Clym and Eustacia.

In his essay Pater insists that pagan worship survives in various forms of ritual, and instances the kindling of fire and the dance as 'the anodyne' administered by 'the religious principle' to 'the law which makes life sombre for the vast majority of mankind'. Here we can see the probable germ for Hardy's creative ideas at the opening of *The Return of the Native*. The heath is the sombre face of life for the more thinking, if not the majority, of mankind; the fire ritual owes far more, as Hardy makes abundantly clear, to paganism than to the Gunpowder Plot; it is accompanied by rustic dancing; and the whole scene marks 'a spontaneous, Promethean rebelliousness against the fiat that [winter] shall bring foul times, cold darkness, misery and death. Black chaos comes, and the fettered gods of the earth say, Let there be light.' Egdon is Eustacia's Hades; she sees in marriage to Clym the means of escaping to a life of gaiety in Paris. Unfortunately Clym has more serious aims; he wishes to enlighten his fellow-men, but he is a blind Prometheus who brings unhappiness to his mother and Eustacia, and fails to realize that the means of enjoying life are, for the majority, more prized than enlightenment.

As seen at the opening of the novel, therefore, Egdon Heath is 'a place perfectly accordant with man's nature – neither ghastly, hateful, nor ugly; neither commonplace, unmeaning, nor tame;

but, like man, slighted and enduring'. Its immensity and mystery had not changed through the ages. Its 'sombre stretch of rounds and hollows seemed to rise and meet the evening gloom in pure sympathy'; its lonely face suggested 'tragical possibilities'. 'The most thorough-going ascetic' (such as Clym) 'could feel that he had a natural right to wander on Egdon'; it reflected his view of life. The scene and its immediate sequel, with their implications, succeed in making such an imaginative appeal that Egdon becomes the supreme entity of the novel, its overtones being intensified in the funereal darkness of its catastrophe. Hardy's highly charged overture was nevertheless daringly experimental. Few can assimilate all its connotations at first reading, yet it sets the tone most appropriate to the theme and tragic narrative of the novel, and leads most impressively by slow artistic gradations to Rainbarrow, 'the pole and axis of this heathery world', and to the focal point which crowns it, the mysterious distant figure of Eustacia, whose first audible notes, 'a lengthened sighing', harmonize with those 'plaintive November winds' which form 'the linguistic peculiarity of the heath'.

The potential advantages of using a scene as a correlative for reflecting a philosophy of life may be better realized perhaps by comparing Hardy's initial presentation of Egdon Heath with his concluding remarks on Elizabeth-Jane's impressions of life in what may be called the postscript of *The Mayor of Casterbridge*. The latter must gain by being read with heartfelt knowledge of what the heroine has suffered, yet its effect is weakened by increasing ambivalence, the author disengaging himself and stepping (as it were) outside the novel to make extraneous comments, as the transfer of 'brief transit through a sorry world' to the preface of his next novel, *The Woodlanders*, confirms.

Natural images such as storm (or wind and rain) and frost are used by Hardy as symbols of mischance or suffering. Frost is employed symbolically at length in *Desperate Remedies* but never more intensively than in *Tess of the d'Urbervilles*, where he reaches his highest level more often and more sustainedly than in any other novel; at such times the poet, philosopher, and novelist are often working in imaginative unison. The incidental thought-image of 'wailing gnats' in the setting which depicts the heroine's dilemma in *Desperate Remedies* becomes a miniature poem in *Tess*. The love of Angel and Tess is more ethereal than earthy. She does not wish to marry him; her desire is for 'a perpetual betrothal' in which everything remains unchanged, summer and autumn, and Angel is always courting her. In such a mood she walks with him in the meadows; looking towards the sun, they see 'a glistening ripple of gossamer webs . . . like the track of moonlight on the sea. Gnats, knowing nothing of their brief glorification', wander 'across the shimmer of this pathway, irradiated' as if they bear fire within them, then pass out of its line, and are 'quite extinct'. The 'quite' underlines her one life, 'the single opportunity of existence ever vouchsafed to Tess by an unsympathetic First Cause – her all; her every and only chance'. The poem-picture is proleptic: so compounded does Tess's initial misfortune become that her life is cut short before it can reach its prime.

Taken in conjunction with one of Hardy's poems, a scene in *Tess* suggests that he had at first hoped to develop it symbolically to promote his philosophy of a First Cause which was not only unsympathetic but blind and unheeding. In 'The Lacking Sense', 'Doom and She', and 'The Sleep-Worker' this indifference is transferred to Nature or the Great Mother, who, as the agent or medium of the Prime Mover, is presented as blind and asleep, working Darwinistically by mindless rote. The birds of 'The Bullfinches', which follows, discuss 'queenly Nature's ways':

> All we creatures, nigh and far
> (Said they there), the Mother's are;
> Yet she never shows endeavour
> To protect from warrings wild
> Bird or beast she calls her child.
>
> Busy in her handsome house
> Known as Space, she falls a-drowse;
> Yet, in seeming, works on dreaming,
> While beneath her groping hands
> Fiends make havoc in her bands.

Alec d'Urberville is presented as Satan or the Arch-fiend. One of Tess's duties is to teach his mother's bullfinches to sing by whistling to them; she does this in her employer's bedroom. Mrs d'Urberville, who sleeps in a large four-post bedstead, is old and blind.

Once while Tess was at the window where the cages were ranged, giving her lesson as usual, she thought she heard a

rustling behind the bed. The old lady was not present, and
turning round the girl had an impression that the toes of a pair
of boots were visible below the fringe of the curtains.

Hardy, who regarded mankind as birds caged in by Necessity or
the force of circumstances, makes it clear that Alec had been there
in ambush.[3]

Bearing a child after her rape, Tess is regarded as a fallen woman.
When she recovers from her ignominy and shame, she has at last
been mastered by that 'irresistible, universal, automatic tendency
to find sweet pleasure somewhere, which pervades all life, from
the meanest to the highest'; it is 'the "appetite for joy" which
pervades all creation'. On 'a thyme-scented, bird-hatching morning
in May', as she walks towards the Valley of the Great Dairies, and
sees the Froom waters as 'clear as the pure River of Life shown to
the Evangelist', her hopes mingle with the sunshine; she hears 'a
pleasant voice in every breeze' and detects joy in every bird's note.
Soon she herself begins to sing, but finds nothing adequate to
express her feelings, except, ironically, the Benedicite (a pagan
'Fetichistic utterance in a Monotheistic setting', Hardy thought),
until the words 'O ye Children of Men, bless ye the Lord, praise
Him, and magnify Him for ever' make her stop short with the
reflection that perhaps she does not 'quite know the Lord as yet'.
(Though apparently mild, these are ambivalent words, conveying
Tess's unsophisticated thought and a weight of authorial irony.)
When she reaches the valley, she stands still, not knowing her
direction, and appears 'like a fly on a billiard-table of indefinite
length, and of no more consequence to the surroundings than that
fly'. Here we have the first phrases of a motif which is last heard
in the final paragraph of the novel, where the words 'the President
of the Immortals, in Aeschylean phrase, had ended his sport with
Tess' echo a comment in *King Lear* (to which Hardy draws attention
in his 1892 preface): 'As flies to wanton boys are we to the gods;
They kill us for their sport.'

The motif recurs when Tess is seen on the cold uplands of
Flintcomb-Ash, after she has been deserted by Angel Clare. Season
and setting are a deliberate contrast to those at Talbothays Dairy
in the days of love and happiness. The scene in which Tess and
Marian 'grub up' swedes has a drab monotony which communicates the extinction of hope:

the whole field was in colour a desolate drab; it was a complexion

without features, as if a face, from chin to brow, should be only
an expanse of skin. The sky wore, in another colour, the same
likeness; a white vacuity of countenance with the lineaments
gone. So these two upper and nether visages confronted each
other all day long, the white face looking down on the brown
face, and the brown face looking up at the white face, without
anything standing between them but the two girls crawling over
the surface of the former like flies.

'So the two forces were at work as everywhere, the inherent will
to enjoy, and the circumstantial will against enjoyment', Hardy
adds.

The human being can choose, but the more deprived a person
is the less freedom of choice he or she enjoys; such choice adds to
the whole network of cause and effect, which continues endlessly,
as it has done from the beginning. Pater presents this 'web' of
universal law, 'penetrating us with a network . . . yet bearing in it
the central forces of the world', at the end of his essay on
Winckelmann; and Hardy refers to it in *The Woodlanders* when he
states that the lonely courses of Winterborne and Marty South
were 'part of the pattern in the great web of human doings
then weaving in both hemispheres'. Logically, proceeding from
antecedent to antecedent, the human mind can posit a First Cause
or Prime Mover, and scientific philosophers at the time of Hardy's
early intellectual development were particularly prone to think in
terms of such an ultimate abstraction. To regard its neutrality (its
indifference to human suffering, for example) as 'unsympathetic'
or cruel is a form of subjective personification which is exceptional
in Hardy's fiction; it is comparable to the Aeschylean impression
that the President of the Immortals took delight in mortal woe. For
a long period Hardy believed that 'the Cause of Things' is 'neither
moral nor immoral, but *un*moral'; ultimately he reached the wise
conclusion that the Scheme of Things (including the Cause) is
incomprehensible.[4]

Chance is the principal determining factor in Tess's brief life,
which is directed by hereditary traits, her feckless parents, and
(above all) by two such extreme types as Alec d'Urberville and
Angel Clare. Yet she is a pure woman, who does no wrong
intentionally, and who is the essence of Christian charity (one of
the virtues of which is long-suffering). That events over which she
has no control lead her first to dishonour, then to abandonment

after marriage, then to a *de facto* marriage with someone she instinctively dislikes (though he has been kind to her and her family), finally to his murder and her early death, constitutes, on the face of it, a highly sensational series of events; in masterly hands, it becomes a tragic indictment of a world which is outwardly Christian. Just before presenting Tess's rape, the author asks where was the Providence of 'her simple faith'; it is the question one should ask at the end of the novel.

There is one scene in which action reflects Hardy's philosophy without comment, and it is his most successful achievement of that kind. This is the account of the wheat-threshing at Flintcomb-Ash. Tess is given the most exhausting task by Groby, the farmer who persecutes her; she has to unbind the sheaves for the 'feeder' of the thresher, and she has no respite, for Groby, having to pay by the hour for the threshing-machinery, is set on using it to the maximum capacity. By the third break during the day, she can hardly walk from the shaking of the machine. When she hears of Alec's arrival, she decides to avoid him by staying on the rick for her dinner; though he is a preacher, and she is officially married, he cannot resist her, and joins her on the stack. When he refers to Angel, who has abandoned her, as 'that mule you call husband', her d'Urberville temper gets the better of her, and she smites him across the cheek with one of her leather gloves, drawing blood. 'Turning up her eyes to him with the hopeless defiance of the sparrow's gaze before its captor twists its neck', she cries, 'Whip me, crush me; you need not mind those people under the rick! I shall not cry out. Once victim, always victim – that's the law!' The zest for life which had caused her to rally and set out for the Valley of the Great Dairies is almost exhausted; later, after her father's death, and the eviction of her family from their home, when it seems that Angel will never return, she becomes Alec's mistress in recompense for his continued kindness to them. This, combined with Angel's 'Too late, beloved' return, reduces her to a frenzy which unhinges her mind and impels her to the murder of Alec, for which she is hanged. A hint of this is probably intended in the anticipated twisting of the sparrow's neck.

The crisis on the wheat stack is the most dramatic pointer to the final exhaustion of, first, Tess's patience when Angel's return makes her think that she has been tricked into spiritual degradation by fate, and, secondly, that renewed will to live after the initial victimization from which all her subsequent suffering springs. This process of exhaustion has its correlative in the gradual wearing-down of Tess's physical energy on the thresher, the 'red tyrant' that has to be served. It is driven by a sooty and grimy engine, the man in charge of which looks equally unpropitious, as if he had come from Tophet. The engine is 'the *primum mobile* of this little world', the world of Tess's suffering. It connotes the Primum Mobile or Prime Mover which had been hypostatized in the pre-Copernican era as the source of life and movement in the universe which it surrounded, this being imagined as a series of concentric revolving spheres, the stars on the outer, earth and man at the centre, as if mankind were the supreme creation in the eyes of God. Hardy, who loved the Church of England, especially its music and architecture, and had at one time hoped to be a country curate, with enough leisure to write poetry, had lost his faith in Christian theology. The Darwinian internecine struggle for existence in nature, and the tragic lot of people, individually or internationally, confirmed his belief that the Cause of Things is blind or indifferent, and that life goes on automatically (he twice uses this term with reference to Tess's rally) or by rote. The threshing-scene illustrates a philosophy of the Ultimate which Hardy presented on a large scale in *The Dynasts*:

> Thus does the Great Foresightless mechanize
> In blank entrancement now as evermore . . . .

Nowhere in Hardy are the particular and the universal, the picture and the philosophy, more synoptically and dramatically fused. The scene provides a splendid example of how (in the words of Pater's essay on Winckelmann) 'the imaginative intellect' of one nineteenth-century artist could command 'that width, variety,' and 'delicacy of resources' which enable it 'to deal with the conditions of modern life'.

8
Tess of the d'Urbervilles

(a) and *Desperate Remedies*

When Hardy began *Tess of the d'Urbervilles* he most probably assumed that there was little future for his first published novel, *Desperate Remedies*. It had appeared in March 1871 and sold very badly; the first American edition appeared in March 1874. A novel which has rarely been given its due appreciation, it uses some of Hardy's most imaginative ideas to develop a critical situation with features which he later decided to turn to more tragical account. Two brief passages from a concentrated sky and landscape scene of psychological import were transferred to *The Return of the Native*, possibly by the end of 1877. Entries in his *Life* suggest that he may have begun writing *Tess* before the end of 1888; clearly his main preparatory work had been completed by the autumn. Composition for its serial version was well under way by 7 February 1889, when he told his publishers that he was too busily engaged with it to undertake anything further. Only three weeks previously he must have been surprised to receive another offer from Ward and Downey to publish a new edition of *Desperate Remedies*. (He had declined such an offer by the same firm out of hand in October 1884.) In his reply of 16 January he said it was 'so long' since he had 'read over' the story that he would like to look into it again, but would reply in two or three days. (Such caution may indicate uncertainty whether it would be to his advantage to have the novel republished in England.) He accepted the offer on 20 January, promising two days later to make any necessary corrections, and completing a short preface before the end of the month. The latter half of this ran:

> but some of the scenes, and at least one or two of the characters, have been deemed not unworthy of a little longer preservation; and as they could hardly be reproduced in a fragmentary form the novel is reissued complete – the more readily that it has for

94

some considerable time been reprinted and widely circulated in America.

In re-reading the novel Hardy had most probably been struck by the wealth of creative ideas in some of its crucial scenes, and, feeling they were wasted in a story which descended to popular sensationalism, decided that, wherever he could, he would develop the most important of them for the enhancement of *Tess of the d'Urbervilles*, to which, in its final form (as opposed to the serial), he rightly attached far greater value.

Fundamental to the heroine's threatened tragedy in *Desperate Remedies* and to the actual tragedy in *Tess*, in which an innocent girl is driven eventually, by force of cruel chance and its consequences, to derangement and death, is the conception that life on earth is the 'single opportunity of existence' for both heroines. Hardy uses these words in both novels, and in no other does he emphasize tragedy in this way. Cytherea's thoughts on the subject are paraphrased from the second of the 'She, to Him' sonnets, which like all his other poems remained unpublished when *Desperate Remedies* was written. Hardy expresses his views the second time as Angel Clare's, those of a conscientious man for whom Tess is 'no insignificant creature to toy with and dismiss', but 'a woman living her precious life', whose 'whole world' depends on her sensations, and came into existence only at her birth:

> This consciousness upon which he had intruded was the single opportunity of existence ever vouchsafed to Tess by an unsympathetic First Cause – her all; her every and only chance. How then should he look upon her as of less consequence than himself; as a pretty trifle to caress and grow weary of; and not deal in the greatest seriousness with the affection which he knew that he had awakened in her – so fervid and so impressionable as she was under her reserve; in order that it might not agonize and wreck her?[1]

Both heroines are the more pitiable because they feel compelled to marry against their will for altruistic motives, Cytherea because she has no one to depend on but Manston for the continuation of her brother's hospital treatment. Alec d'Urberville provides for Tess's destitute family and, when they are evicted after her father's

death, presents them a home on condition that she will live with
him; having no hope after long desertion by Angel Clare, she
consents for their sake. Edward Springrove, with whom Cytherea
is in love, returns too late to prevent her marrying Manston; and
Angel Clare, too late to save Tess from becoming Alec's mistress.
(Cytherea is rescued in the nick of time, as became a Victorian
story slanted to convince a publisher that it would sell.) The
situation is too much for Tess; like Lucy in the romantic story of
The Bride of Lammermoor, she breaks under the strain of suffering
and long waiting for her absent lover, and kills the man she has
been forced to marry. Taking his words from Shelley's 'Epipsychidion', with a change of sense, the appropriateness of which is
clear from Tess's repeated 'too late' when Angel finds her at a
Sandbourne lodging-house, Hardy informed the publisher of the
American serial that his title was 'Too Late, Beloved!'[2]

The men whom circumstances compel the heroines to marry
(legally or *de facto*) are, it should be noted, both sensualists. When
Cytherea consents she feels 'as one in a boat without oars, drifting
with closed eyes down a river – she knew not whither'. The details
of the image summarize a scene in George Eliot's *Romola* which
symbolizes the heroine's state of mind when she has lost all her
illusions about her husband, and leaves him. Hardy changes it to
stress the divorce between soul and body in Tess after sexual
submission to Alec. When she appears before Angel in the doorway
of the Sandbourne lodging-house, he has 'a vague consciousness
of one thing, though it was not clear to him till later; that his
original Tess had spiritually ceased to recognize the body before
him as hers – allowing it to drift, like a corpse upon the current,
in a direction dissociated from its living will'.

Other modifications of imagery used in *Desperate Remedies* relate
to Tess's happiness when in love with Angel during summer in
the Froom valley, and to her desolation in winter at Flintcomb-
Ash after he has abandoned her and emigrated. The colourful
scene in which Keats's wailing gnats float away like sparks of fire
is reduced to a more distinctive and specific picture which stresses
the ephemerality of Tess's happiness during her only opportunity
of existence. As she walks with Angel in the meadows, gnats are
seen irradiated as they wander across a shimmering ray of sunshine.
Their glorification is brief; as soon as they pass out of the beam of
light, they are 'quite extinct'.

Imagery which shows the effect of frost is memorably expressed in both novels. It communicates the harsh indifference of chance, and Cytherea's suffering, before her wedding and almost immediately after, when she discovers that her life and her true lover's are severed by his too-late return. The suffering of Tess at Flintcomb-Ash is more intensive, the wintry weather functioning not only symbolically through the imagination but inflicting physical misery on her, as she and Marian are compelled to work outdoors in appalling conditions; rain driven horizontally by yelling winds strikes them like glass splinters until their clothes are sodden. Visualisation of what Tess endures both in body and spirit, after waiting in vain for a message of hope from Angel, reaches its climax with the arrival, in the succeeding spell of dry frost, of Arctic birds, driven south after unimaginable suffering in polar regions. Tess's suffering is reflected in the tragical eyes of these spectral creatures; the scenes of cataclysmal horror they have witnessed in curdling temperatures that no man could endure form part of the crescendo of imaginative correlatives which heightens the reader's sense of Tess's unrelieved anguish, past and present, and hints at her being on the edge of the unendurable. The question of how much longer she can control her feelings is answered dramatically in the threshing-scene, and fatally when, finding she has been tricked by circumstance into becoming Alec's victim a second time, she, in Hardy's words, kills 'the situation'.[3]

(b) and *Clarissa*

But for Samuel Richardson's novel (1748) *Tess of the d'Urbervilles* might have taken a different course or never have been written at all. Though perhaps disposed to adopt its subject in fiction, since it was based on a tragedy that happened to one of his relatives (perhaps his paternal grandmother), Hardy probably did not think of it until he read *Clarissa*, a novel of inordinate length and some hauntingly moving scenes, the theme of which is influenced very evidently by *Paradise Lost* and less significantly by Shakespeare's poem 'The Rape of Lucrece'. Hardy's essay 'The Profitable Reading of Fiction', which appeared in March 1888, shows that he had read it discriminatingly, aware of its deficiency in 'the robuster touches of nature' found in Fielding, but alert to its structural cunning:

we feel, nevertheless, that we are under the guidance of a hand which has consummate skill in evolving a graceful, well-balanced set of conjectures, forming altogether one of those circumstantial wholes which, when approached by events in real life, cause the observer to pause and reflect, and say 'What a striking history!' . . . No person who has a due perception of the constructive art shown in Greek tragic drama can be blind to the constructive art of Richardson.

Like Shakespeare's, Richardson's story and Hardy's are stories of rape. The image of white as a symbol of virtue in 'The Rape of Lucrece' occurs in a variety of forms in *Clarissa* and *Tess*, and Shakespeare's antithesis of an 'earthly saint' adored by a 'devil' is recurrent in Richardson's novel with its *Paradise Lost* overtones. The 'white hind' image for Lucrece, reinforced by 'The White Hart', the name of the inn where Lovelace lodged when he stage-managed the circumstances which tricked Clarissa Harlowe into leaving home and accepting his treacherous protection, prompted Hardy's poetic association of a heroine born in Blackmoor Vale with the beautiful white hart slain there, according to tradition, in the reign of Henry III. He must have been impressed by Shakespeare's emphasis on the misfortunes created by Opportunity or chance, and it is significant that it is from the introduction to this theme that he adopts a line ('The adder hisses where the sweet birds sing'), changing 'adder' to 'serpent' in anticipation of d'Urberville's Satanic role.[4]

Lovelace's role as a devil is continually stressed. Clarissa is regarded as an angel, and he as Beelzebub or Satan. He recalls Milton's Satan in a number of ways: he is motivated by pride and revenge; he is branded as a reptile or serpent; he enters Clarissa's garden in disguise, and is described as a wall-climber. (Hardy's indebtedness to Richardson for details of the garden which Alec d'Urberville enters by wall-climbing, and Alec's Satanic role, are discussed in a later essay.[5]) Clarissa's one rash act (frequent references to her rashness are intended to recall the rashness of Milton's Eve in plucking the forbidden fruit) is to commit herself to Lovelace's protection in order to avoid a compulsory marriage arranged by her family; when she is indignant at his deceit she says they are recriminating 'like the first pair (I, at least, driven out of my paradise)'. Her virtue is emphasized in terms of whiteness, by the 'virgin white' of her dress, the 'snowy hand' which she waves with 'moving oratory' in addressing her 'destroyer', the white flowing robes which illuminate the dark squalid bedchamber of her imprisonment, and her hands 'white as a lily' just before her death. Tess wears the white muslin dress of the club-walking scene when she leaves home and entrusts herself to Alec, and again on the night of her rape; in her long white nightgown, while she baptizes her child, her countenance is transfigured into 'a thing of immaculate beauty, with a touch of dignity' which is almost 'regal'; subsequently, in times of duress, even after the murder of Alec, her facial whiteness is an oblique reminder of her essential innocence.

Several minor details in *Clarissa* have their resemblances in *Tess*. Lovelace is annoyed because he cannot 'fasten an obligation' on the heroine; nothing, he has found, 'more effectually brings down a proud spirit, than a sense of lying under pecuniary obligations'; he offers Clarissa money and raiment in the hope of making her more agreeable and accommodating. Alec gives presents to Tess as a temptation after violating her; when she realizes his motive, and her folly in accepting them, she loathes herself and returns home, where she makes clothes for her brothers and sisters out of 'some finery' he had given her and she had 'put by with contempt'. The surprising fact that Clarissa could be a 'most elegant dairy-maid' when she stayed with her grandfather, and showed proficiency in all forms of dairy management, may have suggested Tess's happiness as a dairymaid at Talbothays. The comment 'since what is done is done, and cannot be undone' is echoed by her mother when Tess returns home and tells her how her marriage with Angel has been wrecked at the outset by her gratuitous honesty. Another, on a manifestation of Lovelace's hypocrisy, 'But what, dear, will become of us now? – Lovelace not only reformed, but turned preacher', may have weighed with Hardy in deciding Alec's role after Tess's desertion by her wedded husband. Belford's repeated use of '*Devils believe and tremble*' with reference to Lovelace probably accounts for Alec's application of it to himself when he meets Tess, after his conversion, at Flintcomb-Ash. The repeated maxim of Richardson's libertine, 'Once subdued, always subdued' becomes 'Once victim, always victim – that's the law!', a key to Hardy's main theme in *Tess*. The motif of the snarer and the captive bird is recurrent throughout *Clarissa*; by making reformation his stalking-horse, Lovelace has his intended victim in his 'gin', with 'springes' close about her. Images of the latter kind occur in *Tess*; in common with scenes where sleeping birds are doomed (on the

night of Tess's rape), or found bleeding and dying from man's
cruelty (xli), they parallel the heroine's lot, and deepen the sense
of her continued plight and suffering.

Natural background details are relatively rare in Richardson's
novel. Those which are imaginatively inseparable from Clarissa's
rashness when she opens the garden door to Lovelace, only to
become the victim of his machinations, are particularly prominent.
In a neighbouring coppice are overgrown oaks, surrounded with
ivy and mistletoe. Their image, within such a crucial context, may
have dwelt in Hardy's memory, suggesting both the 'Druidical
mistletoe' on the 'aged oaks' in the Chase, where Tess falls a prey
to Alec, and the climactic scene at Stonehenge, where sacrificial
symbolism is associated with Druidic tradition.

In two important respects *Tess* differs from *Clarissa*. Richardson's
heroine is rather too good to be true, too much a model of rectitude
and Christian piety. Tess is not angelic; though a 'pure woman'
who does no wrong deliberately, she is human and makes mistakes,
her weaknesses being hereditary. Her tragedy begins and ends as
a result of self-sacrifices for her family; at these junctures her
decisions are willed. Despite her proneness to accept fate passively
too long, she is admirable in the altruism and endurance which
are part of her nature; in her crisis with Angel Clare, she might
have been, Hardy tells us, 'Apostolic Charity herself returned to a
self-seeking modern world'. Tess's weaknesses and virtues make
her not impossible,

> A Creature not too bright or good
> For human nature's daily food.

An even more important factor for Hardy in the developing of
his novel was his inability to accept the attitude that the only
decent course for a sexually dishonoured woman was to die.
Lucrece's self-immolation may have been an example of Roman
honour; Clarissa, having no wish to live, turns her last thoughts
to preparation for life after death. Such ideas seemed outdated and
unnatural to Hardy. Even he, who sometimes thought it better not
to be born, believed that most people wish to live, and it was most
probably when he was thinking about his main plan for *Tess of the
d'Urbervilles* that he wrote on 16 July 1888:

Thought of the determination to enjoy. We see it in all nature, from the leaf on the tree to the titled lady at the ball. . . . It is achieved, of a sort, under superhuman difficulties. Like pent-up water it will find a chink of possibility somewhere. Even the most oppressed of men and animals find it, so that out of a thousand there is hardly one who has not a sun of some sort for his soul.

Despite a depression which makes her feel at times that 'she could have hidden herself in a tomb', Tess eventually recovers from her ignominy, and sets off 'on a thyme-scented, bird-hatching morning in May' to begin life anew in the Valley of the Great Dairies.

The irresistible, universal, automatic tendency to find sweet pleasure somewhere, which pervades all life, from the meanest to the highest, had at length mastered Tess. Being even now only a young woman of twenty, one who mentally and sentimentally had not finished growing, it was impossible that any event should have left upon her an impression that was not in time capable of transmutation.

The transmutation takes place at Talbothays, leading to her promise to marry Angel Clare before she has taken the opportunity to tell him her 'carking secret', as she has intended:

The 'appetite for joy' which pervades all creation, that tremendous force which sways humanity to its purpose, as the tide sways the helpless weed, was not to be controlled by vague lucubrations over the social rubric.

Her happiness is doomed. Hardy's aim is not like Richardson's, to write a moral story on the storming of good by evil, but to show that even a girl of the best intentions, after coming to grief and starting life anew, can find that anything but fair play is possible at the hands of chance. 'Once victim, always victim', she continues her brief life until circumstances are too much for her, and she is not sorry to relinquish it. Hardy's ultimate purpose is quite the opposite of Milton's in *Paradise Lost*; it is to arraign the ways of 'an unsympathetic First Cause'. Hence his reference to the Aeschylean phrase on the President of the Immortals, and the irony of his remark, ' "Justice" was done', in the last paragraph of the novel.

(c) A Pure Woman

Hardy believed that the First Cause or Immanent Will is unaware of human suffering. To make it 'unsympathetic' creates a dangerous ambiguity: the word may be applied to a Being which *is* unaware and indifferent; it may also be regarded as a personalization which is not inconsistent with the President of the Immortals' having 'ended his sport with Tess'. Although, by the addition of 'in Aeschylean phrase', Hardy had implied a view other than his own, and a figurative use of words, his meaning was misinterpreted by many as an acceptance of the classical tradition that the gods at ease on Olympus derived pleasure from the pains of mortals below. His sub-title, however, was quite unmistakable in intent, and must have seemed cynically provocative to Grundyan readers and Christian theologists, when applied to a woman who, whatever may have been thought of her first 'fall', is a kept mistress and a murderess. So much criticism did it provoke that Hardy, in retrospect, felt it would have been better had it never appeared. *Melius fuerat non scribere*, he wrote in his additional prefatory note of March 1912. This publication of regret may be taken as an unfortunate unsteadying of nerve and judgment, but not as an essential compromise. He did not recant, and the sub-title remained. 'It was appended at the last moment, after reading the final proofs, as being the estimate left in a candid mind of the heroine's character', he wrote in the same postscript. It is in fact the *Leitmotiv* of the novel, and of supreme value in defining Hardy's intention.

A sarcastic review of *Tess of the d'Urbervilles* (mainly a summary of the story which reads like parody) in *The Saturday Review* led to a correspondence in January 1892 between Hardy and two of his friends which leaves no doubt on this question. Writing to Edmund Gosse, he complains that the anonymous reviewer 'suppresses half the title of the story, these being the words without which the aim and purpose of the novel cannot be understood'. His letter to Edward Clodd two days later shows that the omission is 'the second title of the book', which, he maintains, is 'absolutely necessary to show its meaning'. The idea of the sub-title had been an integral part of the story from the outset of its final form. One of Tess's previous names had been 'Sue', and there can be little doubt that Hardy was thinking of a heroine of pure intent in July

1889, when he informed Tillotson & Son (agents for the serial publication of fiction) that the most suitable title for his story would be 'The Body and Soul of Sue'.

Tess is the victim of both chance and character, and, heredity being what it is (another 'cast of the die of destiny', as Hardy writes of the circumstances which determine Marty South's occupation when she first appears), she can do no other than she does in crucial situations. On the more positive side, her character shows moral and spiritual qualities (especially in the ultimate version of the novel)[6] which qualify her admirably to be a tragic heroine in accordance with Hardy's finest conception of tragedy: 'The best tragedy – highest tragedy in short – is that of the WORTHY encompassed by the INEVITABLE.'

It is Tess's extraordinary mischance that her fate is bound up with two such unreliable opposites as Alec d'Urberville and Angel Clare, just as Jude's misfortunes result from relationships with two such extremes as Arabella Donn and Sue Bridehead. Tess's own character is rather unusual; her conscience makes her readily shoulder blame and guilt which more rightly belong to her feckless parents, the most 'shiftless' but well-meaning pair of 'waiters on Providence' in all Hardy's fiction, and a good spring-board for a 'Positivist novel.[7] For them she resigns herself to Alec and employment at the Slopes. He is a libertine; her beauty and a physical maturity beyond her experience and worldly knowledge make her immediately his object. An accession of panic delivers her into the hands of her betrayer. Much later, she submits to the degradation of living with him simply because she has no other choice.

Ethereally Shelleyan, Angel Clare had imagined that, in wooing Tess and 'giving up all ambition to win a wife with social standing, with fortune, with knowledge of the world', he would secure 'rustic innocence'. So convinced is he of her being 'the most honest, spotless creature that ever lived' that he discounts her fears and unwittingly reinforces her proneness to let things take their course until it is too late. His confession on the eve after their wedding leads to hers, and a wave of antipathy washes away all his idealizing sentiment. His vision is 'mocked by appearances', and his affection proves to be 'less fire than radiance':

Within the remote depths of his constitution, so gentle and

affectionate as he was in general, there lay hidden a large logical deposit, like a vein of metal in a soft loam, which turned the edge of everything that attempted to traverse it. It had blocked his acceptance of the Church; it blocked his acceptance of Tess.

At the point of the novel where Angel leaves her, Hardy tells us that a woman more artful and worldly than Tess could probably have overcome his resistance.

But her mood of long-suffering made his way easy for him, and she herself was his best advocate. Pride, too, entered into her submission – (which perhaps was a symptom of that reckless acquiescence in chance too apparent in the whole d'Urberville family – and the many effective chords which she could have stirred by an appeal were left untouched.

The 'greatest misfortune of her life', we are told, was her 'feminine loss of courage at the last and critical moment through her estimating her father-in-law by his sons' just after visiting Emminster vicarage. 'Her present condition was precisely one which would have enlisted the sympathies of old Mr and Mrs Clare.' The opportunity was lost less from ill-chance than from acquiescence in it.

Angel and Tess do not recall Knight and Elfride in *A Pair of Blue Eyes* very strongly, but the resemblance between the two pairs of lovers in the crunch of crisis is close. In both stories the tragic situation created by irresolution, confession, irreconcilability, and submission is 'the chance of things'. Against the 'keen scrutiny and logical power' of Knight, Elfride's 'docile devotion' is 'its own enemy'. 'A slight rebelliousness . . . would have been a world of advantage to her. But she idolized him, and was proud to be his bond-servant.' If only she could be 'the woman she had seemed to be', Knight reflects; 'but that woman was dead and buried, and he knew her no more!' He leaves London for the Continent, just as Angel departs for Brazil. In dramatic fashion the sleep-walking scene shows how the Tess of Angel's vision was also dead and buried. It never occurs to Knight that he owes Elfride 'a little sacrifice for her unchary devotion in saving his life'. In both men the head has developed at the expense of the heart; in both the springs of charity are blocked. This defect of nature is most probably the true explanation of Angel's name: 'Though I speak with the tongues of men and of angels, and have not charity, I am become as sounding brass, or a tinkling cymbal.' In a novel which is imaginatively endowed to appeal above all to charity, it is Tess who is the exemplar.[8]

This does not mean that she is perfect. Her intentions are good, but her willingness to endure is sometimes no more than the weakness of acquiescence or irresolution. She is pure of heart, conscience-ridden from the outset of her tragic career, and ready to abnegate her own wishes and interests for the sake of others. Her last act, choosing the Stone of Sacrifice for her resting-place before her surrender, dramatizes symbolically the role she has chosen to play in one crisis after another. Clare had known that she loved him, 'but he did not know at that time the full depth of her devotion, its single-mindedness, its meekness; what long-suffering it guaranteed, what honesty, what endurance, what good faith'. When he turned adamantly against her, 'she sought not her own; was not provoked; thought no evil of his treatment of her. She might just now have been Apostolic Charity herself returned to a self-seeking modern world.'

In arguing for the abandonment of their marriage before it had begun, Angel's concern for his reputation and what might happen to their hypothetical children if the past became known (as it must, he insists) is too much for her distressed mind:

> She had truly never thought so far as that, and his lucid picture of possible offspring who would scorn her was one that brought deadly conviction to an honest heart which was humanitarian to its centre.

The thought of what could happen makes her decide unselfishly to leave Angel free and return home:

> 'Yes, though nobody else should reproach me if we should stay together, yet somewhen, years hence, you might get angry with me for any ordinary matter, and knowing what you do of my bygones you yourself might be tempted to say words, and they might be overheard, perhaps by my own children. O, what only hurts me now would torture and kill me then! I will go — to-morrow.'

Controversy on Tess's purity must concentrate on her relations with Alec while she is at the Slopes and later at Sandbourne. Many critics have written of her 'seduction' by Alec, who is presented as a tempter before her first and her final degradation. Undoubtedly he wishes to seduce her before and after her 'fall', but she is the innocent victim of rape, and Hardy associates his novel with 'The Rape of Lucrece' and *Clarissa* for that reason. Unfortunately the word 'seduction' is often used synonymously with 'rape'; Hardy uses it in this sense, with reference to Tess, in a letter to Thomas Macquoid (29 October 1891), and refers to Alec as her 'seducer' once in the novel, when she recognises him as the preacher on her way back to Flintcomb-Ash from Emminster. Only at the end, for good, altruistic reasons, and at the point of despair, does she give way to her tempter. It is when her family is on the point of eviction, and she can see no alternative but surrender to Alec, who is ready to provide them a home, with education for her brothers and sisters, that 'a sudden rebellious sense of injustice' makes her, for the first time, include her husband Angel in condemnation of her lot:

> Never in her life – she could swear it from the bottom of her soul – had she ever intended to do wrong; yet these hard judgments had come. Whatever her sins, they were not sins of intention, but of inadvertence, and why should she have been punished so persistently?

By this time the absent Angel had realized the wrongness of his moral judgement. He had matured, and come to the conclusion (with Browning) that character is to be judged not merely by achievements but also by aims and impulses: 'its true history lay, not among things done, but among things willed'.

> No prophet had told him, and he was not prophet enough to tell himself, that essentially this young wife of his was as deserving of the praise of King Lemuel as any other woman endowed with the same dislike of evil, her moral value having to be reckoned not by achievement but by tendency.

Though Hardy had to draw a prudent, rather than a prudish, veil over what happened in the Chase, he leaves the reader in no doubt: Alec was ruthless. There is no question about the ruthlessness; it is a matter of degree: 'Doubtless some of Tess d'Urberville's mailed ancestors rollicking home from a fray had dealt the same measure even more ruthlessly towards peasant girls of their time.' News spreads among agricultural labourers until we hear at harvest-time: 'There were they that heard a sobbing one night last year in The Chase; and it mid ha' gone hard wi' a certain party if folks had come along.' Frenzied by the return of Angel after she has consented to live with Alec, Tess alludes to his cruel compulsion on this occasion: 'O, you have torn my life to pieces . . . made me be what I prayed you in pity not to make me be again!' She herself supplies evidence incidentally: 'suppose your sin was not of your seeking?' she asks the itinerant text-painter when she has left the Slopes and is returning home. Nor is there any reason to think she hides anything from her mother, who later advises her not to tell Angel about her 'Bygone Trouble . . . specially as it is so long ago, and not your Fault at all'. When Tess finally rejoins Angel she tells him she has killed Alec, and that she feared she might do it some day 'for the trap he set for me in my simple youth'. When she is on her way home from the Slopes, Alec admits he has done her wrong: at Flintcomb-Ash he expresses his wish to marry her, 'to make the only reparation I can make for the trick I played you'; she had remained 'unsmirched in spite of all', he says, and for that reason he had never despised her. Angel Clare's testimony is quite unequivocal:

His inconsistencies rushed upon him in a flood. He had persistently elevated Hellenic Paganism at the expense of Christianity; yet in that civilization an illegal surrender was not certain disesteem. Surely then he might have regarded that abhorrence of the un-intact state, which he had inherited with the creed of mysticism, as at least open to correction when the result was due to treachery.

Hardy's comment on Tess when she makes her way to Flintcomb-Ash more than eight months after Clare had left her seems conclusive:

Inside this exterior, over which the eye might have roved as over a thing scarcely percipient, almost inorganic, there was the record of a pulsing life which had learnt too well, for its years, of the dust and ashes of things, of the cruelty of lust and the fragility of love.

Nothing here suggests Tess's willingness to accede to Alec's sexual wishes while she lived at the Slopes; for Hardy there is nothing significant in that episode of her life but 'the cruelty of lust'.

Perhaps it needs to be pointed out that 'love-making' in Hardy never has the connotation it has acquired today. When he implied sexual intercourse, he made his meaning clear: Charles Bradford Raye on his western circuit wins Anna 'body and soul', just as Eustacia gave herself 'body and soul' to Wildeve in the 1895 version of *The Return of the Native*. Love-making in Hardy means no more than courting or wooing. Before they reach the Chase, Alec asks Tess if he has offended her 'often by love-making'; and the 'ethereal' and highly shockable Angel is reassured, after Tess has told him that she cannot marry him, by the thought that 'she had already permitted him to make love to her'. Soon afterwards he remarks, 'I know you to be the most honest, spotless creature that ever lived'.

On the main issue, one scene has led to confusion. It occurs when Alec overtakes Tess, who suspects her pregnancy, and alludes to it as 'the best o' causes' for lying dishonourably and pretending she could return his love. She has left precipitately for home when she feels she is morally slipping; she tells him that she has never loved him, and thinks she never can. Her true feelings are more strongly felt when she has reached home, and heard her mother's astonishment that she has not 'got' d'Urberville to marry her:

Get Alec d'Urberville in the mind to marry her! He marry *her*! . . . She had never wholly cared for him, she did not at all care for him now. She had dreaded him, winced before him, succumbed to adroit advantages he took of her helplessness; then, temporarily blinded by his ardent manners, had been stirred to confused surrender awhile: had suddenly despised and disliked him, and had run away. That was all.

The novel shows clearly that Alec had set out to attract Tess and partially succeeded, that she had allowed herself to be kissed (admitting his 'mastery' to this extent, since she feared him), and accepted gifts from him, after her violation. (He had tried to win her favour previously by providing a new horse for her father, and toys for her brothers and sisters.) She admits that she had been temporarily 'dazed' by him, but tells him she loathes herself for this weakness; if she continued to accept more from him she would soon be his 'creature'; 'and I won't!' she adds. That was the extent of her 'confused surrender'. She had discovered that she was being tempted by Alec's seductive wiles, and it was the horror of this self-discovery that made her pack and leave with secret dispatch: 'I made up my mind as soon as I saw — what I ought to have seen sooner.' As Alec attests much later, she had remained 'unsmirched in spite of all; you withdrew yourself from me so quickly and resolutely when you saw the situation'. Whether the summing-up in 'That was all' is Tess's or Hardy's can make no moral difference; it indicates, in conjunction with the weight of overwhelming evidence elsewhere, no very serious indiscretion by Tess, nothing but what was venial in the circumstances.

Some vagueness at a number of points may have arisen from Hardy's attempt to produce a text which would as far as possible, wherever the story remained unchanged,[9] suit the prudential demands of the serial editor, and be acceptable also to enlightened readers of the book. It does not explain the euphemistic evasiveness of 'the whole unconventional business of our time at Trantridge', which may reflect the converted Alec's embarrassment when, on hearing for the first time of Tess's illegitimate child, he takes upon himself the 'whole blame' for fouling her 'innocent' life. The earlier form, 'the whole blackness of the sin, the awful, awful iniquity', seems more appropriate to an Evangelical preacher.

For its inclusion in the 1895 edition of *Tess* a passage in the July 1892 preface, in answer to hostile reviewers, was revised as follows:

> The more austere of these maintain a conscientious difference of opinion concerning, among other things, subjects fit for art, and reveal an inability to associate the idea of the sub-title adjective with any but the artificial and derivative meaning which has resulted to it from the ordinances of civilization. They ignore the meaning of the word in Nature, together with all aesthetic claims upon it, not to mention the spiritual interpretation afforded by the finest side of their own Christianity.

To this he had previously added 'and drag in, as a vital point, the acts of a woman in her last days of desperation, when all her doings lie outside her normal character.' His former use of 'licensed' for 'artificial' in the above makes it clear that in July 1892 he was captious of the marriage-tie, believing it could be inimical to true love, as he had already indicated in *The Pursuit of the Well-Beloved*, which was yet to be serialized, and was to re-emphasize in *Jude the Obscure* and again in the 1912 postscript to its preface. The reference to Nature is much clearer in the original; it implies that true love and true marriages can exist only between those who are drawn naturally together. Tess's misfortune was not to meet the right man at the right time:

> Nature does not often say 'See!' to her poor creature at a time when seeing can lead to happy doing. . . . Enough that in the present case, as in millions, it was not the two halves of a perfect whole that confronted each other at the perfect moment; a missing counterpart wandered independently about the earth waiting in crass obtuseness till the late time came. Out of which maladroit delay sprang anxieties, disappointments, shocks, catastrophes, and passing strange destinies.

The 'aesthetic claims' which Hardy had in mind arise from the 'beauty' which may be achieved by the presentation of nobility in action. The 'finest side' of Christianity alludes to those virtues which constitute 'Apostolic Charity', of which Tess is seen as the embodiment during trial and tribulation. St Paul's verses on the subject 'will stand fast when all the rest that you call religion has passed away', Jude asserts; without charity or 'loving-kindness' there can be little hope for civilization, Hardy maintains in the Apology to *Late Lyrics and Earlier*.

His reference to Tess's 'last desperation' is excellent, and its omission from the 1895 form of his 1892 preface is a serious loss. That her powers of endurance were being exhausted by the prolongation of Angel's uncommunicative absence, the heavy toll exacted of her by the cruel winter of Flintcomb-Ash, and by d'Urberville's renewed solicitations, is clear from the threshing-scene. The death of her father and her family's eviction because of her reputation make it incumbent on her to act for her younger brothers and sisters. She is left with no option but to make the physical sacrifice and live with Alec. She is still Apostolic Charity in a self-seeking world, and her soul remains unsullied.

Hardy made his most explicit statement on his heroine in an interview with Raymond Blathwayt,[10] who took exception to the sub-title of the novel. Blathwayt could understand its application to Tess's first 'fall', but failed to see how it could refer to the woman who returned to Alec, and thought his murder 'absolutely unjustifiable'. After stressing that hereditary factors had much to do with it, Hardy stated:

> but I still maintain that her innate purity remained intact to the very last; though I frankly own that a certain outward purity left her on her last fall. I regarded her then as being in the hands of circumstances, not morally responsible, a mere corpse drifting with the current to her end.

The claim is unexceptionable. Clearly Hardy makes the crucial distinction between soul and body which had been a factor in the general plan of the novel from the time he planned its serialization. Taking hereditary instinct into account (he refers elsewhere to 'the smouldering ancestral fire in Tess's nature that broke out in the murder'[11]), in addition to innate disposition and the force of circumstances, he might have said, as he indicates in the threshing-scene, that Tess was a victim of the Prime Mover, the First Cause or the Immanent Will.

It seems impossible for Hardy not to have had Tess in mind when writing 'The Blinded Bird'. In the novel her tragic plight evokes images of trapped and suffering birds, as in Richardson's *Clarissa*, where Lovelace imagines the heroine as a caged bird bruising itself against the wires until it submits and sings. The virtues extolled in the poem belong to both heroines, and are explicitly claimed for Tess, who twice wishes herself ensepulchred; its climactic concluding question and answer are really synonymous with the sub-title of *Tess of the d'Urbervilles*:

> Who hath charity? This bird.
> Who suffereth long and is kind,
> Is not provoked, though blind
> And alive ensepulchred?
> Who hopeth, endureth all things?
> Who thinketh no evil, but sings?
> Who is divine? This bird.

9
Hebraism and Hellenism

One would like to know exactly what Hardy thought as his wife read, at his request, not long before he died, this verse from Edward FitzGerald's version of the *Rubáiyát* of Omar Khayyám:

> Oh, Thou, who Man of baser Earth didst make,
> And ev'n with Paradise devise the Snake:
>   For all the Sin wherewith the Face of Man
> Is blacken'd – Man's forgiveness give – and take!

It is, of course, closely linked with the opening of *Paradise Lost*:

> Of Man's first disobedience and the fruit
> Of that forbidden tree, whose mortal taste
> Brought death into the world and all our woe,
> With loss of Eden . . . .

It implies that sins have been wrongly imputed to man, not by God but by Churches, which 'ev'n with Paradise' devised the snake. Hardy had reverted to his old habit of ascribing 'all our woe' to the Unfulfilled Intention, though his later years make it very clear that he did reach the more enlightened attitude of attributing many of our ills to the 'unreason' of man. *Jude the Obscure*, where Sue Bridehead equates her Greek joyousness with sin, after being overwhelmed by the loss of her children, and thinks it is God's will that she should sacrifice herself bodily to her only husband in the eyes of the Church, shows that Hardy had taken into account the snake's association with the sense of sin and shame which, stemming from Pauline doctrine, had recurrently hardened against sex, as it did in Victorian England. For D. H. Lawrence this degrading association constituted the Fall.

The mouthpiece of the Church for centuries, St Paul had created a false distinction between the body and soul, the corruptible and the incorruptible, stressing the virtue of dying unto this life, and of living for the life after death. In *Culture and Anarchy* Matthew

Arnold had dared to suggest that Victorian England suffered from an excess of Hebraism and needed more Hellenism. His Hellenism had both a physical and an intellectual application, though his stress was on the latter. The Victorians would be more fulfilled if they overcame their repressions and their provincialism by cultivating spontaneity and enjoyment in life and a greater flexibility of mind, a willingness to accept new ideas.

Hardy believed in the Christian virtues; he was as much against licence (the abuse of the new thinking, fostered in some by the *Rubáiyát*) as Tennyson in *The Promise of May*. Repeatedly he makes clear his allegiance to Arnold and other Victorians on this issue, but it was a question of living or partly living: E. M. Forster's *A Room with a View* would have gained his immediate approval. If he did not object to the 'sacrifice' of John Keble's morning hymn ('Room to deny ourselves, a road To bring us daily nearer God'), it was because it did not conflict with the Greek ideal of self-discipline: nothing too much, neither too much indulgence nor excessive abstinence. Pauline Christianity is based on a low estimate of human potentialities; it affirms that if there is no immortality we might just as well eat, drink, and be merry, for tomorrow we die. Edward Young repeated the idea even more despairingly in *Night Thoughts*:

> Sense! take the rein; blind Passion! drive us on . . .
> Yes, give the pulse full empire; live the brute,
> Since as the brute we die. The sum of man,
> Of godlike man! to revel and to rot.

Man's duty would be 'to love himself alone'. Almost as much a supporter of 'the religion of humanity' as George Eliot, Hardy could not have dissented from her castigation of a faith centred on other-worldliness with no belief in the necessity of human effort to civilize the world.[1] As Positivists, they made altruism the keystone of their hope for mankind. In a scientific age when the miraculous in religion, including the Resurrection, was denied, Arnold's missionary zeal was more relevant and sensible than St Paul's. He urged the cultivation of man's highest or best self, and, in answer to those who argued as Paul and Young had done, wrote in 'Anti-Desperation':

Hath man no second life? – Pitch this one high!
Sits there no judge in heaven, our sin to see? –
More strictly, then, the inward judge obey!
Was Christ a man like us? Ah! let us try
If we then, too, can be such men as he!

As his Apology to *Late Lyrics and Earlier* discloses, Hardy based his hope for civilization on the survival of the Christianity of Positivism, 'loving-kindness' working hand in hand with science for the benefit of all.

   St Paul's denigration of the corruptible body explains the Puritanism which followed the Renaissance and much that was inhibitory and unhappy in the Victorian era. To some such as Swinburne, who introduced it to Meredith, the hedonistic philosophy of the *Rubáiyát* came like the breath of life; and it was Swinburne's poetry that excited Hardy in London, after his rather strict Church of England upbringing at home. In 'A Singer Asleep' he remembers a 'far morning of a summer day' when he walked in the glaring sunshine 'down a terraced street', and read with 'quick glad surprise' some of Swinburne's passionate early poems. Writing to him on 1 April 1897, he recalls the 'buoyant time' about thirty years earlier when he read his 'early works' as he walked along 'the crowded London streets' in 'imminent risk of being knocked down'. 'A Singer Asleep' suggests that the 'New words, in classic guise' are those of poems or 'tunes' in the first volume of *Poems and Ballads* (1866); the letter gives the impression that he read all the Swinburne he could, including the poetic drama *Atalanta in Calydon* of 1865. He regards Swinburne as the true disciple of Sappho, the poetess whose 'very orts are love incarnadine'. The effect of his poetry on the Victorian public, he writes, was as if 'a garland of red roses' had fallen 'about the hood of some smug nun'. 'If *Atalanta* made the poet Byronically famous, *Poems and Ballads* made him Byronically infamous', James Douglas wrote.

   About the time Swinburne first read the *Rubáiyát* Hardy thought of becoming a parish priest and writing poetry in his spare time. By 1866, after much reflection on scientific discovery and scientific philosophy, he no longer believed in Providence as an arbiter of fate; he had concluded that man is insignificant in terms of space and time, that Chance (including hereditary factors) is largely the determinant of one's destiny, and that human life is limited to existence on earth. How best to live that life was the question posed by Swinburne's poetry. Hardy may have thought Browning an optimist in a Darwinian world, but his enthusiasm for Swinburne must have made him feel that Browning's

> How good is man's life, the mere living! how fit to employ
> All the heart and the soul and the senses, for ever in joy!

was a desideratum, which through the kind of Positivist altruism strenuously advocated by Auguste Comte could become more realizable, given wise leadership, especially in the Church. Hardy's 'debate' on the marriage-tie in relationship to the subject ends despairingly in *Jude the Obscure*. When Lawrence presented the conflict created by the Church between flesh and spirit in *Sons and Lovers*, he had been strongly influenced by the poetry not only of Swinburne but also of George Meredith, who wrote in 'The Woods of Westermain':

> Then for you are pleasures pure,
> Sureties as the stars as sure:
> Not the wanton beckoning flags . . .
> Pleasures that through blood run sane,
> Quickening spirit from the brain.
> Each of each in sequent birth,
> Blood and brain and spirit, three
> (Say the deepest gnomes of Earth),
> Join for true felicity.
> Are they parted, then expect
> Some one sailing will be wrecked.

In an age when the Church related sex to the Fall and preached the corruption of the flesh, Swinburne's challenge brought Hardy a vision of love that was to be enjoyed. 'Anactoria' in *Poems and Ballads* of 1866 asks

> Why hath [God] made us? What had all we done
> That we should live and loathe the sterile sun?

A more explicit passage in the next poem, 'Hymn to Proserpine', must have brought full conviction to Hardy:

> For no man under the sky lives twice, outliving his day.

And grief is a grievous thing, and a man hath enough of his
  tears:
Why should he labour, and bring fresh grief to blacken his
  years?
Thou hast conquered, O pale Galilean; the world has grown
  grey from thy breath;
We have drunken of things Lethean, and fed on the fulness of
  death.
Laurel is green for a season, and love is sweet for a day;
But love grows bitter with treason, and laurel outlives not May.

Love is denied, and time passes, Swinburne concludes; he is
saying with great emphasis what Herrick, a late survivor of the
Renaissance, expressed more lightly in lyrics such as 'Gather ye
rosebuds while ye may' and 'Corinna's Going a-Maying'. Hardy
remembered 'Thou hast conquered, O pale Galilean', and the line
'O ghastly glories of saints, dead limbs of gibbeted Gods!' that
follows the above passage from 'Hymn to Proserpine', in *Jude the
Obscure*.
  Hardy's early Swinburnian zeal emerges in his first published
novel when the heroine's life appears to be on the brink of ruin,
as a result of her altruistic compulsion to marry a sensualist
from whom she naturally shrinks. Cytherea's loveless prospect is
reinforced by a reference to the next poem in *Poems and Ballads*,
'Ilicet' ('It is over'); instead of Eden, she sees 'the fragment of a
hedge – all that remained of a "wet old garden"'. The poem
reflects the joylessness of marriages affected by the constraints of
contemporary Hebraism:

> A little sorrow, a little pleasure,
> Fate metes us from the dusty measure
>   That holds the date of all of us;
> We are born with travail and strong crying,
> And from the birth-day to the dying
>   The likeness of our life is thus.
>
>   *   *   *
>
> They find no fruit of things they cherish;
> The goodness of a man shall perish,
>   It shall be one thing with his sin.
>
> In deep wet ways by grey old gardens

Fed with sharp spring the sweet fruit hardens:
They know not what fruits wane or grow;
Red summer burns to the utmost ember;
They know not, neither can remember,
The old years and flowers they used to know.

The conflict between Hellenism and Christian thinking is an integral part of *The Return of the Native*. Before this novel was really under way, Hardy's studious reading at Sturminster Newton was concentrated for a while on Greek civilization and thought. He noted Auguste Comte's conclusion that the intellectualism of the privileged had been freely cultivated in the midst of popular degradation, and concurred no doubt with John Addington Symonds' view that Greek morality was far less worthy of attention than the moral attitude of Greek philosophers. Unlike Christianity, this was not at odds with the laws of the universe (or nature). It was best summed up in Goethe's 'Im Ganzen, Guten, Schönen Resolut zu leben' (aiming at a life which is whole, good, and beautiful). Hardy believed that in some respects, notably in altruism and Pauline 'charity', Christianity held out finer ideals than Hellenism had done. His 1876 notes suggest that he recognised the opposition of these two cults, and agreed with Symonds on the need for a synthesis 'more solid and more rational then either'.[2] Few would think of making such a subject the theme of a novel, but this is what Hardy attempted in *The Return of the Native*, Hellenic paganism being represented by Eustacia Vye, Christian altruism in the flux of the modern world by Clym Yeobright. The novel shows Hardy's further indebtedness to two essays, the first especially, Pater's on Winckelmann, which first appeared in 1867, and Matthew Arnold's 'Pagan and Medieval Religious Sentiment', which he read in the spring of 1877.

Pater's essay exerted a formative influence on Hardy's creative imagination. His concept of paganism as the basis of all religions, measuring 'the sadness with which the human mind is filled' and beset by 'notions of irresistible natural powers, for the most part ranged against man', leads him to postulate 'the law which makes life sombre for the vast majority of mankind'. From this germ Hardy's opening chapter on Egdon Heath grew, as a symbol of life which is perennially endured. Pagan worship, Pater explains, was an anodyne to this; it was marked by various kinds of ritual, including 'the kindling of fire' and dances. Here we have the suggestion for the first great action in Hardy's story, when ancient ritualism recurs, in the Rainbarrow blaze and the dancing celebrations which ensue on the evening of 5 November, expressing at the approach of winter

> a spontaneous, Promethean rebelliousness against the fiat that this recurrent season shall bring foul times, cold darkness, misery and death. Black Chaos comes, and the fettered gods of the earth say, Let there be light.

Pater's main question is how or whether we can attain the serenity of life which is found in Greek art. 'The longer we contemplate that Hellenic ideal, in which man is at unity with himself', the more we regret the impotence of the modern spirit in a world of 'conflicting claims' and 'entangled interests'. Straining for perfection today 'makes the blood turbid' and 'frets the flesh', whereas the Greek tragedians could confront the discords and discouragements of life with poise and dignity. We have to accept 'the universality of natural law, even in the moral order', a necessity which is 'subtler than our subtlest nerves, yet bearing in it the central forces of the world'. Hardy was familiar with this deterministic concept of the 'web' in the universe at large and in man through hereditary and environmental circumstances. Clym Yeobright, rather like him in his values and aims, is well-meaning but temporarily blind, a modern who, in Pater's words, frets against 'the chain of circumstance'. This and much else, in general, Hardy had in mind when he wrote those apparently simple lines at the opening of 'The Caged Thrush Freed and Home Again':

> 'Men know but little more than we,
> Who count us least of things terrene,
> How happy days are made to be!'

Theocritus, to whose 'blithe and steady poise . . . in a clear and sunny stratum of the air' Pater refers, had been the subject of the essay 'Pagan and Medieval Religious Sentiment'. Arnold is struck by the freedom, naturalness, and animation of the life revealed by Theocritus, and contrasts the cheerful spontaneity of his world with the spiritual ecstasies in which the heart and the imagination took refuge from the senses in the poetry of St Francis. More incidentally he refers to the conflict between Christianity and the pagan spirit by quoting a passage from Heine on 'happier generations' that will 'rise up and bloom in the atmosphere of a religion of pleasure', and will 'smile sadly when they think of their poor ancestors, whose life was passed in melancholy abstinence from the joys of this beautiful earth, and who faded away into spectres' in consequence. 'That is Heine's sentiment, in the prime of life, in the glow of activity, amid the brilliant whirl of Paris', Arnold writes. Not surprisingly, therefore, Hardy calls Clym's home 'Blooms-End' and makes Paris Eustacia's goal.

Eustacia is cast in a Grecian role. 'Where did her dignity come from? By a latent vein from Alcinous' line, her father hailing from Phæacia's isle?' He is described as 'a romantic wanderer – a sort of Greek Ulysses', and she is referred to as Clym's 'Olympian girl'. She is 'the raw material of a divinity', and, with a little preparation, 'would have done well' on Olympus:

> In a dim light, and with a slight rearrangement of her hair, her general figure might have stood for that of either of the higher female deities. The new moon behind her head, an old helmet upon it, a diadem of accidental dewdrops round her brow, would have been adjuncts sufficient to strike the note of Artemis, Athena, or Hera respectively, with as close an approximation to the antique as that which passes muster on many respected canvases.

She lives on Egdon, which is Hades to her; as a result, 'a true Tartarean dignity' sits on her brow. She has 'Pagan eyes, full of nocturnal mysteries'; 'the shady splendour of her beauty' is the surface of the 'sad and stifled warmth within her'. Her great desire is 'to be loved to madness', and she trifles with Wildeve. (When Hardy was seeking a contract for serializing his story, John Blackwood suspected his intentions, and rejected it. Hardy refused to disclose them to Leslie Stephen, and decided not to overstep the mark when it was eventually accepted by *Belgravia*. In the 1895 version of the novel he dared to do what he had probably been tempted to do earlier, stating uncompromisingly that Eustacia and Wildeve had been lovers 'body and soul'. He may have concluded that this cheapened his heroine, for he finally, under no outer pressure, changed 'body and soul' to 'life and soul'.) When Clym Yeobright returns home from Paris, it is 'like a man coming from heaven' to her; her perfervid imagination makes her 'half in love

with a vision'. It is the chance of a lifetime, and her one aim is to
marry him, and escape to Paris.

Clym has no intention of returning to Paris, however; he takes
life very seriously, and hates the flashy diamond business in which
he has been engaged for the gratification of the self-indulgent
and vainglorious. While 'trafficking in glittering splendours with
wealthy women and titled libertines' he had become aware, like
St Paul, of 'creation groaning and travailing in pain'. His studies
had inspired him with altruistic zeal, making him 'a John the
Baptist who took ennoblement rather than repentance for his text'.
He thinks at first of setting up a school; in the end he becomes an
open-air teacher who has yet to realize that 'the rural world was
not ripe for him' and had more material priorities than education.
An ascetic who loves Egdon, and is given to plain living and high
thinking, he is an unsuitable partner for Eustacia, and can tell her
even during their courtship that he is not impressed by her
'sentiment on the wisdom of *Carpe diem*'. When her prospects of
life and happiness in Paris recede, she thinks of the flight of time;
as the sand in her hour-glass slips away, the moon's eclipse grows.
Clym's asceticism and altruism conflict with Eustacia's hedonism.

Their marriage is precipitate; the July sun that fires the Egdon
heather scarlet is an external manifestation of their passionate bliss
in seclusion, but, Clym being earnest in his desire not to delay his
mission, their happiness cannot last long. Disappointed in him,
Eustacia tries to shake off her depression by attending a 'gipsying'
at East Egdon, where she meets Wildeve by chance. The two join
in the communal dancing, and she is exhilarated. In this annual
event, when 'Paganism was revived' in the hearts of the dancers,
'the pride of life was all in all, and they adored none other than
themselves'. The last words, typical of Hardy in their incidentality,
show how far he had moved in his socially ameliorative thought
from those early raptures which Swinburne had excited in him.
He still believed in Swinburne's protests, but he knew they needed
to be counterbalanced by the Christian principles which motivated
Clym for the general good. Like the modern thinker Pater had in
mind, Clym is fully aware of 'the coil of things', the quandary
imposed by 'the defects of natural laws', knowledge of which
makes the 'old-fashioned revelling' more and more difficult for the
conscientious. Thought, the 'parasite', frets his flesh, making his
face, we are told, anticipate 'the typical countenance of the future'
in the expression of life as something to be endured rather than

enjoyed. Incapable of the hedonistic or Hellenist zest for living which is all Eustacia can live for, he, like the general ascetic of the opening chapter, is in harmony with the sombreness of Egdon, which mirrors a kind of life 'distasteful to our race when it was young' and pagan.

The polarization of Hardy's theme, which is one of unresolved conflict, is presented with some degree of artistry in the first and last solitary appearance on the top of Rainbarrow, that of the pagan Eustacia in the gloom of a November evening, and that of Clym in the summer sunshine of a Sunday afternoon before he gives the first of his moral lectures or 'Sermons on the Mount'. It is hardly surprising that the romantic Eustacia has an imaginative appeal which her widowed husband lacks. Each is Promethean; one is a rebel, the other a light-bringer. Clym's 'mental luminousness' is pale in comparison with Eustacia's fire. At the end, when pagan festivities are revived around the maypole, he is too tragically alien to participate. His tragedy extends beyond the narrative intensities. Altogether, as Hardy indicates in advance, his mind is not well-proportioned; he fails to realize that man, whatever else is desirable for his benefit, needs to enjoy life.

The subject recurs briefly in *A Laodicean*, where the heroine reacts against the rigid narrow Victorianism of a nonconformist Church, and cultivates physical beauty through Greek gymnastics. It appears next, more momentously, in *Tess of the d'Urbervilles*. The pagan spirit is revived in Tess when she rallies with the spring, and experiences that 'appetite for joy' which pervades all life. Her singing of the Benedicite was probably 'a Fetichistic utterance in a Monotheistic setting', Hardy writes, adding

> women whose chief companions are the forms and forces of outdoor Nature retain in their souls far more of the Pagan fantasy of their remote forefathers than of the systematized religion taught their race at a later date.

She is drawn to Angel Clare at the dairy-farm through a symbolical garden of weeds and blighted apple trees not dissimilar from that in Swinburne's 'Ilicet'. Its setting in the rich Valley of the Great Dairies is a reminder of how full a life she might have enjoyed had she not suffered a 'corporeal blight' in the eyes of her contemporaries (more specifically, if Angel had been different; both the harp he plays and his playing are inadequate).

This immature man has read much, and prides himself on the modernity of his thought. On one occasion he had lost patience with his Evangelical father, and told him that it might have been 'far better for mankind if Greece had been the source of the religion of modern civilization, and not Palestine'. Taken aback and aggrieved, old Mr Clare 'could not realize that there might lurk a thousandth part of a truth, much less a half truth or a whole truth, in such a proposition'. He preached austerely at Angel for some time, quite unaware of 'the aesthetic, sensuous, pagan pleasure in natural life and lush womanhood' which his son had been enjoying at Talbothays Dairy. This conflict between the forces of Hebraism and Hellenic paganism is made more pointed in the portrayal of Miss Mercy Chant, the prim girl whom Angel was expected to marry; he had just avoided meeting her, her churchiness making his mind fly to those 'impassioned, summer-steeped heathens', the dairymaids in Var Vale, Tess especially.

Soon after meeting her he had thought, 'What a fresh and virginal daughter of Nature that milkmaid is!' and associated her with 'a joyous and unforeseeing past', Hellenic no doubt – 'before the necessity of taking thought had made the heavens gray', Hardy adds poetically with Egdon overtones. So Angel Hellenizes her, calling her 'Artemis, Demeter, and other fanciful names half teasingly'. He worships a vision, not a woman. The result is that, when his illusion of Tess's innocence, of her being Eve before the Fall, is shattered, she is dead to him. He is too centred in the shock of his own disillusionment to regard her as the sufferer who had never tried to deceive him, and too mazed to realize what a self-righteous hypocrite he has become. Deep-rooted resistance paralyses his thought. The superficial irony is that he has willingly lost his sexual virtue, whereas Tess has been the victim of rape; the larger irony is that she is the embodiment of Christian charity in which he is utterly wanting. Self-conceitedly enlightened and progressive in his views, he adopts a typically male attitude, and proves to be indurately Victorian, in a crisis which is to destroy Tess's happiness for life.

Only after wider experience and severe personal suffering does he grow spiritually, and realize the enormity of his cruelty in abandoning Tess. He had long ago 'discredited the old system of mysticism' (Christian theology in particular, with its supernaturalism and beliefs in, for example, transubstantiation and eternal life). He has come to question 'old appraisements of morality', convinced that a person is to be judged by aims and intentions, by 'things willed' rather than by 'things done'. Now, struck by his past 'parochialism' and inconsistencies, he is filled with remorse. 'He had persistently elevated Hellenic Paganism at the expense of Christianity; yet in that civilization an illegal surrender was not certain disesteem.' How then could Tess be blamed when her loss of virginity was the result of 'treachery'? (As early as 1876 Hardy had read in J. P. Mahaffy's *Social Life in Greece from Homer to Menander* that, when a town was captured and the noblest and fairest of ladies became the concubines of their victors, 'such a fate, though felt as a lamentable misfortune, was in no sense a dishonour to the Greek lady, of which she need afterwards be ashamed'.[3])

Tess of the d'Urbervilles indicates that, whatever the importance of Angel's views on the Greek way of life, Christianity has something at least equally valid to offer. It also illustrates, like *Jude the Obscure*, how, in a profoundly emotional crisis, traditional, deep-rooted religious forces (the teachings of the Church for both Angel Clare and Sue Bridehead), rather than 'the reasoned ethics of the philosophers', are likely to decide courses of action.

Hardy remained faithful to both the Christian and the Hellenic ideals. In *Jude* he attacks not Christianity but the illiberalism and inhumanity of the Church with reference to marriage and divorce. When affliction makes Sue bow down to the Church, Jude condemns Sacerdotalism or 'mysticism', but they agree on the supreme value of Pauline charity, as opposed to self-seeking:

'In that chapter we are at one, ever beloved darling, and on it we'll part friends. Its verses will stand fast when all the rest that you call religion has passed away!'

With the theme of this novel in mind, Hardy wrote in November 1893 'The Young Glass-Stainer':

'These Gothic windows, how they wear me out
With cusp and foil, and nothing straight or square,
Crude colours, leaden borders roundabout,
And fitting in Peter here, and Matthew there!

'What a vocation! Here do I draw now
The abnormal, loving the Hellenic norm;

Martha I paint, and dream of Hera's brow.
Mary, and think of Aphrodite's form.'

In a later poem, 'Aquae Sulis', he makes the pagan British goddess
Sul complain that the priests of the abbey which has been built
near her springs and the site of her temple at Bath have scornfully
trampled her dust and despised 'the joys of man whom I so much
loved'.

Hardy's campaign against contemporary marriage laws arose,
no doubt, from the irksomeness of his own marriage bond. There
is ample evidence that he and Emma could not have been enjoying
a life that was whole and good and beautiful, and contrasted
unhappily with the fictional couple who reflect Meredith's ideal in
Diana of the Crossways:

> With her, or rather with his thought of her soul, he understood
> the right union of women and men, from the roots to the
> flowering heights of that great graft. . . . With her, wound in
> his idea of her, he perceived it to signify a new start in our
> existence, a finer shoot of the tree stoutly planted in good
> gross earth; the senses running their live sap, and the minds
> companioned, and the spirits made one by the whole-natured
> conjunction. In sooth, a happy prospect for the sons and
> daughters of Earth, divinely indicating more than happiness: the
> speeding of us, compact of what we are, between the ascetic
> rocks and the sensual whirlpools, to the creation of certain nobler
> races, now very dimly imagined.

Such was the evolutionary optimism of some Victorians. It was
shared by the young intellectual Sue Bridehead, who is first seen
working at Miss Fontover's Anglican shop in Christminster, a
poorly illuminated city, its medievalism of thought renewed by
the Tractarian or High Church movement. She quotes Swinburne
and has read the chapter in Gibbon's *Decline and Fall* on Julian the
Apostate, the Roman emperor who tried to end Christianity and
revive paganism, his dying words being reputedly 'Thou hast
conquered, O Galilean'. When Jude is rejected by Christminster,
he moves to the cathedral city of Melchester, hoping to qualify as
a Church licentiate and become an altruistic curate in some remote
parish or city slum. Sue tells him that 'intellect at Christminster is
new wine in old bottles', and that 'the medievalism of Christminster

must go, be sloughed off, or Christminster itself will have to go'. She contrasts the pagan sensuous love lyricism of the Song of Solomon with the theological interpretation in its chapter-headings, and tells Jude flippantly that he is 'in the Tractarian stage just now'. Like Clym Yeobright (although she is at this time on the Hellenic side of the scales Hardy wishes to see in equilibrium), she yearns for the enlightenment of mankind; 'I did want and long to ennoble some man to high aims', she tells the initiate Jude.

After she has been released by her husband Phillotson, Jude (legally married to Arabella, who had left him) renounces the Church and lives with her. Arabella, returned from Australia with her new husband Cartlett, observes the pair, 'almost the two parts of a single whole', with some envy at the Great Wessex Agricultural Show. One little effect demonstrates their happiness. In the pavilion of flowers, she puts her face within an inch of various kinds of roses to smell them. She tells Jude she would like to put her face 'quite into them', but supposes it is against the rules. He gives her a playful push to effect her wish, and she good-humouredly rejoins, 'The policemen will be down on us, and I shall say it was my husband's fault!' The policeman is the sign of Victorian constraints in this novel. When Jude asks her if she is happy and why, she replies:

'I feel that we have returned to Greek joyousness, and have blinded ourselves to sickness and sorrow, and have forgotten what twenty-five centuries have taught the race since their time, as one of your Christminster luminaries says.'

The luminary is Matthew Arnold, who, while Professor of Poetry at Oxford, had written in 'Pagan and Medieval Religious Sentiment', 'The ideal, cheerful, sensuous, pagan life is not sick or sorry', and declared that the sentiment of this 'religion of pleasure' has 'much that is natural in it', and that 'humanity will gladly accept it if it can live by it'. There were those, such as Tennyson in *Idylls of the King*, who feared it would lead to licence.[4] Christminster cannot accept it; after the loss of her children, while still in her right mind, Sue says:

'We went about loving each other too much – indulging ourselves to utter selfishness with each other! We said – do you remember? – that we would make a virtue of joy. I said it was

Nature's intention, Nature's law and *raison d'être* that we should be joyful in what instincts she afforded us – instincts which civilization had taken upon itself to thwart.'

But what are Sue's instincts? Surely Hardy did not strengthen his case on the question of either Greek joyousness or rigid Victorian marriage laws by associating in marriage two who by heredity are ill-cast for their role, and even more by making the woman epicene and incapable of living married life in accordance with 'the Hellenic norm'. Jude is right: 'I seduced you. . . . You were a distinct type – a refined creature, intended by Nature to be left intact. But I couldn't leave you alone!' It is jealousy which makes her surrender sexually, quite against her instinct, to him. She and Arabella are antithetical types (much as Miriam and Clara Dawes are in *Sons and Lovers*), neither capable of responding fully to Jude in marriage.

The unenlightened medievalism of Christminster persists to the tragic end, the 'crucifixion' of Sue and Jude. It is represented by the 'silent, black, and windowless' walls of Sarcophagus College, which shut out 'the moonlight by night and the sun by day', and symbolize four centuries of gloom and bigotry. Affliction deranges Sue's intellect, 'making opposed forces loom anthropomorphous'; having sinned against God, she must do penance by prostituting herself in re-marriage to Phillotson. Her wedding is a funeral, as Mrs Edlin says. If any other novel presents a more damning indictment of an unnatural marriage which is right in the eyes of the Church, it is Meredith's *Rhoda Fleming*, where father and mother compel Rhoda's sister to marry someone she loathes, anyone for the sake of appearances. Jude's conformity in re-marriage to Arabella is a satirical caricature. He is 'gin-drunk'; Sue is 'creed-drunk'. It is the godly who have no forgiveness, Meredith writes.

10

Hardy and Mrs Henniker

To appreciate the friendship which sprang up between Hardy and Florence Henniker, its origins and the tenor of their early correspondence, one needs to know something of her parentage, background, and upbringing, even about her father when he was a student at Trinity College, Cambridge, where he became one of Alfred Tennyson's best friends.

Richard Monckton Milnes (1809–85), a descendant of Wakefield woollen-manufacturers, was born at Fryston Hall near Pontefract, and educated privately before entering Trinity College. An enthusiast for poetry, he was probably one of the students who contributed to the private publication of Shelley's *Adonais* from a printed text said to have been brought over from Italy by his friend Arthur Hallam. He and Alfred Tennyson became members of 'the Apostles' at the end of October 1829, and about a month later he and Hallam were two of the three representatives of the Cambridge Union who 'drove manfully through the snow' to debate with their opposite numbers at Oxford on the merits of Shelley *vis-à-vis* the alleged superiority of Byron. Hallam described Milnes as witty, frank, light-humoured, unruffled in temper, saucy, but so consistently kind that one ignored 'the extravaganzas of his always random conversation', which was less superficial than it might at first have seemed.

Milnes maintained these affable qualities all his life, and gained many important friends at home and abroad. His travels, which were to take him into Europe, the Middle East, and the United States, began soon after he left Cambridge. He was a talented writer of verse, and an excellent speaker. In 1837 he became M.P. for Pontefract, a position he held until he became the first Lord Houghton in 1863. His political ambitions were doomed to be frustrated, despite his knowledge of foreign affairs, probably because he was more candid than discreet in expressing his liberal views. He played a key part in the choice of Tennyson as Poet Laureate, and did much to promote Swinburne. He was admirably qualified to follow Samuel Rogers in the entertainment of celebrities

127

and friends, which he did at London breakfast parties, first at 26 Pall Mall, then, after his marriage in 1851 to the Honourable Annabella Crewe, at 16 Upper Brook Street – as well as at Fryston Hall. His most permanent contribution to literature probably derives from his *Life, Letters and Literary Remains of John Keats* (1848) and his subsequent editions of Keats's poetry.

Monckton Milnes's wife was the younger daughter of the second Lord Crewe; she had a sweet and charming disposition, and the marriage was a happy one. They had three children: Amicia or Amy, Florence (born in December 1855 and named after Florence Nightingale, whose friendship her father had cultivated not without hope of marrying her), and Robert. Writing to a friend, Milnes describes his daughter Florence in October 1862:

> The second little girl has developed into a verse-writer of a very curious ability. She began theologically and wrote hymns, which I soon checked on observing that she put together words and sentences out of the sacred verse she knew; and set her to write about things she saw and observed. What she now produces is very like the verse of William Blake, and containing many images that she could never have read of. She cannot write, but she dictates them to her elder sister, who is astonished at the phenomenon. We, of course, do not let her see that it is anything surprising; and the chances are that it goes off as she gets older and knows more.[1]

The young poet Swinburne, who loved playing with children, was one of the party in honour of her seventh birthday, when he persuaded her to become engaged to him in ten years' time provided he was rich enough to give her a trousseau of rubies. He probably remembered this playful promise when, at Fryston more than thirteen years later, he came in very excited one evening and embarrassingly *flopped* down on one knee, declaring that her hair had grown much darker.

'I hope you are making the most of your three governesses', her father wrote to Florence in August 1867, when he and Lady Houghton were on a Rhineland holiday with Amicia. His wife being in poor health, he decided to avoid the worst of the following winter in England, and made arrangements to take the whole family by stages from Cannes to Rome, where Joseph Severn, the artist friend who had escorted the dying Keats thither, was now

British Consul, partly as a result of Lord Houghton's recommendation. For several weeks the three children enjoyed an excitingly instructive and memorable holiday. They were present on great occasions within the city, and their father found genuine pleasure in introducing them to scenes with which he had long been familiar in and around Rome. A lover of Shelley, and greatly interested in the works of Keats, he ensured that they were taken to every place associated with them. Of special importance to all was a visit to Casa Margherita, where he and their mother had first met in 1835.

Invited to Paris by Monsieur Thiers, President of the French Republic, in July 1872, Lord Houghton took Florence with him; 'Florey enjoyed her first outing (dining thrice with Thiers, with Lord Lyons, and the Rothschilds), and behaved with great simplicity and *convenance*', he reported; she was only sixteen, but Madame Thiers thought her 'very distinguished'. At Ernest Renan's, she was 'quite struck' by the 'brilliant talk' of this scholarly author of *Vie de Jésus*. A letter to her mother, describing her Paris visit, contains the following passage:

Since papa came I have had several great pleasures. On Sunday an especial one, as he took me to Versailles to dine with M. Thiers. It was delightful, and it interested me extremely to hear him talk. I sat by him at dinner; and afterwards he was so kind, and promised to give me his photograph. We dine there on Thursday again. We were fourteen at dinner; but no ladies except Madame Thiers, her aunt, and sister. There were several officers – among them the General Ducrot, who was celebrated at Sedan. A good many gentlemen came in the evening. The house is beautiful, and guarded by soldiers in quite a royal manner. Yesterday M. Thiers lent us his *loge* in the Assembly, and it was delightful, as there was a tremendous row. It would be impossible to imagine the rage into which some of the deputies got; they looked as if they only longed to fight each other. Gambetta spoke.[2]

Lady Houghton took her daughters with her for the London season of 1873, the last of her life, and they accompanied her to country-houses, notably 'the grand and gloomy Wentworth' of the Fitzwilliams, Trentham, and of course Crewe Hall, from which she drove one day with Florence to Madeley Manor, the home she still loved above all others; they walked round the Bryn as she had

habitually done in her girlhood, and as she did with Richard
Monckton Milnes the day before their engagement in 1851.

Florence and her sister were high-spirited girls who knew when
to observe the *convenances*. Having met numerous people of
distinction from all walks of life at her father's parties and
elsewhere, Florence was well qualified to become a hostess. But
for delicate health (inherited, like her general disposition, from her
mother) and her marriage in 1882 to Arthur Henry Henniker-
Major, youngest son of the fourth Lord Henniker of Thornham
Hall, Suffolk, she might have acquired more fame in such a role.
Her husband was a lieutenant in the Coldstream Guards, and
about to leave on the Egyptian Expedition; they were of the same
age, and their marriage remained stable and true. (Lord Houghton
was disappointed that Florence had not fallen in love with a more
financially advantaged partner.) Arthur Henniker was a dedicated
and successful soldier, not a literary man. When Hardy called on
him and his wife in London early in 1896, Henniker told him an
amusing story, describing the only time he studied poetry; it was
at the time of their engagement, when he bought a copy of Byron,
and struggled manfully through it. He then married, and gave up
reading poetry altogether.

It can hardly be presumed that Florence, after meeting so many
of her father's friends at home and abroad, including politicians
and writers of high standing, would be overawed by the shy
Thomas Hardy, even when he was a famous writer, as he was
when they first became acquainted. Lord Houghton and he met,
not for the first time, in the summer of 1880, when Hardy was
living at Upper Tooting. At clubs and elsewhere they dined
together, Lord Houghton on one occasion introducing him to
James Russell Lowell. Hardy's illness late in the year, when he
was engaged in the writing of *A Laodicean*, made it impossible for
him to accept an invitation to Fryston Hall, as he recalled on 13
July 1893, in one of his earliest letters to Mrs Henniker. Lunching
with her father in June 1883, at the house off Park Lane which
Lord Houghton and his sister Lady Galway had taken for the
season, he met Robert Browning again and the novelist Rhoda
Broughton for the first time. Seeing Browning about to introduce
him to her, his host had hurried forward and done this 'with the
manner of a man who means to see things properly done in his
own house', then walked around, 'pleased with himself as the
company dropped in'.[3]

The first Lord Houghton died in 1885, and his successor Robert (who later became Earl, then Marquis, of Crewe) invited Hardy to Fryston in the summer of 1892, stating that as his sister would be staying with him it would be a great pleasrue to see Mrs Hardy as well. (The second Lord Houghton had lost his first wife in 1887, and did not marry again until 1899.) It is clear from this and a subsequent letter that Mrs Henniker, who had by this time completed two novels and was naturally not without literary ambition, was especially eager to meet the author who, after the publication of *Tess of the d'Urbervilles*, was rapidly becoming the most famous writer of his time. After the death of Hardy's father in July, the invitation was renewed for August. Once again the anticipated meeting had to be deferred, when Lord Houghton accepted the Viceroyalty of Ireland from Gladstone. In January 1893 he sent a copy of his *Stray Verses* to Hardy, who, thanking him in reply, expressed the hope that Mrs Henniker's second novel (*Bid Me Good-bye*) had sold out. The following April the Hardys were invited to stay at Vice-regal Lodge, Dublin, during Whitsuntide, when Phoenix Park would be in 'full beauty'.

As advised by the Viceroy (the Lord-Lieutenant), Hardy and his wife crossed the Irish Sea from Holyhead on 19 May. The previous day they had visited Llandudno, and driven round Great Orme's Head. Recalling that drive, the poem 'Alike and Unlike', published in *Human Shows* years after her death, alludes to a confirmation of differences which kept them apart. As the manuscript indicates, the poet imagines Emma (most unflatteringly represented) reflecting on how this division affected their impressions of the scene:

> But our eye-records, like in hue and line,
> Had superimposed on them, that very day,
> Gravings on your side deep, but slight on mine! –
> Tending to sever us thenceforth alway;
> Mine commonplace; yours tragic, gruesome, gray.

(That the 'division' wrought in the 'autumn' of their lives, as admitted in 'After a Journey', began in the early 1890s is clear from 'The Voice of Things', and confirmed by Hardy's second wife, who in March 1913 refers to his revisiting Cornwall for the sake of the girl he married, and who 'died' more than twenty years previously.) Circumstances were such to make a man of Hardy's temperament susceptible to the courtesies and interest of Mrs Henniker, her brother's hostess.

It was an important occasion for the Lord-Lieutenant. John Morley, the Chief Secretary for Ireland (whom Hardy met on the crossing), was present; and at one of the dinners Mrs Henniker played the zithern. Hardy found time to view public buildings in Dublin, and visit the scene of the Phoenix Park murders. On the last day a party was taken round Guinness's Brewery, all being splashed on the miniature railway with ale 'or possibly dirty water, spoiling Em's and Mrs Henniker's clothes'. Lord Houghton presented a copy of his poems (translations from Béranger) to Hardy before he and Emma departed for Killarney. During their return to Holyhead they 'found on board', among other acquaintances, Mrs Henniker, who was returning to her home at Southsea (her husband, now a captain, being stationed at Portsmouth). A passage omitted from Hardy's *Life* states that the chief significance of his visit to Dublin was his meeting Mrs Henniker, who became 'one of his closest and most valued friends, remaining so until her death many years after'. 'Some of his best short poems were inspired by her', he added.

Before June was over he had read her third novel *Foiled* (1893) and pronounced it clever, quite above what the reviews had led him to expect and, generally as a transcript from human nature, far superior to more highly rated novels such as *The Heavenly Twins*. He did for her what he had done for nobody else, writing 'the true names of the places' in her copy of *Tess*. She sent him copies of some of her verse translations, from French and Spanish poetry; and the thought of one, relating to

> a strange and sweet Affinity,
> That warms two souls in this desert of earth,
> They must claim each other,

assumed such significance to the author of *The Pursuit of the Well-Beloved* that it made its imaginative way into *Jude the Obscure* and eventually, as a contrasting implication, to the title-page of *The Woodlanders*.

He had been to Oxford to witness the Commemoration proceedings in preparation for *Jude*, but his long-laid plans for this novel had become uncertain, and he could not foresee how the course of Sue Bridehead's tragic story and her relationships with Jude were to be affected by his own with Mrs Henniker. That they were kindred souls he was assured when he discovered they had been reading Shelley's 'Epipsychidion' simultaneously, but he was convinced that she could not come to the fore as a writer of fiction unless she overcame her conventionalism. She was a staunch High Anglican, and no doubt he had argued to no avail on the need to become more emancipated and progressive in outlook. In his letter of 16 July 1893 he dares to regret that she has allowed her mind to become so 'enfeebled'; two months later he tells her that, if she means to 'make the world listen' to her, she must be like 'Sarah Grand', author of *The Heavenly Twins*, in saying 'what they will all be thinking and saying five and twenty years hence'.

Journeying up to London from Max Gate on 19 July, he called on her at Southsea, and most probably discussed collaborating with her in a short story. He would think it over, and be delighted to hear from her, he wrote the next day. It is not clear how the proposal was initiated. After a holiday with Emma in Shropshire, and a visit to London, he read the stories which Mrs Henniker included in *Outlines* (1894) with a dedication 'To my friend Thomas Hardy', and suggested slight amendments. On 10 September he sent the 'sketch' for the story they were to work on (then entitled 'Desire', finally 'The Spectre of the Real'), with a 'trifling modification'. Soon afterwards, it seems, he forwarded another, for three days later he hopes she has received the 'skeleton', and tells her that if she does not care for either story he can send others. On 16 September he encourages her to alter the 'Desire' sketch as much as she pleases, and repudiates the contempt she feels he has for her 'rendering' of it.

The next available evidence (in Hardy's letter of 6 October) suggests that Mrs Henniker wrote the first version of the story, and that some of Hardy's criticism hurt her feelings; he assures her that he wishes to continue their joint venture as much as ever, but then asks whether, if he should think of something better, she would mind the 'trouble of writing it out'. On 22 October he tells her that he plans to 'carry out' the alternative ending, since she likes it 'so much better'; again, referring to the sketch-plots she has returned, he wonders whether she would ever like to work out the one she has not adopted. All this seems to indicate his readiness both to provide sketches for the proposed collaboration and to let his partner develop them to the full for his critical comment. (At the time he was preoccupied with final plans for

Jude the Obscure, and even for getting it under way.) Three days later he finds it may be best to 'effect a compromise' between the endings; on 28 October the story is virtually finished. He is having a copy typed, and wishes Mrs Henniker to read it from the beginning (*without* first glancing at the end!) so as to get the intended effect; she must tell him 'quite freely' about anything she dislikes. To observe proportion throughout he has omitted some descriptive details (one which he very much liked was subsequently restored). He invites her to make additions on the bride's preparations for her wedding, substitutes the new title, and suggests that they keep their respective contributions a secret.

Some commentators have judged that Hardy wrote most of the story; there is no proof of that. He clearly played an important part in the evolution of the plot, and in the writing of the conclusion, but nothing suggests that Mrs Henniker did not have a hand in the work at all stages. He was obviously prepared to defer to her; the odds are that she unfortunately deferred too much to him. She was high-principled, and not the kind of person who would allow the story to be published under joint authorship if she had not contributed her share. 'The Spectre of the Real' was sold to a literary agent in November 1893, and revised by both authors in London just before Christmas. It made its first appearance the following year in the winter number of Jerome K. Jerome's *To-Day*.

'The Spectre of the Real' includes elements which are not characteristic of Hardy, especially the Hardy of 1893. In the opening stages especially it reveals an author who gives sustained attention to smoothness of composition, and who has a refreshing eye for colour. Distinguishing features range from the choice of a soldier and a distinguished naval officer in the leading male roles to the frequency of delicate natural observations, of both birds and flowers, which are more typical of Hardy in his less distraught earlier years or in his later life as a poet. The passage which was retained, 'the description of the pool, and the bird tracks' which Hardy felt was to be omitted, though he liked it, comes as a welcome glimpse of the outer world, and as a proof, if proof be needed, that Mrs Henniker was no mean writer. The location and details of the church in which the first marriage takes place seem to confirm that Hardy had taken Mrs Henniker, as he suggested in his letter of 7 June 1893, to study architecture at St Bartholomew's, Smithfield.

The austerer prose style of the contemporary Hardy is felt more in the later stages of the story, in passages marked by plain, simple exactness of diction, and even, once or twice, by a slight ungainliness of expression. His anti-matrimonialism is reflected in a description which anticipates *Jude the Obscure* (v.iv). It occurs when the architectural beauty and repose of the church where the heroine Rosalys waits for her first marriage ceremony are contrasted with the other couples she observes 'on the same errand':

> a haggard woman in a tawdry white bonnet, hanging on to the arm of a short, crimson-faced man, who had evidently been replenishing his inside with gin to nerve himself to the required pitch for the ordeal; a girl with a coarse, hard face, accompanied by a slender youth in shabby black; a tall man of refined aspect, in very poor clothes, whose hollow cough shook his thin shoulders and chest, and told his bride that her happiness, such as it was, would probably last but the briefest space.[4]

Apt quotations, particularly from the Bible, are almost certainly enrichments from Hardy, and the dialogue conveying Jim's growing indifference to his wife after securing her in marriage undoubtedly owes much of its hard coldness to his improvements. It was he who must have remembered the old assumption that a marriage was no longer binding if one partner could not be traced after seven years. (Boldwood had it in mind when he told Bathsheba that, without complete proof of her being a widow, she would be eligible to marry him in about six years' time.) Such an idea may have lingered late among some countryfolk in the nineteenth century, but it seems somewhat incongruously outdated as a motivating force for the marital release of an army officer, and as the axis on which the later part of a story coinciding with the Home Rule debate is to turn.

Jim returns some time after the seven-year span, on reading of Rosalys' imminent marriage to Lord Parkhurst, R.N. (In the magazine version, their meeting is characterized by his blunt and bluff protestations and a sexual ardour to which she succumbs. The revisions made by Mrs Henniker before the publication of the story with others in *In Scarlet and Grey* (1896) omitted the forceful manliness of his embrace, without concealing its implications.) The next morning, after an inadvertent remark which leads to the disclosure that he has a mistress in London, Jim can regard his situation as a joke. The ending provides a series of surprises which tend to indicate Hardy's over-ready recourse to stock devices, the accidental drowning of Jim recalling in some detail that of the returned husband in 'The Waiting Supper'. Rosalys burns 'the renunciatory letter' she had written to her intended husband soon after the departure of the first, and her second wedding takes place according to plan. The sequel is brief, and supplies a calculated shock which some might regard as gratuitous; it is far too abrupt to be successful, though the clue to it is afforded (confirmed, it might be claimed) by the title of the story.

In his letter of 28 October 1893 Hardy told Mrs Henniker that 'all the wickedness' (if the story had any) would be laid on his 'unfortunate head', while 'all the tender and proper parts' would be attributed to her. So it proved when, after the outcry against *Jude the Obscure, In Scarlet and Grey* appeared. Mrs Henniker's stories received higher commendation from the reviewers than 'The Spectre of the Real', and *The Spectator* concluded that Hardy had not been a 'judicious literary counsellor'. On 8 November 1896 he wrote, telling her he was glad to hear the volume was selling well, adding wryly that she must keep 'better literary company' in future. Florence Henniker had most probably realized already that a writer of any consequence must trust her own judgment. She continued to write novels and short stories. She seems to have attempted drama more than once. *The Courage of Silence*, a four-act comedy, was published in 1905. As late as March 1917 she expressed the hope that her new story, which she thought better than her last novel *Second Fiddle*, would soon be published; it was to be dedicated to Thomas Hardy. What happened to it is uncertain. In her time she had given pleasure to many readers, and earned praise from many besides Hardy. 'She wrote fluently and with some skill of the world she knew, the aristocratic world of officers and statesmen in which she lived, and a strain of humour and irony saved her work from the sentimentality of the society novelist.'[5] It was Hardy who wrote a brief anonymous article on her for the benefit of readers of *The Illustrated London News* (18 August 1894), concluding:

> Her note of individuality, her own personal and peculiar way of looking at life, without which neither aristocrat nor democrat, fair woman nor foul, has any right to take a stand before the public as author, may be called that of emotional imaginativeness,

lightened by a quick sense of the odd, and by touches of observation lying midway between wit and humour.

In December 1893, still too unsettled to work steadily on *Jude the Obscure*, Hardy turned his attention to another short story, the main subject of which – based on a psychological fantasy found in a translation of Weismann's *Essays on Heredity* – he may have thought of as early as late 1890. 'Found and touched up . . . "An Imaginative Woman"', he noted.[6] The touching-up must have been considerable, for the Solentsea setting is based on Southsea, where Hardy had visited Mrs Henniker in the summer; and the Marchmills of diverse interests (the husband a thriving, philistine gun-manufacturer, and the wife 'a votary of the muse', Shelley's poetry in particular) have an obvious parallel with Arthur Henniker, an army officer at Portsmouth, and his wife Florence. The island opposite provides a suitable retreat for Trewe, a poet not dissimilar from the Hardy whose experience qualified him to write *The Well-Beloved*.

It seems that on 3 August 1893 Hardy divulged too much of his problems at home, and that, at Eastleigh, a railway junction where they met five days later on their journey to Winchester, Mrs Henniker reproached him for being morbid; 'petty', he preferred to say in his letter of 17 August. The Winchester visit took place most probably because she wished to see the view from the point where Angel Clare and Liza-Lu are imagined watching the black flag raised to mark Tess's execution. Hardy must have been the authority for Hermann Lea's assertion that the George, Winchester, was the scene of 'At an Inn', which records, it seems, the poet's afterthoughts on their being mistaken for lovers when they sought refreshments there in the afternoon:[7]

> Yet never the love-light shone
> Between us there!
>
>   *   *   *
>
> As we seemed we were not
> That day afar,
> And now we seem not what
> We aching are.
> O severing sea and land,
> O laws of men,

> Ere death, once let us stand
> As we stood then!

With Matthew Arnold's 'Isolation' ('Yes: in the sea of life enisl'd')
in mind ('Who renders vain their deep desire? – A God, a God
their severance rul'd'), Hardy falls into the wishful assumption
that their love remains mutual. 'In Death Divided' repeats this
idea, with the Arnoldian overtone metaphorically implied in the
last line:

> The eternal tie which binds us twain in one
>   No eye will see
> Stretching across the miles that sever you from me.

Hardy must have told his second wife Florence that 'A Thunderstorm in Town' and 'A Broken Appointment' (at the British
Museum) were both to be associated with Mrs Henniker.[8] The first
poem is described as a reminiscence of 1893. In it the poet recalls
waiting in a hansom until the lady, immediately the storm ceases,
springs out and makes for her door; he would have kissed her if
only the rain had lasted another minute. So he feels in retrospect;
he records an impulse rather than a probability. 'He Wonders
about Himself' is dated November 1893, and is clearly the poem
which he refers to in his *Life*: 'November 28. Poem. "He views
himself as an automaton".' Hardy is tugged this way and that like
'some fantocine' (as the 'poor puppet' Jude will be in his forthcoming novel), and wonders what next he will be doing; 'Shall I
be rushing where bright eyes be?' The record for December in his
Life shows clearly that he would be, in London, his last engagement
being the revision of 'The Spectre of the Real' with Mrs Henniker.

> Shall I be watching the stars of heaven,
> Thinking one of them looks like thee?

She had sent him photographs, which every day at Max Gate
reminded him of her. The poem ends on an altruistic note; he
wonders whether he cannot, unpuppetlike, 'Bend a digit the poise
of forces, And a fair desire fulfil'. (In the Apology to *Late Lyrics
and Earlier* he assumes that 'the poise of forces' can be affected by
the individual, who has a 'modicum of free will' when the 'mighty
necessitating forces . . . happen to be in equilibrium'.)

In *Human Shows*, the first volume of Hardy's poetry to be published after Mrs Henniker's death, there are two songs which may well have been written with her in mind: 'Last Love-Word', dated 189-, and 'Come Not; yet Come!' Allowance must be made for freedom of poetic fancy, but the closing lines of the first ('When that first look and touch, Love, doomed us two') have an authentic note in complete accordance with all the circumstances of the Hardy–Henniker story in life and literary re-creation. The second song may have been written in 1895 when Mrs Henniker was on holiday in Germany. In his 'sage moments' the poet can say 'Come not near', but the heart speaks otherwise, though 'old fires new burn' and perhaps, in the end, 'tear and overturn' him. 'Tear' recalls the 'time-torn' man of 'A Broken Appointment' (an undated poem), who grieves less for the loss of the expected one's 'dear presence'

> Than that I thus found lacking in your make
> That high compassion which can overbear
> Reluctance for pure lovingkindness' sake . . . .

Hardy's self-pitying nature is disclosed; but more significantly, his realization that Mrs Henniker does not love him:

> You love not me,
> And love alone can lend you loyalty;
> – I know and knew it.

The dramatic fiction of 'The Month's Calendar' may allude to Hardy's disappointment in discovering that his heartfelt yearnings were not reciprocated.

'Wessex Heights', the outcome of Hardy's depression in 1896, when, in the words of his second wife, 'he was so cruelly treated' after the publication of *Jude the Obscure*, shows him hopelessly resigned and almost cynical with reference to Mrs Henniker. Yet the verse in which he lets his feeling get the better of his judgment contains the most important key to his relations with her before their friendship stabilized for life:

As for one rare fair woman, I am now but a thought of hers,
I enter her mind and another thought succeeds me that she prefers;
Yet my love for her in its fulness she herself even did not know;
Well, time cures hearts of tenderness, and now I can let her go.

Commenting on this passage in December 1914, Florence Hardy
wrote to Lady Hoare:

> *She* has always been a sincere and affectionate friend to him,
> staunch and unaltering – and, I am glad to say, she is my friend
> too. There was never any idea of his letting her go – for he, too,
> is true and faithful to his friends, but the *poet* wrote that.

Mrs Henniker could not have perceived Hardy's love, one
suspects, when they met; nor is it apparent in his letters to her.
The later ones denote a durable friendship; the earlier can hardly
be described as those of a lover. Any impassioned tones are those
of a critical mentor; his attentions are almost paternal. He would
never wish to hurt her feelings, and is grateful for every 'nice'
letter she sends him. She is his 'most charming', then his 'dear
little', friend. Soon his shaping imagination conceives her in
Shelleyan terms; she is 'almost a sister'. An allusion to a couple
who are spiritually united (so far as the man is concerned, he adds)
may give a preliminary hint of Mrs Henniker in Hardy's eyes when
he was convinced by 'mutual influence' that they were reading
'Epipsychidion' at the same time. After the revision of their short
story, he writes from Max Gate:

> Of course I shall *never* dislike you, unless you do what you
> cannot do – turn out to be a totally different woman from what
> I know you to be. I won't have you say that there is little good
> in you. One great gain from that *last* meeting is that it revived
> in my consciousness certain nice and dear features which I had
> half forgotten, through their being of that ethereal intangible
> sort which letters cannot convey. If you have only *one* good
> quality, a good *heart*, you are good enough for me.

Her 'ethereal intangible' nature was to enter into Jude's 'tender
thought' for Sue, 'the sweetest and most disinterested comrade
that he had ever had, living largely in vivid imaginings'. Here,

almost certainly, we have the truest expression of Hardy's admiration of Mrs Henniker in 1893; a truth which he could never divulge to her, in letters or speech.

In September 1895 he is surprised to learn that she is reading John Stuart Mill, and still more that she agrees with any of his views. She remained immune to the influence of new scientific or Positivist thinking. As a result of expressing her views more decidedly than she had done in the early stages of their friendship, she appeared to be more intransigent as time passed. Hardy noticed this in 1896; she seemed to have changed a great deal from what she was when she accompanied him to see an 'Ibscene' play in 1893. Even as late as 1911 he laments that their views have drifted 'so far apart'. Yet their friendship did not suffer. In 1904 she was the same to him personally, he says, as she was when he met her in Ireland; ten years later, on the day after his marriage to Florence Dugdale, he addresses her as his 'best friend'. Their interest in each other's work did not diminish.

All her life Mrs Henniker had many friends among the upper classes; through her brother, who became Earl of Crewe in 1895, she met many leading politicians; through her husband, many persons of high rank in the army. She enjoyed company, particularly when she was with her husband — a practical, thorough, just, and genial soldier, and a versatile and highly accomplished sportsman, who won friendship and admiration wherever he went. The social world could not have been completely satisfying to her for long, however. She loved the country and travel; and she was devoted to literature and humane causes. The latter were interests she could share very largely with Hardy, but there were, one suspects, deeper affinities with his genius and character. Her writings indicate not only responsiveness to the sunshine and humour of life but also, to an even greater extent, an underlying awareness of the sad and tragic vicissitudes of mankind.

It is not surprising that Emma Hardy did not care for her, or that only one letter and the shortest of notes have survived from the many which Mrs Henniker must have written to Hardy from 1893 until Emma's death in November 1912. (The question arises whether the poem 'The Thing Unplanned' has any bearing on this. For volume publication Hardy had a habit of giving consecutive order to poems which he closely associated, and 'The Thing Unplanned' follows 'Alike and Unlike' in *Human Shows*, which was published long after Emma's death. Was there a time when her jealousy made him collect letters which Mrs Henniker had agreed to send *poste restante*?)   Florence Hardy expressed astonishment at the first Mrs Hardy's dislike of two such 'warm-hearted, generous kind women' as Mrs Henniker and Lady Jeune. She herself had no cause for jealousy, though perhaps it is significant that she was less sympathetic to Sue Bridehead than to Arabella Donn. In his 1912 preface to *Jude* Hardy admitted that 'there can be more in a book than the author consciously puts there'. Jude's final attempt to break away from Arabella and his rejection by Sue, now a slave to convention, may have derived much of its dramatic appeal from yearnings and inhibitions which Hardy could not escape in times of provocation. Mrs Henniker may have transferred his situation to 'A Statesman's Love-Lapse' (in *Outlines*), one of the novelettes she was working on in the summer and autumn of 1893. With Hardy charity and the philosophy of endurance prevailed: 'Nothing can be done. Things are as they are, and will be brought to their destined issue.'[9] At critical times, Mrs Henniker's intuitive understanding, or his confidence in her, may have helped to sustain Hardy more than anything else: 'if we are not to be the *thorough* friends in future that we hitherto have been, life will have lost a very very great attraction', he told her in October 1893.

A friendship rendered more difficult on one side by the very circumstances which promoted it, and undoubtedly subject in its early phases to strains and doubts on the other, required an unusual degree of reciprocal sympathy to survive. Its preservation for nearly thirty years until broken by death is sufficient warrant for its continuous 'thoroughness' or integrity. The lasting loyalty of Hardy and Mrs Henniker each to the other argues a strong affinity, steady affection, high personal regard, keenly shared interests, and – perhaps the most critical factor of all in the long run – susceptibility to, and respect for, their differences of outlook. Their full story can never be known, but much evidence remains, particularly in Hardy's letters, suggesting that this was the most important and fascinating of all his friendships.

Mrs Henniker died in April 1923 after a long painful illness. She left, her brother Lord Crewe testified, 'a memory of undying youthfulness, of observant humour, of earnest faith and of unchanging affection'. On the previous 9 November she had bequeathed all her letters from Thomas Hardy to his wife Florence, thinking they would be useful to his biographer. There can be no doubt that he and Florence used them to good advantage in compiling his *Life*. How many were lost is conjectural; it seems unlikely from the character of those that remain that any were destroyed by the Hardys. Mrs Henniker may have lost sight of some, and considered others too slight for preservation, but there is not the least evidence to suggest any breakdown in her friendship with Hardy, though their correspondence (perhaps not surprisingly) slowed down in later years.

There are gaps of more than a year each from January 1894 to June 1916, the first and longest coinciding with the period when Hardy was preoccupied with both the serial and volume versions of *Jude the Obscure*, and sometimes much out of favour with his wife.[10] On marriage and religious issues the novel could not have won Mrs Henniker's approval, but she was open-minded, and her relations with Hardy did not suffer a strain. It was published on 1 November 1895; on the 10th he sends her the clues she requested to his Oxford allusions (II.i), and implies that he had written too much to her on his subject while writing some of the story; on the 30th he is making arrangements to meet her at her London home. She travelled considerably, staying with friends in various parts of Great Britain, and going for longer holidays abroad; at such times she may have thought it wiser not to retain correspondence she had answered.

Hardy is very aware of a 'one-sidedness' in their early relations. He seems to allude to the seriousness which markedly tends to disqualify him for the enjoyment of life in high society. He and Mrs Henniker have discussed this handicap, and a 'plan' to overcome it. Whether he can keep it up is questionable, he tells her on 29 June 1893, though he has lunched that day with a lot of people, dines at Lady Shrewsbury's in the evening, and lunches at the Jeunes' the next day, to meet a party including the actress Ada Rehan, whom he would really like to meet. After more of this in London, and a stay with the Milnes Gaskells at Wenlock, he tells Mrs Henniker from Max Gate that the one-sidedness he used to speak of is wearing off. It may have been intensified by the uncertainty of his relations with Emma Hardy, who accompanied him on these occasions.

Hardy could claim Sir George Douglas and Lady Jeune as old friends, and he enjoyed recognition by members of aristocratic families at London gatherings and elsewhere, but he was not a man for publicity and preferred more modest occasions with well-tried (and intelligent) friends. At the end of 1896 he expects Mrs

Henniker will soon return to the 'social distractions' of London;
he has begun to feel he would not mind never seeing London
again. In April 1899 he does not yet know when he and Emma are
going there; he would rather enter a monastery. Two years later
his interests take him further and further from the West End
('barring the residences of a few friends') to older parts of the city
'where dead people have lived'. He instances Sir Arthur Sullivan
and Sir John Stainer, and considers the history of the theatre
nothing compared with the history of the concert room. Living in
the country, he missed great music more than anything else; in
London he attended concerts as often as possible. Although *Tess*
was being produced as an opera at Covent Garden in July 1909,
he was very much depressed by London; he was, in fact, depressed
by life in general, and would not have been sorry to take leave of
it.

County families usually formed their opinions of writers from
gossip and magazines, and Hardy soon discovered that the notori-
ety which reviewers of *Jude* had given him was causing some of
his more aristocratic acquaintances in the country to look askance
at him. In his letter of 24 January 1897 he tells Mrs Henniker he is
glad she enjoyed her stay at Lord Winchester's (in Hampshire),
and goes on to say that Dorset landowners only tolerate an author;
they do not associate with him, 'especially when he is such a
fearful wild fowl as this misunderstood man is supposed to be'.
He then recalls Lady Waldegrave's answer to Browning's proposal,
'We dine our poets, Mr Browning, but we do not marry them.' (It
must have been after re-reading this letter late in life that Hardy
wrote the poem 'A Question of Marriage'.)

It is not surprising that Hardy's letters to Mrs Henniker are
unusually informative and personal; he trusted her, knew they
had common interests (especially in literature), and enjoyed corresponding with her. In September 1895 he regrets that she had not
'after all' accompanied him to places he was using for scenes in
Jude, and recalls a recent visit to Rushmore, where he had enjoyed
the most romantic time since he met her in Dublin.[11] He becomes
an ardent cyclist (cycling in 1898 'more vigorously than ever',
sometimes with his wife, sometimes with his brother Henry), and
tells Mrs Henniker how he and his companion had to push their
cycles two miles uphill while crossing the Mendips one Sunday in
July, on their way to Bristol, which they entered as 'white as
millers' (contrasting with the churchgoers), the back of Hardy's

hands being blistered as a result of wearing no gloves. The next day they attended afternoon service at Gloucester Cathedral, and he tells how the Perpendicular style of architecture was *invented* there (a theory, discounted today, which he was to investigate in 1911 before writing 'The Abbey Mason'). In 1899 the Bishop of Wakefield's denunciation of a play by Pinero for immorality reminded him of how the bishop's predecessor had thrown his copy of *Jude the Obscure* into the fire; it seems, Hardy says, as if there were something in the air at Wakefield that maddens the ecclesiastical mind, making its bishops 'run amuck' intolerantly. There are more important memorabilia among the letters, such as the visit of Hardy and other distinguished authors from Edward Clodd's at Aldeburgh to FitzGerald's grave at Boulge, where he was pleased to find still flourishing in 1901 the rosebush grown from the seed of a rose by Omar's grave. In a graphic account he tells how suddenly in London he was confronted by poster-news of George Meredith's death; it is followed by a choice paragraph on Meredith's weaknesses as a novelist. The finest of Hardy's letters to Mrs Henniker relates to Emma's death; it is wonderfully tempered and balanced, hiding nothing essential. Later (17 July 1914) he refers to the poems he wrote in expiation, feeling he had not 'treated her considerately in her latter life'. Hardy was not a man to minimize his guilt.

Incidental revelations have their value. Such is his admission that, not being able to find a 'motto' for the title-page of *The Woodlanders*, he composed it (one wonders if he did the same for 'The Interloper'). Carols sung at Christmas in 1896 remind him of those sung by the Mellstock choir, and he tells Mrs Henniker that they are the characters he likes best in his novels. Soon afterwards he thinks of all the dead he would like to meet in the Elysian fields, and chooses Shelley, not only for his 'unearthly, weird, wild' genius (and appearance) but for his genuine, earnest 'enthusiasms on behalf of the oppressed'. Fearful that verses which were to appear in *Poems of the Past and the Present* would be criticized for expressing his opinions, he denies that they have any, and asserts more convincingly that the state of the English novel in 1900 is due to the paralysing effect of reviewers on those who would have developed it towards excellence. Like T. S. Eliot later, he sees more scope for forms of dramatic art in the music-halls than in contemporary drama. His criticism of Quiller-Couch's *Oxford Book of English Verse* is in advance of his time. Later he recognised merit in a number of young poets (including Eliot), but in 1913 he was amused to read essays by some of them in which it seemed to be assumed that nobody had ever known how to write poetry until they came along.

In 1899 he is delighted, he tells Mrs Henniker, to find a handsome tribute to her in the *Reminiscences* of Justin McCarthy. (The latter refers to the house in London which is known 'for its gifted and charming hostess'. She is 'an authoress of rare gifts, a writer of delightful stories' who, like her brother, inherits 'a rich poetic endowment' from her father, and one of those uncommon hostesses who, had she been living formerly in Paris, 'would have been famous as the presiding genius of a *salon* where wit and humour, literature and art, science and statesmanship found congenial welcome'.)

The first of Mrs Henniker's extant letters to Hardy (27 August 1906) shows that she had found his 'Memories of Church Restoration' both interesting and amusing. She did not wholly agree with him, particularly on the retention of high oak Georgian pews: they *had far better go*, she thought; they were an eyesore, and would have 'greatly disgusted' the builders of the original churches. She was far from being assertive in expressing differences of opinion; had she been so, Hardy would have been more indifferent to her reception of some of his poems. He fears she will not like the title of *Time's Laughingstocks*, still less some of the verses in it, and asks if he should send her a copy. Later, in March 1911, he warns her that his 'Satires of Circumstance' sequence is likely to appear soon in *The Fortnightly Review*; he does not dare to send her a copy, as he is certain she will not like all or some of the poems. He may have been too apprehensive at times; on this occasion he was probably right, with good reason. Mrs Henniker was interested in all he wrote, whether she agreed with him or not. Her criticism of H. G. Wells's *The New Machiavelli* led him to answer the assumption behind her queries (her usual way of registering differences) as follows (3 October 1911):

I have not read Wells carefully enough to discern his exact theories on the marriage question (if he has any), but you know what I have thought for many years: that marriage should not thwart nature, and that when it does thwart nature it is no real marriage, and the legal contract should therefore be as speedily cancelled as possible. Half the misery of human life would I

think disappear if this were made easy: where there were no
children at the wish of both or either: where there were children
after an examination of the case by a court, and an order for
certain provisions to be made.

Though the question of what should be done for the children of
divorced couples is not inherent in Hardy's anti-matrimonial
fiction, *The Pursuit of the Well-Beloved* shows that his views on
marriage had remained basically unchanged since 1892.

One of the subjects on which Hardy and Mrs Henniker could
write with almost complete unanimity was cruelty to animals. As
early as January 1894 he told her that butchers, drovers, and cab-
drivers were more cruel than vivisectors. Emma and he held an
anti-vivisection meeting at Max Gate in March 1897, but she was
opposed to his being associated with Zola in such a campaign lest
his reputation should suffer. He tells Mrs Henniker that she is
mistaken in supposing he admires Zola's fiction, and that the
animal in human nature should be presented only as a contrast to
the spiritual; obviously he could not have written this without
thinking of *Jude the Obscure*. In 1903 he still considers vivisection a
minor matter compared with the general cruelty of men towards
creatures deemed lower in the scale of creation; he hears them
complaining in railway trucks, and sometimes thinks how unfortunate it was that the human species got the upper hand. Mrs
Henniker, who in 1914 wished some mad woman would set fire
to the new physiological laboratory (where vivisection would be
practised) which had been opened at Cambridge by Prince Arthur
of Connaught, urged Hardy to join various committees for the
prevention of cruelty to animals, but he was too busy for such
work, though later, in 1919, he became a member of the Wessex
Pig Society, after advocating the use of a 'humane killer'. In the
last year of her life she is agonized by the thought of vivisection.
Undoubtedly she stimulated his continuing advocacy of the Golden
Mean, the extension of altruism to all living things. If the wind
blew words, many of them came from Mrs Henniker.[12]

Literature is a common subject in their correspondence, most of
it from Hardy being devoted to their own writings. Having learned
'the tricks of the trade' early in his own career, he soon gives his
friend advice on a publishing offer. He helps her to place short
stories, giving a little 'editorial' improvement to the ending of one
of them (with her approval, it seems).[13] Several times he wishes

they were longer. 'Three Corporals' struck him as the best she had written; he was never more disappointed in reading a tale than when he turned the page and found it ended. On discovering that it was mainly a transcript from life and its 'inconsequence', he recommended that she wrote a series of true stories from military life. He wished there were more of 'Lady Gillian', a charming story with a beautiful opening such as no other woman writer he knew could equal. Regretting the shortness of 'A Faithful Failure', he speaks of the 'suggestive style' of writing which she has quite made her own. Almost six years later, when reading 'His Best Novel' in *The Pall Mall Magazine* of July 1906, he notices the delicate touches of old, and a characteristic she shares with Sir Walter Scott of finishing her story rapidly, as if she felt she might have bored the reader.

Mrs Henniker tried her hand at a play in 1900, and Hardy did not discourage her, though he thought it would be more difficult after novel-writing. He enjoyed seeing a performance of her play *The Courage of Silence* in 1905, assured her that he was interested in G. Worlingworth (her pseudonym as a dramatist) and all his works in 1911, and wished Worlingworth success in 1916. He writes in praise of her last two novels: *Our Fatal Shadows* (1907) and *Second Fiddle* (1912). He considers the first superior in workmanship to her previous novels, and quite convincing and Trollopian, with nothing invented for melodramatic effect (he wishes there *had* been towards the end). He would have let the heroine 'go to the d——' for the man, instead of making her finally decorous and dull; marrying a duke's son she did not love was more immoral than elopement would have been with the married man she did love. He found more maturity of thought and insight in *Second Fiddle* than in her previous novels, and was especially impressed by Mrs Henniker's rare ability in creating a 'real man' such as George. Her method of presenting a story swiftly in 'chronicle' style had much to be said for it, but did not altogether appeal to one who observed the unities before the new mode came in.

War was a subject of special interest to Thomas Hardy; he followed the Boer War with a keen strategic eye, and with special attention to the fortunes of Arthur Henniker and the Coldstreams. Writing on the subject to Mrs Henniker, he reveals a dual capacity: nobody is more alive to the pity and horror of war, yet he admits that few are more martial in spirit when war has to be, or find more pleasure in writing about it in prose and rhyme. (He was thinking about *The Dynasts*, which he had already begun.) The excitement which his grandfather's illustrated edition of Gifford's history of the Napoleonic wars had roused in him in boyhood could easily be reawakened, and he is just as alive to it as he and Mrs Henniker are to equine suffering in battle and military campaigns.) By December 1899, after her attendance at a memorial service to Lord Winchester, who had been killed in action, he has told Mrs Henniker that the British generals by and large lack strategic insight, and that the war is likely to last three years rather than three months. 'How horrible it all is', he writes in February 1900, '. . . and the mangled animals too, who must have terror superadded to their physical sufferings.' He takes pleasure in following the war like a game of chess, but immediately he thinks of it in human terms the romance begins to look 'somewhat tawdry'. On 25 September 1904, when he was occupied with the battle of Jena,[14] he tells Mrs Henniker it was 'a massacre rather than a battle – in which the combatants were *close* together; so different from modern war, in which distance and cold precision destroy those features which made the old wars throb with enthusiasm and romance'. He writes little in these letters on the actual fighting in the 1914–18 war, but sufficiently on the subject to show that he followed it keenly with few illusions, much anxiety, and even with some of the old excitement. 'The war news is exciting almost every day', he writes on Monday, 4 September 1916, after reading the news that a Zeppelin had been brought down near London on Saturday; he thinks the newspapers are too sanguine, however, and adds, 'We have not beaten the Germans by any means yet.' Had Mrs Henniker's husband been involved, there would have been much more on the subject.

Arthur Henniker was a major when he set out with his regiment from Southampton for South Africa in *The Gascon*; during the Boer War he became a colonel; by 1905 he was a major-general. In 1912, while stationed in London, he was kicked by a horse and sustained a broken leg, dying soon afterwards of heart-failure at home, 13 Stratford Place, on 6 February. His wife invited contributions from his many friends for publication in the memorial volume *Arthur Henniker, A Little Book for His Friends*. For this Hardy wrote a poem which he left uncollected:

A. H., 1855–1912

A laurelled soldier he; yet who could find
In camp or court a less vainglorious mind?
Sincere as bold, one read as in a book
His modest spirit in his candid look.

At duty's beckoning alert as brave,
We could have wished for him a later grave!
A season ere the setting of his sun
To rest upon the honours he had won. . . .

Yet let us not lament. We do not weep
When our best comrade sinks in fitful sleep,
And why indulge regrets if he should fall
At once into the sweetest sleep of all?

Hardy's letters show a continual solicitude about Mrs Henniker's health – his concern for his own suggests almost a valetudinarian – and he recommends the Dorset air with little effect until after Emma's death. Florence Henniker first came to Dorchester to attend performances of 'The Three Wayfarers' and 'The Distracted Preacher' in November 1911. She stayed at the King's Arms, but visited Max Gate, it seems; Hardy ends the letter he wrote not much more than a year later, after Emma's death, 'It gave her so much pleasure to have you here.' (There is no doubt that Emma could enjoy being hospitable, but jealous imaginings could have warped her impressions later. Only the previous year, after the Crippen murders trial, she had 'in deadly seriousness' asked Florence Dugdale whether she had noticed how like Crippen Hardy was in appearance, adding that she would not be surprised to find herself in the cellar one morning.[15])

Mrs Henniker was invited to stay at Max Gate by Hardy and his second wife (*née* Florence Dugdale) in June 1914, but four years later he wonders, after dining at the King's Arms and recalling her 1911 visit, whether she will come to Dorchester again. In her reply she reminds him of the walk they took to a number of places, including the Roman arena (Maumbury Rings, no doubt with a scene in *The Mayor of Casterbridge* in mind). She stayed at Weymouth for a holiday in the early part of July 1920, and, after a 'charming and interesting expedition' with the Hardys, met them another day at the County Museum, Dorchester; Hardy had proposed an afternoon outing to Stinsford. 'Wessex' and her company must have pleased her, for she came to stay at the King's Arms towards the end of June 1922, after proposing 'motor drives' each afternoon, one specifically to the country of *The Woodlanders* and 'the old house where Mrs Charmond lived'. Hardy promptly agreed, promising to tell when she came how 'composite' the house of the novel was. Unfortunately the weather was not very favourable. She assures the Hardys in August that her present illness is not the result of the wet weather in Dorset; she had been very well there, and most comfortable at the hotel. On All Souls Day she says she is really better, and hopes to come to Dorchester again; she knows, however, that she must be 'careful for a good while after such a bad illness'. She died of heart-failure on 4 April 1923, and when Hardy read the announcement next day in *The Times* he wrote, 'After a friendship of 30 years!' She was buried by the side of her husband in the churchyard of Thornham Magna, Suffolk, and a simple cross on a three-tiered base (nothing stately as Hardy had imagined in the poem 'In Death Divided') forms a fitting memorial to two who in most respects were as admirably modest in spirit as they were honourable and great.

11

Jude the Obscure: Origins in Life and Literature

Hardy's life was relatively uneventful, and but for his creative imagination and literary successes it would not have been very exciting; it certainly was not very sensational, apart from the effect on the public of works such as *Tess of the d'Urbervilles* and *Jude the Obscure*. Why a story of dreams or aspirations and continued failure, of inveiglement into marriage by seduction, of broken marriages, unmarried lovers who live together and rear children only to find them hanged, of marriages which please God in the eyes of the Church and lead to suicide and spiritual death – why *Jude the Obscure*, in short – should have led early reviewers to deduce that it was 'honest autobiography' must surely occasion surprise. Not until nearly twenty-four years later, when Hardy was roused by a letter from 'an inquirer with whom the superstition still lingered', did he trouble to reply, dictating a letter to his wife Florence, who wrote: 'To your inquiry if *Jude the Obscure* is autobiographical, I have to answer that there is not a scrap of personal detail in it, it having the least to do with his own life of all his books.' When, in the course of preparing his *Life*, he reached the period ending with the 1895–96 reviews of *Jude*, he reverted to this letter, and added:

Some of the incidents were real in so far as that he had heard of them, or come in contact with them when they were occurring to people he knew; but no more. It is interesting to mention that on his way to school he did once meet with a youth like Jude who drove the bread-cart of a widow, a baker, like Mrs Fawley, and carried on his studies at the same time, to the serious risk of other drivers in the lanes; which youth asked him to lend him his Latin grammar.[1]

One can sympathize with Hardy, for the frenetic itch to read autobiography into this novel has never been more blatantly indulged than in relatively recent years. Hardy's first answer was too absolute, of course; his second supplies welcome information, but little to suggest he had given the question careful thought. Yet, though there are scraps of personal detail in *Jude the Obscure*, they are details only, and altogether not very considerable. Three examples come to mind: Hardy's childhood wish not to grow up, as he lay with the sun's rays streaming through the interstices of his straw hat, more accurately reproduced in *Jude* than in the poem 'Childhood Among the Ferns'; Hardy and Jude's reading of the same portions of the *Iliad* in their teens; and the placing of a looking-glass by the window to give the invalid Hardy a view of a glorious sunset, repeated by Sue for Phillotson, as Hardy remembered in his *Life* before denying autobiographical inclusions in his novel. The letter of rejection from T. Tetuphenay of Biblioll College (his Greek name implying the 'hard slap' he administered to Jude) presents a fourth possibility, reported evidence indicating that it could have been a transcript of a reply to Hardy from Benjamin Jowett of Balliol. The probability is that such recollections and adaptations from the author's life comprise less than one per cent of the text.[2] Hardy's architectural interest in stone-masonry, and his clerical aspirations before he became a novelist, are turned wholly to fictional account in Jude's career.

How much of a writer enters the thoughts, feelings, and actions of his characters, of either sex, can never be assessed. Speaking from experience in 'The Three Voices of Poetry', the poet and dramatist T. S. Eliot declares his conviction that the author not only 'imparts something of himself to his characters' but 'is influenced by the characters he creates.' Hardy's views on marriage were not fixed; he indulges them, no doubt, through Phillotson and Sue, but precisely what his views were when he wrote *Jude the Obscure*, and how far they were turned or moulded by the pressures of imaginative circumstance, no one can say, though they were most probably foreshadowed in his serial *The Pursuit of the Well-Beloved*.[3] Undoubtedly the intellectual enfranchisement of the Sue whose intellect 'scintillated like a star' found expression in those Hardyan views which had culminated in his theory of the Unfulfilled Intention:

> that the First Cause worked automatically like a somnambulist, and not reflectively like a sage; that at the framing of the terrestrial conditions there seemed never to have been contemplated such

a development of emotional perceptiveness among the creatures subject to those conditions as that reached by thinking and educated humanity.

Whether Jude's silly lovesick dream, on losing Sue to Phillotson, of her having children in her own likeness reflects one of Hardy's thoughts, as the poem 'To a Motherless Child' seems to suggest, is uncertain; he published the poem as a whimsy, and he must have known that the same idea came to the maudlin hero of Tennyson's 'Locksley Hall'. It is not known whether Hardy's poem was written before or after *Jude the Obscure*.

An imaginative novelist may in some respects, at some stage or other, draw from people he has known in depicting some of his characters. Hardy acknowledges (as his wife Florence told Lady Hoare) that he had one of his uncles in mind when he created Jude; this was John Antell, a Puddletown shoemaker, and a self-educated classical scholar who was occasionally the worse for drink. Nor should Horace Moule, another inebriate, be forgotten; like Jude he was a classical scholar with both 'Christminster' and 'Melchester' connections; according to his friend Hardy, he may have had a bastard son who was brought up in Australia; and like Jude he committed suicide after being irrevocably parted from the woman he loved.

How much of Sue ever existed outside Hardy's imagination is a much more interesting question. The training-college which his two sisters attended at Salisbury ('Melchester') provided the background for one of his sensational episodes. (How fact and fiction can combine to create tradition was illustrated during my first visit to the college more than twenty years ago, when I was told by a young part-time lecturer, who had become an enthusiastic volunteer guide, that one of Hardy's sisters had been an unsatisfactory student, and made her escape from the college by wading through the river that skirts its grounds. Eventually, after a further visit and correspondence with two members of the staff, I was sent copies of Mary and Kate Hardy's college certificates; there was only one word, term after term, for the conduct of both, and not surprisingly it was 'Good'.) Hardy's close kinship with Mary made him acquainted with the College of Sarum St Michael, but it was from his younger sister Kate years later, in 1877–78, that he heard more on its institutional hardships and restrictions; on this subject she felt so strongly that she rather hoped her brother would publish 'how badly we were used'. He revived his training-college impressions by visits to two London colleges for women in 1891, one of them Stockwell College, where his cousin Tryphena Sparks had been trained. Perhaps he owed something to recollections of her experience there; and her early teaching with the headmaster in the boys' half of the schools at Puddletown more probably gave him the idea of placing Sue with Phillotson in a similar position at 'Shaston' (Shaftesbury).

On the train to London in March 1890 Hardy began the ambiguously titled poem 'Thoughts of Phena'. 'It was a curious instance of sympathetic telepathy', he afterwards thought, for at the time of his recalling her Tryphena was dying, as he learned soon after her death. Perhaps one of the precursors of those disharmonies which marred the last twenty years of his married life with Emma had brought back the memory of the girl whose gaiety and affection now assured him that she was another of his lost prizes.[4] The thought (the recurring image of the elusive 'well-beloved') and wakened interest in Tryphena Sparks influenced Hardy's last two novels. In the first preface to *Jude the Obscure* he writes: 'The scheme was jotted down in 1890, from notes made in 1887 and onwards, some of the circumstances being suggested by the death of a woman in the former year.' The postponement of the novel and events of the interim, however, led to considerable changes, as a result of which Tryphena's fictional memorial is to be found in *The Well-Beloved* rather than in *Jude*, most patently, and with hardly any disguise, in the effect of the first Avice's death on Jocelyn:

He loved the woman dead and inaccessible as he had never loved her in life. He had thought of her but at distant intervals during the twenty years since that parting occurred, and only as somebody he could have wedded. Yet now the times of youthful friendship with her, in which he had learnt every note of her innocent nature, flamed up into a yearning and passionate attachment, embittered by regret beyond words. . . . She had been another man's wife almost the whole time since he was estranged from her, and now she was a corpse. Yet the absurdity did not make his grief the less: and the consciousness of the intrinsic, almost radiant, purity of this new-sprung affection for a flown spirit forbade him to check it. The flesh was absent altogether; it was love rarefied and refined to its highest attar. He had felt nothing like it before.

Jude the Obscure was postponed, partly because Hardy's life was too busy and unsettled; mainly, the evidence suggests, because he was unable to finalize his plan for the novel to his satisfaction. Although he had drawn up an outline, he had to make a structural alteration of the opening after embarking on full-length composition, and it was not until 1894 that the novel began to get under way; in January he was 'creeping on a little' and becoming interested in his heroine as she took 'shape and reality', though she was still 'very nebulous'. So he informed Florence Henniker, the 'charming, *intuitive* woman' with whom his friendship began the previous May. An ambitious young novelist, she was not reluctant to encourage his friendship and literary patronage; he was only too ready to give her literary advice and encouragement. At first it was difficult for Hardy to adjust himself socially, but their friendship was based on mutual esteem, and lasted until her death. Beautiful and fascinating, she not surprisingly went to Hardy's head; victim of almost inevitable imaginings, he soon thought he was in love with her. She is the 'one rare fair woman' of 'Wessex Heights', where he tells us that she never knew how much he loved her. Just how the memory of Tryphena Sparks would have helped to create the heroine in *Jude*, had she not, as a result of time and chance, been displaced imaginatively by Mrs Henniker in the creation and development of Sue's character, will never be known. In 1896 Hardy told his friend Edward Clodd that Mrs Henniker had been his 'model' for Sue; his second wife Florence told Professor Purdy that Sue Bridehead was 'in part drawn from Mrs. Henniker'. Sue is presented as an epicene intellectual, sexually cold and fastidious but tantalizingly attractive, a type which had always fascinated Hardy, and which he would have attempted to draw earlier had he not found it so difficult, he told Edmund Gosse.[5] The growing attractiveness of her personality and the progressiveness of her views (his own, not Mrs Henniker's) took charge, the story carrying its author into such 'unexpected fields' that he was uncertain of its future by April 1894, when he urged the cancellation of a publishing contract which had led him to promise 'a tale that could not offend the most fastidious maiden.' When the novel was published in November 1895, he told Gosse that it had not altogether been *constructed*, 'for, beyond a certain point, the characters necessitated it, and I simply let it come'. The way it developed had much to do with Mrs Henniker.

Some of Hardy's thoughts about her are clearly transferred to

Jude. He discovered that he and Mrs Henniker had been reading Shelley's 'Epipyschidion' simultaneously, and attributed his coincidence to their 'mutual influence'. At one point in the novel (IV.v) Jude quotes the poem with reference to Sue:

> A seraph of Heaven, too gentle to be human,
> Veiling beneath that radiant form of woman . . . .

Earlier (III.ix) he sees her in terms of the same poem, 'so ethereal a creature that her spirit could be seen trembling through her limbs':

> An antelope,
> In the suspended impulse of its lightness,
> Were less aethereally light: the brightness
> Of her divinest presence trembles through
> Her limbs . . . .

Before the first flush of his imaginative love had waned, Hardy had endowed Mrs Henniker with this Shelleyan spirituality, a hint of it occurring in a letter of 18 December 1893: one great gain of seeing her recently, he tells her, is that 'certain nice and dear features' in her character, 'half-forgotten, through their being of that ethereal intangible sort', are now revived. Reverting to the passage just quoted from *Jude the Obscure*, we can see how Florence Henniker existed for Hardy at the time of writing: 'the sweetest and most disinterested comrade that he had ever had, living largely in vivid imaginings'. Sue and Jude have 'complete mutual understanding'; they are 'almost the two parts of a single whole', almost the ideal union Hardy had expressed a yearning for at the end of the fifth chapter of *Tess of the d'Urbervilles*. Elsewhere in *Jude* he writes: 'That the one affined soul he had ever met was lost to him . . . returned upon him with cruel persistency . . . .' The tragic irony of this reflection is evident in the title-page epigraph he wrote, his own marriage much in mind, in August 1895, for a new edition of *The Woodlanders*. 'What name shall I give to the heroine of my coming long story when I get at it?' he asked Mrs Henniker when he wrote on Sunday, 22 October 1893. What he wished may be guessed from the appearance of 'Florence' in the signature of Sue's more distant letters to Jude about the time of her first marriage to Phillotson.

It should be stressed that, though she resembles Hardy's impressions of Mrs Henniker in some respects, Sue developed pre-eminently in his imagination. Yet there is one other passage in *Jude* (III.iv) which not only reflects Florence Henniker but bears on the tragic resolution of the novel:

> that epicene tenderness of hers was too harrowing. . . . If he could only get over the sense of her sex . . . what a comrade she would make. . . . She was nearer to him than any other woman he had ever met, and he could scarcely believe that time, creed, or absence, would ever divide him from her.

Hardy and Mrs Henniker differed profoundly in creed; she was Anglo-Catholic and proof against his protestations that as a writer she needed to be twenty-five years ahead of her time. How could she, the daughter of Shelley's champion, he asked in July 1893, allow herself 'to be enfeebled to a belief in ritualistic ecclesiasticism'? He would have to trust to imagination for a woman enfranchised from 'retrograde superstitions'. He was thinking ahead to Sue before tragedy made her retrogressive and conventional in her religious beliefs. Hardy, as a passage on women students (III.iii) in training at Melchester shows (and this is based on observations made at Whitelands Training College[6]), believed that women are the weaker sex, not as well endowed as men to endure suffering and shock. The loss of her children is seen by Sue as a sign of God's anger that she and Jude have ignored ecclesiastical conformity by living together without being officially married. Her prostration below the Cross in the 'ceremonial' church of St Silas, and her declaration that 'Arabella's child killing mine was a judgment – the right slaying the wrong' makes Jude explode with hatred of 'Christianity, or mysticism, or Sacerdotalism, or whatever it may be called'. Her physical self-sacrifice and spiritual death in re-marriage to Phillotson, which is presented as her crucifixion, is not quite Hardy's last comment on the superstition that sanctifies lasting wedlock for incompatible couples whom 'God hath joined together'; Jude's re-marriage is a grotesque satire on the subject. Both are crazed by their losses: one 'creed-drunk', the other 'gin-drunk'. How *Jude the Obscure* would have reached its tragic endings had Hardy not found Mrs Henniker intractably unemancipated in her religion is one of those insoluble questions which are worth asking.

By influencing the character and role of Sue, Hardy's new friendship with Mrs Henniker seems to have contributed a more exciting creative element to *Jude* than any other factor. It is not improbable that some parts of the story had lost their initial inspiration, and grown stale and flat, through long storage. From deep-rooted family associations, chiefly with the paternal grandmother who lived there in her youth, this does not apply to the presentation of 'Marygreen' and the downland country immediately to the north. Hardy remembered the eminent suitability of this terrain for his 'Christminster' story from his first visit to Fawley in Berkshire, over Greenhill Down from Denchworth in the 'Christminster' plain, with his sister Mary in the autumn of 1864, when he sketched the old church. His second visit in the autumn of 1892 revived the scenes, and gave him those new features of school and church which, overtly significant in the opening and closing stages of the novel, are resonant with implications for the whole. Much of *Jude*, however, is characterized by workmanlike, sometimes perfunctory, professional economy of style, with little of the poetic bloom or the severe intensity of tragic tone that are found in *Tess of the d'Urbervilles*.

To offset this, there are dramatic scenes between Jude and Sue which are profoundly moving, some of them the most anguished in Hardy. Yet it is doubtful whether *Jude the Obscure* ranks among the great tragedies. The story and its issues are too closely knit and complicated for one large single action to develop, as in *Tess*. As the first proposed title of the novel indicated, Sue and Jude are simpletons, particularly in not thinking of the need to marry for the sake of their children. It is unfortunate too that Hardy is crude in his satirical depiction of marriage, and that such crudity of event is adduced as a motivating factor for the flouting of marriage conventions by Sue and Jude, who are both authorially manipulated like puppets. Few readers can feel that the tragedy of the novel is inevitable; Hardy makes it too evident from the time when hero and heroine first meet (and subsequently) that, in his calculations, the odds are heavily weighted against them. Jude, we are told, realizes then why he and Sue should be friends, not lovers:

> The first reason was that he was married, and it would be wrong. The second was that they were cousins. It was not well for cousins to fall in love even when circumstances seemed to favour the passion. The third: even were he free, in a family like

his own where marriage usually meant a tragic sadness, marriage
with a blood-relation would duplicate the adverse conditions,
and a tragic sadness might be intensified to a tragic horror.

Again, it is doubtful if the hero has tragic stature, for he capitulates
too readily at critical points; furthermore, the ghastly crucifixion
of the children is an improbable climactic ploy in the predetermined
road-to-Calvary analogue.

Tragedy is heightened when, as in *Hamlet* or *Othello*, we are
made to realize what great human capacities are sacrificed or
overthrown; it is diminished when hope is continually snuffed out,
as it is in *Jude*. From the outset Hardy writes as if he had little
hope: 'But nobody did come, because nobody does; and under the
crushing recognition of his gigantic error Jude continued to wish
himself out of the world.' There is this difference between Tess's
tragedy and Jude's: the main point of the former depends on the
zest for life, the 'appetite for joy', and Hardy imparts it in scene
after scene. Sue is an advocate of 'Greek joyousness', but any
experience of it is stated, never imaginatively realized. In the one
scene of undisturbed happiness between the lovers Sue and
Jude, at the Great Wessex Agricultural Show, there are menaces:
immediate in little Father Time, as Sue recognises; more ominous,
the reader surmises, in Arabella. Marriage blight infects the
philosophic tone of *Jude*; there is always a chilling, killing shadow.
Too much springs from a morbid imagination, and goes a long
way cumulatively to confirm what truth there is in George Eliot's
dictum that 'art which leaves the soul in despair is laming to the
soul, and is denounced by the healthy sentiment of an active
community'. Whatever may be said for Jude's end, that of Sue is
intended to leave the soul in despair. 'How cruel you are!' wrote
Swinburne to Hardy after reading the novel, which made him
yearn for a revival of the *Under the Greenwood Tree* spirit.[7] Hardy's
protest is strong and warranted, but *Jude* as a whole seems steeped
in the essence of *The City of Dreadful Night*:

> Perpetual recurrence in the scope
> Of but three terms, dead Faith, dead Love, dead Hope.[8]

The role of little Father Time at the centre of this tragedy will be
assessed in the context of the last of the literary influences to which
we now turn.

Hardy was 'a born bookworm' on his own admission, and found ideas for his stories in, for example, newspapers (the wife-sale at the opening of *The Mayor of Casterbridge*), essays (images in Pater suggesting early scenes in *The Return of the Native*), the Bible, and fiction (Richardson's *Clarissa* and Scott's *The Bride of Lammermoor* in *Tess of the d'Urbervilles*). Frequently he made imaginative transfers or transmutations by processes of recollection which he may not have suspected at the time of composition; occasionally his borrowings are so extensive they must have been deliberate. A psychologically imaginative writer such as Henry James in his later phase is far less dependent fictionally on background, incident, and external action than Hardy, who in *Jude* appears to have been more than usually committed to incident for the maintenance of a compressed narrative. Literary suggestions may have affected some of the details or descriptions; they may have evoked minor scenes, or even a theme which is sustained through lively dramatic scenes or recurrent background.

As an example of a thought which could be responsible for the introduction of significant detail in *Jude the Obscure*, the following statement from 'The Broad Church', an essay by Leslie Stephen (whose philosophy influenced Hardy's for many years, 'more than that of any other contemporary'[9]), should be considered with reference to the policemen who keep watch in 'Christminster': 'religions are preached, not because they are true, but because they are a highly convenient substitute for police regulations'.

Hardy knew Shelley's poetry intimately; he re-read 'Epipsychidion' at the time when Mrs Henniker was reading it, only a few weeks before he began the full-length composition of *Jude*; and attention has already been drawn to its effect on Jude's sensibility and his spiritualizing of Sue. Perhaps lines from Shelley's poem should be associated with brief scenes in the first two chapters of the novel. In the deep Marygreen well from which the schoolmaster Phillotson had drawn scores of times, and down which he had often peered at the small, remote, shining disc of water, there may be overtones of

> This truth is that deep well, whence sages draw
> The unenvied light of hope; the eternal law
> By which those live, to whom the world of life
> Is as a garden ravaged . . . .

Hardy's abnormally wide-ranging altruism is attributed to Jude in the second scene; its extension into vivid experience as the boy picks his way carefully among the coupled earthworms may have resulted from Shelley's lines

> The spirit of the worm beneath the sod
> In love and worship, blends itself with God.

Thomas Carlyle was another author Hardy read closely in his formative years as a writer, and it seems probable that, in preparation for a novel which began with educational ambition as its main subject ('short story of a young man – "who could not go to Oxford" – His struggles and ultimate failure. Suicide'), he turned again to Carlyle's disguised account of his rural boyhood and his college recollections in *Sartor Resartus*. For evidence that he did so Jude's illusory impression of Christminster (II.vi) may be referred to; he describes it as 'a unique centre of thought and religion', 'the intellectual and spiritual granary of this country', its 'silence and absence of goings-on' being 'the stillness of infinite motion – the sleep of the spinning-top, to borrow the simile of a well-known writer'. In the third chapter of *Sartor Resartus* the fictitious author refers to the gleams he had seen in the eyes of his genius Teufelsdröckh, half-fancying that 'their stillness was but the rest of infinite motion, the *sleep* of a spinning-top'. It is hardly necessary to state that in a book which proclaims the Everlasting Yea childhood is not presented with the bleak disenchantment of *Jude*; nor, as his autobiographical recollections show, was such disenchantment typical of Hardy's. Yet, even in Teufelsdröckh's early years, a dark ring of Necessity and Care was discernible at times; and in this philosophical respect Carlyle has something in common with the author of the 'predestinate' Jude. The actual opening of the chapter on Teufelsdröckh's 'genesis' may have helped Hardy to one part of his final title: 'Unhappily, indeed, he seems to be of quite obscure extraction.' (As the apostle Jude became the patron of lost causes, a link with Matthew Arnold's Oxford – 'home of lost causes' – follows, and Hardy's title assumes synoptic significance, Jude's story being centred chiefly in Christminster, with all that its name ironically implies.) The homestead of the boyhood which Teufelsdröckh recalls in idyllic terms is associated with hogs on the heath and their swineherd's horn, and this could well have been counter-productive in the swine theme of Jude, from the pig-sty by which the hero lay in his boyhood, wishing never to grow up, to his prescient dread that, if Sue finally leaves him, it will be 'another case of the pig that was washed turning back to his wallowing in the mire'. From the pig scenes with Arabella to her father's Christminster home with its 'miserable little pork and sausage shop', where Jude's drunken mockery of re-marriage is celebrated, sexual animalism, the Venus Pandemos to Sue's Venus Urania (iii.vi), pursues its divisive, degrading, symbolic course.

That a disappointed educational ambition eventually took second place in *Jude* is implicit in the first preface, where Hardy refers to his subject as first 'a deadly war waged between flesh and spirit' and secondly 'the tragedy of unfulfilled aims'. His definition of the principal theme as a war between flesh and spirit recalls Tennyson's summing-up of his *Idylls of the King*, in the epilogue 'To the Queen', as a tale 'New-old, and shadowing Sense at war with Soul'. Hardy's admiration of Tennyson's genius for apt expression and imagery may be gauged from the frequency with which he quotes him in *A Pair of Blue Eyes*. Dr Diana Basham[10] drew my attention to the fact that in October 1892 Hardy attended Tennyson's funeral in Westminster Abbey and visited 'Marygreen', where he entered 'a ploughed vale which might be called the Valley of Brown Melancholy', the 'vast concave' that became the scene of Jude's labours for Mr Troutham, the brown surface rising all round to the sky, 'where it was lost by degrees in the mist'. This conjunction of events, she suggested, might account for the similarities we had both noticed in the presentation of the Jude story and that of Arthur, the embodiment of the ideal in man, who is destined to fail through the fleshly weakness which is allegorized first in the secret love of the Queen and Lancelot, finally in its demoralizing effect on the Knights of the Round Table.

Arthur's city Camelot is first seen at a distance by the young idealist Gareth:

> At times the summit of the high city flashed;
> At times the spires and turrets half-way down
> Pricked through the mist.

He is told by Merlin that the city, the ideal, is built to music, that its building goes on though it can never be built, or achieved. Similar features will be found in Jude's distant prospect of Christminster. He sees points of light like topaz, soon veiled in mist; to him it is the heavenly Jerusalem, where Phillotson lives among the 'mentally shining ones'. A faint musical sound of bells is heard in the wind, telling him 'We are happy here!' There is 'beautiful music everywhere in Christminster', he is informed. Hardy allows little scope for idealism, however; nor can one expect that much of the hope associated with music will be attained in a novel which announces in the opening paragraph that Phillotson had never acquired skill with his piano.

On close inspection, the unfortunate but still hopeful Jude finds that his 'city of lights' is one of low-powered lamps, dark corners, obscure recesses, and decrepit buildings. The Christminster chanting of 'Wherewithal shall a young man cleanse his way?' is too ominously juxtaposed with his recollection of 'animal passion', attempted suicide, and reckless drunkenness; the composer of the proleptic hymn 'The Foot of the Cross', which is to move Jude and Sue at a critical juncture, though she afterwards describes it as a 'morbid Good Friday tune', proves to be a soulless commercialist; the transience of Greek joyousness for Sue and Jude, which is linked with music at the Wessex agricultural show, is foreshadowed in little Father Time's remark on the imminent withering of the flowers; an organist plays the anthem 'Truly God is loving unto Israel' before Sue, distraught at finding her children hanged, recognises that the world is not like 'a stanza or melody composed in a dream'; an organ rehearsal for a concert is heard as the dying Jude calls for water; the joyous throb of a waltz enters through the partly opened window as we see him, laid out straight as an arrow; and again, as on the day of his return to Christminster, bells ring out joyously.

Idylls of the King was written to a seasonal cycle, Arthur being born at the beginning of the year, and dying 'at midnight in midwinter'. Hardy had used this kind of poetic parallelism, particularly in tragedy, from *Desperate Remedies* onwards, but its occurrence in *Jude* is limited to Tennysonian antecedents. Guinevere flees through autumn mists, and the last battle is fought in 'deathwhite' mist. Before these events the Tournament of Dead Innocence is marked by wind, rain, and yellow leaf-fall; it is won by Tristram, a knight whose vows are hollow, and to whose taunts Arthur's loyal fool replies:

Swine? I have wallowed, I have washed – the world
Is flesh and shadow – I have had my day.

Jude's remark on the return of the washed pig to his wallowing in
the mire is remarkably close to this. White fog and rain recur
during his last days; in order to see Sue again he willingly risks
death as he makes his way in driving rain to Marygreen, and again
as he returns over the crest of the down by the Brown House 'in
the teeth of the north-east wind and rain'. Shakespeare's 'the wind
and the rain' had acquired symbolic import for Hardy; he uses this
imagery four times with reference to the doom of Jude and Sue,
and Tennyson uses it to similar effect.

Mrs McFall, an advocate of women's emancipation, made her
reputation as 'Sarah Grand' when her novel *The Heavenly Twins*
was published in 1893. She probably knew the stir it was creating
when she called on the Hardys at 70 Hamilton Terrace on 5 June.
'Reaching home Monday at tea-time who should be sitting in the
drawing-room but the author of *The Heavenly Twins*', Hardy wrote,
with little regard for punctuation and syntax. He read the novel,
as is clear from his letter of 29 June to Mrs Henniker. From
Dorchester in September, when, undoubtedly emboldened by *The
Heavenly Twins*, he was trying to make progress with *Jude*, he told
her she must be in advance of her time to make her mark as a
novelist like Sarah Grand, who did not mind offending her
conventional friends. *The Heavenly Twins* could have influenced
Jude the Obscure in various ways.

The fantastically romantic portion of Sarah Grand's inexpertly
constructed novel concerns those 'signs of the times', the twins
Angelica and Diavolo, a mischievous, questioning pair who develop
modern, almost Shelleyan views, which would have appealed to
Hardy. In a somnolent cathedral city, with seventy-five churches,
they expose the mummery of Catholic superstition at their grandfather's castle. They are thoroughly high-principled but, to escape
boredom after her marriage, her husband being away from home
during parliamentary sessions, Angelica disguises herself as Diavolo for nocturnal outings, meets a new mysterious cathedral
tenor, and forms the habit of visiting him late at night; she is an
expert violinist, and he, a practised oarsman. They make long
excursions by boat into the country; one night she plays as if
inspired, and a 'dead white' mist forms over the low-lying
meadows. She falls into the river, and is rescued and carried

unconscious by the tenor to his rooms in the Close. Not until he has taken off the assumed Diavolo's flannel clothing, wrapped him in warm blankets, and embraced him despairingly, until he feels signs of life, and realizes the immediate need for restoratives, does the tenor light a lamp, when he sees the loosened hanging hair and recognises the lady who is his ideal, his cathedral admirer. This episode must have reminded Hardy of the Close and the college attended by his sisters, near the river at Salisbury, probably suggesting Sue's sensational escape from college confinement by wading through the river, and Jude's more realistic administrations in humbler quarters. Similarities are underscored by Sue's 'quite Voltairean' remarks, and by the feeling Jude shares with the disguised Angelica that a delightful companionship could be continued, if only 'the sense of her sex' could remain obliterated or unawakened.

Evadne, the principal heroine of *The Heavenly Twins*, shows exceptional independence of mind and avidity for knowledge; she disapproves of men's attitudes to women in eighteenth-century novels, and considers Tennyson's Arthur more 'wholesome' than his Lancelot. Aware of the 'heredity of vice', she creates a sensation by leaving her husband at the end of their wedding-service, on receiving information about his dissolute past; eventually she agrees to live with him for the sake of appearances, but not as his wife. She distrusts 'womanly women' like her mother, and believes that if women were more 'particular' in their marriages,[11] men would observe higher moral standards. For this reason her husband insists that she shall not participate in feminist campaigns. Inactivity makes her brood, with morbid consequences. She warns her friend Edith, the bishop's daughter, not to marry a dissipated army officer, but her advice is ignored, and Edith bears a syphilitic child:

> She had no smile for him, and uttered no baby words to him – nor had he a smile for her. He was old, old already, and exhausted with suffering, and as his gaze wandered from [his mother to Angelica], it was easy to believe that he was asking each dumbly why had he ever been born.

To Edith the child is so 'monstrous' she wishes to kill it, and is driven mad. Thinking of her tragedy, the disguised Angelica shakes her fist at the cathedral, saying 'I loathe the deeds of darkness that are done there in the name of the Lord.' Sarah Grand was a fearless intellectual; she quotes from Darwin's letters, and even more significantly from Landor:

> Death is not a blow, is not even a pulsation; it is a pause. But marriage unrolls the awful lot of numberless generations. Health, genius, honour are the words inscribed on some; on others are disease, fatuity and infamy.

Everything suggests that Sarah Grand's description of Edith's child contributed to little Father Time. The fear of catching syphilis and of its hereditary consequences was common, with good reason, even among innocent people; and how much Hardy intended to convey by giving Arabella and Jude's son an octogenarian countenance must be conjectural. Dire warnings against Jude's marrying Sue seem to be restricted to temperamental disqualifications which are assumed to be inherited by both. Little Father Time's doom is attributed to both marriages:

> On that little shape had converged all the inauspiciousness and shadow which had darkened the first union of Jude, and all the accidents, mistakes, fears, errors of the last. He was their nodal point, their focus, their expression in a single term. For the rashness of those parents he had groaned, for their ill-assortment he had quaked, and for the misfortunes of these he had died.

The context of the passage, and the undoubted echo of *Paradise Lost* in 'the rashness of those parents',[12] with its allusion to the theological doctrine that Christ was crucified for the sins brought into the world by Eve and Adam, make it clear that Hardy created Father Time as the fulcrum for a Crucifixion analogue which has its miniature tableau in the three hanging children but continues to the end of the novel. The child bears an incredible burden; at times it is as if 'a ground swell from ancient years of night' lifts him, and his Melpomene face looks back over 'some great Atlantic of Time', appearing 'not to care about what it saw'. One might think he bears the sins of the whole world; Sue's conviction that he and her children died to save her from sin plays a key part in the continuation of the Crucifixion parallel.

Sarah Grand's intrepid condemnation of the Church in upholding the 'sanctity' of disastrous marriages must have encouraged Hardy in *Jude*. The diluted Voltaireanism of her proem to *The Heavenly*

Twins looks forward to an equality of the sexes without which 'the best government of nations has always been crippled and abortive'. All this is related to various interpretations of the Cathedral chime, from Mendelssohn's *Elijah* to the words 'He, watching over Israel, slumbers not, nor sleeps.' The frequent recurrence of this musical motif throughout the novel, with significance according to situation and character, is impressive. It is never more devastatingly ironical than when Edith discovers the perfidy of her husband's sexual past; it recalls Hardy's use of 'Truly God is loving unto Israel'. The general role of music in Sarah Grand's novel could have contributed to one feature in the artistic design of *Jude*, and the theme of the chiming bells and death in the final paragraph of the proem seems to be echoed at the end of Hardy's novel. When it was under way, and he found he had to 'let it come', he could often, whether he was observing his general design or not, have had little awareness of the origins of his minor effects and incidentals. He may have been affected by other fiction, contemporary or earlier, but most probably by none to the same extent as by *The Heavenly Twins*.

12

The Well-Beloved

When Hardy began *The Pursuit of the Well-Beloved*, for serialization, he did not know that within a few years he would abandon novel-writing; such a thought was never implicit in his theme. He did know that the 'withering change' which he had contemplated hypothetically with reference to his first love for Emma in 'Ditty' had occurred to him again and again in succeeding years, and had reached the devastating inception of an uncertain phase. He was at the point when he could both question the wisdom of instituting Christian marriage as a mutual pledge or bond for life, and contemplate with self-mockery the frequency with which he had imagined himself falling in love from his early years, either to find 'utter elusion' a factor for making 'a passing love permanent' or only to be disappointed or disillusioned. 'At Waking', written at Weymouth in 1869, records the extinction of the glamour the poet had seen in the 'prize' life's lottery had brought, when realization of the reality, as the 'dead-white' light of day emerges, inculcates a truth akin to that projected at the end of *The Well-Beloved*. Writing not long afterwards in *Desperate Remedies* on those 'echoes of himself' which Stephen Springrove's impressionable heart had found, Hardy almost certainly had in mind his own experience with men friends (chiefly Horace Moule, one suspects) and young women. As Stephen fails to find 'the indefinable helpmate', he concludes that 'the ideas, or rather emotions' which possess him are probably too unreal ever to be embodied in the flesh of a woman, and turns therefore to the heroines of poetical imagination, till Cytherea appears and his heart speaks:

> 'Tis She, and here
> Lo! I unclothe and clear
> My wishes' cloudy character.[1]

This quotation from Richard Crashaw's 'Wishes' proves that Hardy was already fascinated by the Platonic Idea, the theory to which Shelley subscribed, that the perfect exists only in heaven, and that mortals in their transit from eternity to eternity can in general glimpse its manifestations only dimly at best, 'poets' or creators (including artists and statesmen) being the only persons endowed with the divine faculty of seeing forms of the Ideal beyond the veil. Crashaw imagines the 'not impossible she' as the Divine Idea shining through a shrine of crystal flesh; Hardy sees his Well-Beloved as an incarnation in a fleshly house or tabernacle. He had sketched the story many years before its serialization,

> when I was a comparatively young man, and interested in the Platonic Idea, which, considering its charm and its poetry, one could well wish to be interested in always. . . . There is, of course, underlying the fantasy followed by the visionary artist the truth that all men are pursuing a shadow, the Unattainable, and I venture to hope that this may redeem the tragi-comedy from the charge of frivolity.[2]

The more mature Hardy recognised the absurdity of allowing his imagination to be diverted by erotic idealizations with reference to this person and that. In *The Woodlanders* he had ridiculed the shallow metaphysics of the libertine Fitzpiers and his Shelleyan romanticizing of the Idea. He had also stressed the tragedy of the immature Angel Clare's falling in love with his idealization of Tess. No doubt he had this in mind when he wrote on 28 October 1891, only a few weeks before the publication of *Tess of the d'Urbervilles*,

> It is the incompleteness that is loved, when love is sterling and true. That is what differentiates the real one from the imaginary, the practicable from the impossible, the Love who returns the kiss from the Vision that melts away. A man sees the Diana or the Venus in his Beloved, but what he loves is the difference.

He could have been thinking even more perhaps of *The Pursuit of the Well-Beloved*, the serial he had promised as early as February 1890, and on which he was soon concentrating to the exclusion of all other writing.[3]

Hardy was probably more aware than ever of his idealizing propensity in imaginary love-relations. From 1890 to 1897, when he was trying to achieve a satisfactory final form for his Well-Beloved story, discord and unfulfilment in marriage undoubtedly promoted the indulgence of the dream. On hearing of his cousin

Tryphena's death in March 1890 he was quick to regard her as his 'lost prize'; in 1893 he fell more deeply in love with the young, beautiful, *intuitive* Mrs Henniker. (In 1906, after being reminded of Helen Paterson, the illustrator of the serialized *Far from the Madding Crowd* who had married the poet William Allingham soon after his own wedding in 1874, he could tell Edmund Gosse that 'those two almost simultaneous weddings would have been one but for a stupid blunder of God Almighty'.[4] The inclination could not be curbed; it will be found in a very late poem on Louisa Harding, 'To Louisa in the Lane'. It flourished readily in a mind habituated to narrative creation, and not long before his death, much to the annoyance of his second wife, Hardy began a ballad inspired by Gertrude Bugler, the young Dorset actress who reminded him of her dairymaid mother, the original Tess.)

His task in *The Pursuit of the Well-Beloved* was rendered more difficult by the tragi-comedy of his own position with reference to the theme, and he was so dissatisfied with the result that he wished to rewrite the whole. The hostile reception of *Jude the Obscure* (to which he had wisely translated the anti-matrimonial import of his Well-Beloved story) having caused him to forswear further novel-writing, Hardy's most sustained revision of the serial for publication in novel form as *The Well-Beloved* affected the final chapters. Significantly he emphasized the doom or curse of his hero in being at the mercy of the migratory Idea. His problem was to present the imaginative propensity in an absurd fantasy which keeps in touch with the real without sacrificing psychological probability or allowing personal bias and suffering to upset the balance of an artistic whole. The subject was real enough; in a strange and exaggerated form, it was, as he writes in the preface, the recurrence of 'a delicate dream which in a vaguer form is more or less common to all men, and is by no means new to Platonic philosophers'. (More incidentally *The Well-Beloved* shows that women, as one would expect, are also activated by the dream.)

At least one idea which was basic to his projected novel occurred to Hardy early in 1889, when it seemed to him that 'a fine novel or poem of the passage of Time' could be made out of 'the story of a face which goes through three generations or more', differences of personality being ignored. The idea, he adds, was carried out 'to some extent' in *The Well-Beloved*. However serious his original conception may have been, it is clear that his three-generation subject is treated with considerable light-heartedness in both versions of the narrated story. Hardy's views of heredity could not have differed radically from the perceptions of the lovelorn Jude, who, after losing Sue to Phillotson, and resorting practically and vainly to the indulgence of the superstitious hope that 'the phantom of the Beloved' would appear on Old Midsummer Eve, realizes that his dream of seeing her reproduced in her children, should she die or be estranged from him, is foolish, Nature scorning 'man's finer emotions'. 'The consolation of regarding them as a continuation of her identity was denied to him, as to all such dreamers, by the wilfulness of Nature in not allowing issue from one parent alone', Hardy writes.[5] Normally, therefore, the chances that a mother's 'very image' will be repeated in her only daughter and grand-daughter would not be great in his estimation; the chances that the same man would, at intervals of about twenty years, fall in love with all three in such an astonishing succession would be very remote indeed. Peculiar circumstances are adduced, however, to give an inner probability to his extraordinary story.

To heighten dramatic tension in the early stages, Hardy incorporated the antagonism of a Romeo and Juliet theme which he had thought suitable for a novel entitled *Two Against Time* in March 1884. The remark of a sculptor (Hardy's friend Hamo Thornycroft perhaps) 'that he had often pursued a beautiful ear, nose, chin, &c. about London in omnibuses and on foot' was instrumental not only in defining the hero's role but also in suggesting the all-important link with Portland, that single block of peninsular stone which plays a crucial part in the integration of the plot. Its history and peculiar marriage custom have important influences on the course of Jocelyn Pierston's life. (Although his name is 'Pearston' in the serial, 'Hintock Road', his London address, suggests a relationship – as does his later name – to the Idea-obsessed Fitzpiers of *The Woodlanders*.) No doubt Hardy welcomed the opportunity of staging important scenes in a part of Wessex which otherwise would have been little more than a geographical feature at the time of Napoleon's threatened invasion of England.[6]

Readers' credence being proportional to the prestige of the authors whose support they enlist, some critics have exercised their ingenuity to illustrate the 'stonemason's geometry' which the creative mind of the impressionable Marcel Proust discerned in Hardy's novels. Design and artistic patterning will be found in them in varying degrees, but they do not generally belong to the linear stonemason's geometry which Proust sketchily elaborates in an amalgam of miscellaneous perceptions:

> 'Do you remember the stonemasons in *Jude the Obscure*, in *The Well-Beloved*, the blocks of stone which the father hews out of the island coming in boats to be piled up in the son's studio where they are turned into statues; in *A Pair of Blue Eyes* the parallelism of the tombs, and also the parallel line of the vessel, and the railway coaches containing the lovers and the dead woman; the parallelism between *The Well-Beloved*, where the man is in love with three women, and *A Pair of Blue Eyes* where the woman is in love with three men, and in short all those novels which can be laid one upon another like the vertically piled houses upon the rocky soil of the island?'[7]

The parallelism is more apparent at first in *The Well-Beloved* than elsewhere in Hardy, but it arises from a sensible narrative device to accent the 'young man' in the ageing Pierston ('A Young Man of Twenty', 'A Young Man of Forty', 'A Young Man of Sixty') rather than pursue it through a lifetime at the risk of tediousness. This tripartite parallelism is subordinate to a more subtle design which unifies Hardy's themes, keeps his action moving, builds up suspense, and provides relief or contrast in setting, tone, and presentation. The story is simple in outline, but its full effect depends on the significance of minute particulars which are economically presented in more complicated patterning by a professional artist.

The second part of the novel is considerably more substantial than the first and third. Its heroine, the second of the Avice Caros of three successive generations in whom the Idea or Well-Beloved is incarnated, is rather ordinary, but the most real, enigmatic, and amusing of them, and a contrast to the Marcia Bencomb whose role in the opening Romeo and Juliet theme, and in the emphasis on Time's revenges at the end, is of particular importance in rounding off the story and giving it the 'geometrical shape' to which Hardy refers.

The chief differences between *The Pursuit of the Well-Beloved* and *The Well-Beloved* occur at the beginning and the end. The first opens with a chapter, 'Relics', in which the young London sculptor Pearston begins destroying packets of love-letters from girls in whom he had seen the ideal. As there is not time to destroy all of them before leaving for his native island (the Portland peninsula), he wraps up the remaining packages in his raincoat and straps them compactly together to take with him. At home he continues burning them in the garden; the first Avice joins him, and soon discovers that she, to whom he proposes, is 'only one of many' in a 'long row' of predecessors. Pearston meets Marcia Bencomb as in *The Well-Beloved*; they proceed to London, where they are married. Hardy refers to 'the curse of matrimony' and uses the story to inveigh against an 'ill-matched junction on the strength of a two or three days' passion' and the 'formal tie' which makes their marriage 'a cruelty'. They hear 'sardonic voices and laughter' in the wind at night, and the irascible Marcia, feeling trapped for life, and 'her husband's property', declares nothing more absurd in history than inflexible laws based by grey-headed legislators on 'the ridiculous dream of young people that a transient mutual desire for each other was going to last for ever'. The Well-Beloved is dispelled by the marriage-tie.

Forty years later, to please her ailing mother, the third Avice marries Pearston, who has hopefully assumed that Marcia is dead. He is to discover that her physical reluctance in marriage is due not merely to their disparity in years but to her undying love for a French teacher she had met two or three years earlier at Budmouth. She retires early one evening, and he is left 'musing deeply on many things, not the least being the perception that to wed a woman is by no means the same as to be united with her'. He concludes that 'his wife's corporeal frame' is upstairs, and wonders where her 'spiritual part' lurks. The narrative continues:

At eleven o'clock he ascended also, and softly opened the chamber door. Within he paused a moment. Avice was asleep, and his intent ear caught a sound of a little gasping sigh every now and then between her breathings. When he moved forward his light awoke her; she started up as if from a troublous dream, and regarded him with something in her open eye and large pupils that was not unlike dread. It was so unmistakable that Pearston felt half paralysed, coming, as it did, after thoughts not too reassuring; and, placing his candle on the table, he sat down on the couch at the foot of the bed. All of a sudden he felt that he had no moral right to go further. He had no business there.[8]

The conviction grows in him that, 'whatever the rights with which the civil law had empowered him, by no law of nature, of reason, had he any right to partnership with Avice against her evident will'.

The situation has its more sensational parallel in *Jude the Obscure* when Sue leaps out of the bedroom window in instinctive horror at her husband's unexpected approach late at night. He behaves magnanimously in sacrificing his future for the sake of her freedom, but Hardy's bitterness against the 'trap' of the marriage-tie makes Phillotson a conforming sadist in the end, when Sue's broken spirit forces her to submit to God's will. When Pearston knows how much Avice and Leverre are in love, he reasons that 'healthy natural instinct is true law, and not an act of Parliament', and generously settles a large sum of money on her and any children she may have. How wrong, he feels, 'that there should stand a barrier, hard as the stone isle itself' between the two lovers. His youth and spirit have departed, and he decides not to seek new happiness in exile but to commit suicide. He takes an oarless boat, and thankfully finds himself drifting towards the Race, his 'journey's end'. Voices are heard; there is a sudden crash; a bright light shines over him; and he is rescued by the lightship crew. He recovers consciousness in hospital, where his wife Marcia (the widow Mrs Leverre) helps to nurse him. When daylight reveals that Time has turned his Juno into 'the Witch of Endor' he shakes with agonized laughter. The 'Ho-ho-ho!' of the serial ending suggests Hardy's imbalance rather than Pearston's, as the latter grimly considers 'the grotesqueness of things' to which he has finally been brought by his pursuit of the Well-Beloved. Hardy's anti-matrimonial feelings had led him to a climax too heavily embittered and subversive to consort with the lighter tone of his main theme.

Although his more sustained and intensive campaign in *Jude the Obscure* rendered the propaganda bias of *The Pursuit of the Well-Beloved* superfluous in its revised form, *The Well-Beloved* is not without incidental cynicism on the subject of marriage. 'When you have decided to marry, take the first nice person you meet. They are all alike', says the painter Somers, who marries Mrs Pine-Avon 'in cold blood'. After Pierston has helped him to set up a profitable business, Ike and the second Avice, who 'had made an unhappy marriage for love', reach 'that kind of domestic reconciliation which is so calm and durable, having as its chief ingredient neither hate nor love, but an all-embracing indifference'.[9] The marriage of Marcia and Pierston which brings *The Well-Beloved* to its conclusion is based on affection and the wisdom of experience. They are neither romantically infatuated nor passionately in love with each other, but their friendship offers reasonable assurance that they will live contentedly together. The note on which the novel ends is not sour; it is not pitched in quite the same key as that which ends *Far from the Madding Crowd*, but it reflects a similar authorial outlook.

Pierston's first return to the 'Isle of Slingers' took place more than forty years earlier, the reader in the 1890s is asked to remember. The principal action is set therefore about 1850, 1870, and 1890. Hardy displays little interest in the sociological differentials of the periods; in fact he ascribes to 1870 observations of London society which he made much later. In the first part the railway has reached Budmouth; in the second it has extended to the 'island'. It has helped to accelerate the decline of local ballads in favour of the latest songs purchased at fashionable music-sellers, and has played a part, like education, in the extinction of local differences. Pierston soon perceives that those who brought up the first Avice had aimed 'to get her away mentally as far as possible from her natural and individual life as an inhabitant of a peculiar island', to teach her to forget ancestral customs, discard local speech for 'a governess-tongue of no country at all', and 'make her an exact copy of tens of thousands of other people, in whose circumstances there was nothing special, distinctive, or picturesque'. To all appearance, however, the island remains very much the same during the forty years of the action:

> The silent ships came and went from the wharf, the chisels clinked in the quarries; file after file of whitey-brown horses, in strings of eight or ten, painfully dragged down the hill the square blocks of stone on the antediluvian wooden wheels just as usual. The lightship winked every night from the quicksands to the Beal Lantern, and the Beal Lantern glared through its eye-glass on the ship. The canine gnawing audible on the Pebble-bank had been repeated ever since at each tide, but the pebbles remained undevoured.

Pierston's kinship with the island where 'eternal saws were going to and fro upon eternal blocks of stone' is more durable than any of his other attachments. Although, after being three years and eight months away from home, he looks like what he is, 'a

young man from London and the cities of the Continent', his
urbanism sits upon him 'only as a garment' when he makes his
first return. 'What had been familiar' looks so 'quaint and odd'
that he seems to have returned to the Roman isle of Vindilia and
the home of the ancient slingers. Hardy's stress at the outset on
the remote past of the 'hoary peninsula called an island' is no
accident, for, as he points out in his preface (1912), Pierston, the
fantast (one of 'a strange, visionary race'), is the descendant of 'a
curious and well-nigh distinct people, cherishing strange beliefs
and singular customs, now for the most part obsolescent'. Subject to
the elusive, migratory, idealizing Love which had flitted frequently
'from human shell to human shell' ever since his boyhood, Jocelyn
realizes twenty years later that he is more disposed to be happy in
love with one of his island race:

> The Caros, like some other local families, suggested a Roman
> lineage, more or less grafted on the stock of the Slingers. Their
> features recalled those of the Italian peasantry to any one as
> familiar as he was with them; and there were evidences that the
> Roman colonists had been populous and long-abiding in and
> near this corner of Britain. Tradition urged that a temple to
> Venus once stood at the top of the Roman road leading up to
> the isle;[10] and possibly one to the love-goddess of the Slingers
> antedated this. What so natural as that the true star of his soul
> would be found nowhere but in one of the old island breed?

An island where 'for centuries immemorial' people have regarded
inhabitants of the mainland as foreigners or outsiders ('kimberlins'),
and where the custom has been not to marry until fertility is
proved, suggests greater probability for 'the story of a face which
goes through three generations or more':

> And this concatenated interest could hardly have arisen, even
> with Pierston, but for the conflux of circumstances only possible
> here. The three Avices, the second something like the first, the
> third a glorification of the first, at all events externally, were the
> outcome of the immemorial island customs of intermarriage and
> of prenuptial union, under which conditions the type of feature
> was almost uniform from parent to child through generations:
> so that, till quite latterly, to have seen one native man and

woman was to have seen the whole population of that isolated rock, so nearly cut off from the mainland.[11]

When Jocelyn visits Mrs Caro, the first Avice, a girl of seventeen or eighteen, comes bounding into the room and greets him with an unexpected kiss. Her mother rebukes her for such 'impulsive innocence', and Avice becomes self-conscious and guarded in her relations with Pierston. When he kisses her in the old churchyard at Hope, the 'last local stronghold of the Pagan divinities', where 'Christianity had established herself precariously at best', her response is reserved. She and her mother decide it is prudent for her not to join Jocelyn as he walks to Budmouth on the last evening of his holiday, surmising that his father and he as heir may feel that Island Custom should be observed in their courting, his people being 'such old inhabitants in an unbroken line'. (Although Pierston is surprised at the 'antiquated simplicity' which could assume 'that to be still a grave and operating principle which was a bygone barbarism to himself and other absentees from the island', he believes, when he returns after hearing of Avice's death, that, had she accompanied him that evening, 'the primitive betrothal, with its natural result, would probably have taken place', and she would have become his wife.) Circumstances lead to the embodiment of the Well-Beloved in the Junonian Marcia Bencomb, with whom he travels to London and to whom he proposes marriage. Their stone-merchant fathers are bitter enemies; tactless remarks between 'the son of the Montagues' and 'this daughter of the Capulets' when her father opposes their marriage lead to a quarrel and separation. Marcia returns home with her old-fashioned father, who, assuming that Island Custom has been practised, persuades her to postpone marriage and wait to see whether it proves necessary. Pierston realizes how fortunate he is that Bencomb, in his anxiety to avoid a scandal, did not insist immediately on marriage. Gradually, as he wonders whether Marcia will return to him, he beholds 'the mournful departure of his Well-Beloved from the form he had lately cherished'. The time comes when he hears of Avice Caro's marriage to her cousin, and of the Bencombs' departure for a tour round the world, including a visit to a relative in San Francisco.

Twenty years later, at a London society party, he hears that Avice is dead. He is now an A.R.A. For years the study of beauty has been his 'only joy':

In the streets he would observe a face, or a fraction of a face, which seemed to express to a hair's breadth in mutable flesh what he was at that moment wishing to express in durable shape. He would dodge and follow the owner like a detective; in omnibus, in cab, in steam-boat, through crowds, into shops, churches, theatres, public-houses, and slums – mostly, when at close quarters, to be disappointed for his pains.

After being carried 'at one bound over the hindrances of years' by what seemed a sudden burst of inspiration, he had become engrossed in sculpturing his dream-figures, without allowing 'the gusts of opinion' to deflect him from his inherent bias. His 'whimsical isle-bred fancy' had then returned with unprecedented ardour; the Well-Beloved was always near him, recognisable in the liquid sparkle of an eye, the turn of a head, or in the music of a voice. When his art becomes repetitive and his zest for it declines, he has an impression that the Beloved is re-emerging from the shadows, and that the Goddess behind her, pulling 'the string of that Jumping Jill', is 'punishing him anew for presenting her so deplorably'. In pursuit of the Well-Beloved again, he is dining out in grand company when the fatal message comes. The immediate setting gradually dissolves 'behind the vivid presentiment of Avice Caro, and the old, old scenes on Isle Vindilia which were inseparable from her personality'.
When the ladies have withdrawn, 'the soul of Avice – the only woman he had *never* loved of those who had loved him – surrounded him like a firmament'. Soon he finds that 'he loved the woman dead and inaccessible as he had never loved her in life'. Here, supremely in *The Well-Beloved*, Proust found confirmation of his belief: 'we love only that in which we pursue something inaccessible, we love only what we do not possess'. (Pierston is haunted by ghosts; he has been fated to 'see the creature who has hitherto been perfect, divine, lose under your very gaze the divinity which has informed her', each 'mournful emptied shape' stand ever after 'like the nest of some beautiful bird from which the inhabitant has departed and left it to fill with snow'; and, knowing what to expect, he had 'seldom ventured on close acquaintance with any woman, in fear of prematurely driving away the dear one in her'.)[12]
The depth and purity of the emotion stirred in Pierston by Avice's death convinces him that, 'though she had come short of inspiring a passion', she possessed a 'ground-quality' without

which 'a fixed and full-rounded constancy to a woman could not
flourish in him'. A racial instinct such as they had acquired from
their island ancestry was essential for 'the absolute unison of a
pair'. He refuses to stay in London for the Academy night, attends
her funeral, finds her daughter Avice her very image, and wishes,
despite the uncomfortable recollection that he is forty, that he were
illiterate and unknown, 'wooing, and in a fair way of winning',
her. She is a poor, uneducated, unreflecting and matter-of-fact
laundress; he is a famous and wealthy sculptor, a Royal Academi-
cian.

   Back in London, taking his usual walk by the wharves along the
Thames, he meets the second Avice again; fairer than her mother
in face and form, she appeals more to Pierston, who has misgivings
that the migratory Beloved, 'or rather the capricious Divinity
behind that ideal lady', is about to play a queer trick upon him.
The 'gigantic satire' which makes him concentrate his attention on
this girl, rather than on an accomplished and well-connected
London lady, begins when he decides to rent Sylvania Castle for
another holiday on the island. The young Avice is not in the least
moved by him; absorbed in practicalities, she is 'indifferent to,
almost unconscious of, his propinquity'. 'He was no more than a
statue to her; she was a growing fire to him', and he finds a charm
in her 'rejuvenating power' and the cadences of her voice. The
comicality of the sympathy and assistance he proffers her at the
slightest excuse is underlined by her unfailing commonsense.
Jealously watching her elusive movements about the island, he
discovers that she is his 'antitype'. She has had fifteen lovers
already, and tired of each as soon as they became acquainted. 'Of
course it is really, to *me*, the same one all through, only I can't
catch him!' she tells Pierston; she had, she confessed, loved him
for a week, but found him too old. When her attraction to another
threatens her 'ruin' she tells Jocelyn that she would like to leave
the island, and he has no difficulty in persuading her to join his
establishment in London. He becomes her guardian.

   Unfortunately his servants, not expecting his return, have taken
leave for a short holiday. Avice behaves with her usual decorous
indifference towards him. One evening after dusk he sends her
out for stamps, and his protective anxiety makes him frantic before
she returns quite unperturbed, after seeing a little of fashionable
London and purchasing a mouse-trap. She takes her duties conscientiously, having discovered sooty mice in the kitchen. Hearing

the trap click at night, she gets up to secure her prey; her scream when the mouse escapes brings Pierston to her rescue. So the bathos of the ordinary recurs to heighten the absurdity of his visionary eroticism. He puts his arms around her, and asks her to marry him; 'O, Mr Pierston, what nonsense!' she replies. He discovers that she is already married, and that her husband, Isaac Pierston, had left for Guernsey after quarrelling with her. She doesn't care for him, but their marriage was necessary after they had 'proved each other by island custom'. Jocelyn feels that 'Aphrodite, Ashtaroth, Freyja, or whoever the love-queen of his isle might have been' is punishing him sharply. 'When was it to end – this curse of his heart not ageing while his frame moved naturally onward?' He orders Avice to pack, and restores her to her island home. His return in early winter to meet his namesake from Guernsey by pre-arrangement, and effect a kind of reconciliation by setting him up in business, coincides with the birth of Avice's child. In accordance with his wishes, she is named Avice.

After twenty years' severance from the island, Pierston is in Rome, where he overhears an American talking to a friend about an English widow, Mrs Leverre, whom he had recently met in the Channel Islands. (He had known her and her parents in San Francisco; her father was a rich stone-merchant from the Isle of Slingers; she had married a Jersey gentleman, and has a stepson.) Shortly afterwards Jocelyn receives a letter from the second Avice, informing him that her husband Ike has been killed accidentally in his quarry, that she is ill, and that she would like to see him. In about a week he is back on the island, and discovers that she is now well-off. An anxious tone in the second letter she sends him, asking why his visit is delayed, brings him to her. He finds her in his old home, which Ike had bought. She is but a 'sorry shadow' of her former self, and the vision he had warmly expected has departed. To her he appears unchanged, and this is indeed how he feels. If the tragedy of the situation wears a comical aspect, it reaches a more comical climax. Avice the Third is the 'very she', ladylike, 'finer in figure than her mother or grandmother had ever been'. Pierston falls helplessly in love with her. It is as her mother wishes; determined to do the best for her, she and Ike had sent her to school at Sandbourne; a governess now at Sylvania Castle, she submits to maternal pressure and agrees to marry the ageing Pierston. He thinks it expedient to tell her of his love for her mother and grandmother, only to be asked if he had loved her great-grandmother also.

Circumstances lead to Avice's unpremeditated elopement during the night before her intended wedding with Jocelyn. Her balked love for Mrs Leverre's stepson (both of whom have moved from Jersey to Sandbourne) had been suddenly revived, and they had decided to marry without delay, taking an oarless boat (as Pearston in the serial had done) in the hope that the current would take them to the north of the peninsula, where they would then make for Budmouth to entrain for London. They are miraculously saved when drifting towards the Race. Avice's letter of explanation proves too great a shock to her mother's emotional expectations, and hastens her death. Mrs Leverre calls after receiving a note from her stepson, and Jocelyn recognises in her the Marcia whom he had hoped to marry forty years earlier. They soon discover that the young lovers have been safely conveyed to the mainland. Pierston is the victim of 'one of Time's revenges'; Avice the Third has served him only as he served Avice the First.

The following month he lies ill of a fever in his London house. When he has passed the crisis he discovers that Marcia is helping his nurse, and means to stay until he has recovered. The married lovers have called, and are sorry for what has happened. A few days later Pierston realizes that he is no longer the same: his artistic sense has left him. Marcia calls each day, but always veiled; he assumes she is the 'queenly creature' of old, and in his 'revolt from beauty' tells her he wishes she were not handsome. He must allow for lamplight and the beautifying artifices in which she is skilled, she answers; tomorrow, in daylight, he will see the effects of Time. She appears, 'the image and superscription of Age – an old woman, pale and shrivelled, her forehead ploughed, her cheek hollow, her hair white as snow'.

When Jocelyn sees Avice the Third his 'curse' returns, and, 'in the phrase of the islanders', he is urged on again, at the age of sixty-one, 'like a blind ram'. It is as if the new moon, to whom he had often 'bowed the knee', is casting her spell on him. At this point Hardy sees a parallel between his hero's idea of a migratory Well-Beloved and the inconstancy of Shelley's moon: 'ever changing, like a joyless eye That finds no object worth its constancy'. Pierston's worship of it, and its appearances in the narrative suggest its association with 'the love-queen of his isle'. He had hoped to walk with the first Avice to Henry the Eighth's Castle, where they could watch the moon rise over the sea. Lulled into a nap while watching her grave shortly after her funeral, he seems to see her bending over and then withdrawing from it 'in the light of the moon'; he soon discovers that the girl he 'had fancied to be the illusion of a dream' is Avice the Second. When he enters Henry the Eighth's Castle with Avice the Third, thinking of the meeting that might have taken place with her grandmother and 'changed the whole current of his life', the full moon streams down upon them. The island looks sullen in the evening gloom when he returns to marry her. Avice looks up into the light of the full moon as she expects to elope, but, after he has lost her, he sits in growing darkness beside her mother's corpse. He cannot bear light during the chill and fever which keeps him 'swaying for weeks between life and death', and only after a period of artificial light does he recover, being released from 'the curse' into the light of day or the reality of time.

Pierston loses his artistic sense with the removal of the curse, which is implicit in the 'One shape of many names' and effectively synonymous with the Alastor of the poem in which Shelley's poet, as a result of a vision of the Ideal, is driven to his doom, after seeking in vain 'a prototype of his conception'.[13] Jocelyn has deliberately sought the migratory Idea in London society, particularly (for Hardy's narrative purposes) in the designing Mrs Pine-Avon. For this section of the novel Hardy consulted notes made in anticipation of contingencies which might compel him to write stories of 'modern artificial life and manners'. The satirical account of rather empty party-political chatter, animated solely by 'a blunt and jolly personalism as to the Ins and Outs' (ii.i) is based on notes of 19 July 1891. Lord and Lady Portsmouth may have suggested the Channelcliffes (the name, at least); observations made at Lady Carnarvon's on 16 May and 14 June 1887 show that Lady Mabella Buttermead, 'who appeared in a cloud of muslin, and was going to a ball' (ii.i), and Mrs Pine-Avon's 'round, inquiring, luminous' eyes (ii.ii), were derived from Lady Marge W—— and the prettiest of all Lady Portsmouth's daughters. Ellen Terry, whom Hardy saw at Lady Jeune's in January 1891 appears as

a leading actress of the town – indeed, of the United Kingdom and America, for that matter – a creature in airy clothing, translucent, like a balsam or sea-anemone, without shadows, and in movement as responsive as some highly lubricated, many-wired machine, which, if one presses a particular spring, flies open and reveals its works. The spring in the present case was the artistic commendation she deserved – and craved.[14]

The description highlights the artificiality of a society which contrasts with the reality found by Pierston in the Isle of Slingers and his natural kinship with the Caros.

As the 'Protean dream-creature' Pierston pursues is 'a subjective phenomenon vivified by the weird influences of his descent and birthplace', the island integrates the novel. Its hereditary influences and customs rule both his destiny and Marcia's. It had instigated his first use of the chisel in sculpturing. He loves to see white blocks of stone transported to Thames-side wharves after being 'nibbled' from his father's quarry, and he is reminded of the island's quarries by the ruins of Rome. As could be expected of a sculptor, he is most sensitive, when incarnations of the Beloved appear, to form and outline (the 'line and curve' of a body, the 'curve of sound' – in a voice – 'as artistic as any line of beauty ever struck by the pencil'). The underdevelopment of his colour-sense is due as much to the island background of his youth as to his profession: until elms were planted near the site of Sylvania Castle his Channel rock was treeless; it glistens white in the 'colourless sunlight' of summer. Saws seem to work eternally on blocks of stone, while the passage of Time is registered year in, year out, by the tink-tink of chisels in the quarries, which recall Hardy's poem of 1890 'In a Eweleaze near Weatherbury':

> Yet I note the little chisel
> Of never-napping Time
> Defacing wan and grizzel
> The blazon of my prime.

The ageing in Marcia's face which contributes signally to the conclusion of the novel makes its memorable impact through the expression of its human and natural causes in terms of the rock's perennial operations: raspings and chisellings on the one hand, scourges of wind and rain, and extremes of heat and cold.

The effect of time on character is marked. The Marcia who nurses and marries Pierston is not the rather haughty, quick-tempered young woman who left her father angrily at the beginning of the novel. Pierston becomes less the self-seeker and less carefree;

he develops a greater sense of responsibility towards others. Strengthened by regard for her mother and grandmother, his love for Avice the Third is imbued with 'the tenderest, most anxious, most protective instinct' he has ever known.

> Once the individual had been nothing more to him than the temporary abiding-place of the typical or ideal; now his heart showed its bent to be a growing fidelity to the specimen, with all her pathetic flaws of detail; which flaws, so far from sending him further, increased his tenderness. This maturer feeling, if finer and higher, was less convenient than the old. Ardours of passion could be felt as in youth without the recuperative intervals which had accompanied evanescence.

Ardours of passion are spent in the end, but the finer qualities remain.

Pierston's artistic sense is not snuffed out suddenly. He loves the third Avice 'more and more tenderly', but his confidence in their approaching marriage is being undermined, and, as he looks round his 'large and ambitious' studio, 'now being clouded with shades', the countenances of his figures look 'white and cadaverous' (III.v).

> They had never looked like that while standing in his past homely workshop, where all the real labours of his life had been carried out. What should a man of his age, who had not for years done anything to speak of – certainly not to add to his reputation as an artist – want with a new place like this? It was all because of the elect lady, and she apparently did not want him.

Creativity in art is related to ardour for life and the passion for fulfilment in marriage.

The last quotation indicates the danger of reading autobiography in The Well-Beloved as far as artistic creation is concerned. The novel undoubtedly contains glimpses of Hardy, and almost certainly his thoughts on his cousin Tryphena after her death.[15] The peony cheeks of Marcia and 'the Junonian quality of her form and manner' may recall Emma Gifford, but there can be little resemblance between the aged Marcia whom Jocelyn marries and the Emma Hardy who created the discords which were ultimately responsible for the anti-matrimonialism of *The Pursuit of the Well-Beloved* and *Jude the Obscure*.

Pierston's 'bondage to beauty in the ideal' had made him an extraordinary flirt, and more; but there had been nothing dishonourable in his aims or conduct, as Hardy takes pains to stress (more in *The Well-Beloved* than in the serial):

> Nobody would ever know the truth about him; *what* it was he had sought that had so eluded, tantalized, and escaped him; what it was that had led him such a dance, and had at last, as he believed just now in the freshness of his loss, been discovered in the girl who had left him. It was not the flesh; he had never knelt low to that. Not a woman in the world had been wrecked by him, though he had been impassioned by so many. Nobody would guess the further sentiment – the cordial loving-kindness – which had lain behind what seemed to him the enraptured fulfilment of a pleasing destiny postponed for forty years. His attraction to the third Avice would be regarded by the world as the selfish designs of an elderly man on a maid.

The Island Custom imaginings of Marcia's father, with reference to her apparent elopement with Pierston, have been carelessly read as authorial; and some Victorian readers may have agreed with the reviewer in *The World* who stigmatized the novel as sexual and disgusting. Hardy dubbed him 'that Lampsacenian scribbler', and thought his review must have produced 'the amazed risibility' he remembered feeling in his youth at Wilding's assertions in a performance of Foote's comedy *The Liar*. 'There is more fleshliness in *The Loves of the Triangles*' than in the 'phantasmal narrative of the adventures of a Visionary Artist in pursuit of the unattainable Perfect in female form – a man repeatedly stated to be singularly free from animalism', he wrote.[16] Such unexpected absurdity of interpretation must have confirmed his rightness of judgment in renouncing the novel for forms of serious literature which, because they were decidedly less popular, were less liable to attack from Grundyan alarmists.

13

Fictional Autobiography

Ultimately, it may be claimed that the whole creative world of an author's fiction is autobiographical, the record of experience through which he has lived. A valid and sensible distinction may be drawn, however, between the outer world of his experience, the source of his impressions (human and sensory, meditative and philosophical), and the world which he conceives in fiction. Some writers (obviously) depend much more on their lives and experience than others. This dependence may be rather prosaic or photographic, as in the settings of Arnold Bennett; it may result basically in the act of creative recollection, as it does largely in Proust; it may be directed by little more than autobiographical memory, as in the second part of Lawrence's *Mr Noon*. However imaginatively rendered, Lawrence's obsessively self-centred, inchoate and evolutionary, thought-processes figure prominently in his novels; he makes much also of settings which he knew intimately, from Nottinghamshire to Australia, or from Alpine Italy to New Mexico. A writer such as Sterne allows situations and thoughts to drift into dream fantasies that satisfy his imagination.

Hardy's fiction is inventive rather than subjective. When he has a particular landscape in mind, he does not reproduce it for its own sake as Lawrence frequently does; he does not use it to communicate his own feelings, as T. S. Eliot alleged in *After Strange Gods*; it is a re-creation in the light or gloom of an imaginative context. He repeatedly shows that he has the power to create pictorial settings which harmonize with, or comment ironically on, the emotional situations of leading characters. He is not a copyist. His voyage to Plymouth on the *Avoca* supplied some interesting environmental details to illustrate the progress of the steam packet-boat in *A Pair of Blue Eyes*, but they are merely incidental to the reawakening of Elfride's dread that Mrs Jethway's knowledge of her past will wreck her happiness with Knight; Hardy's own experience has been utilized impersonally for the artistic furtherance of an imaginary story. In *The Mayor of Casterbridge* artistic selectivity has precluded detailed or lengthy descriptions of

187

Dorchester, the original of Casterbridge. With rare and incidental
exceptions, Hardy presents only those features, considerably adapted at times for the purpose of the story, which are important in
the development and overtones of his novel. He could rightly
claim, when awarded the freedom of Dorchester in 1910, that,
though not altogether 'a dream-place that never was outside an
irresponsible book', his Casterbridge 'is not a photograph in words,
that inartistic species of literary produce' ('particularly in respect
of personages', he adds). The same could be said of Christminster
in *Jude the Obscure*. Hardy not only selected to give precedence to
the full implications of his story; he modified to impart tone,
colour, and emphasis to his theme. Some writers of fiction such as
Barbara Pym seem to have difficulty in writing beyond the particular
environments of their own experience. Her novels show a bias
towards certain types of character, and the thoughts of her
principals are frequently her own. Hardy is much less circumscribed; his characters are diverse; their development is linked with
changing fictional circumstance. Gabriel Oak and Henchard, Lady
Constantine, Elizabeth-Jane, Tess Durbeyfield, and Sue Bridehead,
all unmistakably different, are almost wholly figments of imaginative creation, like the best of Shakespeare's heroes and heroines
(though not to the same degree, being more related to the
ordinariness of life – which does not exclude extraordinary events).

Autobiographical elements which are consciously drawn from
Hardy's own life do not constitute a large part of his fiction. They
are usually brief and incidental, contributing little significantly to
large-scale movements. In describing how Thomasin crosses the
heath in darkness, and lifts her baby to the top of her head
to protect it from the drenched fronds of the bracken, Hardy
remembered the early childhood experience which he describes in
the last of the 'In Tenebris' poems, when he was benighted with
his mother 'in the midmost of Egdon' and had complete confidence
in her 'watching and ward' as she 'upheld' him (held him up high)
to cope with the heather. He adapts and transfers one of his
juvenile fears to the boy Jude: just as he, while evening darkened
as he was walking home from school and reading *The Pilgrim's
Progress*, was so alarmed by Bunyan's description of Apollyon that
he closed the book and continued his way, terrified at the thought
that the hideous monster might spring out of a tree whose branches
overhung the road, so Jude, as darkness deepens, almost suddenly
extinguishing the distant Christminster lights, and making objects

in the foreground below assume 'hues and shapes of chimaeras';
anxiously descends from the Brown House roof, and runs home-
ward,

> trying not to think of giants, Herne the Hunter, Apollyon lying
> in wait for Christian, or of the captain with the bleeding hole in
> his forehead and the corpses round him that remutinied every
> night on board the bewitched ship.[1]

Hardy read about Herne the Hunter in his adolescence, and it might
be claimed that this reference and the third are autobiographical, but
the subject of fictional autobiography must for all practical purposes
be limited to fictional items in which the author knowingly
revives, or deliberately harks back to, experiences, thoughts, and
associations in his own life. Mere references in the course of
writing, and images (such as those in Hardy from *Robinson Crusoe*)
which serve to give more vivid or exact impressions, are clearly
drawn from recollections of some kind or other. The same applies
to Hardy's architectural terms (both literal and figurative), his use
of paintings to create visual effects (Mr Penny framed in his
window like a shoemaker by 'some modern Moroni'), and all those
references to dances, songs, and sacred music which are found in
his works.

An example of autobiographical literary transference occurs early
in *Jude the Obscure*, when the youthful hero in a burst of euphoria
becomes confident of admission to Christminster, and even aspires
to D.D. status. In this mood he makes a retrospective survey of
his preparatory studies, with special reference to the *Iliad*, of which
he has read two books, 'besides being pretty familiar with passages
such as the speech of Phoenix in the ninth book, the fight of Hector
and Ajax in the fourteenth, the appearance of Achilles unarmed
and his heavenly armour in the eighteenth, and the funeral games
in the twenty-third'. These in fact were the favourite passages
which Hardy listed in the copy of the *Iliad* which he acquired in
1858 (subjoined is the note: 'Left off, Bockhampton 1860'). The
greater facility with Latin which enabled Jude 'to beguile his lonely
walks by imaginary conversations therein' was prompted by
Hardy's recollection of an adolescent familiarity with several books
of the *Aeneid*, and of poems by Horace and Ovid, which led to his
'soliloquizing in Latin on his various projects' in his walks to and
from Dorchester.[2]

An earlier Hardy experience which he used to say stood out more distinctly than any other of its period, and which, he remembered with regret, had reflected a disappointing lack of ambition to his mother when he communicated it to her, was adapted to Jude's state of mind, after his drubbing by Farmer Troutham for being too kind-hearted to the birds he had been hired to scare off a field of newly sown corn. Recalling the original experience, Hardy writes:

> He was lying on his back in the sun, thinking how useless he was, and covered his face with his straw hat. The sun's rays streamed through the interstices of the straw, the lining having disappeared. Reflecting on his experience of the world so far as he had got, he came to the conclusion that he did not wish to grow up. Other boys were always talking of when they would be men; he did not want at all to be a man, or to possess things, but to remain as he was, in the same spot, and to know no more people than he already knew (about half a dozen).

In *Jude* the associations are different. Pig and fog imagery anticipate the main themes of the novel, which relate to marriage as a result of sexual seduction, and the unenlightenment of the Church over the human bondage which follows. The child's painful realization that the survival of one species depends on cruelty to another foreshadows the Darwinian struggle and 'logic' of the living world. The result for Jude is the same as it had been for Hardy in happier circumstances: 'If he could only prevent himself growing up! He did not want to be a man.'[3] Whether Hardy's late poem 'Childhood Among the Ferns' is more exact or more imaginary in its setting must remain conjectural. It records the same thought, the same instinctive disinclination to participate determinedly in worldly competitiveness:

> 'Why should I have to grow to man's estate,
> And this afar-noised World perambulate?'

Jude's early discovery of 'the defects of natural laws' may throw light on Hardy's dictum with reference to Clym Yeobright: 'What the Greeks only suspected we know well; what their Aeschylus imagined our nursery children feel.' Such a generalization on the feeling or insight of children is probably based on Hardy's early disinclination to grow up, and confirmation of this seems to come when he writes a little later of Yeobright's precocious talents and scholarship. The statement that 'At seven he painted the Battle of Waterloo with tiger-lily pollen and black-currant juice, in the absence of water-colours', seems too specific to be imaginary. It may recall a boyhood attempt by Hardy (not necessarily at the same age), after being stimulated by his grandfather's pictorial edition of Gifford's history of the Napoleonic wars, to express in home-manufactured colours a climactic battle which continually made its appeal to his imagination until, late in life after much historical research, he could present it in all its phases towards the end of *The Dynasts*.[4]

At home and in its neighbourhood Hardy in his early years heard many local stories and traditions. To what extent they entered his fiction it is impossible to assess. They may be the subject of biographical surmise, but they are no more autobiographical than narrative features or descriptions incorporated in novels from an author's reading. The nearest Hardy comes to autobiography in this respect is in the preface to *Wessex Tales*, where the 'aged friend' who related the weird episode from which 'The Withered Arm' grew was his mother, the source of the majority of superstitions in his fiction, most of them endemic to the region of her childhood, the country of *The Woodlanders*. The climax of the tale depends on the hanging of a youth because he was present by chance when a rick was fired during the period of rioting and incendiarism by agricultural labourers after the Napoleonic war. The account of this (some of the circumstantial detail of which he included in 'The Winters and the Palmleys') was one which drove the 'tragedy of Life' more deeply into Hardy's mind than any other he heard from his father.[5]

Narrative elements in Hardy may have been indirectly inherited from his grandfather, whose widow remained at Higher Bockhampton, living with Hardy's parents until her death in his seventeenth year. She could remember hearing the news of Louis XVI's execution and of the reign of terror during the French Revolution; she remembered also defensive preparations in the south of England when the Napoleonic invasion was expected, and the beacon alarm on Rainbarrow when a landing was falsely reported (an event Hardy put to good account in *The Trumpet-Major* and 'The Alarm'). He listened excitedly to such stories from his 'gentle, kindly grandmother', who confided in him poignant memories of her life at Fawley in Berkshire during her first thirteen years as an orphan child.[6] He may have remembered her in depicting Mrs Martin, Swithin's aged grandmother in *Two on a Tower*, and probably had her in mind in describing how she 'went straight back into [her] old county again, as usual' when taking a nap:

> 'The place was as natural as when I left it, – e'en just three-score years ago! All the folks and my old aunt were there, as when I was a child, – yet I suppose if I were really to set out and go there, hardly a soul would be left alive to say to me, dog how art!'

Perhaps Hardy's grandmother brought this quaint dialectal greeting (which occurs nowhere else in his works) from her 'old county'; perhaps too the impression he formed of her 'old aunt' played a part in the portraiture of Drusilla Fawley, the great-aunt to whom Jude was sent from Mellstock. Hardy's grandmother, thinking the passage concerned a disobedient woman, may have referred to the verse in Deuteronomy (introduced by the thought of old age and infirmity) which begins 'In the morning thou shalt say, Would God it were even! and at even thou shalt say, Would God it were morning!' Age had probably brought such thoughts to Mrs Martin, who assumes that they would be uttered by Lady Constantine in her loneliness. Lines in Swinburne's 'A Ballad of Burdens', which Hardy read in 1866, may have strengthened (or created) this link:

> The burden of long living. Thou shalt fear
>   Waking, and sleeping mourn upon thy bed;
> And say at night 'Would God the day were here',
>   And say at dawn 'Would God the day were dead'.[7]

Recollections of Dorchester when Hardy was a boy may be found in *The Mayor of Casterbridge*, but the town had not changed greatly when the novel was written, and most of Elizabeth-Jane's market-day observations in the High Street as she made her way with her mother's message to Henchard were no other than Hardy's in the early 1880s when he lived in Dorchester. The action of the novel at this juncture coincides with the period when he attended Mr Last's private school off South Street. After describing how, despite feeble constabulary protest, shopkeepers continued to exhibit their wares across the pavements and into the street, leaving only 'a tortuous defile' for passing carriages, Hardy includes a short paragraph where the autobiographical, the remembered experience, imparts life and humour to what has merely been observed:

Horses for sale were tied in rows, their forelegs on the pavement, their hind legs in the street, in which position they occasionally nipped little boys by the shoulder who were passing to school. And any inviting recess in front of a house that had been modestly kept back from the general line was utilized by pig-dealers as a pen for their stock.

One cannot help feeling that, even if the schoolboy Hardy had escaped being nipped by a horse on such an occasion, he had seen for himself or heard from other boys' accounts the risk run by the unwary.

New life was brought to music in Dorchester by the Scots Greys in the early 1850s, before they left for the Crimea. Their splendid band attracted large crowds from town and country at open-air performances on Sunday afternoons, and they were so popular that they gave a number of concerts in the Town Hall on Thursday afternoons. It seems improbable that Hardy and other members of his family failed to hear them once at least. Their playing of 'The Dead March' in Handel's *Saul* at the funeral of a 'comrade' created 'a profound sensation'. Hardy refers to it in both his early and his latest fiction, first in *Under the Greenwood Tree* (where, in an earlier period, Mr Penny was 'moved in soul' by it), then in 'Enter a Dragoon', where due military honours are paid to John Clark (who had fought in the Crimean War) by their 'fine reed and brass band' in their 'slow and dramatic march through the town to the tune from *Saul*'. This recollection, as late as 1899, suggests that Hardy's memory had been sustained by a stirring experience.

The mural monument below which Hardy sat with his family in Stinsford Church suggested, in the opening chapter of 'An Indiscretion in the Life of an Heiress', a grander design, which

consisted of a winged skull and two cherubim, supporting a pair of tall Corinthian columns, between which spread a broad slab, containing the roll of ancient names, lineages, and deeds, and surmounted by a pediment, with the crest of the family at its apex.

Another memory, of the congregation swaying like trees as they sing 'the evening hymn', is supplied by the opening sentence of the same story, a tragic romance contrived largely from those portions of Hardy's unpublished first novel, *The Poor Man and the Lady*, which had not been included or adapted in his early novels. The occurrence of the same scene in the first of these, *Desperate Remedies*, at a point (xii.8) when the heroine Cytherea fears she is doomed to marry Manston, confirms the probability that it was drawn from the text of *The Poor Man and the Lady*. The congregation at the afternoon service are singing 'the Evening Hymn' (Bishop Ken's 'Glory to Thee, my God, this night'), and Cytherea, as Hardy had done at Stinsford, 'looked at all the people as they stood and sang, waving backwards and forwards like a forest of pines swayed by a gentle breeze'. The attendant imagery is the same as in 'An Indiscretion': the children listlessly trace some crack in the old walls of the church, or follow through the window the movement of a distant bird or bough. The poem 'Afternoon Service at Mellstock' ('Circa 1850', Hardy adds), which was written probably more than forty years later, sets the seal to the autobiographical authenticity of this detail, and affirms the irresistible appeal which the tree imagery retained for its author:

> We watched the elms, we watched the rooks,
>   The clouds upon the breeze,
> Between the whiles of glancing at our books,
>   And swaying like the trees.
>
> So mindless were those outpourings! –
>   Though I am not aware
> That I have gained by subtle thought on things
>   Since we stood psalming there.

Hardy refers to his choirboy days at Stinsford –

> When I was full of wonder, and innocent,
> Standing meek-eyed with those of choric bent,
>   While dimming day grew dimmer
>   In the pulpit-glimmer

– in 'Apostrophe to an Old Psalm Tune'. He recalls it on 'Sunday, August 13, 1916', in 'these turmoiled years of belligerent fire', after hearing the new version, modified years earlier by 'Monk, or another'. There is enough coincidence in the two opening chapters of *A Laodicean* to suggest that they not only reveal the tune but convey the author's own regrets at its passing. It is August when the young architect George Somerset hears 'notes of a familiar hymn, rising in subdued harmonies from a valley below. . . . It was his old friend the "New Sabbath", which he had never once heard since the lisping days of childhood.' Why it had disappeared from all the cathedrals and churches he had known in the meantime 'he could not, at first, say':

> But then he recollected that the tune appertained to the old west-gallery period of church-music, anterior to the great choral reformation and the rule of Monk – that old time when the repetition of a word, or half-line of a verse, was not considered a disgrace to an ecclesiastical choir.

Somerset approaches, and finds that the tune comes from a Baptist chapel. He listens as the New Sabbath proceeds 'line by line, with all the emotional swells and cadences that had of old characterized the tune', and regrets that 'his once favourite air', 'the best in psalm-tunes', had 'gone over to the Dissenters'. All this illuminates Hardy's comment on the tunes sung to the 'Tate-and-Brady' metrical psalms at Stinsford when he was young (and he remembers the 'staple ones', the Old Hundredth, New Sabbath, Devizes, Wilton, Lydia, and Cambridge New): 'upon [which], in truth, the modern hymn-book has been no great improvement'. The context shows,[8] like all the references to the New Sabbath in *A Laodicean*, that he is thinking of both words and tunes.

Whether Hardy attended the celebrations which took place on 30 June 1856 to commemorate the end of the Crimean War and the anniversary of Queen Victoria's birthday is uncertain. His reference in *The Mayor of Casterbridge* to the sports which took place then on Poundbury are so briefly factual that they could have been taken from a programme of events or newspaper in the County Museum library. Less than two weeks later he attended Cooke's Circus in Dorchester, and saw, as he told Rebekah Owen in 1893, Dick Turpin's ride and the death of Black Bess enacted. The dramatic clarity with which this is reproduced in *Far from the Madding Crowd*, even to the carrying out of the gallant horse on a shutter by twelve eager volunteers from the spectators, suggests the re-creation of vividly remembered experience.[9]

Hardy recalled studying 'the *Iliad*, the *Aeneid*, or the Greek
Testament from six to eight in the morning', working at Gothic
architecture all day for John Hicks, and then rushing off in the
evening 'with his fiddle under his arm, sometimes in the company
of his father as first violin and uncle as 'cellist, to play country-
dances, reels, and hornpipes at an agriculturist's wedding, christen-
ing, or Christmas party in a remote dwelling among the fallow
fields, not returning sometimes until nearly dawn'. He must have
remembered details from some of these occasions when he wrote
the opening section of 'The Three Strangers', where, in the boy
'about twelve years of age, who had a wonderful dexterity in jigs
and reels', he recalls the difficulties he used to have when 'his
fingers were so small and short as to necessitate a constant shifting
for the high notes, from which he scrambled back to the first
position with sounds not of unmixed purity of tone'. The writer's
observation on the assembled company conveys the disposition of
his matured sympathies: the majority show a 'princely serenity'
which arises from 'the absence of any expression or trait denoting
that they wished to get on in the world, enlarge their minds, or
do any eclipsing thing whatever – which nowadays so generally
nips the bloom and *bonhomie* of all except the two extremes of the
social scale'. No doubt Hardy's observations at dances where he
had played, and elsewhere, contributed to the dancing and lively
remarks at the tranter's in *Under the Greenwood Tree*. Hardy's
assertion late in life that there was 'no family portrait in the tale'
indicates that readers have always been unguardedly prone to find
too much autobiographical reminiscence in these scenes. The
hipped thatched roof recalls the Hardy cottage at Higher Bockhampton, but no room there was ever large enough to accommodate the dancing and its observers. For these Hardy relied on a
variety of sources, not least the imaginative. His knowledge of the
subject was too great to keep him diffidently tied down to
actual recollections, which were too ordinary and repetitive in the
aggregate for the kind of fiction he wished to create.

The occurrence in *Desperate Remedies* (xv.2) of a recollection from
the Hardy home at Higher Bockhampton seems to be confirmed
by the repetition of part of its imagery in *Under the Greenwood Tree*.
Springrove sits by the fire, looking up at the illuminated darkness
of the chimney, 'where long flakes of soot floated from the sides
and bars . . . like tattered banners in ancient aisles'; seeing two

bright stars in 'the grey March sky' framed by the square opening above seems to cheer him up. Within a similarly spacious fireplace in the second novel, wooden poles have been fixed overhead for the hanging of bacon, and these are 'cloaked with long shreds of soot, floating on the draught like the tattered banners on the walls of ancient aisles'.

The refusal of the heroine in *A Laodicean* to proceed with the baptismal immersion for which she had been prepared, at the service which has drawn Somerset's attention to the Baptist chapel, leads to his challenging the minister Mr Woodwell, who has denounced her Laodicean lukewarmness from the pulpit. He argues learnedly in favour of paedobaptism, a subject familiar to Hardy from arguments which began with his fellow-pupil at the architect Hicks's in Dorchester. This was Henry Robert Bastow, a year or more Hardy's senior, and a Baptist who had become 'very doctrinal' on the subject of adult baptism, at a time when he had resolved on his own re-baptism. So zealous and persuasive was he that Hardy, who 'had been brought up in High Church principles' like Somerset, 'almost felt that he ought to be baptized again'. He obtained what arguments he could from books on paedobaptism, but when Bastow's friends, two sons of the Dorchester Baptist minister Mr Perkins, both 'fresh from Aberdeen University', joined in the controversy, he had to work late at night on his Greek Testament in order to confute his three opponents. For this purpose he bought a copy of Griesbach's edition in February 1860. He must have kept the references he accumulated on the subject, and used them in the case for paedobaptism put forward then and there by Somerset. How it happened that the latter was well prepared is explained: his parents at one time had entertained the idea of his entering the Church (as Hardy's must have done for a while in 1865); he had been acquainted with 'men of almost every variety of doctrinal practice in this country'; and his professional interest in the design of fonts had led him 'to investigate the history of baptism'. The result is ready reference to a series of New Testament quotations, and even more to authorities within the Apostolic tradition, which the author, out of regard for the reader, summarizes in a single paragraph. Hardy admitted that the Baptist minister was one of 'the few portraits of actual persons' in his novels, 'being a recognizable drawing of Perkins the father' as he appeared at the time of the debate which Bastow's zeal for adult baptism had initiated.[10]

Isaac Watts's popular hymn 'O God, our help in ages past' must have been heard by Hardy in several churches by the time he was a young man. It contains the familiar lines

> Time, like an ever-rolling stream,
> Bears all its sons away.

The thought is intrinsic to settings in *Desperate Remedies* and *The Trumpet-Major*. Proverbially associated with a bridge, its occurrence to Hardy as he watched the stream below Grey's Bridge just outside Dorchester can be inferred from a scene in *Under the Greenwood Tree*, where, just after hearing from Dick Dewy that he is engaged to marry Fancy Day next Midsummer, and agreeing that 'the time will soon slip along – Time glides away every day – yes', Mr Maybold, realizing her true attachment, leans over the parapet of Grey's Bridge, watches the gliding water, then tears into tiny fragments the letter he had written to a friend in Yorkshire on the exchange of livings which he had contemplated on marrying her, and sees 'the whole handful of shreds' carried out of sight by the stream.[11]

Before he left home for London in April 1862, 'to pursue the art and science of architecture on more advanced lines', Hardy may not have found his apprenticeship work with John Hicks very arduous or demanding, especially in his earliest years. Such may be the implication of the comments made in *Desperate Remedies* (i.5) on the insignificant progress made in 'the art and science of architecture' by Owen Graye during a shorter period:

> Though anything but an idle young man, he had hardly reached the age at which industrious men who lack an external whip to send them on in the world, are induced by their own common sense to whip on themselves. Hence his knowledge of plans, elevations, sections, and specifications, was not greater at the end of two years of probation than might easily have been acquired in six months by a youth of average ability – himself, for instance – amid a bustling London practice.

'An Indiscretion in the Life of an Heiress' includes an incident which Hardy remembered from the laying of the memorial stone, for the church he had helped to design at New Windsor, by the Crown Princess of Germany on 21 November 1863. Finding her glove daubed with mortar, she returned the trowel with its smeared handle to Arthur Blomfield, Hardy's London employer, impatiently whispering 'Take it, take it!', as Geraldine does when laying the foundation stone of 'a tower or beacon which her father was about to erect on the highest hill of his estate'. Hardy draws considerably from his architectural knowledge in *A Laodicean*, but there is no evidence to indicate that the story recalls any of his architectural experiences. When he told William Lyon Phelps that his novel 'contained more of the facts of his own life than anything else he had ever written', he must have been thinking chiefly of the liberal use he made of records and reminiscences of holiday tours with Emma in western Europe to fill its later pages with background when hero and heroine pursue each other until all ends well. In attaching more importance to 'poetry, theology, and the reorganization of society', the architect George Somerset resembles the young Hardy. For two years both wrote verse which was not 'jumped at by the publishers'; Hardy's 'passion for reforming the world' was very evident in *The Poor Man and the Lady*; and for years he studied to enter the Church. One small episode in *A Laodicean* had its origin in the thunderstorm that spoilt the garden party which Emma and Hardy attended at Mrs Macmillan's in 1879, but how far this occasion contributed otherwise, in scenic detail or event, is uncertain.[12]

One of Hardy's experiences led to a remarkable scene in *The Hand of Ethelberta*, after the heroine decides to visit the country estate of her suitor Neigh one evening. The account was suggested by what Hardy must have seen for himself in 1866 (when he sketched the church) at Findon, Sussex, during a visit to the home of Eliza Nicholls, his London friend. Ethelberta discerns through the fog 'numerous horses in the last stage of decrepitude' in one enclosure. Adjoining this is a smaller one formed of high boarding, through a crevice in which she gains a view of tree trunks in a yard. From the stumps of their branches hang horses' skulls, ribs, quarters, legs, and other joints, ready to appease the voracity of a kennel of hounds. Enough is seen and heard of Neigh's knackery to put paid to his marital hopes. The novel contains brief settings from Hardy's memories of London, the cottage where he and Emma lived at Swanage, the neighbouring coast from the sea, and their honeymoon visit to Rouen. Restricting fictional autobiography to the transfer of Hardy's lived experience (incidents, thoughts, and feelings) to the lives of his characters, we find an excellent example on a minute scale after the lecture heard at Corvsgate (Corfe) Castle, and confirmation of it in 'Days to Recollect', a poem addressed to the spirit of Emma Hardy after her death:

> Do you recall
> That day in Fall
> When we walked towards Saint Alban's Head,
> On thistledown that summer had shed,
> Or must I remind you?
> Winged thistle-seeds which hitherto
> Had lain as none were there, or few,
> But rose at the brush of your petticoat-seam
> (As ghosts might rise of the recent dead),
> And sailed on the breeze in a nebulous stream
> Like a comet's tail behind you. . . ?[13]

Catherine ('Cassie') Pole, with whom Hardy was friendly when he was at Higher Bockhampton in the late 1860s, was a lady's maid at Kingston Maurward House, which provided the fictional setting for the main story of *Desperate Remedies*. Whether Cytherea Graye, Miss Aldclyffe's lady's maid, owes anything to her, and if so, to what extent, must remain an interesting speculation. A link exists, however, between her father and *The Hand of Ethelberta*. When Hardy, early in January 1874, returned from seeing Emma Gifford in Cornwall just in time to accept an invitation from Geneviève Smith to dine at West Stafford rectory, he felt his social inferiority, 'having been denied by circumstances until very lately the society of educated womankind', as he informed her shortly afterwards. Cassie's father, butler at Stafford House, was engaged for the occasion, which Hardy remembered in conceiving the comedy of a social situation when Ethelberta, her origin unknown by her hosts, the Doncastles, is served by her father, their butler:

Impressiveness depends as much upon propinquity as upon magnitude; and to have honoured unawares the daughter of the vilest Antipodean miscreant and murderer would have been less discomforting to Mrs Doncastle than it was to make the same blunder with the daughter of a respectable servant who happened to live in her own house.[14]

There is probably more fictionalized autobiography of an inciden-

tal kind than is usually suspected in *Desperate Remedies*, its hero
being, like the author, an architect, 'a poet himself in a small way',
and 'a thorough bookworm', who despises 'the pap-and-daisy
school of verse', and knows Shakespeare 'to the very dregs of the
foot-notes'. One of Hardy's visual impressions at Weymouth is
transferred to the heroine, as may be seen by comparing lines from
'On the Esplanade' (written probably in 1869):

> The lamps of the Bay
> That reach from behind me round to the left and right
> On the sea-wall way
> For a constant mile of curve, make a long display
> As a pearl-strung row,
> Under which in the waves they bore their gimlets of light: –

with the more succinct and effective 'She surveyed the long line
of lamps on the sea-wall of the town, now looking small and
yellow, and seeming to send long tap-roots of fire quivering down
deep into the sea.'[15]

Hardy realized more and more as he was growing up the
handicap of his upper-working class origin, even at Stinsford
where his incipient friendship with Louisa Harding was frowned
upon by her father, a farmer of means. His genius and innate
superiority exacerbated the sense of social disadvantage he was
made to feel more often in London. Such humiliating experiences
explain the subject of *The Poor Man and the Lady* and its satirical
bias against the middle and upper classes. Some, if not all, of the
feelings Hardy expressed in this novel on this question entered
Desperate Remedies and 'An Indiscretion in the Life of an Heiress'.
In a conversation between Stephen Springrove, the hero of the
former, and the heroine Cytherea, on achieving success, the dictum
'The truly great stand upon no middle ledge; they are either famous
or unknown' is awkwardly introduced, making Stephen add that
they remain unknown when they are sincere, and win fame when
they are convergent (conventional) and exclusive (snobbish). In
the final chapter of the first part of 'An Indiscretion'' (appropriately
epigraphed with the Browning verse which begins with the
acidulous line 'The world and its ways have a certain worth') the
lady, after discovering that her father attaches most importance to
'rank and circumstances' in her suitor, urges her lower-class lover
to aim at success and fame in London, and come back 'a wondrous

man of the world', talking pretentiously on fashionable subjects, on hob-nobbing with big-wigs, on 'vintages and their dates', and on 'epicureanism, idleness, and fashion'. Such is the satirical irony of Hardy's 'truly great' in *her* conclusion 'The truly great stand on no middling ledge; they are either famous or unknown.' Like Springrove, Hardy had learned 'to view society from a Bohemian standpoint', and acquired 'all a developed man's unorthodox opinion about the subordination of the classes'.[16]

This was written after he had fallen in love with Emma Gifford, whose upbringing and background had been socially superior to his, as her father was to declare in very blunt terms. Emma believed in Hardy's genius, and remained loyal to him, expecting no doubt that his growing fame as a novelist would propitiate her father and reconcile him to their marrying whenever their future was assured. This could have been the dominant motive for the appearance of Hardy's name, and the first publicization of his authorship of *Under the Greenwood Tree* and *Desperate Remedies*, on the title-page of his next novel, *A Pair of Blue Eyes*, the story of which originated from the love that sprang up between Hardy and Emma. His journey from Launceston to St Juliot, his arrival at the rectory, the gout which had suddenly afflicted Emma's brother-in-law Mr Holder (and which is transferred to Elfride's father), her singing to her own accompaniment at the piano, her bold pony-riding near Beeny Cliff, and a visit to Trebarwith Strand (xx), are clearly recognisable within the narrative fictionalization. Class-distinction as a marriage impediment is the theme of the first part of the novel. Mr Swancourt, with his habit of quoting Latin at length (a characteristic of Emma's father), is convinced that Stephen Smith (the architect who, like Hardy, had been sent to plan the restoration of the church) is of aristocratic lineage, and therefore his daughter's worthy suitor; he is furious to discover that he is the son of John Smith, a local master-mason (like Hardy's father). When he has married a wealthy widow, he tells Elfride that, after getting mixed up with 'those low people, the Smiths', she may now marry anyone she chooses if she plays her cards well. His wife will move from Baker Street to Kensington, and they will spend 'the usual three months' around Easter in town to join the Fashionable World, which Mrs Swancourt regards critically from their carriage in Hyde Park Row (thereby adding to the satire of a scene which was adapted from *The Poor Man and the Lady*). Stephen is in India, hoping to make the fortune that will qualify him for the hand of Elfride. The social comedy when news of his success and fame reaches St Launce's is keyed up by spirited remarks heard earlier in the novel from Mrs Smith on the merits of her son; they might have come from Hardy's mother.[17]

Henry Knight, who displaces Stephen in Elfride's affections, is a barrister. Hardy admitted drawing his chambers at Bede's Inn from those of Raphael Brandon, the architect for whom he worked temporarily in 1870, in 'the old-world out-of-the-way corner of Clement's Inn'. More than half a century later, in 'To a Tree in London', he remembered the neighbouring soot-laden tree which he described in *A Pair of Blue Eyes*, where it forms a prominent feature in the rapid cinematic presentation of external and internal scenes which are packed with detailed reminiscence.[18]

The theme of jealousy enters the novel with Knight, and was undoubtedly suggested by Hardy's own feelings when he learned that, before his first visit to St Juliot in March 1870, it had been hoped (according to his second wife Florence) that a young farmer would 'secure' Emma Gifford. Hardy's awareness of this during his second visit is the subject of the first verse of 'The Young Churchwarden', which recalls the 'vanquished air' of the one-time suitor as he lit the candles for the evening service at Lesnewth on 14 August 1870. Knight's reading of 'the still small voice' Elijah passage (with Elfride at the organ) arose from Hardy's reading the same, with Emma at the harmonium by the aisle, at the St Juliot evening service on the ninth Sunday after Trinity in August 1872.[19]

Such a recollection was included in *A Pair of Blue Eyes* as much for Emma's sake as for the author's. Confirmation of another in Knight's appearance at the age of thirty (continued later when Elfride thinks he is rather round-shouldered and shows 'a little bald spot' on the top of his head) seems highly probable from a portrait of Hardy about the time of writing. Such personal notes are found elsewhere in Hardy's early fiction, acting as private reminders to those dear to him. In the next chapter he repeats what Emma had told him in her letter of 24 October 1870, 'I suppose I must take you as I take the Bible – find out and understand all I can; and on the strength of that, swallow the rest in a lump, by simple faith.' No doubt Hardy's sisters were pleased that they were remembered, their names being given to Lord Luxellian's two little girls. 'Greenhill' in *Far from the Madding Crowd* could have recalled the author's visit of 1864 with his sister Mary, past the hill of that name on Ridgeway, to Fawley in Berkshire, the village of their grandmother's girlhood (though there is a Green Hill on the heath between Higher Bockhampton and Puddletown). The 'barren down where it never looked like summer' in *Desperate Remedies* was intended for Emma Gifford, recalling her remark on 22 August 1870 when it rained as she sat for Hardy to sketch by Beeny Cliff. The scene in *Under the Greenwood Tree* when Fancy Day floats down the school steps 'in the form of a nebulous collection of colours inclining to blue', looking 'distractingly beautiful' to poor Dick Dewy, who is on his way to a funeral, while she sets off to play at the inaugural service for the new harmonium, was suggested by the metamorphosis of Emma, who played at her brother-in-law's services, 'into a young lady in summer blue' when Hardy returned to Cornwall that very same month. After her death, he included the song 'Should he upbraid' in *A Pair of Blue Eyes* (iii) in memory of days they enjoyed together at Sturminster, where they heard it sung to 'Bishop's old tune'.[20]

As his love for Emma deepened in the summer of 1870, Hardy noticed changes in his relationship to her such as are found in *Desperate Remedies* (end of xiii.5), the novel he completed and revised the following autumn. Springrove had 'long since passed that peculiar line which lies across the course of falling in love'. This is the longing to cherish, when 'the woman is shifted in a man's mind from the region of mere admiration to the region of warm fellowship'. It gives her apparent newness 'in tone, hue, and expression':

All about the loved one that said 'She' before, says 'We' now. Eyes that were to be subdued become eyes to be feared for: a brain that was to be probed by cynicism becomes a brain that is to be tenderly assisted; feet that were to be tested in the dance become feet that are not to be distressed; the once-criticized accent, manner, and dress, become the clients of a special pleader.

Like Springrove's, Hardy's 'impressionable heart' had led him for some years to idealize the well-beloved of his future. As he grew older, he 'concluded that the ideas, or rather emotions, which possessed him on the subject, were probably too unreal ever to be found embodied in the flesh of a woman'. Yet about twenty years later, in *Tess of the d'Urbervilles*, he can still indulge in the Platonic dream of 'two halves of a perfect whole' in love and marriage, as he had done in 'The Waiting Supper'. Such idealism seems to have been countered by a realistic appraisal of marriage from observed actuality, as may be felt in the hauntingly memorable tones of 'To a Bridegroom', an uncollected poem of 1866 which questions whether the lover will keep the vow he promises to observe (according to the Church of England marriage service), 'to love and to cherish' his bride until they are parted by death, whatever the contingencies: 'for better, for worse; for richer, for poorer; in sickness and in health'. Hardy's realistic attitude before his own marriage accounts for the heroine's observation in *Desperate Remedies* that 'Nobody can enter into another's nature truly, that's what is so grievous', the author's disillusioned comment 'Directly domineering ceases in the man, snubbing begins in the woman' in *A Pair of Blue Eyes*, and the unromantic rationalism of his recipe for 'the only love which is strong as death' near the end of *Far from the Madding Crowd*. That this remained more or less his conclusion of the whole matter is borne out in his later novels. At the end of *Two on a Tower* he suggests that loving-kindness is 'more to be prized' in the long run than 'lover's love'. In *The Woodlanders* 'a sympathetic interdependence, wherein mutual weaknesses are made the grounds of a defensive alliance' is given as the foundation of 'an enduring and staunch affection', and in *Tess of the d'Urbervilles* the future happiness of a prospective marriage is said to 'depend upon whether the germs of staunch comradeship underlay the temporary emotion'.[21]

The Hardy who returned to Higher Bockhampton in 1867 was in some respects like his Angel Clare. Each had lost his respect for rank and wealth, and each, after living in London, had acquired an 'aversion to modern town life'. Had both persevered they could have gone to Cambridge, but for each it would have been the misappropriation of a trust, Hardy no longer being able conscientiously to aim at 'a curacy in a country village' (where he could write poetry). Theological studies had made him realize that he could hardly take the step with honour while holding the unorthodox views which he had formed. Like Angel he loved the Church (he remained 'churchy' to the end), though he could not accept the gospel of 'redemptive theolatry' or Article Four (on the Resurrection). To quote the Epistle to the Hebrews (xii.27), both stood for 'the removing of those things that are shaken, as of things that are made, that those things which cannot be shaken may remain'.[22] Hardy refers to this 'wise Epistolary recommendation' in his Apology to *Late Lyrics and Earlier*, glancing regretfully at the Church's failure to fashion 'the religion of the future' by 'joining hands with modern science'.

In the autumn of 1873, when he was at home writing *Far from the Madding Crowd*, 'sometimes indoors, sometimes out'. Hardy 'assisted at his father's cider-making – a proceeding he had always enjoyed from childhood. . . . It was the last time he ever took part in a work whose sweet smells and oozings in the crisp autumn air can never be forgotten by those who have had a hand in it.' In *The Woodlanders* it is associated with Winterborne, a man who, like Hardy's father, was 'As one, in suffering all, that suffers nothing'. To judge by its repetition from *Desperate Remedies*, Hardy's most vivid visual recollection was that of the pomace-shovel shining like silver or polished steel from the action of the apple-juice, and intermittently, while in motion, reflecting the light of the setting sun like bristling stars. The pig-killing in *Jude the Obscure* suggests that Hardy in his youth was familiar with the harrowing sight and sounds of such scenes, a likelihood which seems to find its confirmation in *A Pair of Blue Eyes*, where the reference of Robert Lickpan, the pig-killer, to 'poor deaf Grammar Cates' in the original version suggests the association of pig-killing with Higher Bockhampton and one of the Keats families.[23]

A trace of autobiography seems to inform the ending of one of Hardy's Napoleonic short stories, 'The Melancholy Hussar of the German Legion'. Phyllis, the heroine of the love-story Hardy wove round a local historical event, may have been named after the old lady who, when he was engaged in local research for *The Trumpet-Major* in 1879, showed him where the two deserters were buried near Bincombe Church. He refers to her in his 1894 preface to *Life's Little Ironies*, the first collection in which the story appeared, stating his view 'that she who, at the age of ninety, pointed out the unmarked resting-place of the two soldiers of the tale, was probably the last remaining eyewitness of their death and interment'. *The Trumpet-Major*, Hardy's novel of the Napoleonic era, has a more interesting link with one he knew, the description of the heroine at the beginning being an impression of Mrs Anne Procter as he imagined her when she was young, and as he acknowledged and she herself recognised; she often signed herself 'Anne Loveday' when she wrote to Hardy.[24]

Thoughts and perceptions from the author's past are inevitable incidentals in his fiction, though they may usually be concealed

by transference to dialogue or situation. Hardy's predilection
in poetry is clear from his description of a nervous, tentative
conversation in *The Trumpet-Major*, where, 'as in the works of some
hazy poets, the sense was considerably led by the sound'. In *Two
on a Tower* he draws a simile from his writing-experience to indicate
how impulse gets the upper hand when Lady Constantine is drawn
to the pillar where the young astronomer Swithin is making his
nocturnal observations: 'As the words in which a thought is
expressed develop a further thought, so did the fact of her having
got so far influence her to go further.' Nor can there be much
doubt that Hardy, recurrently a prey to deep dark depression,
writes from experience when he makes Lady Constantine discover
how her marriage to Swithin had ruined his career; how she had,
in his uncle's words, committed a crime:

> Only those persons who are by nature affected with that ready
> esteem for others' positions which induces an undervaluing of
> their own, fully experience the deep smart of such convictions
> against self – the wish for annihilation that is engendered in the
> moment of despair, at feeling that at length we, our best and
> firmest friend, cease to believe in our cause.[25]

Reviews of Hardy's last two novels made him decide, not
surprisingly, to abandon the writing of serious fiction. 'And zest
is quenched by the knowledge that by printing a novel which
attempts to deal honestly and artistically with the facts of life one
stands up to be abused by any scamp who thinks he can advance
the sale of his paper by lying about one', he wrote to William
Archer in 1898. He was thinking primarily of *Jude the Obscure* and
the penalty of writing fictionally in the late Victorian era on 'the
position of man and woman in nature, and the position of belief
in the minds of man and woman'. More particularly he must
have remembered the 'paragraphists' who 'knowingly assured the
public' that *Jude* was 'an honest autobiography', a charge so
absurdly astonishing that he made no attempt to repudiate it for
more than twenty years, when he claimed that, generally speaking,
'there is more autobiography in a hundred lines of Mr Hardy's
poetry than in all the novels'.[26]

This reply (dictated to Florence Hardy) is too sweeping and
ambivalent with reference to 'personal detail'; it is obviously
exaggerated with reference to his poetry. Nevertheless his general

assertion is hardly a distortion of the essential truth, the autobiographical ingredients in *Jude the Obscure* being but a small fraction of the whole. Some of the most important have clearly been given, and little remains to be added. Whatever the early training of Hardy's young cousin Tryphena Sparks (later Mrs Gale) as a pupil teacher contributed to the Sue–Phillotson development, she did not enter the novel, as he first intended (to judge by the 1895 preface, which refers to her death in 1890). Nor, though her dark eyes and hair may have been subconsciously remembered, did her photograph as a girl of twelve in 1863 (which was quite misleadingly held to be the original of that contemplated by Phillotson of Sue as a child). In physique and character Tryphena was quite unlike the epicene Sue. If anyone contributed to the latter it was Mrs Henniker; the extent of such influence was small, a Shelleyan imagining of her which was transferred to Jude, and disapproval of her High Church principles, both to be found in Hardy's letters to her soon after his infatuation began in 1893.[27]

Autobiographically *The Well-Beloved* is more interesting. Its delineation of figures Hardy met in society, especially in London, has already been presented in detail. It suggests that, had he written further novels, he might have been more disposed to make further fictional use of the notes he had made on the 'artificial life and manners' of his time.[28] The novel, however, conveys deeper and more personal emotions. The most moving passage revives and distils the feelings that arose in Hardy when, hearing of Tryphena's death, he remembered her in the distant past. The poem 'Thoughts of Phena' records those feelings, at a time when, with imaginative hindsight, he could regard her as another 'lost prize'. Then, in March 1890, it may have been twenty years since he last saw her, before she left the training-college at Stockwell to become headmistress of a Plymouth school in 1871, just as it was since Jocelyn Pierston had seen the first Avice Caro, whose death revives the past, bringing with it the most refined emotions.

It can occasion little surprise that the hero's repeatedly falling in love includes two experiences from Hardy's own life. The first, at Dorchester, when he was fourteen, is transferred to Jocelyn when he was a boy at Budmouth-Regis, 'standing on the kerbstone of the pavement' outside the Preparatory School. He was 'looking across towards the sea, when a middle-aged gentleman on horseback, and beside him a young lady, also mounted, passed down the street'. Twice she turned and smiled at him, and the smile was enough to fire his heart. The second is the subject of 'I look into my glass', the last of *Wessex Poems*, 1898:

> I look into my glass,
> And view my wasting skin,
> And say, 'Would God it came to pass
> My heart had shrunk as thin!'
>
> For then, I, undistrest
> By hearts grown cold to me,
> Could lonely wait my endless rest
> With equanimity.
>
> But Time, to make me grieve,
> Part steals, lets part abide;
> And shakes this fragile frame at eve
> With throbbings of noontide.

With Pierston it is first seen as 'this curse of his heart not ageing while his frame moved naturally onward'. Then, at sixty, he beholds his face in the glass, and, seeing in it the effect of age and months of despondency, when all seems to go 'against his art, his strength, his happiness', he knows that time opposes him and love, and that time will probably win. Later, while in love with the third Avice, he looks at his mirrored image in the 'cold grey morning light' and asks, 'While his soul was what it was, why should he have been encumbered with that withering carcase without the ability to shift it off for another, as his ideal Beloved had so frequently done?'[29]

Some passages of autobiographical import in Hardy's fiction will undoubtedly have been overlooked; some will be found elsewhere in this volume. More of the kind which follows will remain unsuspected:

> She went to where a swing-glass stood, and taking it in her hands carried it to a spot by the window where it could catch the sunshine, moving the glass till the beams were reflected into Phillotson's face.

Unless Hardy had divulged the origin of this, nobody would have imagined more here than the creation of an intelligent novelist.

He had remembered how, towards the end of the long illness he suffered while engaged on *A Laodicean*, Maggie Macmillan had called, and thought of the same method of enabling him to watch a gorgeous sunset with her and Emma.

Altogether, it has to be concluded that autobiography enters collectively but a small fraction of Hardy's fiction. There is nothing surprising in this if we remember that he aimed at writing 'something more unusual . . . than the ordinary experience of every average man and woman'. Unlike Conrad's life, for example, Hardy's offered little that was colourful and exciting except on a small scale. Some of his short stories, and episodes in his novels, depended on unusual events that came to him from hearsay or reading. For the most part he used his inventive and imaginative powers. Married frustrations enabled him to empathize creatively with some of his later characters, notably Winterborne (as he hinted in his epigraph to *The Woodlanders*) and Jude. His 'constitutional tendency to care for life only as an emotion' drew him to poetry, and there is far more autobiography in his poems, particularly on Emma Gifford/Hardy, than in the whole of his fiction.[30]

14
Hardy's Novel-Endings

'Nearly all novels are feeble at the end', and 'If it was not for death and marriage I do not know how the average novelist would conclude', E. M. Forster writes in *Aspects of the Novel*. If not jaundiced, the view is too dismissive; it might seem to suggest that most of Hardy's endings can hardly be regarded as successful or commendable. Forster thinks the use of marriage as a finale in fiction is 'idiotic', though it could have been anything but that for editors of magazines dependent on serialized fiction in the nineteenth century, when most of their readers were young women who still, like Caroline Helstone in Charlotte Brontë's *Shirley*, had few careers but marriage to which they could hopefully look forward. As late as 1890 Hardy protests in 'Candour in English Fiction' against the insincerity of novels adjusted to 'the regulation finish' that 'they married and were happy ever after'. Critics have complained that Jane Austen responded almost automatically to such a formula, but this young lady knew how to look after herself, how to avoid the conventional and cosy; she was never guilty of a facile ending. Her conclusions satisfy her readers, but marriage never comes without unforeseeable setbacks and suffering, and some of her heroines are of such character or inexperience that one can assume they have yet to learn from mistakes, though they are in too good hands to encounter disaster. Jane Austen can be both amusingly and movingly realistic, especially so at the end of *Emma*.

Novel-endings should seem to be inevitable. In this respect Hardy's compare well with those of his contemporaries. Meredith can sometimes seem off course, notably in *The Ordeal of Richard Feverel*; and Conrad, a superb master of form in some of his shorter stories, can become a victim to technical hesitancy and misjudgment in reaching the *dénouement* of novels such as *Nostromo* and *The Rescue*. Few novelists have the intuitive genius which appears in Turgenev's *Smoke*, enabling him to present scenes with clarity at the outset, to grip the reader while character and action unfold inextricably, and to give no more than is necessary at the end,

leaving the rest to the reader's imagination. One might think that
a novelist is fortunate when he works towards a predetermined
end, as Hardy apparently did in *The Return of the Native*, but the
example of *The Mill on the Floss* constitutes a warning; unless the
plot is disciplined and integrated, the final concatenation of
events may appear arbitrary and unconvincing; it can produce a
tremendous finale without the all-important sense of inevitability.
The contrastingly non-eventful ending of *Middlemarch* will be far
less popular; beside the storm, it is the still small voice, subtle,
sensible, and exquisitely presented.

Hardy's conscientious ability to create well-knit and continually
progressive plots (which seems to have come rather easily to
him more often than not, after painful labour in producing the
astonishingly detailed chronological complications of *Desperate
Remedies*) ensured that his novel-endings were generally adequate
at least. The undisciplined genius of the maturing D. H. Lawrence
made him increasingly careless of form, until he made a late effort
to recover. Depending largely on his own experience for his
subjects (as the continuation of *Mr Noon* testifies to the end), he
often improvised endings, regardless of proportion and unity.
Believing in the demon of creative spontaneity, he preferred to
rewrite wholly rather than revise, and produced three versions of
Lady Chatterley's Lover, with different beginnings and conclusions.
Hardy presents a choice of endings, it may be said, in *The Return
of the Native*, but he does not really choose to balk the issue, as
John Fowles appears to do in *The French Lieutenant's Woman*, by
giving alternative conclusions. How final a novel-ending should
be is becoming more and more the writer's problem. However
much plot may differentiate a novel from the 'slice of life' form, it
should never be so conclusive or catastrophic that it fails to show
that life goes on. If Hardy satisfies in this respect, he never goes
as far as, for example, Barbara Pym in *Jane and Prudence*, where she
leaves the reader wondering what will happen to one of her
heroines; she has reached the end of a phase in her life, but her
future seems rather less certain than that of Gwendolen at the
close of *Daniel Deronda*.

Obviously the more integrated and artistic the plot, the more
the end can be seen retrospectively in the beginning. This could
be illustrated from *A Pair of Blue Eyes* or *The Woodlanders*, or *Tess*,
or *Jude*, but it is not evidence, as it was once fashionable to
emphasize, that Hardy belongs to the the blue-print class of

novelists. He could improvise, as the chapter based on a very recent voyage from London to Plymouth *en route* for St Juliot shows in *A Pair of Blue Eyes*, and make important changes in 1893 before getting *Jude the Obscure* under way, not in accordance with a fixed plan but with one which was subject to direction and modification as seemed best in the course of writing. It was an accident that the plot turned out to be 'almost geometrically constructed', he told Gosse; 'constructed' was the wrong word, he said, 'for, beyond a certain point, the characters necessitated it, and I simply let it come'.[1] Normally he was artist enough to ensure that nothing improbable or discordant resulted. He was not a photographic writer; his vision of life, 'the pattern among general things which his idiosyncrasy [moved] him to observe', included the ironies and cruelties of chance. Probability in art is not the same as probability in life, and the coincidences that lead to the tragic climax of *A Pair of Blue Eyes* must be judged by artistic effect. By such standards they amount to a possibility much less questionable than the two improbabilities which are at the very centre of the plot in *The Return of the Native*, creating the quarrel between Eustacia and Clym's mother, thwarting the latter's attempt at reconciliation, and leading to the flare-up between Clym and Eustacia that produces the tragic ending.

In his first novel, *The Poor Man and the Lady*, Hardy showed more zeal in satisfying his own ends than in attempting to secure the approval of readers. His satire was uncompromising, and the ending, as Alexander Macmillan's observations on the manuscript disclose,[2] followed the events which, with omissions and refinements, Hardy used in 1878 to bring 'An Indiscretion in the Life of an Heiress' to its tragic close. Failure, followed by difficulties and delays, explains why he chose, *inter alia*, happy endings for his next two novels, *Desperate Remedies* and *Under the Greenwood Tree*. Only after the relative success of the second – the first he had tasted – was he emboldened to embark again on a tragically directed plot, and reveal his authorship on the title-page.

Most readers of *Desperate Remedies* must hope that it will end happily for the lovers, the attractive Cytherea especially, who has been denied the marriage of her choice by fate, altruism, and the machinations of Miss Aldclyffe and her illegitimate son Aeneas Manston. Their deaths clear the way for the wedding-bells of the 'Sequel', which brings a welcome return of Hardy's first great comic character, the parish clerk Crickett. The story is rounded off prettily in a brief coda which is soon forgotten, the lovers' kiss on the lake with which it ends re-enacting their first on Budmouth Bay.

So hazardous has it become to hold that the ending of *Under the Greenwood Tree* holds out happy prospects in marriage that the question calls for closer attention. It can be settled only on the evidence of the novel. Critics in this matter have tended to follow D. H. Lawrence, who, with the help of Lascelles Abercrombie's *Thomas Hardy* (1912), wrote a huge essay in 1914, using Hardy's novels as a launching-pad for his developing ideas on the growth of individuality through freedom and fulfilment, especially in sexual love. So strongly and imaginatively did he feel that his views coloured his literary impressions. His 'Study of Hardy', whenever he keeps to the subject, is of little critical value except as a reflection of his own moral outlook and philosophy. He read hastily, and is inaccurate in detail as well as in judgment: Manston is a murderer; Eustacia is of Italian descent; Alec and Tess are cousins. He bunches characters into categories; his 'aristocratic' women (those sexually passionate by nature) include Elfride Swancourt and Marty South with Tess and Arabella. They, and Manston, Troy, Captain de Stancy, and Fitzpiers, might have triumphed in 'heroic' times. In Hardy they are condemned to unfulfilment by 'the bourgeois morality'. Characters are seen as if in new contexts, and Hardy's moral sense and conflict with Victorian conformity are virtually ignored. How much Lawrence disregards and re-creates in accordance with his own self-centred imagination during a later period of western civilization may be seen in *his* Egdon; it is, to use his proliferating epithets, 'the powerful, eternal origin seething with production', 'the eternal powerful fecundity', the Lawrentian 'darkness' to which Clym Yeobright is blind. Had he been Lawrentian, Eustacia would have been happy there. *The Well-Beloved*, with nothing sexually passionate in its ideal theme, is 'sheer rubbish, fatuity' (as is much of '*The Dynasts* conception', Lawrence adds). Breaking convention, the 'lawless' Miss Aldclyffe and the 'fleshily passionate' Manston are much preferred to the 'dull hero' Springrove and the 'nice, rather ordinary' Cytherea, who are destined (within bourgeois conventionalities) 'to happiness and success'. Fancy Day, 'after a brief excursion from the beaten track in the pursuit of social ambition and satisfaction of the imagination, figured by the Clergyman', returns to Dick Dewy, and renounces the imagination. Whatever that means, she is destined to 'carry in her heart all her life many unopened buds that will die unflowered; and Dick will probably have a bad time of it'. It would be an astonishing judgment if Lawrence implied that she would be happier and more fulfilled with Mr Maybold, for the novel surely makes it clear that Fancy is led into temptation partly by parental pressure and partly by 'niceties' which education had made her think important, and that she could not in her restricted circumstances have been as happy had she lost Dick, as once she had feared. Following the inclination of her heart, she is more fortunate than Grace Melbury. Her sounder instinct overcomes the temporary and superficial attraction of a social status which Lawrence normally would have stigmatized as bourgeois.

Under the Greenwood Tree is the happiest of Hardy's novels, the one in which he comes nearest to the idyllic. It raises no serious issues; its humour is often light-hearted. Dick Dewy is not daunted when Fancy's father gives a greater welcome to Mr Shiner, nor need the cry of a bird being killed by an owl be regarded as a very ominous sign when it preludes Dick's overtures to her father as they lean on a piggery rail and contemplate a whitish shape grunting in the straw. The course of love is not intended to run smoothly, but there are no heavily weighted setbacks, and it is Fancy who is under a cloud when she sickens for Dick. Comic irony is at its best when he has to leave in black for his friend's funeral at Charmley as she listens delightedly to his admiration of her hair and apparel before she sets off for the triumphant début as organist which he had set his heart on seeing; he returns a sorry figure, after a walk of four miles, without overcoat or umbrella, in drizzling rain. Writing in such a high-spirited key (as an introduction to Maybold's marriage proposal) sprang from Hardy's happiness in love with Emma Gifford. She, the 'young lady in summer blue'[3] who played the harmonium in St Juliot Church, was the inspiration for the inaugural organ-playing scene which marked the demise of the old Mellstock choir, and for those glances at female vanity which are most humorously expressed by aged observers during the preparations for Dick and Fancy's wedding:

> 'Ah!' said grandfather James to grandfather William as they retired, 'I wonder which she thinks most about, Dick or her wedding raiment!'
> 'Well, 'tis their nature', said grandfather William. 'Remember

the words of the prophet Jeremiah: "Can a maid forget her ornaments, or a bride her attire?" '

Manifestly this type of femininity is so universal that it is not taken seriously by the author, and presages no dissension in marriage. The swarming of bees is an excellent omen, according to folklore and Mrs Penny, who speaks from 'the depths of experience', and probably for her author, when she says, 'Well, 'tis humps and hollers with the best of us; but still and for all that, Dick and Fancy stand as fair a chance of having a bit of sunsheen as any married girl in the land.'

The novel ends with comical irony, quite out of tune with Lawrence's gloomy prognostications. Quite unaware of Fancy's regretted acceptance of Maybold's proposal, Dick tells her they are supremely happy because they enjoy each other's full confidence. Her flirtation with Shiner, which she had confessed, had been too trifling to be considered a flirtation, he assures her. 'We'll have no secrets from each other, darling . . . no secret at all', he continues. 'None from to-day', she answers. The voice of the nightingale (surely no harbinger of unhappiness) is heard, and she thinks of a secret she will never tell. Perhaps Hardy thought of secrets he would never tell Miss Gifford, of, for example, meeting Louisa Harding in the original of the lane Dick Dewy follows at the opening of the novel. Emma Woodhouse thinks it better not to tell Mr Knightley all her follies, and Jane Austen sagely writes:

> Seldom, very seldom does complete truth belong to any human disclosure; seldom can it happen that something is not a little disguised, or a little mistaken; but where, as in this case, though the conduct is mistaken the feelings are not, it may not be very material.

The final statement is very pertinent to the ending of *Under the Greenwood Tree*. Those who think otherwise ally themselves with the abnormally suspicious and over-jealous Knight of *A Pair of Blue Eyes*, who thinks that 'everything ought to be cleared up between two persons before they become husband and wife'. And of him Hardy wrote:

> Knight had in him a modicum of that wrongheadedness which is mostly found in scrupulously honest people. With him, truth

seemed too clean and pure an abstraction to be so hopelessly churned in with error as practical people find it.

The feelings of the lovers at the end of *Under the Greenwood Tree* are unmistakable. They are attuned to the nightingale, which sings 'Tippiwit! swe-e-et! ki-ki-ki! Come hither, come hither, come hither!' It is supererogatory to suggest that this contains a sly allusion to Jaques's parody of the song 'Under the greenwood tree' in *As You Like It*. There is nothing in Hardy's text to indicate that he was thinking, or expected his readers to think, of anything more than the song which he had read over and over again in his favourite book of poetry, *The Golden Treasury*. Its 'Come hither, come hither, come hither' implies that there is nothing more to fear than 'winter and rough weather' (an allusion which incidentally rounds off the novel, taking us back to the wintry wind in the plantation at the opening). For Hardy 'winter and rough weather' symbolize no more than the afflictions which we all expect of life.[4]

More complicated and extended, the ending of *A Pair of Blue Eyes* combines comic elements with a tragic climax of impressive solemnity. Death as a recurrent or thematic note occurs throughout the novel in a variety of forms, sometimes singularly striking, onwards from the song sung by Elfride which closes with the epitomizing words

> O Love, who bewailest
> The frailty of all things here,
> Why choose you the frailest
> For your cradle, your home, and your bier!

At the penultimate stage of the story the sudden desire of leading citizens to cultivate the acquaintance of the working-class Smiths immediately their son's fame reaches St Launce's offsets with satirical humour Elfride's renewed efforts to win back Knight, a lover who is as fastidiously prim and puritanical as he is self-righteously hard and unrelenting. So passionate are her pleas that Hardy in his old age thought he could not do better than versify them for a scene in *The Famous Tragedy of the Queen of Cornwall*.[5] Although *A Pair of Blue Eyes* lacks the qualities of classical tragedy, such as are found in *The Mayor of Casterbridge* and *Jude the Obscure*, it leads to a most moving and unforgettable conclusion. Some will think it strains credulity by its amazing coincidences, a Hardy feature which is amusing when the three lovers of the heroine find themselves on the same train in *The Hand of Ethelberta*, and is equally amusing when the rivals Smith and Knight find themselves on one for Cornwall, each bent on renewing his suit for the hand of Elfride. A passage in *Desperate Remedies* (attributed to Cytherea) suggests that Hardy, who believed in 'the whimsical god . . . known as blind Circumstance',[6] had thought much on the question of coincidence in life and probably in the novel. When two events 'fall strangely together by chance', he writes,

> 'people scarcely notice the fact beyond saying, "Oddly enough it happened that so and so were the same", and so on. But when three such events coincide without any apparent reason for the coincidence, it seems as if there must be invisible means at work. You see, three things falling together in that manner are ten times as singular as two cases of coincidence which are distinct.'

Such is Hardy's contrivance that the reader is as shocked as the prickly pair of lovers when it is disclosed that the dark, richly ornamented carriage which has accompanied them from Paddington contains the coffined body of Elfride, who had married Lord Luxellian. 'False', whispers Knight, who quickly recovers from the withering self-indictment of this hasty, self-centred response to utter his first poised judgment on the girl he had cruelly forsaken (a judgment which recalls Hardy's in the title-page epigraph from *Hamlet*):

> 'Can we call her ambitious? No. Circumstance has, as usual, overpowered her purposes – fragile and delicate as she – liable to be overthrown in a moment by the coarse elements of accident. I know that's it, – don't you?'

Elfride's late history is told by the old parlour-maid Unity in moving limpid prose, and the story ends with a visit by Knight and Stephen Smith, after the funeral, to the Luxellian vault where they had once stood with Elfride, who had now 'gone down into silence' and 'shut her bright blue eyes for ever'. There they see her grief-stricken husband in prayer over her coffin, and promptly withdraw. 'Another stands before us – nearer to her than we', says Knight in a broken voice. Hardy's invention is bold, but the crucial test is the extent to which his words succeed in evoking the appropriate responses. Later readings are likely to confirm the impression that his originality and artistry are remarkable for a novelist at an early stage in his career: the perspectives are excellent; the tone is right; and the whole, profoundly moving. Hardy wisely refused to change the ending for one more cheerful.

Far from the Madding Crowd is a more ambitious work, particularly successful in highly imaginative pictorial scenes of tragic or psychological import, and rather melodramatic. After the death of Fanny Robin, Boldwood's monomania in love, and the shooting of Troy, a quiet ending is needed. It may seem weak, but it is probable in the circumstances, true to the character of Oak and of Bathsheba, who, after recognising her need for the schooling of experience, has been rashly romantic, and has had to pay a fearful price in suffering. After reading the inscriptions on the tombstone of Fanny Robin and Troy, she moves into the church porch to hear the choir-practice. As the children sing 'Lead, kindly Light, amid the encircling gloom' she would give anything to be as they are, and buries her face in her hands, not seeing Oak as he enters, on his way to join the choristers. In the first interval of their talk, she hears from within, 'as from a prompter',

> I loved the garish day, and, spite of fears,
> Pride ruled my will: remember not past years.

Not until she learns that Gabriel thinks of leaving for California, and tenders his notice, does she realize that she cannot dispense with him. His loyalty and worth had been revealed at the same time as Troy's treachery, coming like a lightning-flash as they worked together to save the stacked harvest during the storm. She has, figuratively speaking, to go down on her knees to make him change his mind, and even encourage him to make his marriage proposal. The unromantic realism of the ending may seem disillusioned from an author who completed the novel 'at a gallop' to make preparations for his own wedding, but its sincerity is confirmed in his later fiction, notably in *The Woodlanders* and *Tess of the d'Urbervilles*.[7] The relevant passage runs:

> Theirs was that substantial affection which arises (if any arises at all) when the two who are thrown together begin first by knowing the rougher sides of each other's character, and not the best till further on, the romance growing up in the interstices

of a mass of hard prosaic reality. This good-fellowship –
camaraderie – usually occurring through similarity of pursuits, is
unfortunately seldom superadded to love between the sexes,
because men and women associate, not in their labours, but in
their pleasures merely. Where, however, happy circumstance
permits its development, the compounded feeling proves itself
to be the only love which is strong as death – that love which
many waters cannot quench, nor the floods drown, beside which
the passion usually called by the name is evanescent as steam.

Hardy, it is said, was late in growing-up. It is more relevant, in
view of his early poetry and assessment of life, to think of him
authorially as an old head on young shoulders, rather like his
Father Time. This ending of *Far from the Madding Crowd* should be
remembered when we think of the *dénouement* in *The Well-Beloved*.
The quiet wedding of the 'Conclusion' is completely in key, and
its unbidden celebration by the Weatherbury band, sufficient
testimony to the acceptance of the married couple by the community. All the signs suggest that Bathsheba and Oak are at last
'far from the madding crowd' in Thomas Gray's sense.

For Lawrence *The Hand of Ethelberta* marks 'the zenith' of a feeling
in the Wessex novels 'that the best thing to do is to kick out the
craving for "Love" and substitute commonsense, leaving sentiment
to the minor characters'; it is 'a shrug of the shoulders', 'a last
taunt to hope', and (*The Trumpet-Major* providing a qualified
exception) 'the end of the happy endings'. Initially this may seem
to harmonize with Hardy's thoughts at the end of *Far from the
Madding Crowd*, but close inspection shows that it does not, Hardy's
desideratum being a love which is 'strong as death'. Lawrence's
assessment is true neither to the spirit of *The Hand of Ethelberta* nor
to any work by Hardy; incidentally, it overlooks *A Laodicean* in its
conclusion on happy endings. Hardy's sympathies are with the
lover Christopher Julian, and, though using her to make a mockery
of utilitarian principles pursued at the expense of the heart, he is
sorry for Ethelberta, who sacrifices love altruistically for a large
family of dependants, but who often feels with Shelley that she
could

> lie down like a tired child,
> And weep away the life of care

> Which I have borne and yet must bear,
> Till death like sleep might steal on me . . . .[8]

Nevertheless, the novel is 'A Comedy in Chapters', with much satire of the worldly and commercial, the Darwinian game which Hardy did not care for[9] but which Ethelberta feels she is obliged to play. Climactically a most amusingly satisfying situation arises when members of her working-class family consider it a disgrace that she proposes to marry an old aristocratic roué. The pursuit to prevent this marriage, and (a refinement of a ruse employed by Hardy in his first short story, 'Destiny and a Blue Cloak') Mountclere's outwitting of Ethelberta when she threatens to leave after discovering that his 'Petit Trianon' has been reserved for a former mistress, create excitement and suspense; but the most significant aspect of the conclusion is the revelation that the title of the novel means more than gaining the hand of Ethelberta in marriage. When it comes to playing the 'scientific game', as circumstances dictate, she proves that she is not inexpert; she is the wild duck of the opening scenes, able to fend for herself in the Darwinian struggle to succeed. Though dispossessed by her management, Mountclere's brother admits her skill, and says she has played her cards (her hand) adroitly. After discovering that 'a coronet covers a multitude of sins', she finds it necessary to have the upper hand at Enckworth Court; she becomes 'my lord and my lady both'; and anyone opposing her will find her little finger 'thicker than a Mountclere's loins'. The 'Sequel' shows that her heart is in the right place: Enckworth Court and her family benefit from her reforming zeal and benevolence.

Hardy's early recollection of the recovery of a boy's body (which he had mistaken for a girl's) from the pool below the original of Shadwater Weir 'started the train of thought which led him to write *The Return of the Native*'.[10] His original intention was to end the action with the catastrophe of Eustacia's flight and death. In a footnote to VI.iii he informs us that he did not intend a marriage between Diggory Venn and Thomasin; the former was to have retained his 'isolated and weird character' ('weird' suggesting that he has a hand in destiny), and to have disappeared from the heath mysteriously, 'nobody knowing whither', with Thomasin left a widow. Serialization determined otherwise (at an early stage, for Hardy wrote to his illustrator Arthur Hopkins early in February

1878, the month of the second instalment in *Belgravia*, 'Thomasin, as you have divined, is the *good* heroine, and she ultimately marries the reddleman, and lives happily'). 'Aftercourses' was therefore designed, and it is noticeable that the ending of Hardy's footnote, 'Readers can therefore choose between the endings, and those with an austere artistic code can assume the more consistent conclusion to be the true one', is less unequivocal than the comments he wrote, on his preferred endings and his concessions to magazine-readers, at the end of 'The Distracted Preacher' in *Wessex Tales* and on 'The Romantic Adventures of a Milkmaid' in his own copy of *A Changed Man*.

Some readers maintain that Eustacia commits suicide, but this is hardly confirmed by the novel. She has recovered from the depression which made her contemplate using her grandfather's pistols, and looks forward to escape from Egdon, and to happiness in Paris, even with Wildeve. Her considered willingness to accept his assistance is the purport of her signal on the fatal night (though Hardy is not wholly consistent in this[11]) when she leaves home in darkness so funereal that nothing is visible below the horizon but the light burning in Susan Nunsuch's cottage; cloud and rain have extinguished the moon and stars. The chaos of the elements reflects the chaos of her mind, but she suddenly realizes that she has insufficient money for her journey and cannot accept Wildeve's aid without his company. Not to arouse suspicions at home, Wildeve takes his horse and lighted gig almost a quarter of a mile off, to a point down the road where the only sound which rises above the storm is the roaring of the ten-hatched weir. Eustacia is familiar with the way to Rainbarrow, but not down to Wildeve's inn and its neighbourhood. Her mind is in a whirl; whether she sees his gig-lamps or not, she loses her direction until she stumbles into the whirling weir-pool. The reader has been alerted to the possibility of such an accident by the fear of Thomasin (who knows her way on the heath, however dark the storm) that Wildeve had fallen into the river when returning late from his last visit to Mistover). When Eustacia's body is recovered, it is seen that 'eternal rigidity had seized upon it in a momentary transition between fervour and resignation', as if her last hope had faded into acceptance of helplessness just before her death.

'Aftercourses', the supplement to what may be regarded as a tragedy in five acts, is hardly an anticlimax or a complete success. It may not fit in with Hardy's original 'artistic code', and it is rather too protracted, but in more than one way it helps to give artistic completion to the novel. The marriage of Diggory Venn and Thomasin, two attractive characters, undoubtedly satisfies readers' expectations. Clym plays his expected role at the wedding-service, but is just as naturally indisposed to participate in the celebrations which follow. Convinced that he has driven both his wife and his mother to their deaths (Eustacia to suicide), and is branded like Cain, he feels he would be 'too much like the skull at the banquet',[12] and prefers to prepare the first of his sermons or talks for bringing light to the poor inhabitants of Egdon Heath. Just as the Teutonic rites of the May revel on a bright evening balance Teutonic rejoicings with bonfires and dances on the dark evening of 5 November at the opening of the novel, so the final appearance of Clym, as the preacher on Rainbarrow one warm Sunday afternoon in summer, counterpoises our first view of Eustacia, a lonely figure in the November gloom on the same distant tumulus. Eustacia with her pagan eyes has a romantic appeal which is much greater than that of Clym, although his aims are noble; he is another John the Baptist, who renounces a flashy city career for plain living, high thinking, and the betterment of his fellow men. Such idealism is premature; he has yet to learn that most people attach greater value to material well-being than to enlightenment or culture:

> Yeobright preaching to the Egdon eremites that they might rise to a serene comprehensiveness without going through the process of enriching themselves, was not unlike arguing to ancient Chaldeans that in ascending from earth to the pure empyrean it was not necessary to pass first into the intervening heaven of ether.

If, as chapter II.vi and Yeobright's name suggest, he was intended for a Promethean role, the light he brings is pale. His mother-fixation which is evident in the lines immediately preceding and following the account of the first of his 'Sermons on the Mount' raises the question whether Hardy, who had disappointed his mother by giving up a city career, and perhaps in the choice of his wife, put more into Clym and the ending of *The Return of the Native* than he or Emma Hardy realized.

Unfavourable reviews of *The Return of the Native* made Hardy choose for his next novel, *The Trumpet-Major*, 'a cheerful story,

without views or opinions . . . intended to wind up happily'.[13]
Towards the close the King talks to the heroine Anne Garland by
a mineral spring, after her return from Portland, where she has
watched the *Victory*, with her lover Bob Loveday on board,
disappear over the horizon, destiny-ridden before the battle of
Trafalgar. Mediocre by Hardy standards, with no great action or
character and much comedy of humours rather than of people, it
was very much the kind of novel, with George III 'just round the
corner', that Leslie Stephen would have welcomed for his serial-
readers. The ending creates impatience with the hero's pretence
and continual self-sacrifice in favour of his less steadfast brother,
but all this is outweighed by reference to historical events which
(as with Stanner in an early chapter) supply an extra dimension and
give retrospective poignancy to less sensational though uncommon
happenings at a time of military preparations against a French
invasion. Such resonances find their climax at the very end, with
the chiaroscuro of John, the trumpet-major, seen smiling by the
light of his father's candle, before plunging into the darkness, to
join his companions-in-arms and 'blow his trumpet till silenced for
ever upon one of the bloody battle-fields of Spain'. Beside this the
happy ending which is promised for Anne and Bob makes little
impression. Would it have been different if the story had been
published under Leslie Stephen's editorship? When, after telling
Hardy that the heroine married the wrong man, and hearing him
reply that they usually did, he curtly answered, 'Not in magazines'.

Little more than thirteen chapters of the next novel, *A Laodicean*,
had been written when Hardy was stricken with an illness that
kept him bedridden for months. As serialization had begun, he
was determined to finish it, and dictated the remainder to his wife
until, at the beginning of May 1881, a rough draft was completed
'by one shift or another'. In the later stages, particularly in the
Rhineland portion, he relied so much on his memory and records
of holidays in western Europe that his text exceeded the length he
had guaranteed by a third (his publishers generously paying *pro
rata* for the additional amount, though this had been ruled out in
their contract with the author[14]). The ending of the novel raises
two questions, the first of which may seem very matter-of-fact: to
what extent a writer of fiction is or is not justified in imaginative
departures from the truth when knowingly presenting impressions
or stories of actual places or people. (With reference to the latter,
one thinks of *A Group of Noble Dames* and characters in the fiction

of D. H. Lawrence.) Hardy's Stancy Castle is burnt down by the villain Dare; his Quantock references and his map of Wessex identify it with Dunster Castle in Somerset, though, half ruin, half residence initially, it is almost wholly Hardy's invention, its pictures being recollected from his visit to Kingston Lacy in the summer of 1878, and much of its history and records, where not fabricated, being taken from his huge quarry of antiquity, John Hutchins' history of Dorset; there is no evidence that he ever visited Dunster. Such departures from the real, especially the reduction of the castle to ruins at the end, help to explain why Hardy took pains in his 1912 preface to inform 'the investigating topographist' that his 'sites, mileages, and architectural details' are 'but the baseless fabrics of a vision'.

The second, much more comprehensive, question relates to the theme of this 'story of to-day', with its intrigue, traduction, and travel, leading eventually, after a complicated pursuit, to an all's-well-that-ends-well *dénouement*. In the conversation which concludes it, the hero, George Somerset the architect, tells the heroine Paula that she will recover from the medieval warp which her destroyed castle had given her mind. 'And', she continues inquiringly,

'be a perfect representative of "the modern spirit" . . . representing neither the senses and understanding, nor the heart and the imagination; but what a finished writer calls "the imaginative reason"?'

The finished writer is Matthew Arnold, who, in his essay 'Pagan and Medieval Religious Sentiment' writes, 'But the main element of the modern spirit's life is neither the senses and understanding, nor the heart and imagination; it is the imaginative reason.' His subject, like that of Pater in his essay on Winckelmann, is how to reconcile the inhibitive Christianity of the Victorian era with the life-enjoyment of the Greeks. He quotes a passage from Heine which refers to the hospital atmosphere of the modern world and to 'the factitious quarrel which Christianity has cooked up' between body and soul, before making his distinction between the poetry of later paganism (illustrated from the fifteenth idyll of Theocritus) and that of medieval Christianity, the former living by 'the senses and understanding', the latter by 'the heart and imagination'. To achieve 'that Hellenic ideal, in which man is at unity with himself',

Pater postulates the necessity for 'the imaginative intellect'. Like Arnold, he is thinking primarily of the poet or artist, but his regret that Victorianism had frowned on Hellenism has its link with Clym Yeobright, the intellectual being left in a dilemma, a struggle for a perfection 'that makes the blood turbid, and frets the flesh, and discredits the actual world about us'.[15]

The question of a sane mind in a healthy body is not at the heart of *A Laodicean*, but it is inherent in the Hellenic gymnastics of Paula Power and the sensualism of the prying Captain de Stancy. The heterogeneity of the novel is not far removed from the 'divided aims' of Arnold's 'The Scholar-Gipsy' and his regret for the days when people had '*one* aim, *one* business, *one* desire'. In its transitional world, where technology and engineering are a major force producing a 'nobility of talent and enterprise' opposed to the old effete aristocracy, where Arnold's Dissidence of Dissent is evident among proliferating Churches and 'New Lights', and one school of architects vies with another, *A Laodicean* presents a range of dichotomies which emphasize the problem of seeing life steadily and seeing it whole. Hardy's sense of the poetry and romance[16] in the new engineering is communicated here and there, but the conflict between tradition and increasing diversifications of modernity leads to a divisiveness of mind which is portrayed by the Laodicean vacillations of a heroine with eclectic tastes who strives to adjust and achieve the best. She is happy at the end, yet equivocal over the 'modern spirit', and the new house her husband looks forward to, wishing that her castle were not burnt down and that he was one of the old aristocratic line of the de Stancys. Had Hardy enjoyed the fitness of body and mind necessary for him to fulfil his intentions in this novel, it is doubtful whether the result would have significantly differed, except in its proportions, his aim being to write a story which would illustrate in a variety of ways the need for Arnold's 'imaginative reason' in the welter of contemporary civilization.

The ending of *Two on a Tower*, which fortunately required no such application of a key idea, is the swiftest, and one of the most effective and memorable in all Hardy's novels. Its preliminaries are complicated. Lady Constantine (Viviette) had married the young astronomer Swithin St Cleve secretly, only to discover that her husband, whom she had presumed dead, died after this marriage. For the sake of appearances she postponed its legalization, and, on discovering that Swithin would be disinherited should he marry before the age of twenty-five, and thereby hamper his career, insisted altruistically that he go abroad to prosecute his astronomical studies, as he had intended, and on no account to write to her until the end of that period, lest his purpose weaken. He has hardly left when she discovers her pregnancy; to avoid scandal she accedes to her self-seeking brother's machinations, and marries her former suitor, the Bishop of Melchester. Just over seven months later Viviette bears a son, as Swithin reads in a newspaper sent out to him; later, by the same channel, he learns that the bishop is dead. An astronomer first and foremost, he does not return home until his work near Cape Town is completed; in the meantime he has heard from his grandmother that Lady Constantine's return to Welland House with her boy is expected. He does not take it for granted that the bishop's widow will marry him.

The first person Swithin meets on returning is the vicar Mr Torkingham, from whom he hears the local news. They help to his feet a fair-haired child, who has fallen while climbing over a stile, and Swithin is told that he is Lady Constantine's son. At his grandmother's he meets the organist Tabitha Lark, who has studied music with great success in London during his absence. They are soon chatting vivaciously, Swithin telling her about his astronomical researches and the voluminous notes which need to be rearranged and copied up; Tabitha immediately offers to do this for him. Not until the next morning does he think of going to Welland House. Before setting off, he gazes at the tower where he had practised his astronomy, and where Lady Constantine had fallen in love with him. Seeing somebody on the top, he makes his way there, and hears Viviette talking to her boy. He expects to see the Viviette he left, but he finds another:

Her cheeks had lost for ever that firm contour which had been drawn by the vigorous hand of youth, and the masses of hair that were once darkness visible had become touched here and there by a faint haze, like the Via Lactea in a midnight sky.

Viviette notices at once how shocked Swithin is by her ageing appearance, and quickly senses that his ardour has died. He is, we are told, too much her junior to appreciate the finer qualities she had acquired; he can sympathize with her, but he loves her no longer. She bids him farewell with dignity, and it is not until he is half-way down the tower that he wonders whether he was right to take her at her word. He had come back to England, feeling it was his duty to marry her if she wished to marry him, and, remembering her benevolence towards him, feels disposed to reciprocate her 'loving-kindness'. He returns, embraces her, and tells her he will marry her, as he had intended; she falls in his arms with 'a shriek of amazed joy'. The visible change in her which follows makes her little boy cry, and seek comfort from Swithin, who distractedly tells him he will take care of him. 'O Viviette!' he exclaims again, but there is no reply. He looks up for help, and nobody is in sight save Tabitha Lark 'skirting the field with a bounding tread – the single bright spot of colour and animation within the wide horizon'. When he looks down again his fear is realized:

> It was no longer a mere surmise that help was in vain. Sudden joy after despair had touched an over-strained heart too smartly. Viviette was dead. The Bishop was avenged.

The ending does just enough to round off the novel by reviving its opening scenes; it supplies one shock after another in quick succession; and it indicates all we need to know about the future. Life goes on, and hope is renewed: Tabitha, Swithin's friend for years, is the one 'bright spot of colour' in his life at present. The climax of this tragic finale arose from Hardy's memory of the shock he experienced when, a young man in London, he visited the lady, Julia Augusta Martin, who had been very fond of him, and whom he grew to love when he was a young boy on his visits to Kingston Maurward.[17]

Whereas Viviette's death is a sudden and unexpected tragic event, Henchard's in *The Mayor of Casterbridge* concludes a long tragic action which is dependent less on chance than on his own impulsive character. Ultimately he is as isolated as he made himself at the beginning, but attracts much more sympathy. The man who cast out love now pines for love. Elizabeth-Jane is too unimaginative and unforgiving to understand the situation when this penitent man, guilty of having deceived her from love of her companionship, arrives to congratulate her and Farfrae on their marriage. A shorn Samson, saddened by experience, he leaves, feeling rejected and making no effort at self-extenuation. His gift, a caged goldfinch, is later found starved to death, like all his hopes. Only then does she begin to understand. With Farfrae, who shows his smallness of heart by grudging the anticipated expense of a night's lodging away from home, she searches Egdon for him, and eventually meets Whittle. Only he befriends Henchard at the end. Hardy had remembered how in Hugo's *Les Misérables* another strong man who had committed a crime, before becoming successful in business and a mayor, had only a poor woman to look after him as he lay dying. He associated Egdon Heath with King Lear,[18] and Whittle's loyalty and name may well have been suggested by that of the fool on the heath in Shakespeare's tragedy, the archaic 'wittol' meaning 'fool'. Although Henchard had treated him ignominiously, Whittle could never forget his kindness to his mother in providing coals freely throughout one winter. It is his vernacular account of his master's death which makes the end of *The Mayor of Casterbridge* most moving. Henchard's will reinforces the effect, its poetry following the antiphonal pattern of Hebraic psalms. Only a writer who had known the depths of hopelessness could have conceived the last line, '& that no man remember me'.

Perhaps the additional ending is superfluous. Hardy could not resist it, for his design of the novel, and even more the character of his tragic hero, had been influenced by the masterly analysis of Sophocles' *Oedipus Rex* in John Addington Symonds' *Studies of the Greek Poets*. He may have known the last lines of the choric comment which concludes the play in Lewis Campbell's translation:

I will call no man happy, while he holds his house of clay,
Till without one pang of sorrow, all his hours have passed away.

They have their counterpart in the coda which reflects the stoical outlook on life acquired by Elizabeth-Jane. One phrase from it, 'a brief transit through a sorry world', was repeated almost word for word in Hardy's 1895 preface to his next novel, *The Woodlanders*.

Hardy was not happy with the ending of this novel, telling Symonds in a letter of 14 April 1889 that it was 'rather a failure'. More than three months later, when giving permission for a stage-adaptation of *The Woodlanders*, he writes, 'You have probably observed that the *ending* of the story, as hinted rather than stated, is that the heroine is doomed to an unhappy life with an inconstant husband.' He could not make this abundantly clear, he adds, 'by reason of the conventions of the libraries &c'. He made it clear enough in the 1895–96 edition, prefacing the resigned reflection of

Melbury, her father, on discovering that she has consented to live
with Fitzpiers again, 'It's a forlorn hope for her; and God knows
how it will end!', with the very outspoken and circumstantial

> 'and let her take him back to her bed if she will! . . . But let her
> bear in mind that the woman walks and laughs somewhere at
> this very moment whose neck he'll be coling next year as he
> does hers to-night; and as he did Felice Charmond's last year;
> and Suke Damson's the year afore!'

Then follow stories among his men on couples who make up their
differences, one by the bark-ripper:

> 'I knowed a woman, and the husband o' her went away for
> four-and-twenty year. And one night he came home when she
> was sitting by the fire, and thereupon he sat down himself on
> the other side of the chimney-corner. "Well," says she, "have
> you got any news?" "Don't know as I have", says he; "have
> you?" "No," says she, "except that my daughter by the husband
> that succeeded 'ee was married last month, which was a year
> after I was made a widow by him." "Oh! Anything else?" he
> says. "No", says she. And there they sat, one on each side of
> that chimney-corner, and were found by their neighbours sound
> asleep in their chairs, not having known what to talk about at
> all.'

There is a dry humour about this which is delightful, but it reflects
a disillusionment remote from the youthful zest of Tabitha Lark
with the bounding tread or of the happy couple at the end of *Under
the Greenwood Tree*. In that novel Fancy Day makes the right choice,
despite her educational attainments. Grace Melbury, betrayed by
the superficial refinements of boarding-school training, and by the
ambition of her doting father, is false to her natural inclination
when she prefers Fitzpiers to Winterborne. Despite her husband's
infidelity and their separation, she is won back; she is caught in a
man-trap. If, as seems indubitable, this is the wider, extra-literal
implication of her falling a victim, without physical injury, to the
trap set by Timothy Tangs to secure revenge on Fitzpiers (whom
he rightly suspects of being too interested in his newly wedded
wife, the *ci-devant* Suke Damson), it derives from the inventiveness
of an author who cannot resist a punning conceit. The episode is

developed at some length, and imparts excited suspense when the main action has come to an end, but it is a strange contrivance for a final phase which begins with mourning for Winterborne's death. Grace and Marty South had regularly taken flowers to place on his grave. At the end only Marty, whose woodland affinity with him had been complete, but who had never told her love, is left to pronounce his elegy. Having suffered a life of renunciation ever since shearing her beautiful locks, she is happy that he belongs to her, and her alone, in spirit. 'Now, my own, own love, you are mine, and only mine; for she has forgot 'ee at last, although for her you died!' she begins. Her rustic speech achieves a poetry of devotion which at the very last lifts the end of *The Woodlanders* to the one response commensurate with Winterborne's nobility in unfulfilment and endurance.

Tess of the d'Urbervilles is the story of a girl who recovers after being raped, only to discover that, although, as her author insists, she never did wrong willingly, she is condemned as a fallen woman. 'Once victim, always victim' is her lot; in the end she sacrifices herself to maintain her family, and becomes Alec's mistress. Angel Clare's return too late to save her ('Too Late, Beloved' was the intended title for the serialized novel) maddens her when her will to live is sapped. The climax of *The Bride of Lammermoor* is repeated unromantically, and Tess murders Alec. Her short-lived happiness with Angel at Bramshurst Court (aptly chosen because it was from its original that Dame Alice Lisle was taken to be executed at 'Wintoncester') is an artistic concession similar to that allowed by Shakespeare for the audience's emotional relief in the blissful reconciliation between Lear and Cordelia before the tragic catastrophe. Most fittingly Tess is last seen sleeping on the stone of sacrifice at Stonehenge just before her arrest; from the outset to the beginning of the end she has seen no alternative to sacrificing herself for her family. Her last words, 'I am ready', signify her willingness to die: 'the readiness is all', says Hamlet (repeated in Edgar's 'Ripeness is all' to Gloucester in *King Lear*). The imaginative grandeur and climactic tension of this scene (its traditional association with the Druids recalling the 'Druidical mistletoe' in the 'aged oaks' of the Chase, where Tess's victimization began) make the structuring of the last act of *The Woodlanders* seem rather laboured or clever journey-work.

The final chapter gives a distant view of the Wintoncester prison and the hoisting of the black flag which announces Tess's execution,

as witnessed by Angel Clare and her sister 'Liza-Lu, who appear
'hand in hand' (a first hint of their 'Paradise Lost'), with heads
drooping as in Giotto's 'Two Apostles'. Whether this reference
hints at a resurrection in Angel's life (Hardy thinking of the two
disciples on the road to Emmaus) is uncertain; the fresco fragment
he saw in the National Gallery is now called 'Two Haloed Mourners'
and attributed to Spinello Aretino. Incidental images, the milestone
'standing whitely on the green margin of the grass' and the 'yews
and evergreen oaks', recall critical points in Tess's early life, the
dancing on the green where Angel missed the white-frocked Tess,
and the Chase where her one life was ruined. The sentence
'"Justice" was done, and the President of the Immortals, in
Aeschylean phrase, had ended his sport with Tess', with its echo
of *King Lear*, recalls Hardy's recurrent presentation of her flylike
insignificance in a heedless universe. Unfortunately his figurative
reference to an ancient Greek view of the gods ('the laughter Of
the unalterable gods' in Swinburne's 'Ilicet') has often led readers
to think it represents his own.[19] The final sentence returns us to
Angel and Tess's sister, who had knelt down as if in prayer,
remaining motionless as the black flag waved: 'As soon as they
had strength they arose, joined hands again, and went on'. Such
is the way in which Adam and Eve at the end of Milton's *Paradise
Lost* leave Eden after their fall. Angel will probably marry 'Liza-Lu
in accordance with Tess's wish, but he will never be able to
forget his desertion of Tess in her hour of need, and his heavy
responsibility for her death. The end is grave; it has none of that
brightness of expectation which *Two on a Tower* evokes, but it goes
far to relax the tension, and produce that 'calm of mind, all passion
spent' which Milton and the great Greek dramatists thought
requisite at the end of a tragedy.

When Hardy thought of 'Christminster' he had the Crucifixion
in mind for *Jude the Obscure*.[20] Jude returns to Christminster with
his family, and finds that Remembrance Week has begun; Sue,
expectant, with three young children and no lodging for the night,
regards it as the Feast of the Passover, and thinks their move from
Kennetbridge like 'coming from Caiaphas to Pilate'. Little Father
Time, whose hereditary burden makes him wish he had never
been born, suffers because of his father's sickness, and is anguished
to hear that another child is expected. With ghastly altruism he
hangs the two other children and himself, providing a tableau
crucifixion from which the bifurcating sorrows of Sue and Jude

follow in Crucifixion terms. Overwrought by the loss of her children, Sue believes she is being punished by God for living in sin, and prostrates herself beneath the Cross in an obscure church; 'creed-drunk', she must obey God's will by returning to a husband whose bodily touch repels her. Jude is horrified that an intelligent woman should degrade herself in this way, and the veil of their temple is rent in twain. In remarrying Phillotson she drinks her cup to the dregs, while Jude, 'gin-drunk', remarries Arabella, likewise in accordance with 'true religion', the porcine associations of his wedding celebrations emphasizing the mere sexuality of their *mésalliance*, past and present. He recovers his heroism after this act of cynical despair, when, a sick man, he journeys to see Sue at Marygreen, his battling his way through wind and rain over the downs there and back being no less than a willed suicide, as he admits to Arabella on his return. He dies alone, after calling for water to quench his thirst (a reminder of Christ's thirst on the Cross) and reading verses from the Book of Job which begin, 'Let the day perish wherein I was born', while the organ notes of a concert, and shouts and hurrahs at the Remembrance games are heard at intervals.

> – People frisked hither and thither;
> The world was just the same.[21]

Arabella returns, finds him almost dead, and goes off to see the boat-bumping; she watches the colourful spectacle of the crowded barges, and is pleased to feel the arm of Vilbert, the old vendor of love-philtres, steal round her waist. Instead of going home first, she visits a woman who performs 'the last necessary offices for the poorer dead'. By ten o'clock that night Jude lies covered with a sheet, and 'straight as an arrow' (upright in death as in life), while the 'joyous throb' of a waltz from the ballroom of Cardinal College enters the open window. Two days later Mrs Edlin comes to see him. Applause from the theatre during the conferment of honorary degrees on the Duke of Hamptonshire and such 'illustrious gents' is heard, in satiric conjunction with a visual reminder of Jude's university aspirations and exclusion. His editions of the classics, marked with stone-dust where he had held them in short intervals between his labours, seem to pale to a sickly cast of thought as Christminster bells peal joyously. Hardy's main thrust had been against the indissolubility of marriages between the incompatible. The novel ends with Arabella telling Mrs Edlin that Sue will never find peace until she is dead like Jude. Theirs had been a marriage of true minds, but epicene Sue had always been naturally averse to sexual consent. She was 'intended by Nature to be left intact', Jude tells her after the loss of their children. In thinking they could live together illegally without suffering the consequences, she and Jude had been simpletons, as the first title of the novel implied; a dreamer to the end, he dies thinking that marriage with her was sanctified by Nature. Such is the irony underlying those minute satires of circumstance which sustain the denunciatory animus of two death-bed scenes – one spiritual ('Weddings be funerals', Mrs Edlin says of Sue's), the other final – at the end of *Jude*.

The last of Hardy's novel-endings to be written was that of *The Well-Beloved*, a substantial revision of the pre-*Jude* serial form which had anticipated his animadversions in *Jude the Obscure* on the comprehensive bondage of marriage-laws upheld by the Church. Had it remained like that of *The Pursuit of the Well-Beloved*, its concluding 'Ho-ho-ho!' might have made it appear the Joker in the pack. As it is, some have thought it veils Hardy's kind of Prospero farewell to novel-writing, an unconvincing inference, since his creative light was far from spent, and he was about to begin a more intensive period as a poet. The great financial success of Somers as a popular painter, and the last-sentence swipe at critics who spring up overnight and discern some genius, 'insufficiently recognized in his lifetime', in a sculptor who had already achieved fame, will always have their satirical significance, though they are incidental and secondary to the main thrust of Hardy's fantasy. Son of an affluent and indulgent father, Jocelyn Pierston has lived too much in an ivory tower, turning recurrent idealizations for which he had an innate propensity into art forms of an inevitably restricted nature. His strength as an artist had lain in his weaknesses as a citizen, Hardy points out. As, late in life, his humanity and concern for others increase, his zest and inspiration for his particular form of art declines. Hardy felt strongly that living art depends not merely on the really human, but on the beauty and poetry to be found in the ugly and the unromantic. He knew how tempting it was to pursue his own art and neglect his duties as a citizen, but, with J. H. Middleton, Slade Professor of Fine Art at Cambridge, in mind, he was convinced that it was a handicap to be engrossed in art:

Hardy used to find fault with Middleton as having no sense of life as such; as one who would talk, for instance, about bishops' copes and mitres with an earnest, serious, anxious manner, as if there were no cakes and ale in the world, or laughter and tears, or human misery beyond tears. His sense of art had caused him to lose all sense of relativity, and of art's subsidiary relation to existence.[22]

Truth is 'a naked and open daylight, that doth not show the masques, and mummeries, and triumphs of the world, half so stately and daintily as candle-lights', wrote Bacon; and Pierston is not confronted with the reality of Time's changes until Marcia appears without the benefit of lamp-light and her own 'beautifying artifices'. So overjoyed in his reaction is he at being delivered from the curse of his peculiar life-obsession that he decides to spend his last years in those kinds of altruistic utilitarianism for which he is qualified. Hardy undoubtedly meant to shock the reader by the delayed announcement of this change of interest, but it is questionable whether an anticlimax was intended. *The Well-Beloved* is an imaginative and diverting exercise in deromanticizing a type of Shelleyan–Platonic idealism which appealed to him; it ends rather in the manner of *Faust*, where Goethe, before revealing the dependence of salvation on divine grace, emphasizes the hero's need to transcend his romantic self in schemes which aim at the material welfare and the liberation of mankind. The question, which is related to the ending of *The Return of the Native*, had apparently become rather topical: 'It seems to me', Langham says in Mrs Humphry Ward's *Robert Elsmere* (1888), 'that in my youth people talked about Ruskin; now they talk about drains.'

In retrospect one is struck by the diversity of Hardy's novel-endings; such variety could be illustrated freely, but it suffices to think of it in three chronologically consecutive novels, *The Trumpet-Major*, *A Laodicean*, and *Two on a Tower*. Some may not quite succeed (*The Return of the Native* falls into this category, and probably *A Laodicean*) but none could be condemned as weak. They are never facile or conventional, even the happy endings of *Desperate Remedies* and *Under the Greenwood Tree*. Effectiveness is slightly reduced by an addition in *The Mayor of Casterbridge*, even more by complications in *The Woodlanders*. Given a single final situation, Hardy is at his best perhaps in *Two on a Tower* and *Jude the Obscure*. Some of the minor novels come out well in this assessment; to those already mentioned must be added *A Pair of Blue Eyes*, which provides one of Hardy's most moving tragic conclusions (some might say the most moving of all). The test comes in re-readings: one finds that the imaginative or emotional appeal of most of the finales is never lost; often one discovers more to admire in their artistry. Hardy, as he makes plain in 'The Profitable Reading of Fiction', thought that the novelist, just as much as the sculptor, should aim at 'a beauty of shape' which implies proportion, relevance, and integration. He had come to appreciate 'the constructive art' of Greek tragedies, and knew the critical importance of the ending in a novel as a 'circumstantial whole'. For inventiveness, attention to artistic detail, proportion, and general achievement in this respect, he probably has few superiors among novelists. He was quite incapable of the kind of inartistic misjudgment which mars Edith Wharton's *The Reef*, where the reader's expectations of an ending in keeping with the stature of the novel are mocked by a scene which is bathetically out of place and almost an irrelevance.

15

Symbolism

Although Hardy's pre-novel poems contain a few successes, notably 'Neutral Tones' and 'The Ruined Maid', they are generally so laboured that one must think his later writing benefited more from his assiduous study of the poets, and the plays of Shakespeare, from 1865 to 1867[1] than from his own practice of verse-writing. In his fiction his sensitivity to the imagery and colour of poetry is evident from the first. Frost symbolism occurs occasionally in his early poems, but it is simple and unelaborated; it is developed more creatively in *Desperate Remedies*, where we find the first example of another symbol which Hardy was to develop more than any other in his novels, though the later examples all occur in only one of them, *Tess of the d'Urbervilles*.

This is the garden, usually ruined or weed-infested, deriving ultimately from the thorns and thistles Adam and Eve had to contend with after the mythic Fall, with (in Milton's words from the opening of *Paradise Lost*) 'loss of Eden' and 'all our woe' as the consequence. Hardy hints at this in two scenes, one before, the other after, Tess's 'fall'. Originally his symbol was drawn from Swinburne and Shelley; later, from Milton and Shakespeare. All that remains of the 'wet old garden' in *Desperate Remedies*, when the heroine is anguished at the thought of having to forgo married happiness, alludes to Swinburne's 'Ilicet';[2] the mandrakes which she fancies she can almost hear shrieking in the overgrown hedge derive their significance from Shelley's garden in 'The Sensitive Plant', once an Eden filled with the spirit of Love, an 'undefiled Paradise' of sunshine and sweet-scented flowers which is ruined with the oncome of winter, when 'all loathliest weeds' such as thistles, darnels, agarics, and fungi spring up from 'the wet cold ground'. Only these survive:

> When Winter had gone and Spring came back
> The Sensitive Plant was a leafless wreck;
> But the mandrakes, and toadstools, and docks, and darnels,
> Rose like the dead from their ruined charnels.

The 'mildews and mandrakes' and 'slimy distortions' of 'The Mother Mourns', a poem in which Hardy comments on the Darwinian world in terms of his Unfulfilled Intention theory, are also drawn from 'The Sensitive Plant', as are other details which imply the 'loss of Eden' in three of his major novels: the fungi and rotting leaves of the pestilential marsh by which Bathsheba finds she has spent the night after discovering the worst of her husband Troy (anticipated in the 'atmospheric fungi' of the mist enveloping Yalbury Great Wood, as the coffin containing Fanny Robin and her child is being conveyed to Bathsheba's home); the oozing lumps of fungi (among other natural features of the season), like the rotten liver and lungs of a huge animal, when Eustacia is lost in storm and darkness during her fatal attempt to escape from Egdon; and the fungi, rotting stumps, and other signs of woodland decay, when Grace discovers that Winterborne is at the point of death.[3]

'Paradise' derives from an old Persian word which means a walled enclosure. Milton's Garden of Eden is therefore surrounded by a high verdurous wall, over which Satan has to spring when he enters to entice Eve:

> One gate there only was, and that looked east
> On the other side: which when th' arch-felon saw,
> Due entrance he disdained, and in contempt
> At one slight bound high overleaped all bound
> Of hill or highest wall, and sheer within
> Lights on his feet.[4]

Hardy had the whole scene in mind when he described the enclosure at the Slopes, once a garden but now only a trampled and sanded square; it also is surrounded by a wall which has only one door. Alec d'Urberville, with Tess's seduction, or rape, in prospect, enters by climbing the wall and disturbing the ivy-boughs which cloak it, before he springs from the coping into the plot. His mother's pet poultry (of fashionable breeds, including bantams) is kept in an old thatched cottage overrun by ivy, the boughs of which give its chimney 'the aspect of a ruined tower'. Hardy's stress on the ivy as a parasite suggests the defects of Darwinian nature which extend to man and his more primitive instincts. He took the non-Miltonic elements of his setting from *Clarissa*, another novel of rape. It is by the back door of the walled garden and park that Richardson's heroine is lured from her 'paradise'. Near it, on the inside, is the poultry-yard where she has regularly tended the bantams, pheasants, and peahens she inherited from her grandfather. In the midst of the haunted coppice just outside are the ruins of an old chapel. A 'great overgrown ivy, which spreads wildly round the heads of two or three oaklings' not far from the door, gives the Satanic Lovelace inadequate shelter as he waits hopefully one night in the rain.

The garden at Talbothays which expresses Tess's blighted life as she is drawn to Angel, and anticipates her failure to reach happiness in marriage after experiencing bliss like that of Eden with him, is a development from Hamlet's view of the world as 'an unweeded garden That grows to seed; things rank and gross in nature Possess it merely'. Like those in Shelley's ruined garden, its weeds emit offensive smells; its blighted apple trees, like those of Swinburne's 'Ilicet', suggest the denial of love's fulfilment. Its location in the rich Valley of the Great Dairies, where Tess first sees the Froom as the River of Life, emphasizes the irony of adverse chance both in the past and the future: the maintenance of her renewed zest for life is to depend on Angel, the harpist whose music lures her through the garden. His instrument and execution are both 'poor'.

After Tess's desertion by Angel, just before her father's death and her family's eviction, Alec appears as the tempter. In such a role he quotes from *Paradise Lost*, but the main significance of the scene is its conception in terms of Hell and punishment. Tess, 'once victim, always victim', though of pure intent, will find she has no choice but to live against her will with Alec, for the sake of her destitute family, a fate vaguely hinted at by the oddness of her appearance, in a bleached gown and a short black jacket which suggest 'a wedding and funeral guest in one'. The setting is an allotment at dusk, with smoke and flares from the burning heaped-up weeds and garden refuse. Tess and another worker, whom she assumes to be a neighbour from the next allotment, are now digging so closely that she notices the reflections of fire on the prongs of his fork as well as on her own. (The image is undoubtedly meant to recall the terror she had felt that her child, unless it were baptised, would be tossed in Hell-fire by the arch-fiend with his three-pronged fork.) By chance they approach to throw more weeds on the same fire, and as it flares up she sees that her fellow-worker is Alec d'Urberville, who tells her he has come after leaving presents at her home.[5]

Most of Hardy's symbols were provided by English weather. The earliest and most frequent is that of frost or wintry conditions as a reflection of life's ills and setbacks. Shelley is its main source; it is clearly implicit in 'The Sensitive Plant'; elsewhere, especially in *The Revolt of Islam*[6] and in 'Ode to the West Wind', it is often used with 'If Winter comes, can Spring be far behind?' connotations which are foreign to Hardy. His attitude may be seen in 'Could I but will' and 'A Self-Glamourer'. The dreamer of the former knows that he needs 'head-god' power to call the loved one back to life, and that of a 'half-god' in 'spinning dooms' whereby the frozen scene would flower. The 'frozen scene' has more than a physical sense, as in the second poem, where the distant future disturbs the illusory optimism of one who has chosen to see things far fairer than they are; he has counted his springtime

> Dream of futurity
> Enringed with golden rays
> To be quite a summer surety . . . .

In his subjective world visions have been the verities, so that 'fate and accident' have not appeared to behave 'perversely or frowardly'. Will everything follow suit, he wonders; can his illusions get the better of 'Life's winter snow'? Another unreal subjective world is that of the fickle lover in the song 'I said and sang her excellence', where his ideal ('the very She') is 'a sylph in picture-land, / Where nothings frosts the air'.

Among Hardy's early London poems frost as a symbol occurs in 'Discouragement' and permeates 'Neutral Tones'. One of the last and most remarkable, which he dedicated to A. W. Blomfield before leaving his office in 1867, is 'Heiress and Architect', an ingenious and grimly reductive artifact with the 'Life offers – to deny!' theme, the lady's first wish being denied by the 'arch-designer' (Hardy's First Cause or Prime Mover) in the following words:

> 'An idle whim!'
> Broke forth from him
> Whom nought could warm to gallantries:
> 'Cede all these buds and birds, the zephyr's call,
> And scents, and hues, and things that falter all,
> And choose as best the close and surly wall,
> For winters freeze.'

Soon afterwards Hardy began to write his first novel; it may have included some form of the frost imagery which plays a striking part in *Desperate Remedies*. Cytherea's marriage to Manston is doomed by ill-chance; the night before her wedding she hears branches rattling like dice against her bedroom wall, and dreams she is being whipped with dry bones on strings. She discovers this is the result of a continuing drizzle, a sharp frost, and a strong wind; next morning she sees the branches of neighbouring trees and shrubs heavily laden with icicles, some broken, a large one torn off, and others bowed to the ground. She had never thought they could 'bend so far out of their true positions without breaking' or that she could 'so exactly have imitated them'. Her true lover, at last free from his former engagement, arrives too late to prevent the wedding; and they meet, severed by a stream which runs as 'obtusely as ever' beneath 'a large dead tree, thickly robed in ivy', and now 'considerably depressed by its icy load of the morning'. The Darwinian ivy is not there by chance; it is a reminder of the struggle for existence which compels Cytherea to marry Manston for the sake of her brother. The river as a symbol of time, indifferent to human fate, is seen earlier in this novel, as elsewhere in Hardy's fiction.[7]

In subsequent novels frost and winter imagery are used incidentally, but not more insistently or with very pronounced effect until we reach *The Woodlanders* and *Tess of the d'Urbervilles*. It occurs significantly when Lady Constantine ponders whether she will have courage to meet her impending trial, 'despising the shame' until Swithin's return from the southern hemisphere; soon, however, 'fear sharp as frost' settles upon her (as it does on the narrator in the poem 'Family Portraits'). When Henchard, after leaving Casterbridge alone, resumes his old occupation of hay-trussing, he has lost his zest for life, and reflects:

'Here and everywhere be folk dying before their time like frosted leaves, though wanted by their families, the country, and the world; while I, an outcast, an encumberer of the ground, wanted by nobody, and despised by all, live on against my will!'

The Woodlanders opens with theme-notes of winter in association with death. It begins with a scene bespeaking 'a tomb-like stillness', and its first morning emerges as 'the bleared white visage of a sunless winter day . . . like a dead-born child'. 'Winterborne', the

name of its hero, is indicative of mischance and suffering. As a
pictorial image of the almost unendurable, frost reaches its most
intensive climax with the Arctic birds at Flintcomb-Ash, 'gaunt
spectral creatures with tragical eyes' that forget their polar suffering
in 'dumb passivity' as they concentrate on the present, seeking
food in the 'desolate drab' exposed field where Tess and Marian
have to hack up swedes during an unusually severe spell of frost.
The fruitless mission which Tess subsequently makes to Emminster
vicarage, in the hope of getting in touch with Angel Clare, is
marked by the rustling of shrubs on the lawn in a frosty breeze,
and by the rattling of ivy leaves which it has turned 'wizened and
grey'.

   Frost and winter symbolism continues in Hardy's poetry to the
end. In 'Before Knowledge' he imagines two lovers for whom
adverse circumstances would have been more tolerable had they
known in advance that the converging lines along which they had
moved were bound to meet:

> Then well I had borne
> Each scraping thorn;
> But the winters froze,
> And grew no rose;
> No bridge bestrode
> The gap at all;
> No shape you showed,
> And I heard no call!

'Standing by the Mantelpiece' presents Hardy's friend Horace
Moule as the speaker, just before the suicide occasioned when his
fiancée broke off their engagement; he refers to the 'wintertime'
close around him that 'might have shone the veriest day of June'.
The full tragic force of this metaphor is found again at the opening
of 'In Tenebris', where Hardy's deep depression (caused as much
by domestic circumstances as by the critical reception of *Jude the
Obscure*) assumes wintry imagery in almost death-bell tones:

> Wintertime nighs;
> But my bereavement-pain
> It cannot bring again:
> Twice no man dies.
>
> Flower-petals flee;

But, since it once hath been,
No more that severing scene
  Can harrow me.

Birds faint in dread:
I shall not lose old strength
In the lone frost's black length:
  Strength long since fled!

Leaves freeze to dun;
But friends can not turn cold
This season as of old
  For him with none.

'The Something that Saved Him' may allude to this period, when
'unseeing the azure', he went on to 'white winter' without knowing
May. 'The Frozen Greenhouse', suggested by a recollection of
plants 'frozen dead' at St Juliot, is principally an expression of the
poet's sense of bereavement after his wife Emma's death: the frost
of the present is 'fiercer' than that recalled during his re-visit, and
she is 'colder' than the iced plants that had been neglected
overnight. Five out of six consecutive pieces in *Poems of the Past
and the Present* relate to winter, some of them clearly showing that
extra-literal sense which is summed up in 'the Frost's decree' of
the villanelle 'The Caged Thrush Freed and Home Again'. The
thrush informs his 'tribes in treen' that, unable to 'change the
Frost's decree' or 'keep the skies serene', men know little more
than they 'How happy days are made to be'. The question in 'The
Darkling Thrush' is whether they know as much. Here, with the
poet's fervourless outlook reflected in a landscape 'spectre-gray'
with frost, and in weakening daylight made desolate by 'Winter's
dregs', the joyous song of an aged and 'blast-beruffled' thrush
leaves him wondering whether natural life does not, after all, offer
more grounds for hope than he has found. The disillusionment of
his last volume of poetry is hinted at in the title 'Winter Words'.

If fog as a concomitant or symbol of depressing circumstances
was in Hardy's mind when he included mists among the elements
which showed Egdon at its most intensive, nothing remarkable
came of it before *The Woodlanders*. At one point in the story (xiii) it
assumes a special significance when, with Norse overtones of
unfulfilment, it combines with evening darkness to form a 'gloomy

Niflheim' for Winterborne. As a means of indicting the Church, to which its general significance extends, Hardy uses it in *Jude the Obscure* to emphasize the tragic unenlightenment of the deranged Sue, whose intellect had once, 'scintillated like a star'. Disaster having made 'opposing forces loom anthropomorphous', she superstitiously decides that she must sacrifice herself to Phillotson, her husband in the sight of God. The obscurity of the church in which she prostrates herself beneath the Cross is maintained by the Christminster fog. She and Jude are seen moving through the latter like 'Acherontic shades' when he escorts her to the cemetery, where she bids him farewell by the graves of those who had died to 'bring home' to her the error of her former views; it persists when she leaves him for Phillotson; and it reaches climactic satirical force when this couple are about to be remarried at Marygreen:

> 'Where is the church?' said Sue. She had not lived there for any length of time since the old church was pulled down, and in her preoccupation forgot the new one.
> 'Up here', said Phillotson: and presently the tower loomed large and solemn in the fog.

This fog had travelled up from the lowlands around Christminster, and was dripping from the trees on the green when the bridal pair set off with Gillingham from Mrs Edlin's. Three months later Jude, after his 'gin-drunk' marriage, leaves his sick-bed at Christminster to see Sue at Marygreen. He is exhausted by the driving rain on the hills as he walks the last five miles, and he battles his way back in the teeth of the cold north-east wind and rain, wet through but indifferent, willing his own death, as he tells Arabella on his return. The persistence of the wind and rain as an image in the immediate sequel stresses its poetic or symbolic import. Sue feels she has sinned in seeing Jude and discovering that she loves him still. She decides therefore, as she tells Mrs Edlin, whom she persuades to stay for the night, that she must do penance by making her postponed physical surrender to Phillotson that night. Her reiterated expression of determination to drink her cup to the dregs is given additional tragic weight by the juxtaposition of the widow's comments on the unusual force of the wind and rain. 'Weddings be funerals 'a b'lieve nowadays', she says as she calls attention to it a third time, after finding that Sue has entered Phillotson's bedroom.

Hardy seems to have been feeling his way towards this particular symbol of life's tribulations in *The Return of the Native*. Egdon Heath reaches its most intensive moods often in winter darkness, tempests, and mists, when it is 'aroused to reciprocity', the storm being 'its lover, and the wind its friend', he tells us in his preliminary chapter, anticipating the orchestration of its grande finale when Eustacia attempts her nocturnal escape. On a miniature scale the same symbolism plays its role in the storm that wrecks a plantation enclosed from the heath in the year of Clym's birth, and counterpoints his anguish after quarrelling with his mother before impulsively marrying Eustacia.

The symbol grew from the recurrent echo in Hardy's mind of the combined refrains in Feste's song at the end of *Twelfth Night*:

> With hey, ho, the wind and the rain,
> For the rain it raineth every day.

He seems to have recalled the last in the burden of 'An Autumn Rain-Scene', where the final verse suggests that, whatever life's vicissitudes (and they incline to misfortune in this poem), death brings release. The same thought underlies 'A Drizzling Easter Morning', where the poet questions two theological assumptions, that Christ died 'a ransom for many' and that the Resurrection spells the hope of eternal life. As in 'Friends Beyond' and 'Jubilate', he maintains that people do not wish to live after death. He stands in wind and rain among the churchyard graves, while a loaded waggon moves slowly along the road, stressing what Wordsworth describes as 'the heavy and weary weight Of all this unintelligible world':

> I stand amid them in the rain,
> While blusters vex the yew and vane;
> And on the road the weary wain
> Plods forward, laden heavily;
> And toilers with their aches are fain
> For endless rest — though risen is he.

As Hardy writes in 'Nature's Questioning',

Meanwhile the winds, and rains,
And Earth's old glooms and pains
Are still the same, and Life and Death are neighbours nigh.

How nigh they are is implicit in the design of 'During Wind and
Rain', where past and present are juxtaposed stanza by stanza. By
their movement alone, especially in 'He, she, all of them – yea',
the first five lines of each convey jollity or happy expectations from
improvements and change. The brightness of these pictures of the
past (which Hardy found, after her death, in his first wife's
recollections of family life at Plymouth during her youth) is offset,
in the last two lines of each verse, by poignant regret arising from
present knowledge of the destructive effect of Time. The refrain,
which alternates 'Ah, no; the years O!' threnodically with 'Ah, no;
the years, the years', suggests that the poet's dream of a living
past is continually interrupted as he is dragged back to the
harshness of reality, which makes him imagine (in the final line of
each verse) how, during wind and rain at Plymouth, where
happiness and high expectations had prevailed, 'the sick leaves
reel down in throngs', 'the white storm-birds wing across', and
'the rotten rose is ripped from the wall'; how, finally, down the
inscribed names on the tombstones of all whom he has recalled,
'the rain-drop ploughs'. The erosiveness of Time reaches an
inexorable climax in the slow insistence of Hardy's rasping last
word.

Hardy uses the rainbow or iris-bow frequently as an indication
of romantic hope or of illusion, the former probably from Hope's
'iris of delight' in Shelley's *Hellas*, the latter from an agnostic view
of God's covenant in Genesis to maintain seed-time and harvest,
and not destroy mankind again by flooding the earth. At the
opening of *Desperate Remedies* he mentions 'sudden hopes that
were rainbows to the sight' but proved to be only mists. When
Eustacia's 'perfervid' imagination makes her fall 'half in love with
a vision' raised by Clym's return from Paris, she has a wonderful
dream in which she finds herself dancing with a man in silver
armour; she is in paradise. Suddenly they dive into a pool on the
heath, and come out 'somewhere beneath into an iridescent hollow,
arched with rainbows'. This 'La Belle Dame sans Merci' motif ends
much later on a note anticipating disillusionment, when Clym
awaits her in a ferny hollow, where there is 'neither bud nor
blossom, nothing but a monotonous extent of leafage, amid which

no bird sang'. The scene contrasts with that of 'The Hollow amid the Ferns', where Troy's bedazzlement of Bathsheba seems to her first of all 'a sort of rainbow', which, ominously perhaps, is 'upside down in the air'.[8]

Hardy distinguished repeatedly between romantic 'lover's love' and those deeper mutual qualities which are necessary for lasting attachment or successful marriage. In the poem 'The Well-Beloved', as well as in the novel of that name, his subject is illusory love, the dream, the vision, or the Idea, which is doomed soon to fade. It is to be found in 'At Waking', and it is adduced satirically with reference to the amorist Fitzpiers, who tells Winterborne that love is subjective, 'joy accompanied by an idea which we project against any suitable object in the line of our vision, just as the rainbow iris is projected against an oak, ash or elm tree indifferently'. It makes no difference who the 'young lady' is, he continues. Nobody who has read Hardy's mature views on marriage in his fiction (including *The Woodlanders*) and elsewhere could think it possible that he would agree with this superficial theorist who argues shallowly from German philosophy in accordance with inclinations which are shown for what they are worth.

The 'rainbow iris' illusion is quite foreign to 'The King's Experiment', an odd presentation (in terms of 'Doom and She') of how the world changes for one truly in love when the loved one dies. The circumstances here are more tragic, but the psychological truth is that of 'The Lover's Journey' in Crabbe's *Tales*:

> It is the Soul that sees: the outward eyes
> Present the object, but the mind descries;
>
> *   *   *
>
> Our feelings still upon our views attend,
> And their own natures to the objects lend:
>
> *   *   *
>
> But Love in minds his various changes makes,
> And clothes each object with the change he takes;
> His light and shade on every view he throws,
> And on each object what he feels bestows.

'Her Apotheosis' is the song of a 'faded woman', who recalls a period when she was unusually attractive, and 'an iris' ringed her with 'living light'. In 'The Absolute Explains' Hardy remembers the 'glad days' of pilgrimage to St Juliot, and 'that irised bow Of years ago' when he and Emma Gifford were in love. 'Rainbow-rays embow' the day of their first meeting, as he remembers it forty-three years later, not long after her death, in 'Looking at a Picture on an Anniversary'. As an index of illusions about Darwin-ian nature and life, the image occurs in 'To Outer Nature' and 'On a Fine Morning'. In the former, which appeared in *Wessex Poems* with an illustration of flowers hanging dejectedly around the top of a vase with fallen petals at its base, Hardy looks back to early days when he believed that God's love animates all Nature:

> O for but a moment
> Of that old endowment –
>   Light to gaily
>   See thy daily
> Iris-hued embowment!

In the second of these poems (which might be one of Hardy's 'songs') the speaker (or singer) asserts that happiness does not come from seeing life realistically,

> But in cleaving to the Dream,
> And in gazing at the gleam
> Whereby gray things golden seem.

He therefore prefers to see shadows as unfolding lights, and

> As no specious show this moment
> With its iris-hued embowment;
>   But as nothing other than
>   Part of a benignant plan;
> Proof that earth was made for man.

The impression that Wordsworth is the target here gains support from the association of the iris-bow with 'the Dream' and 'the gleam', suggesting that Hardy's rainbow symbol had, as one of its origins, 'Intimations of Immortality':

There was a time when meadow, grove, and stream,
The earth and every common sight,
  To me did seem
  Apparelled in celestial light,
The glory and the freshness of a dream.
It is not now as it hath been of yore; –

   * * *

   The Rainbow comes and goes,
   And lovely is the Rose,

   * * *

 But yet I know, where'er I go,
That there hath past away a glory from the earth.

   * * *

Whither is fled the visionary gleam?
Where is it now, the glory and the dream?

Hence, in a *A Pair of Blue Eyes* (xxxii), the dying away of the 'iridescence' in a preliminary scene which foretells the passing away of 'a glory' when Knight's 'dream' of Elfride is no longer what it has 'been of yore'.

16

Hardy as a Thinker

It must be obvious to readers of the poems Hardy wrote from 1865 to 1867 that the fundamentals of the main beliefs he was to hold for life were already fixed. Just what he read in the years immediately following his departure from home for London in April 1862 is not known; what evidence exists is scattered, but it suggests that he devoted much time first to literature (chiefly poetry), then to philosophy. He had clearly made a study of much scientific and agnostic thought by 1865, and yet in the summer of that year, after the failure of attempts to persuade magazine-editors to accept any of his poems, he indulged the idea of taking a degree at Cambridge in order that he could become a rural curate and write verses in his spare time. Not long after this the young man who had dreamed in childhood of being a parson, and for whom Stinsford Church had been the centre not only of his religious, but also of his musical, literary, and artistic education,[1] decided that his heterodox beliefs no longer allowed him conscientiously to pursue a course with such pleasant prospects in view.

The new world of space and time as revealed by astronomers and geologists had been familiar to him from articles in magazines and journals for several years. How much he studied Sir Charles Lyell's *Principles of Geology* (1830–33) is not known, but it seems very unlikely that he would neglect such an epoch-making book, and the cliff-hanger scene in *A Pair of Blue Eyes* bears testimony to an informed interest in the subject. Familiar with 'nature red in tooth and claw' on Egdon Heath and in the woods near his home, he was 'among the earliest acclaimers of *The Origin of Species*', though he was never one to share Darwin's sense of grandeur in a view of evolution which signified the survival of the fittest at the expense of the weak. *Essays and Reviews* (1860) by 'The Seven against Christ', as its authors were designated, did something to unsettle Hardy's more orthodox beliefs, and make him receptive, at a later stage, to the 'higher criticism' (historical and scientific studies of the Scriptures which had developed strongly in Germany). Yet in 1865, soon after its publication, when he was thinking of a career in the Church, he read the *Apologia* of John Henry Newman, who had been foremost in the Tractarian movement, and hoped to be convinced by him, because, as he says, his friend Horace Moule liked him so much. He found the style charming but the logic faulty, 'being based not on syllogisms but on converging probabilities'; later he described it as 'a poet's work, with a kind of lattice-work of logic in places to screen the poetry'. He found far more conviction in John Stuart Mill's treatise *On Liberty*, 'which we students of that date knew almost by heart'. The work, which Hardy was to remember in *Jude the Obscure*, argues with passionate intelligence for the freedom of the individual conscience in all matters, and affords a splendid example of what it was designed to promote, 'the entire moral courage of the human mind'. It could not have been long after 1865 that Herbert Spencer's *First Principles* (1862), a book containing ideas on evolution which were worked out before the publication of *The Origin of Species*, began to exert a deep influence on Hardy, who found it most stimulating, acting upon him 'as a sort of patent expander' when he was 'particularly narrowed down by the events of life'. More than any other work, it may have habituated Hardy to think in terms of the First Cause.[2]

His interest in Positivism probably began about this time. He may have met Professor Beesly, one of the translators of Auguste Comte's massive work on the subject, and a prominent member of the Reform League, which had its offices below Blomfield's, where Hardy worked until the summer of 1867. Apart from studies of his work, some translations had already appeared, and Hardy closely examined sections of the 1865 translation of Comte's *A General View of Positivism*, which he borrowed from Horace Moule. Comte was an agnostic; he neither affirmed nor denied God. Basing his principles on the belief that nothing is knowable beyond the phenomena of the universe, where all is subject to unalterable laws, he holds that our obligations are to the human race, and to all sentient beings. The key to his religion is altruism (a word he invented); it was to become Hardy's Golden Rule, extending to all living things. For Comte capitalists were parasites, doomed to disappear. Education and science were to be fostered for the progress of mankind, and religion needed to be founded on scientific truth. He believed that abstract reasoning was beyond the capacity of all but a few, and the promotion of the new religion depended on its appeal to the heart. The artist in stimulating moral energy or will through imaginative feeling for the furtherance of social justice and amelioration was of the highest importance. (*Tess of the d'Urbervilles* and the novels of George Eliot illustrate what Comte had in mind.) Had this 'religion of humanity' become, as Mill thought it would, 'the religion of the Future', it would have proved more effective in the modern western world than religions based on supernatural theologies which only minorities are prepared to accept. On this question Hardy wrote pertinently after hearing of George Eliot's death:

> If Comte had introduced Christ among the worthies in his calendar it would have made Positivism tolerable to thousands who, from position, family connection, or early education, now decry what in their heart of hearts they hold to contain the germs of a true system.

There can be no doubt from his essay 'Utility of Religion' (and his subsequent 'Theism') that Mill was much impressed with Comte's ideas. They contributed to his *Utilitarianism* (1861), which Hardy quotes at some length in *The Hand of Ethelberta* (xxxvi), a novel inspired to a considerable degree by altruism and anti-mammonism. For many years he read much on philosophy in contemporary journals, without changing significantly his essential views. Resemblances and coincidences of thought, especially in German philosophers, Schopenhauer and Hartmann in particular, have been given exaggerated importance with reference to beliefs which Hardy had held in common with Mill and others before he had made his mark in literature. When Helen Garwood in 1911 sent him a copy of her doctoral dissertation *Thomas Hardy, an Illustration of the Philosopher Schopenhauer*, he informed her that the views reflected in his works showed harmony with Darwin, Huxley, Spencer, Hume, Mill and others, all of whom he used to read more than Schopenhauer. There is no evidence that he made a systematic or lengthy study of Schopenhauer or any German philosopher during the formative period of his thought.

Hardy's 'constitutional tendency to care for life only as an emotion' did not dispose him to logical thinking any more than it did to 'a science of climbing' in his career. Poets, Shelley and Swinburne especially, did more to sway and sustain his beliefs than abstract philosophy. There had been a time, no doubt, when, like most Victorians, he had set great store by Tennyson, a poet who never ceased to search for truth, and included astronomy and geology among his muses, without losing his faith in the Incarnation and the immortality of the soul. Though the Poet Laureate's vehement opposition to Positivism did not become publicly explicit until later, it supplies a measure of the extent to which Hardy's sympathies with the tenets of *In Memoriam* must have failed in the late 1860s, however much he admired its poetry. Long before he wrote his 'An Ancient to Ancients', he could have said, 'The bower we shrined to Tennyson . . . is roof-wrecked.' Shelley's notes to his early poem 'Queen Mab' are sufficient to indicate that Hardy's new enlightenment came indirectly from the eighteenth century as well as from Victorian heterodoxies; an acknowledgment of its direct influence has already been given in Hardy's reference to Hume. Shelley's note 'Even love is sold' created an impetus which was regenerated in the writing of *Jude the Obscure*, and the same may be said of Swinburne's liberating influence on Hardy in 1866.

Hardy's abstract reasoning sometimes conflicts with the more powerful feelings of his imaginative intellect, notably in *Tess of the d'Urbervilles*, where casual, detached thoughts are introduced on the heroine's grief and sense of shame during her pregnancy, at home after her rape. It is hard to conceive a passage more irrelevant to the novel than this:

> alone in a desert island would she have been wretched at what had happened to her? Not greatly. If she could have been but just created, to discover herself as a spouseless mother, with no experience of life except as the parent of a nameless child, would the position have caused her to despair? No, she would have taken it calmly, and found pleasures therein. Most of the misery had been generated by her conventional aspect, and not by her innate sensations.

The hypothetical position is absurd, with a mother who has had 'no experience of life except as the parent of a nameless child', living in a kind of vacuum which can have none of the conventional attitudes of western civilization. Wherever she had been, the Tess of the novel would have cared greatly. Her misery had been generated by the most painful sensations, though convention had contributed to her subsequent suffering.

Whatever her attitude to convention, people would have continued to blame her for her illegitimate pregnancy. She was regarded as an immoral woman in her village, and her family's subsequent eviction, after her father's death, was due to this reputation. Yet Hardy regards her as the dupe of fancy, misled by 'a cloud of moral hobgoblins'. 'She had been made to break an accepted social law, but no law known to the environment in which she fancied herself such an anomaly.' As a victim of rape, she had not even broken a social law; nor can one equate, as Hardy does, the human world in which she lived with the natural world of 'skipping rabbits on a moonlit warren'. He premises his remarks with the philosophical statement 'for the world is only a psychological phenomenon', as if convinced by Berkeleyanism, and as if Alec d'Urberville, Tess's unborn baby, her family, and the people of the village where she sought to conceal her shame, had no existence except in her mind. Elsewhere he claims that but for 'the world's opinion' her experience would have been 'simply a liberal education', and that her 'passing corporeal blight had been her mental harvest'. The novel, with its 'Once victim, always victim' theme, suggests that it was anything but passing, despite her rally. It may have made her more tolerant, as it did toward Angel when he made his confession after their wedding, and it may have given her greater powers of endurance, but the novel does not suggest that it changed her character greatly. It made her appreciate Angel's protective care during their courtship, but the most significant 'mental harvest' resulting from her 'corporeal blight' is to be found when Tess is stung into action in the threshing-scene. Its consequences are becoming too painful to contemplate or endure. Hardy's authorial comments are usually integrated with the novel-world of his projection; when he detaches himself to make external comments, as he does very signally in *Tess*, he is on dangerous ground. It is no wonder that D. H. Lawrence wrote, 'Two blankly opposing morals, the artist's and the tale's. Never trust the artist. Trust the tale.'[3]

There can be no denying the power of Hardy's indictment of illiberal marriage-laws in *Jude the Obscure*; it motivates the tragic conclusion after a catastrophe which, we are expected to believe, is the result of hereditary causes. There seems to be a 'logical' weakness in the 'case' Hardy presents; it would have been more cogent had it been based on the less exceptional. In a passage which purports to be Jude's reflection when he finds he is falling in love with Sue, Hardy clearly anticipates the catastrophe which precipitates the tragic endings of the two lovers. He has loaded the dice so heavily against them that all seems predetermined. Jude thinks of 'crushing reasons' why he should not allow himself to fall in love with Sue. The first is that he is already married; the second, that they are cousins; the third, that marriage in his family has usually meant 'a tragic sadness'. The whole combination of circumstances could produce 'a tragic horror'. Later, when she is engaged to marry Mr Phillotson, Jude and Sue are 'possessed by the same thought . . . that a union between them, had such been possible, would have meant a terrible intensification of unfitness'. Even if we accept this deterministic complex and its consequences, Hardy weakens his case for marriage-reform by basing it on an abnormal marriage. Sue and Jude are drawn to each other; they have a spiritual kinship, and enjoy intellectual companionship. She is an epicene, however, and instinctively revolts against sexual marriage; her marriage behaviour is abnormal from first to last.

On 9 May 1881 Hardy wrote down his conclusions 'after infinite trying to reconcile a scientific view of life with the emotional and the spiritual' (an excellent expression of his aims as a thinker and artist). Later, in *The Woodlanders* (vii), he referred to this view as 'the Unfulfilled Intention, which makes life what it is'. The 'general principles' he reached relate to natural laws. 'Law', he says,

has produced in man a child who cannot but constantly reproach its parent for doing much and yet not all, and constantly say to such parent that it would have been better never to have begun doing than to have *over*done so indecisively; that is, than to have created so far beyond all apparent first intention (on the emotional side), without mending matters by a second intent and execution, to eliminate the evils of the blunder of overdoing. The emotions have no place in a world of defect, and it is a cruel injustice that they should have developed in it.

If Law itself had consciousness, how the aspect of its creatures would terrify it, fill it with remorse!

The hypothetical 'second intent and execution' signifies the removal of all the defects of the natural law. In 'The Mother Mourns' Hardy imagines Nature's regret that man has become aware of them; that this regret is his own is clear from 'Before Life and After', where he yearns for the return of man's primitive or natural state before consciousness evolved. He admitted that he was 'So Various', but how he, who countered the charge of pessimism by insisting that

he was an 'evolutionary meliorist', could be so regressive in outlook
is remarkable rather than unimaginable; the life of emotion to
which he surrendered as a poet made him subject to inconstant
moods:

> A time there was – as one may guess
> And as, indeed, earth's testimonies tell –
> Before the birth of consciousness,
> When all went well.
>
> None suffered sickness, love, or loss,
> None knew regret, starved hope, or heart-burnings;
> None cared whatever crash or cross
> Brought wrack to things.
>
>   *   *   *
>
> But the disease of feeling germed,
> And primal rightness took the tinct of wrong;
> Ere nescience shall be reaffirmed
> How long, how long?

Hardy expresses the same thought when the Spirit of the Pities in
The Dynasts laments 'the intolerable antilogy' of 'making figments
feel'. What hope, we might ask, could there be for the progress of
civilization if people were not keenly alive to injustice and suffering?
Hardy's unusual awareness of their incidence is manifest in his
fiction and *The Dynasts*. The complete pessimism of his regressive
mood came from the same source, but it is not typical. Hardy did
not share the kind of evolutionary optimism which made Shaw
conclude *Saint Joan* with 'O God that madest this beautiful earth,
when will it be ready to receive Thy saints? How long, O Lord,
how long?', but, however opposite he seems in 'Before Life and
After', his Positivism usually made him more sympathetic with
such a hope than with any desire for the return of mindless
primitivism.

He must have been considering his Unfulfilled Intention theories
when he concluded *The Return of the Native*, where (vi.i), in a more
typical, aggressive mood, he vents his blame for human mischance
on his abstract ultimate the First Cause. He criticizes Clym Yeobright for not being like 'the sternest men' (with whom he must be
identifying himself), and for not continuing to maintain that 'he

and his had been sarcastically and pitilessly handled'. 'Human beings', he continues,

> in their generous endeavour to construct a hypothesis that shall not degrade a First Cause, have always hesitated to conceive a dominant power of lower moral quality than their own; and, even while they sit down and weep by the waters of Babylon, invent excuses for the oppression which prompts their tears.

The accusation is not open-minded. It suggests a writer obsessed with wrongs inflicted on the human race, and blind to other natural laws which seem slowly to assuage distress (a subject considered by Wordsworth at length, both in time and in *The Excursion*, from personal suffering far greater than Hardy had ever known at this stage of life). However mistakenly optimistic Yeobright is in the altruistic aims he is to pursue, he has risen to higher things than self. In his zeal to attack the low morality of his First Cause, Hardy has forgotten altruism. He has, as he was often to do, assumed that all is attributable to a Prime Mover, making no distinction between the unknown Creator of the universe and the spirit of good at work among men, the Johannine God, Matthew Arnold's 'stream of tendency that makes for righteousness'. Additionally, as he was to realize much later, he is blaming his First Cause for man's mistakes.

Hardy's awareness of his changeability of mood and thought may be seen in the consecutive arrangement of 'I said to Love' and 'A Commonplace Day' in *Poems of the Past and the Present* (1901). 'Too old in apathy', he ends the former with ' "*Mankind shall cease.* – So let it be", I said to Love.' In the second poem Hardy reflects, as the dull wet day draws to its end, that it marks nothing important achieved by him, or by anyone else as far as he knows. Yet, it may be, in someone somewhere, some impulse inspired by 'that enkindling ardency from whose maturer glows The world's amendment flows' has arisen but

missed its hope to be
> Embodied on the earth;
> And undervoicings of this loss to man's futurity
> May wake regret in me.

Belief in the 'world's amendment' as a result of noble impulses kindles Hardy's expression, but the closing lines disclose a more qualified assurance and zeal than the subject engenders in George Eliot at the end of *Middlemarch*.

Yet, at the end of *The Dynasts*, in 1907, Hardy did offer hope of the world's amendment. It seemed to him that 'the Unconscious Will of the Universe' was 'growing aware of Itself', and he claimed that this idea was his own, stating categorically that he had 'never met with it anywhere'. *The Dynasts* ends rather ambivalently, however; the intellect says one thing, the heart another. The Years insist that the Immanent Will still goes on

> Moulding numbly
> As in dream,
> Apprehending not how fare the sentient subjects of Its scheme.

It is the Pities who, after expressing the view that it would be better for mankind utterly to cease rather than continue its sufferings, suddenly experience signs of the change:

> But – a stirring thrills the air
> Like to sounds of joyance there
> That the rages
> Of the ages
> Shall be cancelled, and deliverance offered from the darts
> that were,
> Consciousness the Will informing, till It fashion all things fair!

In *The Dynasts* the Will is seen working on, or in, people. It is the unreasoning force which sways the ambitions of Napoleon, moving him inexorably, for example, to undertake his disastrous Russian campaign. It is

> A Will that wills above the will of each,
> Yet but the will of all conjunctively;
> A fabric of excitement, web of rage,
> That permeates as one stuff the weltering whole.

Part of this web of rage is revealed in Berlin, when Prussia is provoked to war. No 'voice of reflection' is heard; 'the soul of a nation distrest' is 'aflame', almost as unconscious as the Will of the part it plays in 'the weltering whole'. The idea that the human race can learn from its errors and sufferings, and that nobler, humanitarian, impulses (represented by the Pities) will gradually prevail is completely intelligible, but how the universe, the 'web Enorm' of space and time, and how the laws of heredity and Darwinian nature, can be affected, how consciousness can inform the Immanent Will as a whole, till it fashion *all* things fair, is another question. There had been so much theorization on the Will, especially by German philosophers, that it had become a fashionable subject, one which Hardy could not resist, though its furtherance was founded on fancy and abstract reasoning. Hardy argued that

> what has already taken place in a fraction of the whole (*i.e.* so much of the world as has become conscious) is likely to take place in the mass; and there being no Will outside the mass – that is, the Universe – the whole Will becomes conscious thereby: and ultimately, it is to be hoped, sympathetic.[4]

The orthodox Christian assumes that God is both the creator of the universe and the spirit at work for righteousness in mankind. No warrant for such an assumption has yet been produced; the universe, including nature on this planet, is activated by unalterable law, with consequences affecting heredity and diseases in all species. The human link affects but an infinitesimal part of the whole, and consciousness working for amelioration on earth has no known relationship with a universe which is beyond its comprehension.

The outbreak of the 1914–18 war made Hardy regret ending *The Dynasts* as he had done. It destroyed his 'belief in the gradual ennoblement of man', and 'gave the *coup de grâce* to any conception he may have nourished of a fundamental ultimate Wisdom at the back of things'. In 'Fragment' (*Moments of Vision*, 1917) he implicitly attributes his former hope to the effect of traditional Christian belief in God (referred to 'vaguely, by some' as 'the Ultimate Cause', Hardy adds, knowing the weakness of his former abstract terminology, especially in 'the First Cause', compared with 'the Immanent Will'):

> 'Since he made us humble pioneers
> Of himself in consciousness of Life's tears,

It needs no mighty prophecy
To tell that what he could mindlessly show
His creatures, he himself will know.

'By some still close-cowled mystery
We have reached feeling faster than he,
But he will overtake us anon,
    If the world goes on.'

It will be seen that the theorizing here combines Hardy's heterodoxy
with a providential Christian assumption.

Hardy's more cautious later views seem to verge on Necessitari-
anism. He agreed that people have a 'modicum of free will . . .
when the mighty necessitating forces – unconscious or other' are
in equilibrium (which simply means when we have the opportunity
to reflect and make a choice), but insisted that the Cause of Things
is unmoral, 'an indifferent and unconscious force' that 'neither
good nor evil knows' and is 'loveless and hateless'. It conforms
neither to the Pities' hope nor to the old Greek view of 'the
President of the Immortals'. Hardy was becoming tired of the
charge that he believed in a Prime Mover who was like 'a malignant
old gentleman, a sort of King of Dahomey. . . . "What a fool one
must have been to write for such a public!" is the inevitable
reflection at the end of one's life', he wrote to Alfred Noyes in
December 1920. His conclusion was that 'neither Chance nor
Purpose governs the universe, but Necessity', a view, he held,
close to Spinoza's 'and later Einstein's'.[5]

The most important change in Hardy's views is recorded in
'Thoughts at Midnight'. Some of it was written on 25 May 1906,
but the most radical part runs contrary to the philosophy which
permeates *The Dynasts*, and was probably written in the 1920s when
Hardy, like many others, clearly saw that peace was threatened
by the vengeful policy-making of the victors after the 1914–18
war. The author who had regarded Jude as his 'poor puppet', and
who had portrayed Napoleon and the Prussian people helplessly
swayed by the Immanent Will, now upbraids mankind for acting
like puppets, and not with intelligent anticipation:

Acting like puppets
Under Time's buffets;
In superstitions
And ambitions
Moved by no wisdom,
Far-sight, or system,
Led by sheer senselessness
And presciencelessness
Into unreason
And hideous self-treason.

They are not sinned against, but the sinners:

God, look he on you.
Have mercy upon you!

The charge against the human race is repeated in 'We are getting to the end', where Hardy is almost in despair to think that nations may be 'tickled mad by some demonic force' into war again. He does not oppugn the Immanent Will; the madness or unreason is human:

We are getting to the end of visioning
The impossible within this universe,
Such as that better whiles may follow worse,
And that our race may mend by reasoning.

More remarkable is the change in Hardy's thought on the subject of death. In his prime he was certain that there was no life-to-come, and that the only kind of immortality that could be claimed depended on posthumous memories. In 'A Sign-Seeker' he asserts the finality of death: 'When a man falls he lies.' Positivistic immortality is the subject of 'Her Immortality', 'His Immortality', and 'The To-Be-Forgotten', the last two poems stressing the brevity of life-after-death for ordinary people, however good, compared with that of the famous:

For which of us could hope
To show in life that world-awakening scope
Granted the few whose memory none lets die,
But all men magnify?

Yet, after the death of Emma in 1912 and of his sister Mary in 1915, the old assurance has gone. In 'Paradox' he is prepared to believe that the latter's spirit, though lost to them, is co-present, views the vicinity, and is aware of what befalls them: 'Yea indeed, may know well; even know thereof all'. In 'He Prefers Her Earthly', thinking of Emma the fearless pony-rider of St Juliot, he wonders if she is present in the 'glory-show' of an 'after-sunset'; she may be, 'for there are strange strange things in being', stranger than he knows. If she is there, how different she must be, he muses:

> Changed to a firmament-riding earthless essence
> From what you were of old.

In 'A Woman Driving' he asks:

> Where drives she now? It may be where
> No mortal horses are,
> But in a chariot of the air
> Towards some radiant star.

This is not just the poeticizing of the non-rationalist poet who believed in 'spectres, mysterious voices, intuitions, omens, dreams, haunted places, etc.' The Hardy who in 1890 wrote that he had been looking for God all his life, and was confident he would have found him had he existed, who later, in 'A Sign-Seeker', denied the possibility of securing the 'blest enlightenment' of glimpsing a phantom parent or friend, seeing him smile, and hearing him softly breathe the desired reassurance, 'Not the end!', believed that on the Christmas Eve of 1919, he did see a churchyard ghost, after placing a sprig of holly on his grandfather's grave at Stinsford. The phantom wore eighteenth-century dress, and said, 'A green Christmas'; when Hardy followed it into the church it vanished.[6] We have moved far from the novelist who insisted for two of his heroines, one early, one late, that life on earth was her 'single opportunity of existence'.

Hardy, whatever his extravaganzas, had come to realize that man's knowledge and perceptiveness were too limited to fathom the mysteries of the universe. There had been a time when theorizing of the kind he summarizes in 'Nature's Questioning' had been publicized and debated as if all things were intelligible to rationalists. It was because Hardy was no longer an unqualified devotee of rationalism that his friend Edward Clodd prized his genius less highly. Hardy had realized that even scientific theory is fallible, because its conclusions are man-made. When he wrote 'Drinking Song' he must have thought with Tennyson that in the vast sum of things 'Our little systems have their day; They have their day and cease to be.' From Thales of ancient Greece onwards he selects famous thinkers whose conclusions, once considered absolute, are now discounted or doubted, among them Darwin's theory of man's evolution from the brute. Having been too absolute himself, Hardy was ready in December 1920 to admit that 'the Scheme of Things is, indeed, incomprehensible', and to argue, as he had done in 1917, that his many statements and representations on the subject (with their inconsistencies) were mere 'seemings' or impressions of the day. He protested that he had no philosophy, 'merely what I have often explained to be only a confused heap of impressions, like those of a bewildered child at a conjuring show'. 'It is my misfortune that people *will* treat all my mood-dictated writing as a single scientific theory', he concluded. Hardy's changes of view are often mood-dictated, especially in his poetry; often they proceed from modifications of beliefs which he had held firmly for long periods.

17

Literary Allusion and Indebtedness

'People are always talking about originality; but what do they mean? . . . If I could give an account of all that I owe to great predecessors and contemporaries, there would be a small balance in my favour', Goethe told Eckermann. Hardy made no such general admission; he indicated writers who were great masters and examplars to him, and emphasized that he was a 'born bookworm'. That, and 'that alone', was unchanging in him, he added (at the opening of the chapter 'Student and Architect' in his *Life*). It may not occasion surprise therefore to find that his works contain frequent literary references, allusions, and quotations; that other writers' images gave him narrative and scenic ideas; and that, like Emily Brontë in *Wuthering Heights*, he sometimes, as a means of furthering his own fiction, adapted or borrowed episodes, situations, and details from literature which impressed him.

The efflorescence of quotation which marks the scene in *Desperate Remedies* where Edward Springrove and Cytherea Graye fall in love illustrates not only Hardy's habit of culling evocative phrases from poetry, especially from *The Golden Treasury*, but also the risk of surfeiting the reader with uncritical excesses. One of his favourite poems, Browning's 'The Statue and the Bust', from which he was to draw more effectively in his later fiction, supplies the first quotation, and it is introduced with a precision which is outweighed by its awkwardness. The 'reasoning' of 'Sweet, sweet Love must not be slain' expresses Cytherea's anxiety for Stephen in a style which is intended to be feminine but is no more than sentimental poeticizing of a weakened Elizabethan vintage. Lines in Keats's 'Ode to a Nightingale' –

> Where but to think is to be full of sorrow
>   And leaden-eyed despairs,
> Where Beauty cannot keep her lustrous eyes,
>   Or new Love pine at them beyond to-morrow

– contribute to the sentimental continuation of the above, as Cytherea's young violet eyes 'pine at' Stephen 'a very, very little', and to the conclusion, which expresses the view that the 'brighter endurance of woman' is due more to 'a narrower vision that shuts out many of the leaden-eyed despairs in the van, than to a hopefulness intense enough to quell them'.

Milton's question in 'Lycidas' whether it is better to 'meditate the thankless Muse' or 'sport with Amaryllis in the shade' excites the thoughts of both lovers, for whose supreme happiness Hardy finds denotation in 'The bloom of young Desire and purple light of Love' from Thomas Gray's 'The Progress of Poesy'. Their kisses combine with sounds from the bay and shore in 'many a voice of one delight', the scene recalling the first of Shelley's 'Stanzas Written in Dejection near Naples'. Later, uncertainty about their future makes Cytherea forget 'herself to marble like Melancholy herself' as she glides pensively along the pavement, Hardy abstracting part of the image from Milton's 'Il Penseroso', and assuming the reader's familiarity with the whole:

> Forget thyself to marble, till
> With a sad, leaden, downward cast
> Thou fix [thine eyes] on the earth as fast.

Then, after telling us that traces of tears are visible on her drooping eyelashes as she slept, he adds from *The Passionate Centurie of Love* by the Elizabethan poet Thomas Watson

> Love is a sowre delight, and sugred griefe,
> A living death, and ever-dying life.

The disconnection here, which leaves the thought conjecturally authorial, suggests that Hardy, in his callow eagerness to excel, attached too much impressiveness to poetical quotation, and that, had he been more mature and independent-minded, he could sometimes have expressed himself more adequately, concisely, and pertinently in prose.

In comparison with his own brief but poetical description of the reflected promenade lights, with their 'tap-roots of fire quivering down deep into the sea', the above quotations create a cumulative sense of adventitiousness or bedizenment, of being accretive rather than integral to conception; it is as if he is suffering from a

compulsive addiction, and has to introduce them, however effectively. Literarary quotation, allusion, and reference remained for
all that a significant part of Hardy's outlook and style. They were
for him an essential part of an author's role, becoming a novelist,
who, like others before him, Sir Walter Scott especially, expected
readers to appreciate the best of traditional culture, including
classical literature, Shakespeare, and the Bible, and to be alive to
the best and most significant in the greatest of modern writers.
Hardy in his day could assume such responses; by literary reference, quotation, hints, and echoes, he could awaken overtones
that would help to stimulate, define, and enrich perception,
thought, and imaginative feeling. In the modern world of haste
and change and mass-media, where few have time to think or read
for themselves, where, for example – and this has a special
importance for the Hardy reader – the 'authorized version' of the
Bible, for centuries our common inheritance, is rarely read or
heard, the question must arise how much a writer nourished in
the cultured tradition loses by non-realization or partial realization
of his deepening or expanding overtones. Explanation is no
substitute; nothing can equal the illumination that comes from
immediate awareness and integration of meaning.

   'The Impercipient' and 'At an Inn', which occur consecutively
in *Wessex Poems*, illustrate the problem. The second probably
presents no difficulty, but the significance of its conclusion assumes
a richer meaning if the allusion to Arnold's 'Isolation' is instantly
communicated:

> Yes: in the sea of life enisl'd,
> With echoing straits between us thrown,
> Dotting the shoreless watery wild,
> We mortal millions live *alone*. . . .
> Now round us spreads the watery plain –
> Oh might our marges meet again!
>
> Who order'd, that their longing's fire
> Should be, as soon as kindled, cool'd?
> Who renders vain their deep desire? –
>   A God, a God their severance rul'd;
> And bade betwixt their shores to be
> The unplumb'd, salt, estranging sea.

Little can be made, however, of the 'inland company' pointing
upward to a 'glorious distant sea' in the first poem, unless
one fully appreciates Wordsworth's 'Intimations of Immortality'.
Hardy's poem gains by knowledge of a further Wordsworth
reference, and by appreciation of its relatedness to *The Pilgrim's
Progress* and *In Memoriam*, well-known works in tens of thousands
of homes when it appeared in 1898. The impact made by the poem
will be more exciting the better one realizes the faith inspiring
Bunyan's Shining Ones who live 'upon the borders of heaven'
where the sun shines night and day; how, too, after losing his
greatest friend, Tennyson wrestled with his doubts for years before
recovering faith ('And all is well, though faith and form Be
sundered in the night of fear'). It helps also to realize the allusion
to Wordsworth's *Excursion*, another work concerned with the
recovery of faith, where the despondent Solitary protests
(iv.1083–5):

> Alas! such wisdom bids a creature fly
> Whose very sorrow is, that time hath shorn
> His natural wings!

'Intimations of Immortality' explains the happiness of childhood
in terms of the Platonic belief that the soul exists in heaven before
birth, and that the older we grow the further we move from such
a state, though we have compensations, one of them being the
memory of childhood experiences which seemed 'Apparelled in
celestial light, The glory and the freshness of a dream':

> Hence in a season of calm weather
> Though inland far we be,
> Our Souls have sight of that immortal sea
> Which brought us hither,
> Can in a moment travel thither,
> And see the Children sport upon the shore,
> And hear the mighty waters rolling evermore.

In his novels Hardy makes several references or allusions to this
poem, most imaginatively in *A Pair of Blue Eyes*, where both in the
preliminary scene and the narrative discourse he shows how the
glory and the dream in Knight's love of Elfride die away. For
Eustacia they depart from Wildeve when she hears that he is no

longer coveted by Thomasin. The 'season of calm weather' has its
echo at the end of *The Mayor of Casterbridge*. Wordsworth's idea
that 'Heaven lies about us in our infancy', and that we come
'trailing clouds of glory . . . From God, who is our home' is seen
as a ghastly satire by Tess, when she and her poverty-stricken
family are forced to leave home. 'To her and her like, birth
itself was an ordeal of degrading personal compulsion, whose
gratuitousness nothing in the result seemed to justify, and at best
could only palliate', Hardy adds. In the smiles of the boy Jude,
when his mind is already set on Christminster, he sees the
'beautiful irradiation' of the young which gives rise to 'the flattering
fancy that heaven lies about them then'. The 'glory', accompanied
by Wordsworth's visionary 'gleam', which the dreaming boy sees
in his distant view of the city, proves to consist of lamps which
wink their yellow eyes dubiously at him when he arrives there in
early manhood.[1]

Reference has already been made to Robert Browning's 'The
Statue and the Bust', a poem prized by Hardy for rating the moral
conformity of the faint-hearted lower than magnanimity, however
unconventional. 'The world and its ways' having 'a certain worth',
the intended elopement is postponed, and passion declines with
increasing age. Browning imagines the 'frustrate' ghosts of the
lovers as they 'sit and ponder What a gift life was, ages ago'; the
sin he imputes to them is 'the unlit lamp and the ungirt loin', in
consequence of which they 'see not God'

> Nor all that chivalry of his,
> The soldier-saints who, row on row,
> Burn upward each to his point of bliss.

Only a reader familiar with Browning's poem can appreciate to the
full Hardy's adaptation of its main theme in 'The Waiting Supper'.
The Bathsheba who looks on the past 'over a great gulf', as if she
were like 'the mouldering gentlefolk of the poet's story', and can
'sit and ponder what a gift life used to be', assumes greater interest
because, unlike her opposite, she is not 'frustrate', her suffering
being the result of a rash, impulsive marriage. Winterborne's
'frustrate ghost' provides another interesting contrast, his self-
denial being part of a character Hardy clearly admires. When Jude
gives up the Church for Sue, he tells her his 'point of bliss is not
upward', like that of the 'soldier-saints', but 'here'. Browning's

poem accentuates Sue's degradation after her mental breakdown, when she insists that the loss of her children is God's punishment for sin. Penance demands that she conform by returning to her husband Phillotson, and, since 'the world and its ways have a certain worth', she must be remarried, though (in the eyes of Jude and of Hardy) the ceremony sanctifies her prostitution.[2]

Burns's 'To a Mouse' provided an apt parallel to tragic chance in the affairs of men, and Hardy's allusions to it were no doubt readily recognisable. The 'best-laid schemes' and 'I . . . guess and fear' occur in *Desperate Remedies*, and Elizabeth-Jane's reluctance to tempt Providence is expressed as 'that fieldmouse fear of the coulter of destiny despite fair promise'. Joseph Poorgrass's 'multiplying eye' derives, less obviously perhaps, from Burns's 'Death and Doctor Hornbook':

> The rising moon began to glowre
> The distant Cumnock hills out-owre:
> To count her horns, wi' a' my pow'r,
> I set mysel;
> But whether she had three or four
> I cou'd na tell.[3]

Whether Hardy wished readers to notice that the horned moon and its reflection, as observed by Oak after the loss of most of his sheep, depend for features and expression, even to the extent of the two hundred dead, on a passage associated with a curse in 'The Ancient Mariner' is questionable. He may have created the scene from unconscious memory, or he may have been so impressed imaginatively by all the attendant details of the curse suffered by the mariner that he took a curious satisfaction in adapting them to his narrative, believing, as T. S. Eliot did, that the writer is fully justified in stealing for the purpose of re-creation.[4]

Solomon Longways' 'Why *should* death rob life o' fourpence?' is one of the most memorable utterances in Hardy. It repeats with justificatory emphasis Christopher Coney's question after digging up, and spending at the Three Mariners, the four ounce pennies which had been used for closing Mrs Henchard's eyes before her burial. The universality of the question is given a proverbial quality by its simple brevity and concreteness. It is Hardy's invention, all the more admirable for its quintessentializing mutation of an argument in a sharp exchange at the opening of Dickens' *Our Mutual Friend*:

> 'Why, yes, I have', said Gaffer. 'I have been swallowing too much of that word, Pardner. I am no pardner of yours.'
> 'Since when was you no pardner of mine, Gaffer Hexam, Esquire?'
> 'Since you was accused of robbing a man. Accused of robbing a live man!' said Gaffer, with great indignation.
> 'And what if I had been accused of robbing a dead man, Gaffer?'
> 'You COULDN'T DO IT.'
> 'Couldn't you, Gaffer?'
> 'No. Has a dead man any use for money? Is it possible for a dead man to have money? What world does a dead man belong to? T'other world. What world does money belong to? This world. How can money be a corpse's? Can a corpse own it, want it, spend it, claim it, miss it? Don't try to be confounding the rights and wrongs of things in that way. But it's worthy of the sneaking spirit that robs a live man.'

Other Hardy short stories besides 'The Waiting Supper' are given point and imaginative emphasis through reference or allusion to literary contexts. The final anguish of 'The Marchioness of Stonehenge' is a notable example, in its evocation of King Lear's 'How sharper than a serpent's tooth it is To have a thankless child.' David's lament for Saul and Jonathan supplies the ending of 'The History of the Hardcomes': 'The two halves, intended by Nature to make the perfect whole, had failed in that result during their lives, though "in their death they were not divided".' Luke Holway's contrition in 'The Grave by the Handpost' is made more poignant by the Biblical words inscribed for him on the memorial stone he wished to be erected to his father, 'I am not worthy to be called thy son.' More moving is the Biblical reference at the end of 'Old Mrs Chundle', when the unexpected makes the curate realize how he has sinned in thought and deed; stunned at the completeness of his misjudgment, he goes out 'like Peter at the cock-crow', kneels down in the dust of the road, and prays for forgiveness.

No literary influence permeates Hardy's work more than that of the Bible, and so much did its stories appeal to his imagination

that, in 'Zermatt: To the Matterhorn', he can write about some of
its miraculous events as if he believed in their occurrence:

> Yet ages ere men topped thee, late and soon
> Thou didst behold the planets lift and lower;
> Saw'st, maybe, Joshua's pausing sun and moon,
> And the betokening sky when Caesar's power
> Approached its bloody end; yea, even that Noon
> When darkness filled the earth till the ninth hour.

(The 'betokening sky' recalls a scene in Shakespeare's *Julius Caesar*.)
Hardy was a rationalist most of his life but, as an imaginative
writer, especially in poetry, he believed in the value of tradition,
and was not averse to the supernatural ('spectres, mysterious
voices . . . haunted places, etc., etc.').[5]
  Hardy was also highly impressed by the artistry of Biblical
narratives. On Easter Sunday, 1885, just before concluding *The
Mayor of Casterbridge*, he was moved to write on the subject, having
come to the conclusion that the convincing qualities of these stories
were due not so much to their actual truth as to 'the actuality of a
consummate artist who was no more content with what Nature
offered than Sophocles or Pheidias'. Considering the recognised
writers of his time in both fiction and history, he commented:

> how few stories of any length does one recognize as well told
> from beginning to end! The first half of this story, the last half
> of that, the middle of another. . . . The modern art of narration
> is yet in its infancy.

More than two years later he selected 'the chapter of the Bible [2
Samuel, xviii] containing the death of Absalom' as the finest
example of narrative prose, 'showing beyond its power and pathos
the highest artistic cunning'. His references, beginning with the
name 'Endorfield' in *Under the Greenwood Tree*, show that Saul's
visit to the witch of Endor was one of his favourite Old Testament
narratives.[6] The attraction of stories relating to Saul and David led
Hardy to draw considerably from them in *The Mayor of Casterbridge*
for the creation of both character and incident. Love which turns
to jealousy and hatred between Henchard and Farfrae is based on
the Saul–David relationship, the younger successful man being
introduced as 'ruddy and of a fair countenance' in both the novel

and the first book of Samuel (xvii, 42). So Hardy provides his clue, which is supported in Henchard's visit to the weather-prophet, whose prescient readiness is likened to that of Samuel when he receives Saul. Furthermore, Saul's love of music, his gloomy fits, his strength and stature, his anger, and his resolve to murder his rival are all developed with reference to Henchard and Farfrae in several scenes, some powerful, some highly imaginative, all memorable.

Scriptural references, quotations, and allusions are particularly numerous in *Tess of the d'Urbervilles* and *Jude the Obscure*. However incidental some may be, the full significance of the former, the gravamen of Hardy's figurative charge against the President of the Immortals, cannot be fairly assessed without realization of the composite character of Pauline 'charity', and the extent to which it is displayed by the heroine. In *Jude* it is the action, especially when Jude and Sue return to Christminster, which gains from Biblical overtones; the full intensity of the tragedy, and of its satire against the Church, cannot be felt without a continual awareness of the extent to which they are conceived as a Crucifixion theme. Nothing can be more challenging to a belief in Providence than Hardy's expression of Jude's Christminster dreaming in terms of the Holy Ghost alighting on Jesus in the form of a dove ('I'll be her beloved son, in whom she shall be well pleased') when he is rudely brought back to reality by a smack on the ear from the pig's pizzle thrown by Arabella. Sue's crucifixion is emphasized by her repeated determination to drink her cup to the dregs; that of the dying Jude by his thirst. Her declaration, when she rejects her embroidered nightgown for 'sackcloth' in preparation for remarriage to Phillotson, that it is 'an accursed thing . . . fit for the fire' has a Scriptural overtone which was once familiar. One may not lose much by not recognising it, but it is a deprivation to miss the authorial thrust or the emotional heightening of most of Hardy's Biblical allusions.[7]

Few contemporary authors would have written 'rejoiced with great joy', or thought of the lover entering Swithin 'like an armed man' and casting out the student; nor would Hardy, unless he had found Scriptural phrases and imagery most expressive. Familiarity with the Bible in his day had various effects on his writing. It encouraged him to go beyond reference and quotation to allusion; he expected readers to recognise the spying implication when Ethelberta tells Picotee that they have visited Neigh's Farnfield estate 'to see the nakedness of the land'. It made him assume that

readers visualized Biblical narrative as he did: the exaltation of
Grace Melbury's face after her visit to Mrs Charmond is likened
by Giles to that of Moses when he came down from the Mount;
that of her father, after having hopes of Grace's divorce raised by
Fred Beaucock, reminds him of Stephen when 'beheld by the
Council, with a face like the face of an angel'. More importantly
the Bible echoed many of Hardy's profounder thoughts, and for
that reason contributed effectively to his style, especially at more
tragic points. When, for example, Lady Constantine cannot get in
touch with Swithin, and is afraid their child will be born out of
lawful wedlock, she wonders whether she can meet her impending
trial, 'despising the shame', until his return, which is likely to be
long delayed owing to the conditions of his uncle's will. After
encountering her brother and telling him her plight, she creeps
into the house, 'bowed down to dust' by what she has revealed.
Two passages, one on the whole creation groaning and travailing
in pain, the other on things true, lovely, and of good report, are
notable for their recurrence in Hardy's late fiction and his later
poetry; the second expresses the grounds on which what hope he
had for the world was based.[8]

Hardy uses expressions from *The Book of Common Prayer* less
frequently but with equal aptitude, as the following example from
A Pair of Blue Eyes may indicate. The demolition of the church
tower, just after Elfride quotes 'Thou hast been my hope, and a
strong tower for me against the enemy' to Knight, ominously
foreshadows the ultimate severance of their relations, but the full
effect of Hardy's intended irony will be missed if it is not known
that the prayer 'Be unto them a tower of strength' follows the
betrothal rites in the Church of England service for the solemniza-
tion of matrimony.[9]

Hardy's adaptation of features in Victor Hugo's *Les Misérables* to
the opening of *The Mayor of Casterbridge*, its subsequent situations,
and more especially to the development of its tragic conclusion, is
so astonishing in its scope that one might be tempted to call it
plagiarism (an offence of which he was more justifiably accused
with reference to an amusing but relatively insignificant drill-scene
in *The Trumpet-Major*). Perhaps he intended a hint of acknowledge-
ment in his mention of the *misérables* who tended to haunt the
remoter of the two bridges on the lower side of Casterbridge (xxxii).
Significant influences of Richardson's *Clarissa* and Scott's *The Bride
of Lammermoor* have already been discussed, in addition to those

of essays by Walter Pater and Matthew Arnold, Sophocles' *Oedipus Rex*, Milton, *Paradise Lost* in particular, and George Eliot, notably in *Under the Greenwood Tree* and *Far from the Madding Crowd*.

Although Hardy quotes explicitly or implicitly from Shakespeare more than from any other author, his influence tends to be incidental. That of *King Lear* is not always specific, but it is suspected in the choice of the heath scene, with Whittle as sole attendant, for Henchard's death. It may have suggested the gift of the caged goldfinch which Henchard, at a time when he is completely in disgrace with fortune, intends as a wedding-gift and peace-offering to Elizabeth-Jane.

> We two alone will sing like birds i' the cage;
> When thou dost ask me blessing, I'll kneel down
> And ask of thee forgiveness.

Mrs Yeobright's words, not long before her death, 'Can there be beautiful bodies without hearts inside? . . . I would not have done it against a neighbour's cat on such a fiery day as this!' open with the gist of a question asked by Antonio in *Twelfth Night* (near the end of III.iv), the remainder (like Clym's subsequent 'which a dog didn't deserve' and 'like an animal kicked out') originating from Cordelia's

> Mine enemy's dog,
> Though he had bit me, should have stood that night
> Against my fire.

Mr Torkingham's description of the 'nameless something' on Lady Constantine's mind as 'a rooted melancholy, which no man's ministry can reach' gains from recognition of its origin in Macbeth's

> Canst thou not minister to a mind diseas'd,
> Pluck from the memory a rooted sorrow?

By accident or design, the letter addressed by Marian and Izz Huett to Angel Clare begins with Iago's words to Othello: 'Look to your Wife.' Less familiar allusions, such as the words of the apothecary in *Romeo and Juliet* (v.i) when Jude, addressing the crowd at Christminster on Remembrance Day, says it was his poverty and not his will that consented to be beaten, may easily be overlooked, more so than Dare's remark about his father's lacking advancement (like Hamlet). When Sue rends her embroidered nightgown, her tears resound through the house 'like a screech-owl', with a suggestion of the unnatural and of foreboding, the full force of which cannot be felt unless its association with a shroud at the end of *A Midsummer Night's Dream* is summoned up. Her second wedding to Phillotson is indeed a funeral.

From his early years as a writer Hardy was influenced in thought and expression by Thomas Carlyle. In 'We are getting to the end', the importance of which as a reflection of Hardy's later thinking is emphasized by its penultimate position in his posthumously published collection of poems, he revives the image of the caged bird and its human significance in Carlyle's essay 'Goethe's Helena': 'The Soul of Man still fights with the dark influences of Ignorance, Misery, and Sin; still lacerates itself, like a captive bird, against the iron limits which Necessity has drawn round it.' The image occurred to him when he contemplated the rich and poor in the 'wheel' and 'roar' of London: 'All are caged birds; the only difference lies in the size of the cage.' The bird caught in the toils of circumstance sometimes expresses the plight of his heroine, especially in *Tess of the d'Urbervilles*. Carlyle's imagery is often poetic, and there can be no doubt that the simile of the lovers who, in 'The Duchess of Hamptonshire', leap together 'like a pair of dewdrops on a leaf' came from *Sartor Resartus* (II.v), where the souls of the lovers, 'like two dew-drops, rushed into one'.

Well-known poems by Wordsworth and Keats, particularly those in *The Golden Treasury*, account for many quotations and allusions in Hardy, but some may be overlooked. The church clock in *Desperate Remedies* (x.3) echoes the 'bewildered chimes' of 'The Fountain' by the former; and a line in 'The Two April Mornings', a companion poem, is recalled when Christopher Julian, after seeing the last of Ethelberta, stood long lost in thought, and 'did not wish her his'. Johnny Nunsuch's gaze into the face of the dying Mrs Yeobright, 'like that of one examining some strange old manuscript the key to whose characters is undiscoverable' derives from Keats's 'The Eve of St Agnes', where Porphyro looks into the aged Angela's face.

> Like puzzled urchin on an aged crone
> Who keepeth clos'd a wond'rous riddle-book.

Only a reader appreciative of Keats's 'In a drear-nighted December' will sense the overtones of the phrase 'glued up by frozen thawings' in *The Woodlanders* (xvii). (The wailing gnats of 'To Autumn' have a significance which has already been shown.)

Hardy's admiration for Swinburne's poetry never waned. He must have read *Tristram of Lyonesse* soon after its publication in 1882, for he quotes from it in his first edition of *Two on a Tower* (xxxvi). His enthusiasm for Swinburne's strictures against the Victorian Church, and in favour of more natural, joyous living, began in 1866, if not earlier; but it was not until *Jude the Obscure* that he dared to repeat them challengingly. In retrospect it pleased him to think that the onslaught on his novel was 'unequalled in violence' since the publication of *Poems and Ballads* in 1866, and that, when they met in June 1905, Swinburne could quote with amusement from a Scottish paper: 'Swinburne planteth, Hardy watereth, and Satan giveth the increase.'[10]

Nevertheless, it was Shelley who exercised a greater influence on Hardy than any other poet; and hints of his indebtedness to him, including quotations, occur from first to last, from Shelley's well-known poems in *The Golden Treasury* and from his major works. Hardy's familiarity inclines him repeatedly to Shelleyan expression; he expects his reader to catch the resonance of 'Stanzas Written in Dejection near Naples' when Ethelberta longs 'like a tired child' for the time when her work is over, and she can await death placidly. The 'solid media of cloud and hail shot with lightning' in 'A Tryst at an Ancient Earthwork' springs from imagery in 'Ode to the West Wind', as does the figurative language of 'disperse like stricken leaves before the wind of next week' in the Apology to *Late Lyrics and Earlier*, or the simile comparing Angel Clare's normal propensities, at the time when he turns against Tess, to 'dead leaves upon the tyrannous wind of his imaginative ascendency'.

The influence of Shelley's first major poem, 'Queen Mab', and its notes, to which Hardy's attention was drawn at an early stage of his literary career, must have been great. In their astonishing range of revolutionary thought, they must have appealed to his imagination, and done much to enlarge and mould his scientific thought and philosophy. The suffering endured by Arctic birds before driven south to Flintcomb-Ash may have developed partly from Shelley's image of nature's ruthlessness in the 'ceaseless frost' of the Polar regions (if his use of frost as a symbol of adversity originated from this context, it was amply reinforced in *The Revolt of Islam*). Shelley's notes impressed on Hardy the principle of Necessity as an immense chain of cause and effect throughout the universe, and started or confirmed higher-critical thoughts on the unlikelihood that the Spirit pervading the 'infinite machine' with its plurality of worlds 'begat a son' upon the wife of a Jewish carpenter (the subject of Hardy's 'Panthera'). Shelley's views on marriage coincide with those expressed by Hardy in *The Pursuit of the Well-Beloved* and *Jude*:

> Love withers under constraint: its very essence is liberty: it is compatible neither with obedience, jealousy, nor fear: it is there most pure, perfect, and unlimited, where its votaries live in confidence, equality, and unreserve.

Sue Bridehead sums them up from lines in Thomas Campbell's 'How delicious is the winning':

> Can you keep the bee from ranging,
> Or the ringdove's neck from changing?
> No! nor fettered Love from dying
> In the knot there's no untying.

How Hardy drew creative ideas from Shelley's 'The Sensitive Plant' and 'Epipsychidion' has already been shown. In *Jude the Obscure* (VI.ix) he presents him as 'the Poet of Liberty', a phrase which applies to much in Shelley's poetry, especially his drama *Prometheus Unbound*. Its lyrical choruses suggested the role of the aerial spirits in *The Dynasts*. Some are sung by 'Gentle guides and guardians . . . of heaven-oppressed mortality', and in them Hardy's Spirit of the Pities may be found. They appear as the flower of man's intelligence, like the Chorus at the end of Part First of *The Dynasts*, coming 'from the mind Of human kind Which was late so dusk, and obscene, and blind', and representing man's highest Thought, Wisdom, Art, and Science. Hardy's Shade of the suffering Earth has its origin in Shelley's drama, and the Fore Scene echoes a Shelleyan note when the Chorus of Pities sings to aerial music:

We would establish those of kindlier build,
    In fair Compassions skilled . . .
Those, too, who love the true, the excellent,
And make their daily moves a melody.

In *Prometheus Unbound*, and elsewhere in Shelley, music and
musical imagery reflect happiness and the ideal; and accordingly
Hardy's Spirit of the Pities maintains, after the battle of Trafalgar
and Nelson's death, that

                    Things mechanized
    By coils and pivots set to foreframed codes
    Would, in a thorough-sphered melodic rule,
    And governance of sweet consistency,
    Be cessed no pain.

Perhaps the expression of uncertain hope at the end of *Hellas*,
Shelley's second and more specific drama on human liberation,
weighed with Hardy when he chose to end his epic drama more
hopefully than historical impartiality (or the Spirit of the Years)
warranted.

A singular example of the influence of Shelley's imagery on
Hardy's creative imagination is to be found in 'Neutral Tones', one
of his most remarkable poems, completed before he left London
in 1867. It has been associated with Rushy Pond and, more
surprisingly, with the Berkshire original of the frozen pond where
Jude Fawley thinks of committing suicide. Fictional biography has
linked it with Hardy and this and that girl in his early life. Such
assumptions appear to characterize an age which makes little
allowance for a writer's imaginativeness. In his later years Tennyson was 'driven mad' by the identification of Lincolnshire places
with poems such as 'The Miller's Daughter'; he would have been
more incensed had he been aware of the Lincolnshire habit of
identifying Maud with Rosa Baring. 'Why do these fellows give
me no credit for *any* imagination? The power of poetical creation
seems totally ignored by them. All this modern realism is hateful!'
he exclaimed. One might equally ask how Hardy could have written
all his fiction, had he been confined to the world of living
experience. The 'She, to Him' sonnets of 1866 show that he could
imagine and dramatize situations which probably occurred to him
as a result of being shocked by the effects of age on Mrs Martin, a

lady whom he had loved when he was a very young boy.[11] He was also, it should be remembered, imaginatively sensitive (as 'The Darkling Thrush' proves) to what he read in poetry and elsewhere.

One stanza on love in Shelley's lyric 'When the lamp is shattered' haunted Hardy's imagination during his early years as a writer:

> Its passions will rock thee
> As the storms rock the ravens on high;
> Bright reason will mock thee,
> Like the sun from a wintry sky.
> From thy nest every rafter
> Will rot, and thine eagle home
> Leave thee naked to laughter,
> When leaves fall and cold winds come.

He quotes the first four lines in *Desperate Remedies* (vi.1), and there can be little doubt that

> Bright reason will mock thee,
> Like the sun from a wintry sky

as a chapter-epigraph in the second part of 'An Indiscretion in the Life of an Heiress' was retained from Hardy's unpublished first novel *The Poor Man and the Lady*. He included

> O love! who bewailest
> The frailty of all things here,
> Why choose you the frailest
> For your cradle, your home, and your bier?

from the same poem in *A Pair of Blue Eyes* (iii), in accordance with its main theme; and remembered it much later when describing how 'cold reason' came back to 'mock' Tess for answering her friends with superiority when she returned from the Slopes. Confirmation of its early influence on Hardy's imagination is found in 'Neutral Tones'.

He had already associated winter and frost with setbacks; in 'Discouragement', for example, an earlier poem than 'Neutral Tones', he regards the various handicaps of heredity as 'frost to flower of heroism and worth' and 'fosterer of visions ghast and grim'. His 'God-curst' sun comes from the fusion of Shelley's mocking sun with the image and thought of lines in Swinburne's 'Anactoria', which Hardy read soon after its appearance in the 1866 volume of *Poems and Ballads*:

> Him would I reach, him smite, him desecrate,
> Pierce the cold lips of God with human breath,
> And mix his immortality with death.
> Why hath he made us? what had we all done
> That we should live and loathe the sterile sun . . .?

Swinburne's sterile sun accords with Hardy's whole poem; it goes far to explain its title, which he probably had in mind when, in *Tess of the d'Urbervilles*, he described the forlorn spot called Cross-in-Hand, attributing to it a new kind of beauty, 'a negative beauty of tragic tone', far different from the landscape charm sought by artists and sight-seers. In the composition of his poem, Hardy in London may have begun with a particular pond and an imagined situation in mind; his setting is, however, the product of images which developed in association with Shelley's thoughts on love in 'When the lamp was shattered' until they were united in a tone-poem of negative beauty. The conjunction of winter, fallen leaves, the inimical sun, bird imagery, and a sense of mockery in two such brief poems can be no accident.

There are obvious differences, especially in rhythm. The final verse of Shelley's lyric is fiercely keen, as befits a storm and its effects at the outset of winter. It is generalized, monitory, and anticipative, the rather shrill verse moving swiftly and relentlessly, with sharp incisive momentum, to the slow, stressed insistence of an ending indicative of worse to come. Hardy's poem is retrospective and particularized: the former lovers stand by a pond; the sun is God-curst; the leaves have fallen from an ash, and are grey. In this frosty scene there is little motion; what life it has is no more than a final flickering before the extinction of love. Eye-movement and words are hinted at, but the smile of the deceiver is on the point of expiry; it is 'the deadest thing Alive enough to have strength to die'. The mockery that leaves the victim of wrecked love in Shelley's poem 'naked to laughter' appears only momentarily in Hardy as 'a grin of bitterness' which vanishes 'Like an ominous bird a-wing'. The eyes give the impression not so much of an individual as of the eternal woman, with 'eyes that rove Over tedious riddles of years ago'. Hardy has succeeded, as T. S. Eliot was to do more habitually, in creating an original poem largely from derivatives fused and localized by his imagination. The relationship of Shelley's images has been shifted in 'Neutral Tones'; their association in a new complex of rhythms, setting, and the dramatic humanization of a universal subject, has given the poem a remarkable individuality. So strong is it, in fact, that it does not echo Shelley or any other author; it is unique.

18

The Hero of *The Dynasts*

Although, as Hardy says, *The Dynasts* is presented on an 'intermittent plan', and he assumes in his reader a sufficient familiarity with the subject 'to fill in the junctions required to combine the scenes into an artistic unity', it has an artistic wholeness quite independent of such imaginary links. Any attempt to read it purely on the historical plane would soon lead to recurrent disjunction; it would become a technical impossibility, for innumerable links indispensable to the coherence of this epic-drama belong to extra-dimensional media which transcend its historical confines, however vast, although they impinge occasionally on the consciousness of some of its personages. The history is provided by varying means, sometimes reported, sometimes descriptive, often in dramatic form; it provides most of the subject, but it is basic to something more important, and that is the vision of a poetic philosopher, who not only subjects terrestrial events to the thoughts and feelings of spirits in an Overworld but makes these observers the agents whereby, in cinematic style, our point of view is continually moved, from air to earth, from long range to close-up, from country to country, sometimes with recordings of military movements, sometimes with hints of their ultimate outcome, in a 'panoramic show' of unprecedented range.

To think of a hero without reference to Hardy's philosophical vision of events, regarding *The Dynasts* as if it were an epic like *Paradise Lost* or a drama like *Macbeth*, or both, could therefore limit vision, make us see things out of context, and distort values. Fundamental to all those aspects of Hardy's outlook which are represented by the spirits of the Overworld is the conception of a Prime Mover of events throughout the whole universe, an Immanent Will which acts mechanically, unconscious of human life and suffering. Napoleon, who is more central than any other human character to the action of *The Dynasts*, admits his subjection to such a force. At Tilsit he tells the Queen of Prussia that it baffles his intent, and harries him on, whether he will or not; it dominates him. His star is to blame, not himself; it is unswervable. When he

282

informs his wife, the Empress Josephine, that the need for an heir to the throne of France compels him to seek a new marriage, he feels they

> are but thistle-globes on Heaven's high gales,
> And whither blown, or when, or how, or why,
> Can choose us not at all!

On the banks of the Niemen, at the start of his Russian campaign, he feels he is as much compelled by fatality as Russia. An impulse which has influenced him since the battle of Lodi Bridge (1796) moves him on willy-nilly, oftentimes against his better mind. He is there by laws imposed inexorably on him:

> History makes use of me to weave her web
> To her long while aforetime-figured mesh
> And contemplated charactery: no more.

When, with defeat at Waterloo, he knows his last imperial gamble has failed, and the Spirit of the Years intimates 'Sic diis immortalibus placet', he concurs:

> Yet, 'tis true, I have ever known
> That such a Will I passively obeyed![1]

Though for long a glorious and magnetic hero in the eyes of the French, it is not thus that he is portrayed by Hardy. If character is fate, Napoleon falls because his vaulting ambition has o'erleaped itself like Macbeth's. His first act, when he crowns himself in Milan Cathedral, betrays his pride and hubris: when his naval strength is broken by Villeneuve's defeat off Cape Trafalgar, he comments, 'Well, well; I can't be everywhere', and consoles himself with the assurance of victory at Austerlitz. At the end his thought, unlike that of any other national hero in *The Dynasts*, is on himself, where it has always been: how much more secure his fame would have been had he been killed in battle like Nelson, Harold, Hector, Cyrus, and Saul. Once his aim had been no less than to 'shoulder Christ from out the topmost niche In human fame'. Whatever allowance Hardy makes for his being an instrument of the Will that works nations into combative ardour and unreasoning folly,

he sees him finally as one of relative insignificance in the full
course of time, which cannot be excluded from the dimensions of
The Dynasts:

> Such men as thou, who wade across the world
> To make an epoch, bless, confuse, appal,
> Are in the elemental ages' chart
> Like meanest insects on obscurest leaves
> But incidents and grooves of Earth's unfolding;
> Or as the brazen rod that stirs the fire
> Because it must.

Nor, although England eventually succeeds as Napoleon's arch-
enemy and 'master mischief-mind', is it Hardy's purpose to set up
his country in the role of hero. His altruism would not allow
him to present England with the conscious pride displayed by
Shakespeare in *Henry the Fifth*. Though two national heroes, Nelson
and Wellington, are sometimes the centre of attention in two great
battle episodes, the maimed, dead, and dying (which extend at
times beyond the human) are not overlooked; often they are the
subject of Hardy's intensest vision. He does not spare the carnage,
French, British, or Russian, or the agony of those doomed to be
frozen to death in the retreat from Moscow. His principal human
subject is poor mankind, the suffering and waste of nations driven
to frenzy and 'demonry' in a prolonged dynastic struggle caused
principally by Napoleon's megalomaniac ambition.

But for the evolution of his cinematic technique, with aerial
spirits as guides and commentators, Hardy could not have coped
as successfully as he did with the immensity, the minutiae, and
the complexities, of his scheme. Whether they speak or remain
silent, they accompany us as we read, from viewpoint to viewpoint,
creating our 'migratory Proskenion'. Sometimes, when there is
little or no dialogue, with only scene and dumbshow, for example,
the transitions are swift. If there are longueurs in *The Dynasts*, they
occur during relatively protracted scenes of conventional drama
(notably in Part Second) when the subject is less conducive to
external comment. The spiritual guides and commentators help to
provide dramatic relief, though this is not their main purpose.

Before evaluating the role of each of the leading spirits, it may
be helpful to illustrate their general function. *The Dynasts* begins
and ends, very significantly, with the entry of 'the Ancient Spirit

and Chorus of the Years, the Spirit and Chorus of the Pities, the Shade of the Earth, the Spirits Sinister and Ironic with their Choruses, Rumours, Spirit-Messengers, and Recording Angels' in the Overworld, from which they (and we) look down on the prone and emaciated figure of Europe, the Alps forming its vertebrae, the peninsular plateau of Spain its head, with the lowlands, hemmed in by the Arctic Ocean and the Ural mountains, looking like a grey-green garment. Before this view is disclosed, and before reference is made to the dynastic struggle which is to continue with Napoleon's attempt to shatter the naval strength of England under Nelson, the spirits talk of the unconscious workings of the Immanent Will throughout the universe; it is the ultimate and inevitable point of reference throughout *The Dynasts*. Given 'free trajection' of their 'entities', they move down through space to 'the surface of the perturbed countries', where, with them, we see 'the peoples, distressed by events which they did not cause, . . . writhing, crawling, heaving, and vibrating in their various cities and nationalities'. A light of preternatural penetration reveals how life and movement in 'all humanity and vitalized matter' depends on the Prime Volitions of the Will. The scenes of the terrestrial tragedy which follows show the 'pulses' of this 'Cause'.

Recurrent views near and far stress the sufferings of individuals and their insignificance in the continuum of Time and Space. We watch a vast Austrian army moving towards the Inn river; its 'silent insect-creep' is described by a recording angel as if it were no more than the movement of molluscs on a leaf. Before the battle off Cape Trafalgar we have a bird's eye view of the opposing fleets; for close-ups of the fighting we move twice from Villeneuve's flagship to Nelson's, the second transition taking us to the cockpit of the *Victory* to watch the death of Nelson after Villeneuve's surrender; the scene then 'overclouds' and the spirits comment to aerial music. Walcheren (2.ii.viii) is seen as a marshy island, the evening sunshine lying like 'yellow sheaves across the vapours that the day's heat has drawn from the sweating soil'. On closer view, 'brass-hued and opalescent bubbles' are seen rising from the trodden ground; the skeletoned men appear, one of them falling now and then, and being carried away to a roofless hospital. Only through the spirits, especially the Spirit of the Pities, is the full tragic situation explained and expressed. An enormous procession of carriages containing courtiers and nobility leaves Vienna, when Maria Louisa is conveyed to France to become Napoleon's wife and bear him an heir. It is seen below as 'no more than a file of ants crawling along a strip of garden-matting'; we follow it to Munich, where roofs and houses appear like 'the tesserae of an irregular mosaic', and eventually to Courcelles, where 'the point of sight' descends to earth for a dramatic presentation of the meeting between the Emperor and his future bride. At the beginning of his disastrous Russian campaign, Napoleon, 'diminished to the aspect of a doll', rides ahead of his suite over the swaying bridge across the Niemen, and is proleptically obliterated in the darkness of a thunderstorm. His winter retreat from Moscow is visualized and auditioned with wonderful crescendo: first a flake of snow, then another and another till all is 'phantasmal grey and white' as the caterpillar shape of the French army creeps nearer and grows more attenuated, minute parts of it being left behind and flaked over until they are no more than 'white pimples by the wayside'; as the point of vision descends, the mournful taciturnity which prevails is broken by sounds of 'wind-broken and lacerated horses', and of their incessant flogging. At the crossing of the Beresina we see hordes of Russians 'assailing eighteen thousand half-naked, badly armed wretches, emaciated with hunger and encumbered with several thousands of sick, wounded, and stragglers'. Further skeleton-like stragglers are overtaken in the next scene, where our vision ranges from frost-bitten features and eyes oozing with pus to stars in Orion which flash like stilettos as the frost stiffens. Such features are but a few details in the astonishing magnitude of an artistically conceived work which presents only a 'flimsy riband' in the 'web Enorm' of 'those artistries of Circumstance' woven numbly as in dream by the Immanent Will.

It is not always easy to discriminate between the roles of some of the minor spirits. The Spirit of Rumour, or its chorus, more often than not shares with the Recording Angels the task of reporting strategic movements on land or sea, or preparatory movements for battle, occasionally the course of battle itself. (There is so much recourse to this function that, for the sake of variety, it is sometimes given to the Spirit of the Years and even, at climactic points of suffering or destruction, to the Pities.) Less prominent and necessary, the Shade of the Earth (almost synonymous at times with Nature), aware of its inhabitants' pains and dread, is in travail but helplessly in thrall to the Immanent Will (a reminder of poems by Hardy such as 'Doom and She'). Though clearly concerned with what may happen to It (*The Dynasts* opens with her question 'What of the Immanent Will and Its designs?), she is left a listener in the After Scene when hopes are raised.

Less contributory than the Rumours and Recording Angels, but more significant in the final evaluation of *The Dynasts*, are the Spirits Sinister and Ironic. Together they play a Mephistophelian role, which was far from being unattractive to Hardy, always quick to see the irony of things. The Spirit Sinister's delight in misfortune and bloodshed disgusts the Pities, with whom Hardy is supremely in sympathy, but he knew, like the Spirit, that 'War makes rattling good history', and there can be nothing but a private authorial joke in an altercation on the Unfulfilled Intention (Hardy's belief in which is introduced by the Shade of the Earth), when, after being told by the Spirit Sinister that any attempt made to prove there is any right or reason in the universe could not be accomplished before Doomsday, the Spirit of the Year wishes he could move the Immanent Will to chain and imprison him (the 'Iago of the Incorporeal World') for a thousand years, as it is said he did his 'like' (the Satan of Revelation, xx.2). Here Hardy alludes to the kind of contemporary condemnation of himself which associated him and Swinburne with the work of Satan. Among several amusing comments by the Spirit Ironic are three of more general import. The first, in the Fore Scene, a declaration that what appears as a terrestrial tragedy to the Spirit of the Pities is a comedy, registers with perhaps too severe a detachment Hardy's allusion to Horace Walpole's epigram that life is a comedy to those who think but a tragedy to those who feel. The second, when the Pities pray that the battle of Austerlitz may be brought to a speedy issue with the minimum of suffering, is a reminder of slaughter on a much larger scale when prehistoric species were exterminated in the course of evolution. The third, with reference to the Congress of Vienna,

> Where every Power perpends withal
> Its dues as large, its friends' as small,

is contained within the larger irony of 'a war of wits' between the victorious allies when preparations are being secretly made for Napoleon's escape from Elba.

It is the Spirit of the Years who indicates the setting and substance of the initial scenes, and so habituates us to the process of continual change, in the historical drama. Above all, however, he speaks, as far as he can, on the ultimate Cause, the Immanent Will which 'no mind can mete'. Nothing, he prologizes, has indicated that 'cognizance has marshalled things terrene' since the beginning of life, or will do 'in my span'. After introducing us to Milan Cathedral, just before Napoleon's self-coronation, he refers to Christianity as one of those local cults which last in 'brief parentheses',

> Beyond whose span, uninfluenced, unconcerned,
> The systems of the suns go sweeping on
> With all their many-mortaled planet train
> In mathematic roll unceasingly.

To this ancient, who is seen as the 'Eldest-born of the Unconscious Cause' by the Spirit of the Pities, the butchery at Borodino is but 'A fabric of excitement, a web of rage' in 'the weltering whole' of a dynastic struggle which shows

> A Will that wills above the will of each,
> Yet but the will of all conjunctively.

When the Pities agree with their leader that the Will is to be condemned for quickening sense in those doomed to suffer, the Spirit of the Years rebukes them for blaming the Impercipient, and urges them to stay their judgment until the end of Time (as if, after all, change for the better might come).[2]

Like the Shade of the Earth in this exchange (and Hardy in his Unfulfilled Intention theory), the Pities regret that mankind ever became sensitive to pain and wrong; they lament 'the intolerable antilogy Of making figments feel'. This had happened by 'luckless, tragic Chance', according to the Spirit of the Years, who regards the Spirit of the Pities as a youth with much to learn, when he fails to realize that Napoleon is subject to the Will and cannot be deflected from his course. To him the Pities, with their 'naïve and liberal creed' are 'great-hearted young Compassionates' who forget the Prime Mover. Undoubted successors to Shelley's 'guides and guardians' of 'heaven-oppressed mortality' in *Prometheus Unbound*, they tell the Shade of Earth that, rather than allow Napoleon to pursue his tainted career,

> We would establish those of kindlier build,
> In fair Compassions skilled,
> Men of deep art in life-development;
> Watchers and warders of thy varied lands,
> Men surfeited of laying heavy hands
> Upon the innocent,
> The mild, the fragile, the obscure content
> Among the myriads of thy family.
> Those, too, who love the true, the excellent,
> And make their daily moves a melody.

In the cathedral ceremony at Milan the Spirit of the Pities sees only pomp and vaingloriousness; he still regrets the tainting of those 'large potencies' shown by Napoleon when his aim was to 'throne fair Liberty' in place of Privilege, and yearns for the loving-kindness of early Christianity. His kinship with Hardy is clear.[3]

The denizens of the Overworld, who have power, it seems, to transport us with imaginative immediacy to whatever part of the earth they wish to visit (in both exterior and interior scenes), are present throughout the whole action. We are far more in touch with them than with any human character, and collectively they fulfil the most crucial role in Hardy's presentation of Napoleonic history. Some merely record for our information; of those who for the most part comment on what is scenically or dramatically displayed, the Spirit of the Years and the Spirit of the Pities are much the most important. Only through them does Hardy express his serious views. If we really read *The Dynasts* we shall identify with them; the history we contemplate is seen *sub specie auctoris*.

It may be difficult always to identify with the Spirit of the Years. He appeals to the intellect, and his views on the Immanent Will are repetitive and mechanical; Hardy is expressing old thoughts rather as if they came by rote, without freshness and vitality. Some readers (and the author knew that such reaction to his heterodoxy was inevitable) will find them unacceptable, and applaud the Spirit of the Pities (1.i.vi):

> I feel, Sire, as I must! This tale of Will
> And Life's impulsion by Incognizance
> I cannot take.

Only at one point are readers likely to question the rightness of the Pities, however, and that is when they echo Hardy's view that it would have been better had the Will not made humanity alive to natural defects, injustice, and suffering. Even so, this agreement has the value of stressing where Hardy's sympathies lie in *The Dynasts*. His 'constitutional tendency' was 'to care for life only as an emotion', and, though his horror of war is repeatedly conveyed in the detail of the scenes, it is through the Pities that he expresses most acutely and powerfully his feelings on the carnage, the waste, and the unreason, of war. Their attitude throughout on this subject wins the reader's approval, and no human character can vie with them for the role of hero in this drama. It is in their choral lyrics, which are accompanied by aerial music, that they strike the deepest chords, strongly with reference to battle, and very significantly elsewhere, as in their lament at seeing the Prussian nation aflame against all judgment:

> Yea, the soul of a nation distrest
>   Is aflame,
> And heaving with eager unrest
>   In its aim
> At supreme desperations to blazon the national name!

Space is found for only one verse on the successful resistance of Prussians and Russians in the massacre at Eylau (February 1807), and that is given to the first semichorus of Pities:

> Snows incarnadined were thine, O Eylau, field of the wide white
>   spaces,
> And frozen lakes, and frozen limbs, and blood iced hard as it
>   left the veins:
> Steel-cased squadrons swathed in cloud-drift, plunging to doom
>   through pathless places,
> And forty thousand dead and near dead, strewing the early-
>   nighted plains.

Lengthier and equally moving are the lyrics on the soldiers wasted and dying after long inactivity in the fetid atmosphere of Walcheren, and on the bravery of the British who fought victoriously, mostly to die, at Albuera. In the second, after alternating semichoruses, the full chorus concludes:

Hide their hacked bones, Earth! – deep, deep, deep,
Where harmless worms caress and creep. –
What man can grieve? what woman weep?
Better than waking is to sleep! Albuera!

During the battle of Borodino the attention of the Spirit of the
Pities is drawn not only to the agony and crazed cries of the
fighters but also to horses 'maimed in myriads' and 'tearing round
In maddening pangs'. 'It is enough. Let now the scene be closed',
the Spirit of the Years decides. Surprisingly perhaps, the most
popular lyric in *The Dynasts*, on the dread and destruction affecting
smaller forms of life, after preparations for battle have been made
on the eve of Waterloo, is given mainly to the Spirit of the Years;
it is factual, and a reminder of T. S. Eliot's maxim that the most
artistic poetry results not from expression of the emotions but by
virtue of escaping from them.[4]
    Among the clouds with the other spirits, high above the road
from Smolensko to Lithuania, the Spirit of the Pities asks questions
which have universal overtones for those of a philosophical or
religious mind:

Where are we? And why are we where we are?

The very sound and movement of these words help to evoke a
sense of the lost and helpless on two levels, the first in anticipation
of those who perish or suffer far from home during the French
retreat from Moscow, the second echoing the perplexity of honest
thinkers on human life in the universe of time and space. The line
must have been prompted consciously or otherwise by Shelley's
Adonais (xxi):

Whence are we, and why are we? of what scene
The actors or spectators?

As if to confirm their supreme importance in its design, the
chorus of Pities brings *The Dynasts* to its memorable conclusion.
This, it will be seen from clear hints with reference to the Immanent
Will, did not come as a late inspiration, but was an integral part of
Hardy's final plan from the outset. At the very opening of the Fore
Scene the Spirit of the Pities dares to suggest that 'Sublunar shocks

may wake Its watch anon'; the chorus of Pities concludes Part
Second more hopefully:

> Yet It may wake and understand
> Ere Earth unshape, know all things, and
> With knowledge use a painless hand,
> > A painless hand!

To give it pride of place again at the end of the whole work seems
to confirm the impression that it speaks, more than the Spirit of
the Years, for Hardy. The one is positive; the other, relatively
negative. The conclusion is beyond the reckoning of the Years,
but, to adapt earlier words of their chorus, it is the topmost cyme
crowning the last entablature of *The Dynasts*. Few who have followed
the long course of thought and feeling evoked by the human
scenes and the reactions of the spirits within this drama can fail to
respond to the wish expressed in the intimation

> > That the rages
> > Of the ages
> Shall be cancelled, and deliverance offered from the darts that
> > were,
> Consciousness the Will informing, till It fashion all things fair!

19

Reflections on Hardy's Poetry

The title immediately raises the question whether poetry is restricted to the artistic forms of verse. Leslie Stephen, writing to Hardy (who had noted in 1885 that his approval was 'disapproval minimized') on the pleasure he had found in reading *Wessex Poems*, told him how he had 'admired the poetry which was diffused through the prose' when *Far from the Madding Crowd* came out under his serial editorship. In Hardy's fiction from the first, and very strikingly in *Desperate Remedies*, it was to remain, not just in succinct felicities but in larger wholes of setting and human situation, emerging exquisitely or intensely in comparative imagery, or voicing the deeper overtones of life and death. In this respect there are passages in *Tess of the d'Urbervilles* and scenic notes in *The Dynasts* which have greater imaginative distinctness than appears in the majority of Hardy's poems. Verse, whether rhymed or unrhymed, has other graces, however: deft and intricate stanzaic craftsmanship, memorability, and, above all, aptness of emphasis and subtleties of movement.

During the period when he wrote his early verse in London, Hardy immersed himself in English poetry, and was drawn particularly to Shelley. Great as was his heady enthusiasm for the passion of Swinburne's pagan anti-Victorianism, he seems never to have been intoxicated as a practitioner by his euphonious excesses or larger rhythmical sonorities; he preferred the dramatic roughness and conversational lyricism of Browning. Convinced by the argument in the preface to *Lyrical Ballads* that poetry should draw from 'the real language of men', he was influenced also by Wordsworth, as can be seen in 'The Widow Betrothed', which he first thought of about 1867. Yet, with the exception of 'Domicilium' (also Wordsworthian), a poem which belongs to an earlier period, the surviving poems of 1865–67 suggest that Hardy soon discovered the need to achieve his own style, whatever the labour and cost (the disappointment of non-publication). He seems independently to have reached convictions which were confirmed later by Stephen's observations on the poetic folly of imitating anyone. Whatever 'Neutral Tones' owes to Shelley, it is certainly not imitative; nothing comparable in movement will be found in the earlier poet.

The early poems indicate furthermore that Hardy had the courage to prefer sense to sound; if the sound echoes the sense, so much the better; to give it priority was weakness and evasion. It is as if he had already adopted the stance which earned his approval in June 1924, when, after having illustrated his mastery of stanzaic pattern in an astonishing variety of forms, he noted from Mark Rutherford: 'We do not want carefully constructed pieces of [verse] mosaic. Force is what we need.' This, one assumes, does not necessarily imply energy but life at all events, as opposed to lulling, mellifluous verse. Hardy had shown that he could write with sustained lyrical lightness and ease in 'Regret not me', where the style conforms to the subject. For the same reason it varies considerably throughout Hardy's poems.

It is excusable to wonder whether Tennyson would have been proud to have written 'Beeny Cliff', which is set to the 'Locksley Hall' metrical pattern, or whether Hardy would have been pleased to have composed Edward Thomas's 'Adlestrop'. Few more lyrical poems than the latter can be found in a conversational style. It begins quietly, and ends most evocatively, yet, with the exception of a little rhyming and a single repetition, its language is that of ordinary speech. The revolution in poetry which Hardy and Thomas helped to bring about, Hardy especially, may be gauged from a comment on 'Adlestrop' in E. A. Greening Lamborn's *Poetic Values: A Guide to the Appreciation of 'The Golden Treasury'*, first published in the year of Hardy's death. (Hardy's ambition to have one of his poems in *The Golden Treasury* was not achieved in his lifetime.) The comment indicates how long established prejudices can persist, making the imaginative ear tone-deaf:

Adlestrop is an attempt to immortalize a moment's experience. . . . But it is doubtful if it is a successful attempt. It is emphatic, with its curt, staccato phrasing; but it is not therefore impressive and memorable, for the words are commonplace; except the name of the station and the trees and flowers they have no charm of melody or magic of rhythm to haunt us after they have trembled into silence.

Haunting melody and magic are just what later generations must have found in the climax of this unusually rhythmical poem:

> And for that minute a blackbird sang
> Close by, and round him, mistier,
> Farther and farther, all the birds
> Of Oxfordshire and Gloucestershire.

For an example of the poetry of ordinary speech, where the words follow a conversational idiom, one could hardly do better than turn to the ending of 'The Oxen':

> Yet, I feel,
> If someone said on Christmas Eve,
> 'Come; see the oxen kneel
>
> 'In the lonely barton by yonder coomb
> Our childhood used to know',
> I should go with him in the gloom,
> Hoping it might be so.

'Beeny Cliff' has a grander rhythm, but it is never Virgilian;[1] its language is often simple, but the metre changes it from speech ('And the sweet things said in that March say anew there by and by'), and many of its telling effects depend on such poetic artifices as 'alliteration's artful aid' (the waves 'engrossed in saying their ceaseless babbling say', 'purples prinked the main'). Speech rhythms do not coincide with art as fully as in the apparently artless lines quoted from 'The Oxen', and the poet's craft is manifest, showing dexterities which give the impression of supreme linguistic naturalness in 'As we laughed light-heartedly aloft', and of massive and continuous solidity (as opposed to 'that wandering western sea') in 'bulks old Beeny' and 'looms that wild weird western shore', both images characterized by 'chasmal beauty', both introduced with heavy inversion, and both reinforced alliteratively, the second with three strong consecutive stresses. As at the end of 'The Going', the utmost emotion is concentrated in a word as simple as 'so': 'The woman I loved so, and who loyally loved me'. To attempt further exploration of stylistic detail in artistic conformity with sense within the contrasts of scenery and in association with life and death would be tedious. 'Beeny

Cliff' illustrates a range of those artistries which help to create the texture of many of Hardy's poems.

Alliteration is used with intensifying effects in *The Dynasts*, especially in the verse of the Spirits. Overpartiality for this device is apparent; in the Talavera scenes, Hardy is intent on making us hear the striking of the hour during the preliminary fighting ('Talavera tongues it as ten o' the night-time') and visualize one effect of the scorching western sun on the battlefield ('Last, the swealed herbage lifts a leering light'). Most readers of Hardy are familiar with a small number of songs and choruses from *The Dynasts*; it is unfortunate that they usually do not include two of the most finished, both by the Pities, at Walcheren and Albuera. The feeling imparted by the second, which is more taut and tense, as could be expected for a battle, is heightened by a judicious use of alliteration and repetition. The former gains immensely from a variety of alliterative forms. Soldiers who had 'withstood the blasting blaze of war' are doomed to lie feverish or dying on a marshy delta island, where 'the fen-lights flit' and humidity 'solves' them to its 'softness'. They remain helplessly inactive, 'pent pithless' there during 'the aggressor's arrogant career', a phrase which, with its rolling, almost crashing sound, contrasts with the lines that immediately follow:

> Here, where each creeping day the creeping file
> Draws past with shouldered comrades score on score,
> Bearing them to their lightless last asile,
> Where weary wave-wails from the clammy shore
>   Will reach their ears no more.

Turned to good use, its sound echoing the sense, alliteration is not to be scoffed at. At the end of 'Reminiscences of a Dancing Man' it contributes so successfully to visual and rhythmic effects that it does not call attention to itself. When it does, it invites parody and usually gets it.

Poetic artistry extends to the structuring of stanza and poem. In 'Long Plighted' (arising from 'The Waiting Supper', with the theme of Browning's 'The Statue and the Bust') all the opening lines of the verses consist of the hesitant postponing question, followed by a single word, which, repeated in each consecutive pair of stanzas, helps to unify the whole, as does the rhyme which runs throughout and ends each verse. The question-and-answer design of 'Memory and I' may seem simple, but the key words 'youth', 'joy', 'hope', 'faith', 'love' could not all have sprung readily to mind, to cover such a time-span of tragic chance. The story of 'John and Jane' (not uncommon, the names suggest) is summed up in the lengthening final lines of the stanzas, and in the changes which accompany the rhymed repetition in the opening lines, from 'boisterous place' and 'laughing face' to 'gruesome place' and 'skull's grimace'. The four verses of 'During Wind and Rain' have much in common, most significantly the light notes of happiness in the opening lines and the painful sense of loss wrought by time in the last two, stressed by the repeated contradiction at regular points of the alternating 'yea' and 'aye' by 'Ah, no; the years'. Two generalizations follow from these examples. The first is that close attention to such formal features must have commended itself to one whose architectural training developed a lasting regard for design within the constituent parts as well as the whole. The second is that Hardy did well to open his first volume of poetry with 'The Temporary the All', the first words of which, 'Change and chancefulness', have a positional emphasis which is repeated in 'chance and change' at the end of the preface to his next volume.

The irony of chance is a recurrent motif in Hardy's poetry, as the titles of his next two volumes, *Time's Laughingstocks* and *Satires of Circumstance*, confirm. A series of brief poems in the latter (with the same title), issued light-heartedly in 1911 from notes jotted down 'some twenty years' earlier,[2] suggests the cultivation of a mode which suited his humour or addiction. They are generally too sketchy and reflex to do him justice. Other poems, such as 'The Slow Nature', reflect the deeper tragic ironies; some appeal to varying levels of humour. 'In the Days of Crinoline' is a joke or scoff on the level of parish scandal, whereas 'The Ruined Maid', an early poem, shows Hardy's satirical humour at its best. 'The Curate's Kindness' combines tragedy with comedy in excellent dramatic narrative. With its series of surprises ending climactically, 'Ah, are you digging on my grave?' has more to offer than the predictable and unrelieved irony of the poem from which it may initially have originated, 'Is my team ploughing?', Hardy's favourite in A. E. Housman's *The Shropshire Lad*.

The first of Hardy's collected poems contains the peculiar word 'outshow'. It might be considered to be on a par with 'outshine', until one becomes familiar with his habit of coining verbs by the addition of adverbial prefixes ('creep out' = 'outcreep' in 'Winter

Night in Woodland'), as in 'outlean', 'outshade', or 'outshape' in 'After the Last Breath', and 'outshrill' in 'Last Words to a Dumb Friend'. 'Outskeleton' for 'present skeletal outlines of' in 'Rome: Building a New Street in the Ancient Quarter' anticipates the 'gaunt anatomy' of 'Time's central city'. As he did not hesitate to use archaic words, it is possible that Hardy had met the sixteenth-century use of 'outshow' for 'show forth', but it is just as likely (considering his practice) that he invented it. He was very bookish and scholarly, and, though some of his less orthodox poetic diction was drawn from his folk heritage, it was derived equally or more from the Dorset dialect of Barnes's poetry; even more, from earlier English poets and from foreign languages, French especially (as in 'last asile').

Hardy was crotchety, nevertheless, in his arbitrary use of words, sometimes to the detriment of his poetry. His coinage of verbs with the prefix 'un', not in the usual sense exemplified in 'undo' but as a general negative ('unbloom' = 'not bloom') leads to occasional awkwardness, as in (except where otherwise stated the following examples are from *The Dynasts*) 'His projects they unknow, his grin unsee!' (1.vi.i), 'Express in forms that now unbe' (1.vi.iii; cf. 'I'd have my life unbe' in 'Tess's Lament'). Many readers will have little difficulty with 'fineless' for 'endless' (1.i.ii), but how many can accept 'voidless' for 'unavoidable' (3.iii.i)? The risks run by Hardy can be illustrated from simple examples of his neologistic ventures: 'Where the sun ups it' in 'The Wind's Prophecy' and 'To usward' (2.iv.vii). Nothing can quite justify the use of 'outsetter' for a composer who 'sets out' music in 'Apostrophe to an Old Psalm Tune', or of 'outleant' in 'The Darkling Thrush' ('The Century's corpse outleant'), where, providing the rhyme rather than the sense, it is used, as in 'Honeymoon Time at an Inn', for 'extended' (cf. 'his form extend' in 'End of the Year 1912'). Had he wished, Hardy could have avoided such infelicities.

Of a different kind, though determined by rhyming convenience, is the clumsy, momentarily stultifying, inversion 'They know Earth-secrets that know not I' which mars the excellence of 'An August Midnight'; it seems astonishing that Hardy could allow this final line to remain unchanged more than two years before publication. Another disconcerting inversion concludes 'To Outer Nature', where 'Passed the hodiernal!' must mean 'the hodiernal being passed'. Here the rhymes, double with light (feminine) endings throughout the poem (and almost triple in 'sempiternal', 'hodiernal'), are an important part of the tripping measure which prevails, conforming to a carefree state of youthful non-Darwinian illusion, that 'iris-hued embowment' when nature seems irradiated with love. Such rhymes suit light or satirical verse, and have their place no doubt in such a poem as 'Thoughts at Midnight'; they are more effective when the mood is more lively and varied. Whether such quirkish rhymes as occur in 'Under the Waterfall' and 'Drinking Song' –

> The purl of a runlet that never ceases
> In stir of kingdoms, in wars, in peaces;

> Copernicus, and righted that.
> We trod, he told,
> A globe that rolled
> Around a sun it warmed it at.

– were included according to 'the principle of spontaneity', of concealing art by apparent carelessness, knowing that, as in architecture, 'cunning irregularity is of enormous worth',[3] must remain tantalizingly conjectural. There is nothing humorous in the first poem to justify the oddity of 'peaces', whatever may be said on the light-heartedness of 'Drinking Song' in defence of the second hazardous rhyme.

'The whole secret of a living style and the difference between it and a dead style, lies in not having too much style – being, in fact, a little careless, or rather seeming to be, here and there. . . . Otherwise your style is like worn half-pence – all the fresh images rounded off by rubbing, and no crispness or movement at all', Hardy wrote late in life.[4] The colloquial 'anyhow' in 'She Revisits Alone the Church of Her Marriage' exemplifies the intermittent uses of such 'careless', liberating artistry. It will be found at greater length in 'A Countenance', where the easy conversational manner is more broken, less smoothly rhythmical, than in 'The Oxen':

> Her laugh was not in the middle of her face quite,
>   As a gay laugh springs,
> It was plain she was anxious about some things
>   I could not trace quite. . . .
> And her lips were too full, some might say:
> I did not think so. Anyway, ...

Here, except in the lift of the second line, hardly anything is done to emphasize the rhythm. Such a style, found more frequently in Hardy's later poems, is often the concomitant of unromantic, or what might conventionally be assumed to be unpoetical, subjects.

Perhaps it should be said that Hardy's rounding-off by rubbing has no necessary link with Gerard Manley Hopkins' 'Parnassian', which is often assumed to be *par exemple* Tennysonian. All poets are capable of it; it consists of verse which is written '*on and from the level* of a poet's mind' when he is uninspired, when, as Hardy would say, the style is dead. 'Great men, poets I mean, have each their own dialect as it were of Parnassian', Hopkins continues; and it is found in Hardy, not least when he writes on, for him, such a worn-out abstract subject as the Immanent Will in *The Dynasts*. It is Hardy, not the husband, whose words fail to carry conviction, between a lively opening and ending in 'The Forbidden Banns', as he continues in old ballad measure:

> When low her husband said,
> 'I would from the bottom of my heart
> That father was not dead!'

The exclamation mark cannot bring the words to life.

'There is enough poetry in what is left [in life], after all the false romance has been abstracted, to make a sweet pattern', Hardy wrote in June 1877, instancing Hartley Coleridge's 'She is not fair to outward view'. An additional note on the latent but 'hitherto unperceived beauty' which is to be seen by 'the spiritual eye' is related to his belief 'that the beauty of association is entirely superior to the beauty of aspect, and a beloved relative's old battered tankard to the finest Greek vase'. When he wrote eleven years later 'To find beauty in ugliness is the province of the poet', he did not imply the only province, only that a living poet would find moving subjects in areas and items where to the common eye no poetry is. For him, as for the Pities, poetry lurks wherever 'pit-pats poor mankind'.[5] It is greatly to Hardy's credit that he perceived this truth at a relatively early stage in his career, emphasized it continually, and set an example in enlarging the bounds of poetry. His perceptions were sharpened, it should not be forgotten, when he was maturing as a novelist. Two days after completing *The Mayor of Casterbridge*, he wrote: 'The business of the poet and novelist is to show the sorriness underlying the grandest things, and the grandeur underlying the sorriest things.' It needs little reflection to appreciate that any of Hardy's major tragic novels gives far greater scope for the realization of such aims than a brief poem. Artistically developed, the novel can stir the reader more often and with a cumulative strength quite beyond the range of a short poem, which, whether it moves intensely or not, focuses attention in such a way that its subject excites generalizing thought. A few lines in *Jude the Obscure* (III.i, second paragraph) are given a local habitation and a name in 'An East-End Curate': 'the humble curate wearing his life out in [a] city slum – that might have a touch of goodness and greatness in it; that might be true religion . . .'. Several of Hardy's poems have subjects which would not have been deemed suitable for verse by most poets (cf. 'A Gentleman's Second-Hand Suit', 'The Gap in the White', 'The Pink Frock', 'The Rejected Member's Wife', and even 'A Circular', the subject of which attains significance through its tragic irony of association).

'Is not the noblest poetry of prose fiction the poetry of every-day truth?' Wilkie Collins asked in his introduction to *Basil* (1852), a novel which probably had a strong influence on features of Hardy's early fiction. Later, as Wordsworth had done in his famous preface, George Eliot drew attention to the poetry of scientific discovery, even of railways. The evidence of 'Afterwards' and of Hardy's poems in general does not suggest that Hardy was as alert as Charles (Tennyson) Turner to the poetry latent in common manifestations of new technology, or gave himself as much time to consider it, especially in little everyday things. It is an important feature in the complex of *A Laodicean*, where the poetry of the telegraph wire is incidental, and the view of a railway tunnel is admired for its own sake, with emphasis on the romance of 'science, steam, and travel'. In 'After a Romantic Day' a railway cutting is given 'poetry of place' by the moonlight, even more by the associated feelings of the observer. The 'charmless scene' of 'In a Waiting-Room' is irradiated by the excitement of children over a picture which raises expectations of what their seaside holiday holds out for them and their mother. 'The Change', one of the most moving of Hardy's recollections of Emma Gifford, evokes a London railway-station scene. Two of the three images which dominate 'Nobody Comes', in the gathering darkness outside Max Gate, are the telegraph wire which 'Intones to travellers like a spectral lyre Swept by a spectral hand', and a car with glaring headlights that 'whangs along in a world of its own', leaving the poet alone by his gate.

Hardy's arrangement of his poems – with the obvious exception of clearly defined but relatively short subdivisions within some of his volumes – suggests that the majority are 'pieces occasional and various', though links will be found in this general miscellaneity to explain the juxtaposition of poems in a number of very brief sequences. The variety is such that it is well-nigh impossible to select a typical poem. Among his best – and 'The Going', 'The Voice', 'After a Journey', 'Beeny Cliff', and 'At Castle Boterel' (from one of the exceptional groups) have been omitted – the following call for inclusion: 'Neutral Tones', 'The Colonel's Soliloquy', 'The Darkling Thrush', 'The Ruined Maid', 'Autumn in King's Hintock Park', 'To Carrey Clavel', 'The Homecoming', 'The Dead Quire', 'The Convergence of the Twain', 'Regret not me', 'The Oxen', 'During Wind and Rain', 'Paying Calls', 'Afterwards', 'Queen Caroline to Her Guests'. (The order of these poems shows no preference; it is that of their appearance in *Collected Poems*.) No two of them are alike in form, mood, or subject. They are humorous or tragical; they vary from narrative to lyrical, from the dramatic lyric and dramatic soliloquy to the descriptive–philosophical; some almost defy categorization. However they are paired, they are strikingly different.

In judging the range of Hardy's poetry, the vast dimensions of *The Dynasts* should not be overlooked. After devoting six years to this achievement, his major ambition, he could relax and write short poems whenever he pleased on whatever appealed to him. So it must have seemed until the death of his first wife, when the radiant recollection of his old love was brought sharply into poignant focus by remorse for his neglect of her in later years. Rarely had his feelings been so deeply moved by his own experience, and rarely has a poet shown the elegiac integrity which is to be found in 'Poems of 1912–13'. Verse-writing soon became an anodyne, a continuation of his retirement hobby, which he pursued happily (however grave the subject) to the end, anticipating that each of his last four volumes of poetry would be his final one, as their concluding poems indicate, first and most memorably with 'Afterwards' in *Moments of Vision*.

Despite the range of vision of many of Hardy's poems (on altruism, for example, in 'The wind blew words'), and despite the vividness and variety of its human interest, his poetry derives

strength and special appeal from certain overriding limitations. In
Poems of the Past and Present he maintains a long barrage against an
impercipient First Cause and the Unfulfilled Intention, on behalf
of a Positivist religion of humanity. In his subsequent poetry he
continually returns to the suffering and cruelty consequent on the
blindness of the Prime Mover or Immanent Will; and it is fortunate
that there are times when he gives the subject relief in dramatiza-
tions of fanciful, and even amusing, originality. Analysis of the
poems published after his wife's death will show that, wholly or
partially, directly or indirectly (sometimes veiled in fiction), three-
tenths are devoted to his deceased wife and her grave. Posthumous
love had indeed become 'the monopolist'. As Hardy aged, the
dead in their buried state (Emma, his parents, and his sister Mary
especially) gained increasing hold on his imagination, once a source
of humour on this subject (as in 'Friends Beyond'), now

> a gallery portrait-lined,
> And scored with necrologic scrawls,
> Where feeble voices rise, once full-defined,
> From underground in curious calls.[6]

Travel and two wars occasioned a large number of poems, but
Hardy's verse nowhere suggests the more objective range of
Browning or, whatever its historical perspectives, the imaginative
overtones which ironically relate a spiritual past and the worldliness
of western civilization in Eliot's 'Gerontion' and *The Waste Land*.
Such is the cumulative fascination and power of Hardy's personal
poetry, however, that it creates a live interest in his biography.
Caring for life 'as an emotion' had made him both novelist and
poet, and he must have been encouraged when, on 1 July 1879,
he copied down from Leslie Stephen 'The ultimate aim of the poet
should be to touch our hearts by showing his own . . . .' Lesser
poets might have stumbled under such guidance; Hardy's lapse into
self-pity in 'A Broken Appointment' reveals a danger. Fortunately his modesty and judgment were usually in control of his
sincerity; he was not one to parade or exploit his personality, and
he rarely forfeits the reader's sympathy.

At the beginning of the twentieth century it was assumed that
Hardy was a greater novelist than poet; today the contrary view is
usually maintained. Often it comes from people who know little
of his writings beyond a slim selection of his poems, or anthology

pieces, or, in an age of mass-mediated culture rather than of reading for oneself, recordings of a limited number of his poems by theatrical or film celebrities. Where differences exist as great as those between the relatively large and complex form of a typical Hardy novel and the brief concentration of almost any Hardy poem, there can hardly be a valid basis for judgments on the whole of his work in one genre *vis-à-vis* the other. Philip Larkin, who had tried both forms, thought it 'harder to write a good novel than a good poem'.[7] Hardy's novels contain innumerable poetic elements, some in remarkable abundance. He drew from them for images in his poems, just as he found subjects for poetry in recordings which he included in his *Life*. The image of sea-waves sounding 'like the huzzas of multitudes' in *The Hand of Ethelberta* (xlv), for example, occurs in 'The Voice of Things' and 'The Wind's Prophecy'; another from the same novel (already given in 'Fictional Autobiography') in 'Days to Recollect'; and that of 'the May month when beech trees have suddenly unfolded large limp young leaves of the softness of butterflies' wings', from *The Woodlanders* (xlvii), in 'Afterwards'.

However far Hardy advanced the use of demotic English in poetry, he seems to have been at one with Wordsworth in eschewing the grosser forms of diction. Words on a graffiti level which are crassly expressive to the illiterate, or to youths who wish to be regarded as manly, are quite alien to his writing. Though they have commended themselves to some modern poets, they do nothing to further the success of a writer who is sensitive and discriminating in his use of language, whose every venture

> Is a new beginning, a raid on the inarticulate
> With shabby equipment always deteriorating
> In the general mess of imprecision of feeling,
> Undisciplined squads of emotion.

It is not wholly to be wondered at that Eliot, alarmed at the danger of '*servitude* to colloquial speech and to current jargon' in 1947, found much to admire in Milton, whose verse he had once condemned, and thought that poets might profit from a study of the literature in their own language, and the literature and grammatical structures of other languages. After an innovative period which had gone too far, the time had come to create poetry from 'new and more elaborate patterns' of the established diction.

Hardy's study of English literature and other languages had equipped him well for the furtherance of his idiosyncratic style in verse, though his linguistic coinages and his arbitrary use of words against all common usage are not always commendable.

His propensity to make poetry out of what Eliot describes as 'the unexplored resources of the unpoetical' affects not only his language but also his figurative or comparative imagery. The latter occurs often in architectural terms, sometimes in common observations of the everyday world. They are particularly striking in 'Overlooking the River Stour', where swallows are seen (like animated crossbows) flying in 'curves of an eight' and a moorhen darts out from the bank, 'Planing up shavings of crystal spray'. In 'Once at Swanage' the sea, roaring high and low behind the headlands, suggests

> the slamming of doors,
> Or a regiment hurrying over hollow floors.

At the opening of 'Suspense' the images become daringly ordinary:

> A clamminess hangs over all like a clout,
> The fields are a water-colour washed out,
> The sky at its rim leaves a chink of light,
> Like the lid of a pot that will not close tight.

Ezra Pound thought Hardy's success as a poet was 'the harvest of having written' his novels first. Perhaps it would be equally true to say that it was due to his musical ear and his musical upbringing. Like Wordsworth at Alfoxden, he recognised 'a latent music in the sincere utterance of deep emotion', and it was for this reason that he mingled not only the language but also the less regular measure of speech with the more regular movement of his stanzaic norms.[8] The finest modulations of his poetry (variations affecting pitch, movement, syllabic length and stress, as in 'Up the cliff, down, till I'm lonely, lost') can be judged only by the inner ear. Hardy often composed deliberately to music (once to marching, in 'Men Who March Away'), sometimes to hymn tunes, more frequently to song and dance. So habitual was the practice, he may have done this unconsciously in the elegiac 'Rain on a Grave', which beats to a dance rhythm, especially at the end, as do 'Great Things' and several poems where it is clearly in harmony with the subject.

Hardy told V. H. Collins that one reason for making a practice
of publishing nearly everything he completed in verse was the
discovery that poems he did not care for were sometimes highly
regarded by his readers. Long before this, in January 1899, he had
written:

> No man's poetry can be truly judged till its last line is written.
> What is the last line? The death of the poet. And hence there is
> this quaint consolation to any writer of verse – that it may be
> imperishable for all that anybody can tell him to the contrary;
> and that if worthless he can never know it, unless he be a greater
> adept at self-criticism than poets usually are.

Views will change from age to age, and there will always be
readers, no doubt, who will wish Hardy had published less. If
some of his poems are slight and third-rate, he has at least fifty,
any one of which is worthy of inclusion in a representative
anthology of English poetry. F. R. Leavis once asserted that 'any
real claim he may have to major status rests upon half-a-dozen
poems alone': 'Neutral Tones', 'A Broken Appointment', 'The Self-
Unseeing', 'The Voice', 'After a Journey', and 'During Wind and
Rain'. At the other extreme, and far nearer a true assessment, we
have Philip Larkin, who did not 'wish Hardy's *Collected Poems* a
single page shorter'; he could read him 'for years and years and
still be surprised', a 'marvellous thing to find in any poet', he
added.[9] (It is equally true of most of Hardy's prose.) Larkin
responded personally and poetically; in style, subject, and thought,
Hardy had a special appeal for him. Whatever their kinship, Hardy
did not share Larkin's rather depressing negativism, his denial of
so much in life. Pessimism may have darkened Hardy's last years,
as he saw western Europe heading for disaster, but he did not lose
his concern and reverence for humanity. The Spirit of the Pities
and his general altruism remained strong in him; though 'too old
in apathy' for much in life, he was still the poet of 'The wind blew
words' and 'Afterwards'; still also one with the poet who wrote:

> Let me enjoy the earth no less
> Because the all-enacting Might
> That fashioned forth its loveliness
> Had other aims than my delight.

20

At the Year's End

Charles Lamb felt that every man has two birthdays which 'set him upon revolving the lapse of time, as it affects his mortal duration'. One is special to the individual; the other, New Year's Day, marks 'the nativity of our common Adam'. He had never, he writes, heard the bells which ring out the Old Year without 'a gathering-up' of his mind 'to a concentration of all the images that have been diffused over the past twelvemonth', all that had been 'done or suffered, performed or neglected'. Hence the 'ring out the old, ring in the new' syndrome, the traditional Janus reckoning, accompanied by New Year resolutions, and the kind of moral stocktaking found, for example, in Pepys's diaries or Sir Walter Scott's *Journal*. On 1 January 1826 Scott writes:

> These solemn divisions of time influence our feelings as they recur. Yet there is nothing in it – for every day in the year closes a twelvemonth as well as the 31st December. The latter is only the solemn pause, as when a guide, during a wild and mountainous road, calls on a party to pause and look back at the scenes which they have just passed.

At the end of 1826 he finds melancholy in 'the regular recurrence of annual festivals'. 'We meet on such occasions like the survivors of some perilous expedition, wounded and weakened ourselves, and looking through the diminished ranks of those who remain, while we think of those who are no more.' No wonder that Lamb, with a similar prospect before him, 'reluycted' at 'the inevitable course of destiny'. Scott was ageing; his next year ends in 'trouble and sickness'; his prospects are gloomy but, having made his audit, he is thankful to God, and hopeful:

> I am now perfectly well in constitution; and though I am still in troubled waters, yet I am rowing with the tide, and less than the continuation of my exertions of 1827 may, with God's

blessing, carry me successfully through 1828, when we may gain
a more open sea, if not exactly a safe port.

Such faith in times of trouble is not characteristic of Hardy at
the year's end, or at any other time. He has left evidence which,
though relatively infrequent and vestigial, points to his habit of
self-auditing both on birthdays and at the end of the year. In 1887
he writes a cryptic note: 'The forty-seventh birthday of Thomas
the Unworthy', without a hint of what he rues having done or left
undone, during a year which he described as 'fairly friendly' in
retrospect. Late in life he could record the honours which befell
him on his birthdays. He tempers his eightieth with a number of
reflections on life, beginning

> When, like the Psalmist, 'I call mine own ways to remembrance',
> I find nothing in them that quite justifies this celebration.

He looks back over his lifetime, and cannot think that people have
changed for the better despite unprecedented material advances.

Although, with one exception, he never indulges in the traditional retrospective surveys at any length, it may be of interest to
follow the changes and vicissitudes of his life by reference to what
he records, particularly in his *Life*, letters, and poems, about the
endings of selected years, periods which knit Christmastide with
the New Year as a festive season.

During the early childhood of Thomas Hardy and his sister Mary
the Higher Bockhampton community was large enough for us to
assume that in those days (when games, song, and dance were
necessarily localized, traditional, and homespun) they were not
neglected during this season, either at home or in the neighbourhood. The young boy of 'The Self-Unseeing' who danced ecstati-
cally to the jigs, hornpipes, reels, waltzes, and country-dances
which were played in the evenings by his father must have been
excited by the unusual festivities of Christmas–New Year periods.
He remembered them at 'the house of hospitalities' just down the
lane at Higher Bockhampton.[1] Neither here, much less in his own
small home, could the tranter's party of *Under the Greenwood Tree*
have taken place; impressions for this were gained at home and in
the neighbourhood, some from what he saw later at country
celebrations and parties elsewhere, and some even from fiction.
As a choir-boy, he would know the excitement of carol-singing

round the parish with instrumental players, though the stringed choir of the novel belonged to a past which was already becoming romantic in the mind of a youth eager for anecdote and hearsay, especially of the unusual.

To what extent, if any, Hardy's end-of-the-year junketings were affected by the ups-and-downs of his father's business is wholly conjectural. In early adolescence he often returned cold and tired in the morning with his father after 'merry minstrellings', on one occasion after playing six or seven hours as second violin to him. It was bitterly cold, the encrusted snow glistening in the moonlight, when they saw a white human figure apparently headless in the hedge. Tired out, with fingertips tingling from pressing the strings, the boy Hardy would have hurried home past this ghastly apparition, but his father, finding the man drunk, in a long white smock-frock, with his head hanging forward, roused him from his stupor, lest he were frozen to death. They supported him to his cottage, where he was received with a torrent of abuse from his wife, who promptly floored him. This extraordinary encounter may or may not have taken place during 'the twelve days of Christmas', but it serves to show how the youthful Hardy, in one way or another, was learning 'what life was', as his mother thought he should, when he accompanied his father to provide music for celebrations which included New Year's Eve parties. The events of the poem 'Winter Night in Woodland' seem to belong to an earlier period, but the cruel customs it denotes of 'bird-baiters' and poachers in the Christmas season continued in the vicinity of Hardy's home during his youth, and the boy who did not wish to grow up undoubtedly saw and heard much that he would willingly have shunned. If, as 'The Oxen' suggests, he and Mary heard at home the old belief that cattle knelt down on Christmas Eve, they thought with awe of such occurrences in the barton at the bottom of Higher Bockhampton lane.

Horace Moule had probably returned to his Fordington home for the Christmas–New Year period when he gave Hardy copies, first of *The Golden Treasury* in January 1862, then of *The Thoughts of the Emperor M. Aurelius Antoninus* on New Year's Day 1865; both of these books were highly prized by Hardy all his life. A passage which was omitted from his early autobiography makes one wonder whether he could have met Louisa Harding, whom he admired before leaving home for London, at Christmastide in 1862 or 1863. She was the daughter of a Stinsford farmer who thought

him socially inferior, and frowned on their association. In the first
version Hardy states that their attachment 'may have lasted a year
or longer', and that they used to meet 'down to his 23rd or 24th
year on his visits to Dorset from London'. Yet the final text tells
us that he spoke only once to her as they passed (this occasion
being recalled in his late poem 'To Louisa in the Lane').[2] In 1863
he looks forward to rejoining his sister Mary (then teaching at
Denchworth, north of Wantage, Berkshire) at home, and having
'a bit of a lark' after Christmas; two years later, as two pencil
sketches by him show, he spent Christmas with her at Denchworth.
Meetings with relatives at Puddletown, particularly at the Antells',
were frequent, often at the end of the year, in the 1860s.

In 1870, when he fell in love with Emma Lavinia Gifford, he was
still engaged in architecture, but his main ambition was the
publication of his first novel. He had made strenuous efforts before
sending his second venture, *Desperate Remedies*, off to Tinsley in
December 1870, most of the manuscript a fair copy made by Emma
in Cornwall. Having aimed high and most poetically in parts of it,
he had allowed his complicated plot to descend to rather crude
sensationalism for commercial gain, and it was this adulteration
which worried him at the end of the year, after bringing to mind
on 15 December the words of Hamlet, 'Thou wouldst not think
how ill all's here about my heart: but it is no matter!' So severely
was it criticized in *The Spectator* the following April ('a desperate
remedy for an emaciated purse' being especially galling because it
was too near the truth) that Hardy, reading the review on his way
home from Dorchester, sat on the stile in Kingston leaze and
wished he were dead. (Having discovered, no doubt, what Hardy
had written in the meantime, John Hutton, the reviewer, wrote
on 29 April 1873 to admit the severity of his censure.)

At the end of 1872, feeling much happier after the publication
of *Under the Greenwood Tree*, Hardy was at work finishing *A Pair of
Blue Eyes* when he received an invitation from Leslie Stephen, who
had found much to admire in *Under the Greenwood Tree*, to write a
story for *The Cornhill Magazine*. He was even more delighted when,
returning from a visit to Emma in Cornwall on New Year's Eve
1873, he bought a copy of *The Cornhill* at Plymouth, and found the
first part of his serialized story, *Far from the Madding Crowd*, given
pride of place at the beginning of the magazine, with a striking
illustration by Helen Paterson. Emma's delight and surprise must
have been even greater when she, without whose encouragement

he might never have chosen a literary career, received this copy, for he had given her no idea of his new novel.

Its success enabled them to marry soon after its completion in 1874. At the end of 1875, when they were living at Swanage, he was busy with the completion of *The Hand of Ethelberta*. The following Christmas, after settling at Sturminster Newton, they stayed at Higher Bockhampton with Hardy's parents. He was anxious to begin *The Return of the Native*, and spent some of his time there renewing impressions of the heath and views from Rainbarrow, especially at dusk, for the opening chapters of the novel. Probably during this visit he made the ground-plan sketch of 'Mr C's house' (near the communal well at Higher Bockhampton) with Eustacia Vye's house at Mistover Knap in mind, though it is difficult to see how ultimately it played a necessary part in its description. He returned to novel-writing with renewed zest early in the New Year, after a period of recuperation and intensive reading, and sent the first fifteen chapters (with Avice as the name of his heroine) to John Blackwood on 12 April. After further unsuccessful attempts to place his serial, he adjusted his plans and recast all he had written. By the end of 1877, after the publication of his delightful children's story 'The Thieves Who Couldn't Help Sneezing' in *Father Christmas*, and before the conclusion of their 'Sturminster Newton idyll', Hardy had decided that for practical purposes as a novelist he must live in London; Emma agreed, and her brother thought she would benefit socially by such a move.

At Tooting a year later he seems to feel the need of reassurance. In November, when *The Return of the Native* was published in volume form, he felt before it was light one morning that he lacked sufficient staying-power to hold his own in the world. His thought on New Year's Day runs:

A perception of the FAILURE of THINGS to be what they are meant to be, lends them, in place of the intended interest, a new and greater interest of an unintended kind.

He had been devastated to find that his efforts to achieve a major success with his novel had failed. The reviewer in *The Athenaeum* rated it 'distinctly inferior to anything of his' he had read, and more specific charges were already making Hardy wonder how he could follow his true artistic self in such unpropitious times.

Even so, by the end of the year (1879) Hardy was becoming a

recognised literary figure in London. In December, attending the inaugural meeting of the Rabelais Club at the Tavistock Hotel, in a cheerless room which the thick fog had penetrated, he succeeded poorly in his own estimation. A year later he was bedridden, Emma acting as amanuensis as he continued *A Laodicean*, the serialization of which had just begun. After writing to her private secretary, to suggest that Queen Victoria might be interested in the appearances of George III in *The Trumpet-Major*, he had been pleased to send her a copy. It was a period when he had time to reflect on his reading. News of George Eliot's death late in December set him thinking on the force Positivism might have been if Comte had included Christ among his 'worthies'. He read Arnold, and disagreed with his views on literary provincialism, though he was soon to find Arnold's desideratum, 'the imaginative reason', applicable not only to Wordsworth's contention that the more perfectly the natural object is reproduced, the more poetic is the picture, but also to the theme of his current novel.

Though the Hardys moved to Wimborne in June 1881 for the sake of his health, they were very active, receiving an unexpected number of social calls, taking an extensive tour in Scotland, and assisting in Shakespeare readings. They met many of their friends in London in December, when Hardy visited the Royal Observatory at Greenwich, after completing an application to the effect that he wished to ascertain whether a hollow memorial pillar with an interior staircase could be adapted for astronomical purposes, and how it could be roofed without interfering with observations, all of which was strictly true for *Two on a Tower*, plans for which were well advanced. On New Year's Eve he and Emma were guests at a ball given by Lady Wimborne at Canford Manor. (This undoubtedly was a grand occasion, and some recollected details of it may have filtered into the extraordinary dance episode of 'The Romantic Adventures of a Milkmaid', to which Hardy must have been giving much thought one year later.) 'Thus ended 1881 – with a much brighter atmosphere for the author and his wife than the opening had shown', Hardy wrote years later in his *Life*.

After two years at Wimborne they moved to Dorchester, a step 'they often regretted having taken', though 'the bracing air brought them health and renewed vigour'. Apart from lengthy visits to London in the spring and summer for many a year, and holidays abroad, they were to live here for the rest of their lives. Hardy did much research in local history at the museum, besides more general reading, before embarking on *The Mayor of Casterbridge* in 1884. On the previous New Year's Eve he was busy planting trees on the exposed land he had bought for the building of the home which he was to name Max Gate. What a change for him in January when he was in London, meeting Henry James, his old friend Edmund Gosse, the sculptor Hamo Thornycroft, and the painter Alma-Tadema, to whom he talked about the Roman remains which were being discovered on the site of the house he had planned!

Still living in Shirehall Lane (a house which his visitor Gosse described as rambling, and one of which a townsman said 'He have but one window, and she do look into Gaol Lane'), he was not content to hear the bells of St Peter's ring out the Old Year of 1884, but had to climb up to the belfry with the ringers, as the night-wind 'whiffed in' through the louvres, and clamber with them over the bells to watch them fix the mufflers (noticing how the tenor bell had been brightly pitted by its battered clapper). After this he observed the ringers in action, and the red, green, and white sallies bolting up like rats through the holes between the beams overhead. His interest in bell-ringing had been evident at the end of *Desperate Remedies*.

Depression returns at the end of 1885. He had noticed it in November when labouring over his plot for *The Woodlanders*. On 21 December he senses 'the Hypocrisy of things'; the child is completely unaware of it, and older people, 'more or less according to their penetration', though even they rarely perceive that '*nothing is as it appears*'. New Year's Eve finds him unusually sad; he does not disclose the underlying reasons, but wonders whether all his efforts to create a home at Max Gate will be worth while, and remembers the advice of Marcus Aurelius which Horace Moule had inscribed in his presentation copy of *The Thoughts*: 'This is the chief thing: Be not perturbed; for all things are according to the nature of the universal.' He may well have had doubts, much less well-founded than those which worried him when he forwarded the manuscript of *Desperate Remedies* to his publishers, about the reception of *The Mayor of Casterbridge*, a novel which opens sensationally and which, for the purpose of weekly serialization, contains a frequency of exciting and suspenseful incident, once or twice little above the level of popular magazine fiction in substance. On 2 January 1886, the day the first instalment appeared in *The Graphic*, he writes: 'I fear it will not be so good as I meant, but after all, it is not improbabilities of incident but improbabilities of character that matter.' (Anthony Trollope had written similarly in his *Autobiography*.)

Hardy is not very cheerful at the end of 1886, though he tells Gosse that he is trying to maintain the spirit of the 'Merry Christmas' greetings he sends him. He is disconcerted because a critic in *The Saturday Review* has deemed a sentence in *The Mayor of Casterbridge* on a rather improbable method of improving bad flour a justification for sneering at the whole work, and wonders whether reviewing can ever be conducted on such a sound system that books in their entirety are no longer judged by iotas such as a slip in a date or quotation.

At the end of 1887, the year in which he finished *The Woodlanders* and outlined plans for *The Dynasts*, he notes that nothing has been heard from Max Gate to indicate that it is New Year's Eve – 'no bell, or band, or voice'. He does some annual stocktaking, which includes telling indications of the literature he had consulted or read (he should have added 're-read'):

> The year has been a fairly friendly one to me. It showed me and Em the south of Europe – Italy, above all Rome – and it brought us back unharmed and much illuminated. It has given me some new acquaintances, too, and enabled me to hold my own in fiction, whatever that may be worth, by the completion of 'The Woodlanders'.
>
> Books read or pieces looked at this year:
>
> Milton, Dante, Calderon, Goethe.
> Homer, Virgil, Molière, Scott.
> The Cid, Nibelungen, Crusoe, Don Quixote.
> Aristophanes, Theocritus, Boccaccio.
> Canterbury Tales, Shakespeare's Sonnets, Lycidas.
> Malory, Vicar of Wakefield, Ode to West Wind, Ode to Grecian Urn.
> Christabel, Wye above Tintern.
> Chapman's Iliad, Lord Derby's ditto, Worsley's Odyssey.

The new acquaintances were nearly all celebrities and members of aristocratic families he, sometimes with Emma, had met in London.

Whether Hardy had begun writing *Tess of the d'Urbervilles* before the end of 1888 is uncertain; he had given it a great deal of preparation during the autumn, and on 10 December he writes a note which, though it suggests something more personal, something unfortunate and unavoidable, possibly at Max Gate, is conceived with reference to the same Ultimate as the misfortunes of Tess:

> He, she, had blundered; but not as the Prime Cause had blundered. He, she, had sinned; but not as the Prime Cause had sinned. He, she, was ashamed and sorry; but not as the Prime Cause would be ashamed and sorry if it knew.

Hardy's parenthetical comment, 'The reference is unexplained', when, during the compilation of his *Life*, he was confronted by this note, may genuinely indicate his inability to remember what occasioned it. On New Year's Eve he and Emma were most probably looking forward to their imminent departure for London, where one of the main objectives was a visit to the Old Masters at the Royal Academy.

1890 was a year in which Hardy received absurdly Grundyan complaints from editors about stories he had to bowdlerize for publication. The work involved in this was trivial compared with the expedients he knew he would have to employ, after repeated rejections of the story, to produce a version of *Tess* which would be acceptable for serialization. No wonder, therefore, that on Christmas Day he is already half-dreaming of the time when he can turn to poetry: 'While thinking of resuming "the viewless wings of poesy" before dawn this morning, new horizons seemed to open, and worrying pettinesses to disappear.' He observed the New Year's Eve tradition of looking outdoors just before midnight, and was 'confronted by the toneless white of snow spread in front, against which stood the row of pines breathing out: "'Tis no better with us than with the rest of creation, you see!"' If the bells of Fordington Church rang out the old year, and rang in the new, he could not hear them.

At the end of 1891, after the appearance of *Tess* in volume form, and of 'The Son's Veto' in a Christmas number, Hardy thanks H. W. Massingham for his generous article on his novel in *The Daily Chronicle*, and for recognising that virility in fiction poses no necessary threat to sound morality. He had felt ever since writing *Two on a Tower*, he says, that the 'doll of English fiction' must be destroyed if the novel is to have any future. He could hardly have foreseen, he was to write with hindsight, that with the publication of *Tess of the d'Urbervilles* his own future as a novelist had reached 'the beginning of the end'.

The pleasure that Hardy's picture of the year's end in 1893 suggests may have been real enough; if so, it occurred during a period when his relations with Emma were repeatedly subject to strain. After finishing his London engagements when he and Mrs Henniker revised 'The Spectre of the Real',

> he spent Christmas at Max Gate as usual, receiving the carol-singers there on Christmas Eve, where, 'though quite modern, with a harmonium, they made a charming picture with their lanterns under the trees, the rays diminishing away in the winter mist'. On New Year's Eve it was calm, and they stood outside listening to the muffled peal from the tower of Fordington St. George.

Two years later some of the reviews of *Jude the Obscure* had begun to throw Hardy into emotional turmoil, and he pens a statement which if intended to be self-justificatory (as it must have been, since it was a comment on 'one or two' of the reviews), ends unconvincingly and evasively:

> Tragedy may be created by an opposing environment either of things inherent in the universe, or of human institutions. If the former be the means exhibited and deplored, the writer is regarded as impious; if the latter, as subversive and dangerous; when all the while he may never have questioned the necessity or urged the non-necessity of either . . . .

The expression 'things inherent in the universe' is more indicative of Hardy's obsession with the Primal Cause than of anything else; taking heredity into account, both tragedies are explicable in human terms. The first alternative is intended more for *Tess*; the second, more obviously for *Jude*.

The following year Hardy was in disgrace with fortune at home and abroad. It was the year of the third 'In Tenebris', of 'The Dead Man Walking' (a poem seared by the memory of the hatred kindled against him in his 'Love's heart'), and of 'Wessex Heights' (a cry for freedom from the 'mind-chains' that clanked with the injustices of reviewers against *Jude*). Thoughts of his own birthday made him write: 'Every man's birthday is a first of April for him; and he who lives to be fifty and won't own it is a rogue or fool, hypocrite or simpleton.' His Christmas is dull, but it satisfies him, he tells Mrs Henniker, because it is free from 'positive sorrows'. Relief is brought by villagers who sing the carols he loved when they were sung by the old 'Mellstock' choir (at Stinsford).

It was not all doom and gloom with the Hardys in their last twenty years together; far from it. In 1897 they attended parties and performances in London, their season from Max Gate including a tour in Switzerland to boot. With the publication of *The Well-Beloved* his writing of prose fiction had virtually ceased. He had some short-story commitments; 'The Grave by the Handpost', which appeared in an 1897 Christmas number, illustrates how far Hardy's Christmas stories diverged from Dingley Dell celebrations and other Dickensian fare. It is the story of a father's suicide and burial (with, it was said, a stake through his coffinless body) at crossroads, concluding with the son's suicide at the same spot. Carol-singers and musicians arrive by chance as the burial of the first is completed; afterwards, with time to spare and no one but the dead to hear them, they think it accordant with Christmas to play a carol over the grave, choosing one with the lines, 'He comes the prisoners to release, In Satan's bondage held.'[3] When the son hears these words sung at Christmas years later, after returning from the Peninsular War, he walks to his father's burial-place and shoots himself. The subject is grimmer than the events on moonlight nights at Christmastide in 'What the Shepherd Saw' (written for a Christmas number in 1881), a story of murderous jealousy which ends with the local tradition of flitting shapes seen at night during Christmas week, with the gleam of a weapon and the shadow of a man dragging a dead body.

Another Christmas story by Hardy appeared for Christmas 1881 as 'Benighted Travellers', a romantic tale with a happy ending, its heroine's name being changed (after the publication of *The Mayor of Casterbridge*) from 'Lucetta' when it was included as 'The Honourable Laura' in *A Group of Noble Dames*. The most delightful of Hardy's Christmas stories in prose, apart from 'The Thieves Who Couldn't Help Sneezing', is 'A Tradition of Eighteen Hundred and Four', first published as 'A Legend . . .' in *Harper's Christmas*, 1882; so well told is it that many readers believed Napoleon's fictional reconnoitring on the south coast to be an actual tradition. Much later reflections on the discord between contemporary realities and the Christian message of old, 'Glory to God in the

highest, and on earth peace, good will toward men', were to find
bitter expression in Hardy's verse.

Wessex Poems, Hardy's first volume of poetry, came out in the
middle of December 1898. Having laboured manifestly over the
style of several of them at different periods (a third of them having
been written before he began novel-writing), he endeavours to
make light of his uneasiness by telling Gosse that the poems were
'lying about', and he didn't know what to do with them. That his
poetic style weighed on his mind is clear from a sentence in
his letter to Gosse which, after rightly inveighing against the
'mellifluous preciosity' of fashionable contemporary verse, ends
with the claim that content is more important than form. Whatever
he feared, he was buoyed up by generous criticism from Swinburne
and William Archer, though he seems to have attached more
importance to a letter which he received from Leslie Stephen before
the end of the year, expressing gratitude at being remembered as
a friend, and stating that the volume had given him genuine
pleasure.

Christmas 1899 was unlike any Hardy had so far experienced.
The Boer War, which he followed with avid interest, was going
very badly for the British. He had thought it likely to break out
when he wrote 'Murmurs in the Gloom' on 22 September:

> 'O Dynasties that sway and shake us so,
> Why rank your magnanimities so low
>> That grace can smooth no waters yet,
>> But breathing threats and slaughters yet
>> Ye grieve Earth's sons and daughters yet
>>> As long ago?
>
> 'Live there no heedful ones of searching sight,
> Whose accents might be oracles that smite
>> To hinder those who frowardly
>> Conduct us, and untowardly;
>> To lead the nations vawardly
>>> From gloom to light?'

Since then he had watched one night in wind and rain the
departure of troops from Dorchester, seen the embarkation of 5000
soldiers at Southampton, and written some of his best war poems,
including 'Drummer Hodge'. Two others appeared in December,

and a third, 'A Christmas Ghost-Story', on 23 December in *The Westminster Gazette* (not on Christmas Eve, as indicated in *Poems of the Past and the Present*). In this the phantom of a dead soldier moans nightly to Canopus:

> 'I would know
> By whom and when the All-Earth-gladdening Law
> Of Peace, brought in by that Man Crucified,
> Was ruled to be inept, and set aside?
> And what of logic and of truth appears
> In tacking 'Anno Domini' to the years?
> Near twenty-hundred liveried thus have hied,
> But tarries yet the Cause for which He died.'

For these sentiments Hardy was taken to task by the editor of *The Daily Chronicle*, who thought that the soldier could not have been one of the brave who died on the Tugela front. On Christmas Day Hardy replied in most scholarly style with references to Homer, Virgil, the book of Samuel, Dante, and Hamlet, asserting the propriety of making a disembodied spirit, which had nothing left to defend, express a universal feeling, especially in a poem for Christmas reading.

He was anxious to complete two short stories, his last in prose, in fulfilment of long-standing promises. He began 'Enter a Dragoon' in November, but did not make much progress with it owing to 'a distressing nausea and headache'. The second was designed for *The Sphere*, a magazine which was to make its first appearance in January. Hardy informed Clement Shorter, its editor, that he would begin 'shaping the story' ('A Changed Man') on New Year's Day. Its fiction was to be woven around true and memorable accounts of the valiant work performed at Fordington by Henry Moule, the vicar, during 'the cholera years', especially the epidemic of 1854. Both stories were finished before the end of January.

There seems to have been some uncertainty about whether the century ended on 31 December 1899 or 1900; and Hardy's emphasis on the latter has been found in what appears as the odd irrelevancy of 'End of the Nineteenth Century' (capitalized) at the close of the 1899–1900 chapter of his *Life*. It is sometimes claimed that he wrote 'The Darkling Thrush' in 1899 on the assumption that this was the last year of the century. The evidence given is that when copying up the poem for the publication of *Poems of the Past and the Present* he subscribed 'The Century's End', adding '1899', which he crossed out for '1900'.[4] This alteration may confirm an uncertainty that had existed, but the faltering cannot be assumed to imply more than a moment's uncertainty at the time of copying, since Hardy had taken steps to ensure that the poem was published at the most appropriate time in *The Graphic*, where it appeared on 29 December 1900 with the title 'By the Century's Deathbed'. The later subscription 'December 1900' may be accurate, but the still later '31 December 1900' is so patently false that one wonders how reliable some other datings may be.

Internal evidence suggests that the poem was written during the latter part of 1900. Hardy's copy of John Keble's *The Christian Year* shows that he had long been familiar with many of its poems, and there can be little doubt that the initial inspiration for 'The Darkling Thrush' came not from Keats's 'Ode to a Nightingale' but from Keble's 'The Twenty-first Sunday after Trinity', where, in the 'dreary blast' of a grey autumnal evening, a redbreast warbles a 'cheerful tender strain', though its 'joyous prime' be spent, 'And on the world's autumnal time, 'Mid withered hues and sere, its lot be cast'. 'That', Keble reflects,

> is the heart for thoughtful seer,
> Watching, in trance nor dark nor clear,
> The appalling Future as it nearer draws:
>
> *   *   *
>
> Contented in his darkling round,
> If only he be faithful found,
> When from the east the eternal morning moves.

Hardy's change to midwinter and the thrush was most probably occasioned by the striking contrast of a memorable descriptive passage in W. H. Hudson's *Nature in Downland*, which appeared in the summer of 1900:

> Mid-winter is the season of the missel-thrush . . . when there is no gleam of light anywhere and no change in that darkness of immense ever-moving cloud above; and the south-west raves all day and night, and day after day. . . .

Most noticeable is the coincidence in Hudson's account of the thrush's song in wind and gloom with the manner in which Hardy's 'blast-beruffled' bird *flings* his soul upon a darkening world:

> you must believe that this dark aspect of things delights him; that his pleasure in life, expressed with such sounds and in such circumstances, must greatly exceed in degree the contentment and bliss that is ours, even when we are most free from pain or care, and our whole beings most perfectly in tune with nature. . . . The sound is beautiful in quality, but the singer has no art, and flings out his notes anyhow; the song is an outburst, a cry of happiness . . . .

By comparing the bird's pleasure in life with man's, Hudson implicitly raises the question which was at the heart of Hardy's subject at the outset. His contrast is greater than Hudson's; if he is in accord with the scene ('every spirit upon earth' seeming as 'fervourless' as he), he is far removd from 'beings' who are 'most free from pain or care' and 'most perfectly in tune with nature'. Hardy the poet is rarely in tune with nature; he is too conscious of its Darwinian aspects. The mood of his poem may be wholly poetic, a pose for artistic purposes which are excellently fulfilled. It could have been induced by the poems which influenced him, including Matthew Arnold's 'Dover Beach' and its 'darkling' connotations. The prolongation of the Boer War and its casualties could have had their effect. Even the weather could have contributed; on 30 January 1899 he had written: 'Frost has always a curious effect upon my mind, for which I can never account fully – that something is imminent of a tragic nature.' What is significant is the poet's uncertainty, reflecting a maturity and wisdom transcending the assurance he had acquired at an early stage about life and the universe. It is seen in 'An August Midnight', written in 1899, which ends with the reflection that the insect-life which has engaged his attention is aware of 'Earth-secrets' unknown to him; and again in 'The Year's Awakening' of February 1910, which asks how it is that the 'vespering' bird and the crocus root know that spring is on the way when winter is most severe. 'The Darkling Thrush' is not an expression of Hardy's hope; it admits the possibility that his hopelessness (the general pessimism with which he was later charged – wrongly, he thought) may be invalid, that the carolling thrush (an apt metaphor for the Christmas season) is, like the other vespering bird and the crocus, in tune with nature, whereas he, the reasoner, is not (a thought which may lie behind the debate posed in 'Night in the Old Home').

Hardy prepared the manuscript of *Poems of the Past and the Present* in the summer of 1901. In many of these poems, following Arnold's idea that the distinguishing feature of the greatest poets is 'their powerful and profound application of ideas to life', he had done what he hoped to do after concluding from the reception of *Jude the Obscure* that readers of fiction did not wish to be disturbed by heterodox views in any form. Perhaps he could express 'ideas and emotions which run counter to inert crystallized opinion' more fully in verse, he wrote in 1896:

> To cry out in a passionate poem that (for instance) the Supreme Mover or Movers, the Prime Force or Forces, must be either limited in power, unknowing, or cruel[5] – which is obvious enough, and has been for centuries – will cause them merely a shake of the head; but to put it in argumentative prose will make them sneer, or foam, and set all the literary contortionists jumping upon me, a harmless agnostic, as if I were a clamorous atheist, which in their crass illiteracy they seem to think is the same thing. . . . If Galileo had said in verse that the world moved, the Inquisition might have left him alone.

His temerity made him extremely gloomy in September 1901 about the reception of his second volume of verse, as he told Gosse, who, on receiving an inscribed copy from Hardy in November, read it eagerly. He thought the poems went 'straight to the very heart', and enjoyed many of them, including 'The Darkling Thrush', immensely. The war poems were technically the best that had been published, the only ones which had 'gone below the drum and tinsel'; 'The Souls of the Slain' was inexpressibly great. For him Hardy was the most admired writer among his contemporaries; the 'sheer intensity' of his sympathy made him 'helplessly uncritical', and he would always read him with 'the old tingling pulse'. Gosse did not mention any of the poems in which Hardy had tried to assert views influenced by Darwinism, Positivism, and other forms of rationalism, but he gave Hardy some of the confidence in himself which made him write on New Year's Eve:

> After reading various philosophic systems, and being struck

with their contradictions and futilities, I have come to this: *Let every man make a philosophy for himself out of his own experience.* He will not be able to escape using terms and phraseology from earlier philosophers, but let him avoid adopting their theories if he values his own mental life. Let him remember the fate of Coleridge, and save years of labour by working out his own views as given him by his surroundings.

This probably suggests overconfidence. Hardy may already have begun the presentation of his philosophy in *The Dynasts*.

Part First of *The Dynasts* was ready for publication in December 1903, but, owing to copyright law (the American edition not being ready), the work could not be published until January 1904, after the title-page had been reprinted with the amended date. Christmas, he had told his friend Edward Clodd, no longer meant much to him; it raised an increasing number of 'frustrate ghosts' without a corresponding increase of friends. His letter of 2 January 1906 shows that Florence Dugdale, who was to be more than a friend to Hardy and Emma, had visited Max Gate near the end of 1905, when he had expected Part Second of *The Dynasts* to be published, only to find his hopes thwarted by a political crisis. Two years later he was correcting the proofs of Part Third.

Writing to Mrs Henniker in December, on the shortest day of 1906, he tells her that some of his verses will appear in the January *Fortnightly Review*, and that he does not propose to send her a copy, since he is certain she will not like them. He alludes to 'New Year's Eve', a poem of peculiar inappropriateness to the season; there is no relief to its pessimism. After opening its brief duologue with God's statement that he has completed another year, the poem continues:

> 'And what's the good of it?' I said,
>   'What reasons made you call
> From formless void this earth we tread,
> When nine-and-ninety can be read
>   Why nought should be at all?
>
> 'Yea, Sire; why shaped you us, "who in
>   This tabernacle groan" –
> If ever a joy be found herein,
> Such joy no man had wished to win
>   If he had never known!'

Hardy takes his place with the preacher of 'vanity of vanities; all is vanity'. No wonder he received a letter from the Philippines at the end of 1905, telling him he was like 'some terrible old prophet crying in the wilderness'. The poem ends with a recrudescence of Hardy's Unfulfilled Intention theory, God expressing surprise that man has developed a consciousness and an ethical sense which he had never known. Hardy then presents God as he had continually done since the beginning of the century: always impercipient (allowing for the poetic licence of brief awakenings for dramatic purpose in Hardy's poetry) and working unconsciously 'Eternal artistries in Circumstance', as the Spirit of the Years announces in an introduction to the bloody struggle of *The Dynasts*. When Clodd wrote to him about his poem, Hardy adverted to Herbert Spencer's 'feeling' that 'it is paralyzing to think what if, of all that is so incomprehensible to us (the Universe) there exists no comprehension anywhere'. As an example of creating God in man's image, this is as remarkable as it is absurd. Hardy was wiser years later when, taking up a defensive position, he argued that the views expressed in his poems were only *seemings*, and that the Scheme of Things was incomprehensible.[6]

The weather at Max Gate on New Year's Eve 1907 was 'dreadfully dull', with sleet descending and snow on the ground. Hardy had probably been taken aback to find that his ballad 'A Sunday Morning Tragedy' had been rejected by both *The Fortnightly Review* and *The Nation*. It appeared in the first (December 1908) number of *The English Review*, the editor, Ford Madox Hueffer (Ford), having founded the magazine, it was said, in order to publish this poem. Hardy had thought of producing it as a play, but come to the conclusion that the subject (a fatal attempt at abortion which proves to have been unnecessary) would not be tolerated on the contemporary stage. The poem was included in *Time's Laughingstocks*, Hardy's third volume of poetry, which appeared in December 1909 when he was in London. He returned with the usual sore throat to Max Gate, and had to stay in bed until the New Year. So attached was he to the old custom of hearing the bells at midnight that he sat by his bedroom fire on New Year's Eve, straining successfully to hear in the chimney the muffled peal at Fordington Church.

It was almost the same with him the following Christmas after returning from London, but he recovered, paid a visit to the American fleet in Portland Roads, and went on board the battleship

Connecticut, the captain and several officers being afterwards received at Max Gate. On 29 December Hardy and Emma went on board the English *Dreadnought*, and thence to a dance on the American flagship *Louisiana*, to which they were welcomed by Admiral Vreeland. Earlier Hardy had been distressed by the death of his 'study cat' Kitsey (commemorated, with the Roman graves which had been found at Max Gate, in 'The Roman Gravemounds').

Although very well and happy early in December 1911, when he journeyed with Miss Dugdale and his sister to Bath, Bristol, and Gloucester, before composing 'The Abbey Mason', he was worried and saddened as the year closed by the serious decline in health of his sister Mary, the playmate of his early years. His distress must have been slight compared with his state at the end of 1912 after the shock of Emma's death and (most probably) the discovery of her notebooks, one enclosing the generally benign recollections of their courtship years, the others reserved for splenetic, vindictive outpourings, the worst thoughts she had harboured against him. Did Hardy already contemplate revisiting Cornwall in March, to arrive there on the anniversary of his first visit, in expiation of his neglect of her when he sought refuge in his Max Gate study and elsewhere? His poem 'End of the Year 1912' suggests a distanced, tranquillized recollection of one whose songs were once heard at Max Gate while the six Fordington bells ushered in the New Year:

> You were here at his young beginning,
>   You are not here at his agèd end;
> Off he coaxed you from Life's mad spinning,
>   Lest you should see his form extend
>   Shivering, sighing,
>   Slowly dying,
>   And a tear on him expend.
>
> So it comes that we stand lonely
>   In the star-lit avenue,
> Dropping broken lipwords only,
>   For we hear no songs from you,
>   Such as flew here
>   For the new year
>   Once, while six bells swung thereto.

On 16 January 1913 Florence Dugdale informs Clodd that Hardy, despite reading and re-reading Emma's voluminous diaries, which contain bitter denunciations of him from about 1891 until a day or two before her death, looks well and seems cheerful. His sister Kate has told her that he has regained the happy laugh he had when he was a young man.

A crisis arose at Max Gate when Emma's niece Lilian Gifford returned for Christmas. The question was who was to be in charge; Miss Dugdale, who had been acting as Hardy's secretary and general assistant for some time, decided that the matter must be settled in a week, and the result was their sudden marriage in February. In November, more than three months after the outbreak of the 1914–18 war, *Satires of Circumstance* appeared, eight days before the staging of scenes from *The Dynasts* by Granville-Barker began at the Kingsway Theatre, London. Florence attended the first performance, sitting next to John Masefield and his wife. Hardy, who had seen an early rehearsal, was unfit to travel, and did not see the play until about three weeks later. 'Dorchester is more or less full of soldiers and German prisoners', he writes on Christmas Day; he sees no end to the war. A newspaper editor had invited him to send Christmas greetings to his readers, but it was too difficult a puzzle for him, he answered, the times being 'an absolute negation of Christianity'. The war killed all his belief in 'the gradual ennoblement of man' as he had expressed it in 'The Sick Battle-God', and made him regret that he had ended *The Dynasts* on a hopeful note. Furthermore it gave 'the *coup-de-grâce* to any conception he may have nourished of a fundamental ultimate Wisdom at the back of things'. Events seemed to support his views on necessitation with a modicum of free will, and his surmise that 'the never-ending push of the Universe was an unpurposive and irresponsible groping in the direction of the least resistance'. 'A sad vigil, during which no bells were heard at Max Gate, brought in the first New Year of this unprecedented "breaking of nations".'[7]

A chance event the following year produced 'A New Year's Eve in War Time'. In the customary style Hardy had opened the door to 'let in' 1916. As he listened to the wind droning in his pines and the grating of the weathercock, he heard the clattering of a horse along the road. The rider passed Max Gate at great speed just as the clock was about to strike midnight, and the poet was reminded of the horse ridden by Death in Revelation and of the continuing war. The birth of the New Year is accompanied by a moan from the trees:

> Maybe that 'More Tears! –
> More Famine and Flame –
> More Severance and Shock!'
> Is the order from Fate
> That the Rider speeds on
> To pale Europe; and tiredly the pines intone.[8]

'At the Entering of the New Year', also written during the 1914–18 war, contrasts old style and new, the former being recalled with relish by Hardy, who remembers how delightfully the New Year was hailed in song and dance, the music throbbing to allemands, heys, and poussettings, while the 'measured booming' of the contrabasso was audible to anyone within the parish bounds, including furtive poachers as well as shepherds at midnight lambings. Now we may listen for the peal of muffled bells, but the war makes us think of 'bereaved Humanity', which seems to loom like a mantled ghost in the grey as it sighfully wishes the New Year will never be born.

What hope could a new year bring? Hardy was 'scarcely conscious of New Year's Day' in 1917. At the end of November *Moments of Vision* was published; 'Afterwards', as its conclusion, suggests that the poet felt he could not live much longer. Writing to Sir Henry Newbolt on New Year's Eve, he said he could not remember parting from an old year with less reluctance than from the present one. He did not sit up in the usual way, but went to bed at eleven. The wind being in the east, he made no effort to hear the bells before midnight, and 'slept in' the New Year like his parents, Emma, and sister Mary 'out there', across the valley, under the yew in Stinsford churchyard. He was thinking of his poem 'Looking Across' and its conclusion:

> Tired, tired am I
> Of this earthly air,
> And my wraith asks: Why,
> Since these calm lie,
> Are not Five out there?

On 30 December 1918, not long after the end of the war, he wrote to Sir Henry Newbolt again, thinking of 'Men Who March Away' and of how, in the September sunshine, he had despondently surveyed a row of 'young fellows in straw hats who had fallen-in' in front of the County Hall. The war had lessened his interest in the human race, he added. He did not see the New Year in, nor did he at the end of 1919. A young poet had written to him for advice, and, thinking of his own complete failure to obtain publication of his early poems for years, he recommended beginning with *imitative* verse, adopting the manner of any accepted recent poet, say Wordsworth or Tennyson; it is fatal, he continued, 'to begin with any original vein you may be blest with' or not to pay great attention to the mechanics of verse. Reviewers did not know that 'dissonances, and other irregularities, can be produced advisedly, as art', and can charm the ear more than 'strict conformities'; they had either forgotten or never heard that *Ars est celare artem.* Just before Christmas he had been honoured with an invitation to lecture at Yale University, a possibility quite beyond his experience, age, and temperament; he declined the offer, as he had declined other invitations to the States. That same month he had performed a far more agreeable function at Lower Bockhampton, when he opened the club-room which had been built as a war memorial. He may have been looking forward to receiving his honorary degree of Doctor of Letters at Oxford in February.

Christmas 1920 was much happier. Not only did carol-singers come and sing old Bockhampton carols; there was a visit of the mummers, who performed 'Saint George's play' from T. H. Tilley's adaptation of *The Return of the Native*, which had been staged in Dorchester during November. The lights of Max Gate welcomed them; the singers, grouped round the fiddlers and their elevated lantern, sang their carols outside; and then all trooped in for the performance of the play in the drawing-room. It was, Florence Hardy wrote to Sydney Cockerell, a most exciting Christmas. One of the party told her that he had never seen Hardy look so young and happy. After the performance, both talked to the players, recalling incidents in local productions of *The Mellstock Quire*, *The Trumpet-Major*, and 'Wessex Scenes from *The Dynasts*', and the recent occasion when the stage-lighting failed and Clym and Eustacia had to pause in the proposal scene until lighted candles could be fixed. Hardy privately hoped that his dramatization of *Tess of the d'Urbervilles* would be staged in Dorchester (Tilley thought that local public feeling at the time would be against it); he intimated to Eustacia (Gertrude Bugler) that he would like to see her play the part of Tess. The next afternoon Florence found him writing a poem; as expected, it was dismal, but he worked with gusto, which was always a sign of his 'well-being'. His high spirits seem to have lasted until he saw the New Year in at least, his *Life* recording that he sat up to hear the bells, 'which he had not done for some time'. His poem 'At the Entering of the New Year' appeared in *The Athenaeum* that day; he had told the editor John Middleton Murry to print the first part only, if he thought the second too pessimistic. Two years later, after having his brother Henry and his sister Kate (a much livelier couple than he and Mary) to '1 o'clock dinner' and tea, he must have felt tired, for he did not sit up. He had been busy working on 'The Absolute Explains', a long poem in which he surveys the past, notably the years when he was in love with Emma Gifford, in the light of Einstein's theory of Time; significantly he is advised not to look into the future. Post-war developments seem to have impressed on Hardy the need once again to lay the blame for international failure or looming disaster on the 'unreason' of man rather than on an abstraction such as the Absolute or the Immanent Will. 'Christmas: 1924' expresses grave fears:

> 'Peace upon earth!' was said. We sing it,
> And pay a million priests to bring it.
> After a thousand years of mass
> We've got as far as poison-gas.

Two other late Christmas poems present satires of circumstance relating wholly or partly to casuals on their way to the Union at Dorchester. 'Christmastide' seems to present no more than an irony, with the poet striding despondently in the rain when greeted cheerily with 'A merry Christmas, friend!' from a sodden tramp who breaks into song. 'A Nightmare, and the Next Thing' is more elaborate, creating a rather Conrad-like vision which indicts the post-war western world in a willed confrontation, not a reluctant one as in the restricted and familiar view of 'The Reminder' in *Time's Laughingstocks*. Six girls on their way to a dance see nothing nightmarish in the foggy street, or 'anywhere'. The phantasmal street scene suggests the Nether Glooms of 'To My Father's Violin';

'anywhere', the mind of the poet, who is thinking of his imminent death.

Late in 1924 *Tess of the d'Urbervilles* was performed by 'The Hardy Players' at Dorchester and Weymouth, Mrs Bugler acting the part of Tess with such moving success that Hardy was delighted. His attentions created gossip and jealousy among some of the players, jealousy even more in Florence Hardy. Christmas was 'as cheerful as may be', her husband informed his friend A. C. Benson, Master of Magdalene College, Cambridge; he had long ago passed the point when anniversaries became 'the saddest days of the year'. The news that Gertrude Bugler wished to take the opportunity that seemed to emerge of repeating her success on the 'professional stage' in London made him feel anxious and responsible. With the New Year, which he and Florence heard announced for the first time on radio by Big Ben and London church bells, tension grew, especially when Frederick Harrison, the manager, invited Gertrude to play at the Haymarket. When Cockerell arrived on 10 January he soon found Max Gate under a cloud of jealousy and discontent as a result of Hardy's infatuation. Florence was not satisfied until, after behaving absurdly, she had done enough to make Mrs Bugler in February think it best to decline the role.

One reason given by Mrs Hardy for wishing Gertrude Bugler (who was ignorant of the comic situation which had arisen) not to play the part of Tess in London was that if she did Hardy would travel at great risk to his health to see her performance. He did not go when the play was produced in London, first at Barnes Theatre, then at the Garrick, from which on 6 December the company came to perform as best they could before the Hardys in their drawing-room. Two weeks later the young war poet Siegfried Sassoon was on a visit to Max Gate when news came of the death of his uncle, Hardy's friend Sir Hamo Thornycroft. On 23 December, his sister Mary's birthday, Hardy thought of her 'out there' and of the world's indifference to her life. On New Year's Eve he and Florence sat up to hear a special broadcast programme of events heralding and celebrating the start of 1926: 'dancing at the Albert Hall, Big Ben striking twelve, singing Auld Lang Syne, God Save the King, Marseillaise, hurrahing'. The wireless had brought new excitement to Max Gate.

One of the household who enjoyed the wireless was Wessex, the fierce little terrier whom Florence brought to Max Gate in 1913; it was often turned or kept on to please him. At first Hardy did not care for him; he was a disturber of the peace. Soon Wessex became his pet, and he spoiled him, feeding him with goose and plum-pudding one Christmas. When Lady Cynthia Asquith visited Max Gate in 1921, she found him on the table 'contesting' every forkful of food she tried to take. He may have been 'A Popular Personage at Home' (except with the servants), but he was the terror of most callers and visitors, bit the postman three times and had two of his front teeth kicked out in consequence, and was the despair of his mistress, who often thought of having him 'put down'. This did not happen until 27 December 1926, when age and infirmity made it necessary, much to the distress of his master, who noted after the terrier's burial in the Max Gate pets' cemetery: 'Wessex sleeps outside the house the first time for thirteen years.' Some of Hardy's friends thought 'his life was definitely saddened' by the loss of his most constant companion at home and on local walks. He did not sit up to see in the New Year.

In 1927 the Balliol Players came for the third time to perform a Greek play on the lawn at Max Gate. It was a year in which Hardy had visits from several distinguished friends and was taken on visits by Florence near and far. He often spoke of his early years, and said that 'if he had his life over again he would prefer to be a small architect in a country town, like Mr Hicks at Dorchester'. He had achieved all he wished to do, though he wondered whether it had been worth while. His one ambition, as far as he remembered, had been to have some poems in 'a good anthology' like *The Golden Treasury*. He continued working, and had another collection of poems (*Winter Words*, published posthumously) almost ready for the press. On 11 December he sat down at his writing-table, and felt for the first time in his life quite unable to work. He was anxious that his poem 'Christmas in the Elgin Room' should be copied and sent to *The Times* (where it appeared on the 24th). Gosse wrote immediately in its praise, and Hardy replied on Christmas Day. He was in bed, 'living on butter-broth and beef-tea', the servants much concerned (though he was relieved) that he was unable to eat any plum-pudding. He did not go downstairs alive again. On 26 December he was thinking of the Nativity and the murder of the innocents, and Florence read the Biblical accounts and articles in the *Encyclopaedia Biblica* to him; there wasn't any evidence that the gospel story was true in any detail, he commented. As the year ended she opened the window, hoping he would be pleased to hear the bells. He could not, and did not seem to be interested.

The severity of the winter intensified, and deep snow lay around.
Thoughts of the past drifted into Hardy's mind, with evocations
of deep regret for his shortcomings with Emma. Near the end
thoughts of another kind led him to dictate short and somewhat
inchoate verses in answer to attacks he had resented from 'the
literary contortionist' G. K. Chesterton, who in 1913 had dubbed
him 'a sort of village atheist brooding and blaspheming over the
village idiot', and from George Moore, who had described him as
'one of George Eliot's miscarriages' in 1886, and disparaged his
writings and prose style in 1924.[9] As Hardy's strength diminished
he could no longer listen to prose. In the middle of one night he
asked Florence to read aloud Walter de la Mare's 'The Listeners';
one evening he followed intently as she read Browning's 'Rabbi
Ben Ezra' at his request. He did not express what he thought. A
few hours before his death, as the afternoon grew dusk on 11
January, he requested one particular verse from the *Rubáiyát*, which
she read.[10] There may have been Swinburnian overtones in this,
but it seems an odd reversion, a gesture of Promethean defiance,
quite inconsistent with the line of intelligent thinking which had
led Hardy to proceed, with reference to nature and the universe,
from belief in the Impercipient to the conclusion that the Prime
Mover is unknowable. More significant had been the emphasis in
his later life on man's 'unreason' in the perpetuation of evil. The
very title of his last volume of poetry seems to express the ebbing
of faith in the human race at the end of his life. 'We are getting to
the end of dreams!' he concludes in the penultimate poem:

>   the end of visioning
> The impossible within this universe,
> Such as that better whiles may follow worse,
> And that our race may mend by reasoning.

His tune was more manly in the days when he defended himself
as a meliorist, not a pessimist, and adopted a Positivist creed:

> The truth should be told, and the fact be faced
> That had best been faced in earlier years:

> The fact of life with dependence placed
> On the human heart's resource alone,
> In brotherhood bonded close and graced

With loving-kindness fully blown,
And visioned help unsought, unknown.[11]

Supplement

(a) Hardy and Heredity

The lottery of birth weighed heavily on Hardy's mind during his early years in London; more than anything else it conspired to create his literary poor-man-and-the-lady complex. The hereditary 'hap of birth' in general gave him food for deeper thought in 'Discouragement', a poem which engaged his intermittent attention from 1865 to 1867, if not earlier. It may have been stimulated originally by lines in *Hamlet* (I.iv, 23–6), and cannot be excluded from the larger incidence of 'Crass Casualty' in 'Hap' (1866). Where was the Providence of his Christian faith, he must have asked himself.

Scientists having established that inbreeding produces weaker or defective offspring, the Church began to frown on the marriage of cousins. The question could have been brought home to Hardy about this period, when, it is believed, his mother forbad or opposed his engagement to his attractive cousin Martha Sparks.[1]

The pleasing irony that the most conspicuous mark the sailor Bob Loveday brought back after all his travels about the world was 'an increased resemblance to his mother, who had lain all the time beneath Overcombe church wall', appealed so much to Hardy late in life that he made it the subject of his poem 'The Rover Come Home'.[2]

During his last years as a novelist Hardy emphasized the importance of heredity more persistently. When, in February 1889, *Tess of the d'Urbervilles* was already under way, it struck him that 'The story of a face which goes through three generations or more, would make a fine novel or poem of the passage of Time.' From this grew both *The Well-Beloved* and the poem 'Heredity' ('I am the family face . . . The eternal thing in man, That heeds no call to die'). Tess's fate is decided not merely by adverse circumstances but by hereditary traits, notably 'reckless acquiescence in chance' and, when her endurance is tried to the utmost, passionate (even violent) outbreaks of the old d'Urberville temper.

334

Not until after the death of his cousin Tryphena (much the youngest of the Sparks sisters) did Hardy set seriously to work on the main plot of *Jude the Obscure*, which turns on 'the tragic issues of two bad marriages, owing in the main to a doom or curse of hereditary temperament peculiar to the family of the parties'. One of these marriages is between cousins. (Hardy had probably remembered his attachment to Martha Sparks; his poem 'Thoughts of Phena' simply shows the rousing of a retrospective and imaginary love for another 'lost prize'.) It is assumed that their parents' disastrous marriages make such a union doubly dangerous. The fatal story of their common ancestor (a variant of 'The Winters and the Palmleys', which was originally set in the Melbury area, and therefore most probably based on a story handed down by Hardy's mother) makes Sue feel that a tragic doom hangs over their family like that of the house of Atreus; or of Jeroboam, the theological Jude adds. It is overheard by little Father Time, the instrument of their woe, a child born, it seems, to inherit their ancestral gloom and suffer for all his parents' mistakes and misfortune.[3] This crux in the tragedy of *Jude*, together with 'The Forbidden Banns', suggests that the subject of heredity could work morbidly in Hardy's imagination.

Late in 1890, after the planning of *Jude* but long before its composition, Hardy found time to read the 1889 translation of Weismann's *Essays on Heredity*, which provided the germ for his story 'An Imaginative Woman', based on a hereditary assumption (a psychological fantasy) which Hardy must have regarded as a novelty for his readers, though it is essentially akin to popular superstitions going back to the tradition in Genesis of Jacob's outwitting his uncle Laban by placing ringstraked rods before strong cattle at the time of conception, so that they brought forth 'ringstraked, speckled, and spotted' for his gain.

With its continual emphasis on the influence of heredity and circumstance on the heroine, *Tess of the d'Urbervilles* must raise the question of how much room Hardy left for the exercise of individual free will. In 'The Pedigree' (1916), where the moon casts an inauspicious spell, the speaker sees the long line of his ancestry, alike in mien, build, and brow, dwindling back through time, and concludes

> That every heave and coil and move I made
> Within my brain, and in my mood and speech,

had been 'long forestalled by their so making it', the first of them being 'the primest fuglemen' of his line, determining all his actions. The same hereditary determinism is found in 'Family Portraits' (first published in 1924, and later much revised). Puppetlike motions are seen in the narrator's ancestors, but the link between their 'law-lacking passions' and his, and his fears for the future (written at a time when Hardy cared little for life) suggest very strongly that the adumbrated drama of the remote past is imaginary (whatever hints may have occurred to him in tracing his own pedigree). In surmising that 'endeavours to balk future pain' might succeed were the past uncovered, the poem approaches the confines of Eliot's *The Family Reunion*, and holds out more hope than 'The Pedigree'.

(b) Hardy's Titles

Hardy found almost a thousand titles for the whole of his works, including short stories and essays, and the vast majority of his poems (apart from the many chapter-headings which are worthy of consideration in this context). In this respect, it is doubtful if any other author coped with more consistent skill or more frequent felicity. Sometimes they are so artistically turned that they command immediate admiration; more often, especially with the poems, their appropriateness is such that we assume they came as naturally as leaves to a tree, forgetting the adage that 'True ease in writing comes from art, not chance.' Many of the titles came readily no doubt to Hardy; some (nobody can gauge the proportion) must have teased him repeatedly out of thought. Much time passed in the composition of each before he could decide finally on titles for *Tess* and *Jude*. A title can give an author more difficulty than any item in the book or poem to which it relates.

'Two on a Tower' was one Hardy afterwards disliked. He changed 'The Mellstock Quire', which is more appropriate to the main story, to 'Under the Greenwood Tree' because titles from poetry were fashionable.[4] His next two were of that order, 'A Pair of Blue Eyes' from a song in Sheridan's *The School for Scandal*, and the startlingly ironic 'Far from the Madding Crowd' from Gray's 'Elegy'.

For a time he had been fascinated by 'A Winning Tongue Had He', which initially he had in mind for *A Pair of Blue Eyes*; the verse of its origin (from 'The Banks of Allan Water' by M. G. Lewis, a popular song set to a traditional air) occurs in the manuscript, most probably as the initial theme-song, 'O Love, who bewailest . . .' being substituted for it in the first edition (iii). The same verse is found in *Far from the Madding Crowd* (xxiii), and the title would obviously have been much more appropriate to this novel (for which it may have been considered) than for the story of *A Pair of Blue Eyes* as it stands. In 1927 Hardy could not remember any connection between this novel and 'A Winning Tongue Had He'; such a title would have been quite unsuitable, he stated.[5] What his original plan was remains unknown.

Quotations continue in the titles of his poems, but not on a large scale. Among the more obvious are 'The Selfsame Song', 'And There was a Great Calm', 'In Death Divided' (unlike Saul and Jonathan), 'In Time of "the Breaking of Nations"' (Jeremiah), and 'According to the Mighty Working' (from the Church of England burial service). The significant allusion to the tragedy overhanging Oedipus in 'Where three roads joined' (from J. A. Symonds, *Studies in the Greek Poets*) is often missed.

The complete absence of repetition in such a large number of titles is a mark of Hardy's inventiveness and punctilious selective care. He would not have substituted 'On the Doorstep' for 'Staying and Going' had he not remembered that he had discarded the poem 'On the Doorstep' from the 'Satires of Circumstance' series in his previous volume.

One interesting feature in the title of his poems is the use made of the third person pronoun or pronominal adjective to give a general significance, sometimes when the poem relates closely to the poet: 'She, to Him', 'His Immortality', 'He Fears his Good Fortune', 'Her Apotheosis', 'She Revisits Alone the Church of Her Marriage'.

The last is an example of those slightly longer titles which are poetical in their very sound and movement; others which spring to mind are 'At Lulworth Cove a Century Back', 'Winter Night in Woodland', 'The Maid of Keinton Mandeville', and 'Evelyn G. of Christminster'. The same is true of 'When I set out for Lyonnesse', one of those opening-line titles chosen when nothing finer in sound or sense was forthcoming.

If Hardy emulated anyone in the titles of his poems it must have been William Barnes. One could not imagine his using the kind of title which we associate with the eighteenth century, though still to be found in poets of the nineteenth: 'Ode: On the Pleasure arising from Vicissitude' (Gray); 'To a Mouse, on Turning her up in her Nest with the Plough, November, 1785' (Burns); 'Lines: Composed a few miles above Tintern Abbey, on revisiting the banks of the Wye during a tour. 13 July 1798' (Wordsworth); 'Supposed Confessions of a Second-Rate Sensitive Mind' (Tennyson). These are hardly poetical; some are matter-of-fact, with biographical value; with them, the prose-writer has taken over. Hardy's 'After Reading Psalms xxxix., xl., etc.' approximates to them, and we must be grateful for his clues. His titles, from the most simple and unobtrusive, are rarely out of tune with his poems. Sometimes they go further, strengthening the imaginative impact of their subjects, none more intensively perhaps than 'Neutral Tones', one of his earliest.

(c) *The Mayor of Casterbridge* and *Les Misérables*

Hardy honoured Victor Hugo. He read his poetry as well as his prose, sent a card for a wreath at his funeral, and wrote, at the invitation of a Continental newspaper, the following tribute for the centenary of his birth: 'His memory must endure. His works are the cathedrals of literary architecture, his imagination adding greatness to the colossal and charm to the small.' The implications of the cathedral metaphor are particularly true of *Les Misérables*.

This novel had great appeal for Hardy; he read it in C. E. Wilbour's translation once or twice from 1887 to 1889.[6] *The Mayor of Casterbridge* gives ample proof that he had read it earlier in French; if he intended the word *misérables* as a hint, it gives no idea of his borrowings. Resemblances between the two novels show that Hardy was influenced particularly by the final scenes in the life of Hugo's hero Jean Valjean. In the following notes on comparable features, references to *Les Misérables* are given at the beginning, and those to *The Mayor* at the end.

(i) (Fantine) The hero of each story is physically strong, successful in business, and becomes a mayor, after committing a crime.

(ii) (Jean Valjean, IV.i) When Javert, the police inspector, contemplates suicide he goes to one of two bridges, very close together over the Seine, and leans over the parapet in deliberation. The scene could have suggested the two bridges for the *misérables* of two different classes at Casterbridge (xxxii).

(iii) (Ibid.) Javert's prospects are unendurable, and the darkness is complete as he leans over the whirlpool. In Hardy's novel there are two scenes with these features: the first (xxxii) draws attention to the deep pool called Blackwater, and reveals a landscape which grows blacker until it is like a picture 'blotted in with ink'; in the second (xli) Henchard's prospects are unendurable, and the land ahead is as darkness itself as he proceeds to Ten Hatches, intent on drowning himself.

(iv) The ex-mayor lives for Cosette. She is not his daughter, but all his fortune is hers when she marries Marius. Henchard is ruined, but all he has in life is the girl he once thought his daughter, Elizabeth-Jane.

(v) (Ibid., VI.ii) Jean Valjean is not missed at the wedding-banquet, so happy are the young lovers (xliv).

(vi) (Ibid., VI.iv) Can Valjean's past remain a secret? If it is revealed, he will he disowned and have nothing to live for. Rather than lose Elizabeth-Jane, Henchard lies (xli).

(vii) (Ibid., VII) After Valjean's confession, Marius, who had always been suspicious and afraid of him, turns against him, and regards him as an 'outcast'. Valjean pleads to see Cosette, and would willingly enter by the back-door. He visits her in the basement, but his reception gets colder and colder with every succeeding visit. Cosette's married happiness makes her forget him when his visits cease. (Cf. xlv, Elizazbeth-Jane begs her husband Farfrae to help her find Henchard, and make his life 'less that of an outcast'; xliii, 'He proceeded to draw a picture of the alternative, . . .'; xliv.)

(viii) (Ibid., VII.ii) He is a 'remorseful Cain' (xliii).

(ix) (Ibid., IX.ii) As he lies dying in his poor tenement, he has only the portress, 'this good woman', to attend him. The doctor says he is dying from the loss of a dear friend. With this one can compare the loyal service of Whittle, Henchard's death in an abandoned cottage on the heath, and the effect of his rejection by Elizabeth-Jane (xlv).

(x) (Ibid., IX.iv, v) After Marius has discovered the true story of Valjean, he and Cosette hire a fiacre to bring him back. Hugo's ending is a happy one, though Valjean dies. Unlike Hardy, both believe in Providence (xlv).

(xi) (Ibid., IX.v) Cosette, looking forward to Valjean's return, tells him how pretty her garden is and of her sorrow that a nesting redbreast has been killed. It would be charming to live together and hear the birds in the trees, he replies. Then he announces his imminent death, and immediately refers to the redbreast. The symbolism is simpler than that of the caged goldfinch which Henchard brings as a peace-offering and wedding-present (xliv), and which is left to die like all his hopes.

Bishop Bienvenu and his life of compassion (Fantine, I–III) must have been held in high veneration by Hardy, who believed more and more firmly with the years that only brotherhood and loving-kindness stood between man and disaster. The bishop's pity for all God's creatures, including the spider and the ant, recalls 'An August Midnight'.

Hugo's preface to *Les Misérables* must have made a strong impact on Hardy. 'So long as there shall exist, by reason of law and custom, a social condemnation, which, in the face of civilization, artificially creates hells on earth . . . so long as ignorance and misery remain on earth, books like this cannot be useless.' This apologia would commend itself as a charter to Hardy when he was contemplating *Tess of the d'Urbervilles* and *Jude the Obscure*, and there is an echo of it in 'Why do I?', the last poem in *Human Shows*.

Notes

Reference Abbreviations

CP	Collected Poems	PBE	A Pair of Blue Eyes
D	The Dynasts	RN	The Return of the Native
DR	Desperate Remedies	TD	Tess of the d'Urbervilles
FMC	Far from the Madding Crowd	TM	The Trumpet-Major
HE	The Hand of Ethelberta	TT	Two on a Tower
JO	Jude the Obscure	UGT	Under the Greenwood Tree
L	A Laodicean	W	The Woodlanders
MC	The Mayor of Casterbridge	WB	The Well-Beloved

Letters R. L. Purdy and M. Millgate (eds) *The Collected Letters of Thomas Hardy* in 7 vols, Oxford, 1978–88.

Life Alternative references are given to (1) F. E. Hardy, *The Life of Thomas Hardy*, London and New York, 1962, and (2) M. Millgate (ed.), *The Life and Work of Thomas Hardy*, Basingstoke and London, 1984.

Millgate Michael Millgate, *Thomas Hardy: A Biography*, Oxford, 1982.

Purdy Richard Little Purdy, *Thomas Hardy: A Bibliography*, Oxford, 1968 edition.

Chapter 1   The Ranging Vision

1. *CP*. After Reading Psalms xxxix., xl., etc.
2. *Life* 146–7/151.
3. The quotations in this paragraph are from Hardy's general preface of 1912, 'The Profitable Reading of Fiction', *Life* 104/107, the preface to *Lyrical Ballads*, and *W*.i.
4. See 'Winckelmann' and 'Conclusion' in Walter Pater's *Renaissance* studies.
5. R. G. Cox (ed.), *Thomas Hardy, The Critical Heritage*, London and New York, 1970, pp. 277–8.
6. *Life* 226/236–7.
7. Quotations from *WB*.ii.viii and *JO*.v.iii.
8. *Aspects of Literature*, London, 1920, p. 130.
9. *CP*. 'We are getting to the end', He Resolves to Say No More.
10. Apology to *Late Lyrics and Earlier*.
11. *FMC*.xliii.
12. See note 4 above, Arnold's essay 'Pagan and Medieval Religious

Sentiment', Supplement (c), and the Index (for more on other references).
13. See the later essay on *Tess of the d'Urbervilles* (ch. 8).
14. From 'The Profitable Reading of Fiction'.
15. See Keats's letter to J. H. Reynolds, 19 February 1818. The poem begins, 'O thou whose face hath felt the Winter's wind'.
16. *CP*. In the Old Theatre, Fiesole; *Life* 188/195, 193/200.
17. *Life* 252/268, 386/417.
18. Arnold, 'Pagan and Medieval Religious Sentiment'; Pater, 'Winckelmann' (note 4 above).

Chapter 2   Hardy and George Eliot

1. Cf. *The Mill on the Floss*, VI.vi and MC.xvii.
2. See *Middlemarch*, xxxi; *Felix Holt*, iii; *MC*.iv and the opening paragraph of ix.
3. Thomas Carlyle's essay 'Goethe's Helena' and George Eliot's 'Mr Gilfil's Love-Story', iii (*Scenes of Clerical Life*).
4. *Daniel Deronda*, xvii and *TD*.xli; *Middlemarch*, liii and *TD*.xlvi.
5. *Daniel Deronda*, lvi; J. W. Cross, *George Eliot's Life*, entry for 29 December 1862; I Corinthians xiii, 1–13; *JO*.VI.iv.

Chapter 3   Psychological Pictorialism

1. For the references in this paragraph, see *Life* 52/53, *DR*.viii.4, *Life* 184/191, *W*.ii, xxiv (the last suggested by Alistair Smart in 'Pictorial Imagery in the Novels of Thomas Hardy', *The Review of English Studies*, 1961, and punctuated according to Dale Kramer's edition, Oxford, 1981).
2. *DR*.ii.4, *PBE*.xiv, *TT*.xviii.
3. Cf. 'single opportunity of existence', *DR*.xiii.4 and *CP*. She, to Him (II).
4. *DR*.iii.2 (allusion to Gray), xii.6 and TD.lv.
5. *RN*.III.v.
6. *PBE*.xxxii.
7. Hardy wrote down the details during a night of thunder and lightning at Higher Bockhampton, Cf. F. A. Hedgcock, 'Reminiscences of Thomas Hardy', *The National and English Review*, October 1951.
8. The Ancient Mariner, iii–iv, ll. 206–29, 248–62.
9. Hardy's scene is attributed to a town and military station many miles north of Weatherbury, but it was most probably conceived with the river on the north-east side of Dorchester in mind, the County Gaol above it to the left, and the meadows and Fordington (Durnover) Moor to the right. This may account for Troy's saying, 'We are all of us as good as in the country gaol till to-morrow morning.' With the description compare the opening pages of *Middlemarch*, xxviii.
10. Hardy provides clues to this scene near the end of the next chapter,

xxxii, but the extent of Bathsheba's indecisiveness is not fully disclosed until xxxvii.

11. *W*.xxix; cf. *PBE*.xxix epigraph.
12. Cf. *RN*.I.i and *Life* 120–1/124, 185/192. The colourful scenery of 'Beeny Cliff' is not as characteristic of Hardy's poetry as the settings of 'Neutral Tones' and 'The Darkling Thrush'.

Chapter 4   *Two on a Tower*

1. See *The Thomas Hardy Year Book* no. 5, 1976, p. 9. There is a tradition that the Moules' telescope was mounted on the tower of Fordington Church. Whether it happened or was merely proposed, it suggests impressions that may have entered into the conception of *Two on a Tower*.
2. Cf. Robert Gittings, *The Older Hardy*, London, 1978, p. 26.
3. *Life* 151/155–6; cf. *Letters* I.96. Although it is in the Charborough Park region, Hardy disguised the setting principally by choosing for the site of his tower that of an obelisk memorial in the plantation capping Weatherby (or Weatherbury) Castle, an ancient hill-fortress, aptly described in the name 'Rings-Hill'.
4. Purdy 44n and *Letters* I.110.
5. *Life* 150/154.
6. *Letters* I.110 (to Gosse, 10 December 1882).
7. See Hardy's 'Candour in Fiction' (1890).
8. By adding the date (7 July) and 'Viviette yielded to all the passion of her first union with him' (xxxvi), and 'I ought not to have consented to that last interview: all was well till then!' and the date of birth (xl). This was first pointed out by J. C. Maxwell in *The Thomas Hardy Year Book*, no. 2, 1971.

Chapter 5   Mephistophelian and Satanic

1. The name is retained in the Lower Wessex version, published in *A Changed Man*, 1913; it could have been suggested by Pallington, east of Tincleton, the Stickleford of the story as it was published in the summer number of *The Graphic*, 1883. Simon Gatrell, in *The Thomas Hardy Journal*, October 1987, suggests Ilsington Wood to the northeast of Tincleton.
2. *King Lear* III.iv, c.140 (Edgar).
3. For the references, see *RN*.I.ix opening and VI.iii footnote.
4. See *DR*.viii.4, *W*.ii, and John Ashton, *Chap-books of the Eighteenth Century*, London, 1882, p. 41.
5. See *L*.II.v and Job i, 7; *L*.II.ii; and, for the following paragraph *L*.II.vii.
6. *Fantasia of the Unconscious* v.
7. *Letters* I.259. For more on this, see the later essay 'Symbolism' (ch. 15).

Chapter 6   The Uniqueness of *The Woodlanders*

1. *Life* 127/131.
2. *Thomas Hardy: A Critical Study*, London, 1924, p. 67. (First edition, 1912.)
3. Desmond Hawkins, *Thomas Hardy*, London, 1950, p. 64.
4. *Thomas Hardy: The Novels and Short Stories*, London, 1949, p. 141.
5. *Life* 165/171–2 and *W*.xl, xliii.
6. He did. See *Letters* iii.190.
7. *Life* 220/230.
8. Quotations from *W*.iii and *Life* 177/183.
9. Cf. *CP*. At Waking.
10. First pointed out in the author's *Thomas Hardy: Art and Thought*, London, 1977, p. 109; cf. Mary Jacobus, 'Tree and Machine: *The Woodlanders*' in Dale Kramer (ed.), *Critical Approaches to the Fiction of Thomas Hardy*, London, 1979.
11. Cf. *Letters* ii.85.
12. *Life* 185/510, 357–8/– and *Letters* iv.212.
13. David Lodge, Introduction (p. 1), New Wessex Edition of *The Woodlanders*, London, 1975; Ian Gregor, *The Great Web*, London, 1974, pp. 167–8.
14. *Life* 185/192.

Chapter 7   Philosophy in Fiction

1. Leslie Stephen, *Essays on Freethinking and Plainspeaking*, London, 1873, p. 165.
2. See note 4 to 'The Ranging Vision' above.
3. Cf. *TD*.ix, *Life* 171/178, and note 3 to 'Hardy and George Eliot' (ch. 2) above.
4. *Life* 409–10/439–40.

Chapter 8   *Tess of the d'Urbervilles*

1. *TD*.xxv and note 3 to 'Psychological Pictorialism' (ch. 3) above.
2. Cf. Epipsychidion, ll. 131–2, *TD*.lv, and *Letters* i.196.
3. *Life* 221/231.
4. For the white hart and 'the serpent hisses', see *TD*.ii, xii.
5. See the opening pages (on the garden) in 'Symbolism' (ch. 15).
6. For the gradual ennoblement of Tess's character in successive texts, see J. T. Laird, *The Shaping of 'Tess of the d'Urbervilles'*, Oxford, 1975.
7. Hardy's Positivist friend Frederic Harrison wrote to him on 29 December 1891, describing *Tess* as a 'very beautiful book', deserving 'verbal attention as much as a poem of Tennyson'. It would be ranked as his finest work, though it was too 'bold, original, and incisive' for 'our Pharisaical Philistines. To me it reads like a Positivist allegory or sermon.'

8. For the quotations in this and the next paragraph, see I Corinthians xiii, 1–13.
9. After the first two Phases had been typeset for Tillotson & Son, and Hardy had refused to recast the story, the contract between them was cancelled. An agreement was at length reached for serialization in *The Graphic*. For this everything relative to Tess's rape was excluded; she returned home after discovering that she had been tricked into a bogus marriage with Alec; no child was born.
10. In *Black and White*, 27 August 1892.
11. To Harley Granville-Barker: *Letters* vi.362.

Chapter 9   Hebraism and Hellenism

1. In 'Worldliness and Other-Worldliness: The Poet Young'. This essay appeared in *The Westminster Review* at the time (January 1857) when Marian Evans had just begun writing fiction, for which she assumed the name of 'George Eliot'. The passage by Edward Young occurs in *Night Thoughts* vii.
2. Cf. Lennart Björk, *The Literary Notes of Thomas Hardy*, Göteborg, 1974, pp. 53ff. (text). Hardy made a close study of J. A. Symonds, *Studies of the Greek Poets* (2nd series), London, 1876.
3. See Björk, *The Literary Notes of Thomas Hardy*, pp. 53–4 (text) and 276, 277 (notes). The above passage is a late addition to *TD*.xlix, and not in the manuscript.
4. See 'The Last Tournament', 275–358, and Jude's fear (vi.iii) that, if Sue leaves him, 'it will be . . . another case of the pig that was washed turning back to the wallowing in the mire', an image drawn from II Peter ii, 22.

Chapter 10   Hardy and Mrs Henniker

1. T. W. Reid, *The Life, Letters, and Friendships of Richard Monckton Milnes, First Lord Houghton*, London, 1890, vol. ii, pp. 85–6.
2. Ibid., ii.268.
3. *Life* 138/142, 159/165.
4. The story, from *In Scarlet and Grey* (1896), is reproduced in *The Thomas Hardy Year Book*, no. 13, 1986, with notes by Jeffrey S. Cramer.
5. Purdy 343.
6. *Life* 230/240 (Weismann) and 260/276.
7. Cf. Millgate 340n and note 39 on p. 603, which indicates Florence Hardy as the indirect source for this information.
8. Cf. Purdy 345.
9. *JO*.vi.ii, from Aeschylus, *Agamemnon*.
10. Perhaps Hardy's marital unhappiness reached its nadir the following year, in 1896, when he wrote the third of the 'In Tenebris' poems, in which he wishes he had died in early childhood; the thinly disguised autobiography of 'The Dead Man Walking', which contains the lines

'And when my Love's heart kindled In hate of me'; and, against Arnold's 'Dover Beach', 'Sept. 1896 – T. H./E. L. H.', alluding to the lines 'Ah, love, let us be true To one another! . . .'

11. See *Life* 269/286 and *CP*. Concerning Agnes (Mrs Grove, another lady for whom Hardy was pleased to act as literary adviser).
12. Cf. *Life* 224/235, 349/376–7; *CP*. 'The wind blew words'; *Letters* II.94 (to Mrs Henniker, on the pig-killing scene in *Jude*).
13. *Letters* II.71–2 (to Clement Shorter).
14. *D2.I.iv.*
15. Florence Dugdale to Edward Clodd, Brotherton Library, University of Leeds.

Chapter 11 *Jude the Obscure*: Origins in Life and Literature

1. *Life* 274/289–90, 392/425.
2. *Life* 15–16/20, *JO*.I.ii; W. R. Rutland, *Thomas Hardy: A Study of his Writings and their Background*, Oxford, 1938, pp. 21–2, *JO*.I.vi; *Life* 148/152, *JO*.IV.vi; R. L. Purdy, letter in *The Times Literary Supplement*, 3 October 1942, *JO*.II.vi.
3. See the inset quotation from a letter (3 October 1911) to Mrs Henniker in the previous essay (ch. 10), and the essay on *The Well-Beloved* (ch. 12).
4. Cf. *CP*. Thoughts of Phena, and Purdy 220 or *Letters* III.218.
5. *Life* 272/– or *Letters* II.99.
6. *Life* 235/246–7.
7. *Life* 270–1/288–9.
8. James Thomson's poem was published in 1874: see the second section.
9. *Life* 100/102 and Leslie Stephen, *Essays on Freethinking and Plainspeaking*, London, 1873, p. 9.
10. My interest in the possible influence of *Idylls of the King* on *Jude* grew in the autumn of 1982, when I was preparing *A Tennyson Companion*, London and New York, 1984. Dr Basham forwarded me her article on the subject in February 1983; it is included in *The Thomas Hardy Society Review 1984*.
11. Cf. Harold Orel (ed.), *Thomas Hardy's Personal Writings*, Lawrence, Kansas, 1966, and London, 1967, p. 249 ('The Tree of Knowledge').
12. *JO*.VI.ii and *Paradise Lost* ix.780ff.

Chapter 12 *The Well-Beloved*

1. Quotations from *DR*.i.2 and x.4.
2. *Life* 286/303–4.
3. *Life* 239/251, Purdy 94, and *Letters* I.249.
4. *CP*. Thoughts of Phena, *Life* 254/270 (cf. *CP*. Wessex Heights, 'Yet my love for her in its fulness she herself even did not know'), *Letters* III.218 (or Purdy 220).
5. See *Life* 217/226 and *JO*.III.viii.

6. *Life* 164/171, *Letters* II.169. Napoleon's threatened invasion provides the background to most of *TM*, and is the main subject of *The Dynasts*, Part First.

7. From the second part of 'The Captive', vol. 10 of *Remembrance of Things Past*, C. K. Scott Moncrieff's translation, London, 1941, pp. 235, 236.

8. From chapter xxviii; omitted unfortunately from the New Wessex Edition.

9. *WB*.II.x and II.xiii; III.vi and III.i.

10. On Jordon Hill, the scene of *CP*. The Well-Beloved in some editions.

11. For the two quoted passages see *WB*.II.iii, III.ii.

12. See *WB*.II.iii; Proust, 'The Captive' (note 7 above), p. 245; and *WB*.I.vii. The bird image comes from Wordsworth's sonnet 'Why art thou silent!'

13. Cf. *WB* title-page and II.i, from Shelley, *The Revolt of Islam* I.xxvii.

14. Reference to *Life* 291/309–10; inset quotation from *WB*.II.ii (cf. *Life* 232/244).

15. See the passage from *WB*.II.iii in the previous essay.

16. Cf. *Letters* II.154–9 and *Life* 286/304. *The Loves of the Triangles* (1798) is a parody of Erasmus Darwin's *The Loves of the Plants* (1789).

Chapter 13   Fictional Autobiography

1. Cf. *Life* 441–2/476 and *JO*.I.iii.

2. See W. R. Rutland, *Thomas Hardy: A Study of his Writings and their Background*, Oxford, 1938, pp. 21–2, and *Life* 28/32.

3. *Life* 15–16/20 and *JO*.I.ii.

4. See *RN*.III.i and *Life* 16–17/21.

5. Newman Flower, *Just As It Happened*, London, 1950, p. 92.

6. *CP*. One We Knew, The Alarm; *Life* 420/453.

7. In Hardy the association between Deuteronomy xxviii, 67 and the sadness of old age is found in *DR*.xi.3 and *TT*.ii.

8. Cf. *Life* 10/16.

9. See Millgate 61–2.

10. *Life* 27/32, 29–31/33–5, 50/52–3, and *L*.I.vi, vii.

11. Cf. *DR*.xii.6, *TM*.i, The Waiting Supper vii (in *A Changed Man*), and *UGT*,IV.vii.

12. Cf. *Life* 48/50, where Hardy wrongly gives 1865 as the year; Millgate 81; and, for further details, Ellen Dollery, *The Thomas Hardy Journal*, 1987, p. 38. See also Edmund Blunden, *Thomas Hardy*, London, 1951, pp. 48–9; *L*.I.i, iv (end); *Life* 53/54, 61/63, 128/131.

13. See *HE*.xxv and Robert Gittings, 'Findon and *The Hand of Ethelberta*', *The Thomas Hardy Society Review 1984*, pp. 306–7; also *HE*.xxxi, the brief paragraph beginning, 'Then the lecture ended'.

14. Millgate 149–50, *Letters* I.26, and *HE*.xlii.

15. Cf. *DR*.ii.3, iii.2; and *Life* 27/31 (born bookworm), 53/54 (Shakespeare).

16. Cf. *DR*.iii.2 and xi.4.

17. For Emma's father and Latin, see Evelyn Hardy and Robert Gittings (eds), *Emma Hardy, Some Recollections*, London, 1961, p. 18.

18. Cf. the opening of *PBE*.xiii and *Life* 77/80.
19. Cf. *Life* 156–7/162, *PBE*.xix, *CP*. Quid Hic Agis?, and I Kings xix. The evidence for the service at Lesnewth, the village with which St Juliot was paired for church duties, is found in a deletion on the MS of *CP*. A Young Churchwarden and a note in Hardy's prayer-book.
20. *PBE*.xiii, xviii; Evelyn Hardy, *Thomas Hardy's Notebooks*, London, 1955, pp. 31–2; *DR*.xv.3; cf. *CP*. 'It never looks like summer', The Figure in the Scene; *UGT*.iv.v and *Life* 78/81; cf. *Life* 118/122 and *CP*. The Maid of Keinton Mandeville.
21. Cf. *DR*.x.4, *TD*.v end, 'The Waiting Supper' iv, *DR*.xiii.4, *PBE*,xxvii, *FMC*.lvi end, *TT*.xli, *W*.xxviii, *TD*.xxv.
22. Cf. *TD*.xviii and *Life* 50/52–3, 376/407.
23. *Life* 96/99, 248/262; *DR*.viii.3; *W*.xxviii; *JO*.i.vi, x; *PBE*.xxiii; *UGT*.i.ii (Grammer Kaytes's).
24. *Letters* vi.315.
25. *TM*.xvii; *TT*.iv, xxxv.
26. See *Letters* ii.206, the end of 'Candour in Fiction' (January 1890), and *Life* 274/289–90, 392/425.
27. Cf. *Letters* ii.23–4, 26, 44 and *JO*.iii.vi.
28. See the latter part of the essay on *The Well-Beloved* (ch. 12), and cf. *Life* 104/107, 291/309–10, 305/328.
29. *Life* 25/29; *WB*.i.vii, ii.xii, iii.iii, iv.
30. See *JO*.iv.vi; *Life* 148/152, 252/268, 87/89.

Chapter 14   Hardy's Novel-Endings

1. *Life* 271/– and *Letters* ii.93.
2. See Charles Morgan, *The House of Macmillan*, London, 1944, pp. 88–9.
3. Cf. *Life* 78/81 and *CP*. Love the Monopolist, which was begun in 1871, with *UGT*.iii.iv, iv.i and v.
4. Cf. R. P. Draper's introduction to *Thomas Hardy: Three Pastoral Novels*, London, 1987, and Swinburne's 'nightingales are louder for love's sake' in 'Anactoria' (*Poems and Ballads*, 1866).
5. This was discovered by Richard Snell. See his article 'A Self-Plagiarism by Thomas Hardy', *Essays in Criticism*, January 1952, and compare scene xiv of the first edition of the play (scene xvi of the 1924 edition) with *PBE*.xxxiv, xxxv.
6. Cf. 'Fellow-Townsmen' viii (in *Wessex Tales*) and *DR*.ix.3.
7. *W*.xxviii and *TD*.xxv.
8. Cf. Shelley, 'Stanzas, Written in Dejection near Naples', and *HE*.xxvii end.
9. *Life* 53/54, 87/89, 104/107.
10. Gertrude Bugler, *Personal Recollections of Thomas Hardy*, Dorchester, 1962.
11. Compare the end of v.v and the opening of v.ix. In the former the passage 'If I wish to go . . . escape me' was added to the MS, with 'assistance' for 'company'. The change to 'company' suggests Hardy's final intention, though his later text still shows some reluctance on

Eustacia's part (v.vii) and Wildeve's uncertainty about what they will do.

12. See the ballad of 'Alonzo the Brave and the Fair Imogene' by M. G. ('Monk') Lewis, 1775–1818.
13. Hardy to John Blackwood (who had looked askance at the early chapters of *RN*), 9 June 1879 (*Letters* I.65).
14. Edmund Blunden, *Thomas Hardy*, London, 1951, p. 48.
15. Cf. *RN*.II.vi opening and III.i.
16. See the end of the essay 'Hardy and George Eliot' (ch. 2).
17. Cf. *Life* 41/43 and 18–20/23–5.
18. See Hardy's prefaces to *RN* (1895) and *TD* (1892); also 'The Withered Arm' v (in *Wessex Tales*).
19. Cf. *Life* 243–4/256–7, where the reference to Aeschylus, *Prometheus Bound* (l. 169) is given, and *D3*.VII.ix, where the view is given as outdated ('As earthlings used to say'). For a rare example of Hardy's writing in this way, see the inset quotation beginning 'To cry out' in the essay 'At the Year's End' (ch. 20).
20. Hardy's 1895 preface shows that he had worked out plans for *JO* in 1890, from earlier notes. He changed 'the Marquis of Trantridge' in *A Group of Noble Dames* (vi) to 'the Marquis of Christminster' for volume publication in 1891. 'Christminster' at the opening of *DR* did not appear before 1896.
21. From *CP*. Just the Same.
22. *Life* 226/236–7.

Chapter 15   Symbolism

1. Cf. *Life* 48–54/51–5.
2. See the excerpts quoted in the essay 'Hebraism and Hellenism' (ch. 9).
3. *Life* 149/153, *FMC*.xliv (cf. xlii), *RN*.v.vii, *W*.xlii.
4. *Paradise Lost* iv, 131–43 and 172–83.
5. See *TD*.1 and xiv. Alec quotes *Paradise Lost* ix, 626–31.
6. See IX.xx–xxviii.
7. For the frost imagery see *DR*.xiii.1 and 4; for the river, *DR*.xii.6, *UGT*.IV.vii, *TM*.i, and 'the Waiting Supper' viii.
8. *Hellas*, l. 43; Genesis viii, 21–2 and ix, 11–16; *DR*.i.5; *RN*.II.iii, III.v (cf. 'And no birds sing' in Keats's poem).

Chapter 16   Hardy as a Thinker

1. Robert Graves, *Goodbye to All That*, London, 1957 (first published in 1929), ch. 28. Though Hardy's statement is given in the form of a generalization, there can be no doubt that it applied to himself as much as to anyone.
2. See *Life* 33/37, 48/50, 330/355; Edmund Blunden, *Thomas Hardy*, London, 1951, p. 110; *Letters* II.24–5.

3. See *TD*.xiv, xiii, xv, xix, and Lawrence, *Studies in Classic American Literature*, 'The Spirit of Place', for the passages referred to or quoted in the last two paragraphs.
4. Quotations in this paragraph are from *D*3.i.v, *D*2.i.iii, *D*3. After Scene, *Life* 335/360–1.
5. Cf. *Life* 337/363–4, 409/439, and the Apology to *Late Lyrics and Earlier*.
6. *Life* 369–70/400, 224/234, and Florence Hardy to Sydney Cockerell in *Friends of a Lifetime*, ed. Viola Meynell, London, 1940.

Chapter 17 Literary Allusion and Indebtedness

1. *PBE*.xxxii, *RN*.i.xi, *MC*.xlv, *TD*.li, *JO*.i.iv and ii.i.
2. *FMC*.xlix, *W*.xlvi, *JO*.iv.v and vi.iv.
3. *DR*.x.1 and xvi.1, *MC*.xiv, *FMC*.xlii.
4. See note 8 to 'Psychological Pictorialism' (ch. 3) above.
5. *Life* 369–70/400.
6. *Life* 170–1/177; Harold Orel (ed.), *Thomas Hardy's Personal Writings*, Lawrence, Kansas, 1966, and London, 1967, p. 107; I Samuel xxviii.
7. For the last reference (*JO*.vi.v) cf. Joshua vi, 18 and vii, 1 and 15.
8. *L*.iii.iii (cf. I Chronicles xxix, 9), *TT*.xv (Proverbs vi, 11), *HE*.xxv (Genesis xlii, 9), *W*.ix (Exodus xxxiv, 29) and xxxvii (Acts vi, 15), *TT*.xxxviii (Hebrews xii, 2 and Psalm xliv, 25); Romans viii, 22 and Philippians iv, 8.
9. *PBE*.xxxi and Psalm lxi, 3 (Church of England service version).
10. *Life* 270/288, 325/349; cf. *CP*. A Singer Asleep.
11. *Life* 41/43, 18–20/23–5, 101–2/104–5.

Chapter 18 The Hero of *The Dynasts*

1. *D*2.i.viii, ii.vi; *D*3.i.i and vii.ix.
2. *D*. Fore Scene and *D*1.i.vi, ii.ii, *D*3.i.v, *D*1.v.iv.
3. For the contents of this paragraph, see *Life* 149/153 (the Unfulfilled Intention), *D*1.i.vi, iv.v, v.iv, i.vi, Fore Scene (three references), and i.vi.
4. For the lyrics in question, see *D*2.i.iii, i.vii, iv.viii, vi.iv, and *D*3.i.v, vi.viii.

Chapter 19 Reflections on Hardy's Poetry

1. Cf. Donald Davie, 'Hardy's Virgilian Purples', *Agenda*, spring–summer Hardy number, 1972, pp. 138–56.
2. See *Life* 367/396 (where Hardy refers to these 'caustically humorous productions') and *Letters* iv.151.
3. Cf. *Life* 105/108 and 300–1/323.
4. *Life* 105/108.
5. *Life* 114/117–18, 120–1/123–4, 213/222, *D*2.iii.i.

6. From *CP*. In a Former Resort after Many Years.
7. *Required Writing*, London and Boston, 1983, pp. 95–6.
8. Cf. *Life* 311/334.
9. For Leavis, cf. *The Southern Review*, summer 1940, p. 92; for Larkin, *Required Writing*, pp. 174, 176.

Chapter 20   At the Year's End

1. Cf. *CP*. The House of Hospitalities.
2. Robert Gittings, *Young Thomas Hardy*, London, 1975, p. 56; Millgate 87; *Life* 26/30 and 502.
3. From Philip Doddridge's well-known Church of England hymn 'Hark, the glad sound, the Saviour comes', sung to Ravenscroft.
4. See Dr Bernard Jones, 'Hardy and the End of the Nineteenth Century', *The Thomas Hardy Society Review 1981*.
5. See note 19 to 'Hardy's Novel-Endings' (ch. 14) above.
6. Cf. *Letters* iii.244 and *Life* 374/405, 375/406, 377/408, 410/440.
7. *Life* 368/398. Cf. *CP*. In Time of 'the Breaking of Nations' and Jeremiah li.20.
8. Cf *Letters* v.199 and Revelation vi,8.
9. Chesterton in *The Victorian Age in Literature*, and Moore in *Confessions of a Young Man* and *Conversations in Ebury Street*. Cf. J. M. Murry's trenchant defence of Hardy against Moore in *The Adelphi*, April 1924.
10. See the opening of 'Hebraism and Hellenism' (ch. 9).
11. From *CP*. A Plaint to Man.

Supplement

1. Millgate 59.
2. Cf. *TM*.xv.
3. See *JO*.v.iv, the Atlantic paragraph in v.iii, and the paragraph beginning 'The boy's face expressed' in vi.ii.
4. Cf. *Life* 151/155 and 86/88.
5. Florence Hardy to Howard Bliss, 17 September 1927, Princeton University Library.
6. (Hardy's tribute) *Life* 311/334; (translation readings) Lennart Björk, *The Literary Notes of Thomas Hardy*, Göteborg, 1974, pp. 185, 195 (text) and 399, 409 (notes; cf. entry 243).

Index

Turner, Charles (Tennyson) 301
Turner, J. M. 40, 78

United States, the 12, 328

Victoria, Queen 312
Virgil 9, (*Aeneid*) 189, 196, 295, 319
Vreeland, Admiral (U.S. fleet) 325

Walpole, Horace 287
Ward, Mrs Humphry 235
Watts, Isaac 198
Weismann, August 137, 335

Wells, H. G. 146
Wessex (the Hardys' dog) 330–1
Weymouth 150, 169, 201, 330
Wharton, Edith 235
Winchester 137, (Wintoncester) 231
Wordsworth, William 1, 9, 37, 245, 248–9, 257, 267, 268, 275, 293, 301, 304, 305, 312, (Tintern) 314, 338

Young, Edward 113

Zola, Émile 147